Dictionary of Genocide

Volume 1: A–L

SAMUEL TOTTEN
and
PAUL R. BARTROP

With contributions by
Steven Leonard Jacobs

GREENWOOD PRESS
Westport, Connecticut • London

Library of Congress Cataloging-in-Publication Data

Totten, Samuel.
  Dictionary of genocide / Samuel Totten and Paul R. Bartrop ; with contributions by Steven
Leonard Jacobs.
     p. cm.
  Includes bibliographical references and index.
  ISBN 978-0-313-32967-8 (set : alk. paper)—ISBN 978-0-313-34642-2 (vol. 1 : alk. paper)—
ISBN 978-0-313-34644-6 (vol. 2 : alk. paper)
  1. Genocide—History. 2. Crimes against humanity—History. I. Bartrop, Paul R. (Paul
Robert), 1955– II. Jacobs, Steven L., 1947– III. Title.
  HV6322.7.T68   2008
  304.6'6303—dc22   2007028430

British Library Cataloguing in Publication Data is available.

Library of Congress Catalog Card Number: 2007028430
ISBN: 978-0-313-32967-8 (set)
         978-0-313-34642-2 (vol. 1)
         978-0-313-34644-6 (vol .2)

First published in 2008

Greenwood Press, 88 Post Road West, Westport, CT 06881
An imprint of Greenwood Publishing Group, Inc.
www.greenwood.com

Printed in the United States of America

The paper used in this book complies with the
Permanent Paper Standard issued by the National
Information Standards Organization (Z39.48-1984)

10 9 8 7 6 5 4 3 2 1

The authors dedicate this book to all past and present victims of genocides and mourn their loss, and those scholars and other activists who are aggressively working on the eradication of this ongoing human tragedy.

Contents

List of Entries

Acknowledgments

Samuel Totten wishes to acknowledge the initial interest and enthusiasm of Drs. Israel W. Charny, Eric Markusen, and Henry Huttenbach in this project.

Paul R. Bartrop would like to acknowledge, with gratitude, the research assistance of Eve Grimm, Morgan Blum, and Jordana Silverstein. He is especially thankful to Margaret Iaquinto, of Bialik College, Melbourne, for the dedication and enthusiasm she brought to the task of guiding him through the necessary intricacies of advanced information technology—sometimes literally saving the day when the project could otherwise have been in jeopardy. Finally, he would like to extend his gratitude to all the students who, since 1998, have passed through the Comparative Genocide Studies elective at Bialik College and who have taught him so much about the need to be precise whenever we are discussing genocide.

Introduction

The idea for the development of this *Dictionary of Genocide* was conceived by Samuel Totten in the late 1990s. This was at a time when an ever-increasing number of scholars in various fields (international law, sociology, political science, history, and psychology, among others) were turning their attention to the seemingly insuperable problem of genocide.

Cognizant of the fact that scholars in different fields often used certain key terms in different ways and that many new terms germane to genocide prevention and intervention were being coined and/or used in various and often extremely different ways, Totten concluded that there was a critical need for a dictionary that accurately, clearly, and concisely delineated genocide-related terminology. It seemed that such a dictionary would make a contribution to the relatively new but burgeoning field of genocide studies and would thus be useful not only to scholars but also to government officials, intergovernmental personnel, and university students.

When a term is defined or understood in various ways by different individuals, groups, and/or organizations, it results in miscommunication. Furthermore, without a clear definition that is agreed upon by most, *if not everyone*, it is difficult, if not impossible, to discuss and analyze, let alone ameliorate, an issue or problem in an effective manner. Indeed, the misunderstanding as to what a specific term means can lead not only to disagreements but also to lengthy and acrimonious debates and arguments as well as missed opportunities to solve critical situations. Ironically, there does not exist a more classic example of such misunderstanding in the field of human rights than the debate over how to define the term *genocide*.

The definition of *genocide* used in the United Nations Convention on the Prevention and Punishment of the Crime of Genocide (UNCG) is the one definition that is internationally recognized by individual states, intergovernmental organizations, ad hoc tribunals such as the International Criminal Tribunal for the former Yugoslavia (ICTY), the International Criminal Tribunal for Rwanda (ICTR), and the International Criminal Court (ICC). That said, numerous scholars have devised their own definitions of *genocide* in an attempt to make the definition either more inclusive (e.g., including groups not covered under the UNCG, such as "political groups") or more exclusive (e.g., limiting the focus to mass murder versus such harmful acts as causing "serious mental harm"). As a result of both the limitations of the UNCG's definition and the many new definitions devised by scholars, there has been an ongoing debate over which definition, if any, is the "best." As many have pointed out, though, while certain alternative definitions to the UNCG may be more useful for analyzing whether a situation constitutes genocide, the *only* definition that has authority within international law is that of the UNCG. It is therefore this definition that is used in prosecutions of those alleged to have committed genocide.

The following definition is that which is found in the UNCG, the latter of which was adopted by Resolution 260 (III) A of the United Nations General Assembly on December 9, 1948:

> In the present Convention, genocide means any of the following acts committed with intent to destroy, in whole or in part, a national, ethnical, racial or religious group, as such:
>
> (a) Killing members of the group;
> (b) Causing serious bodily or mental harm to members of the group;
> (c) Deliberately inflicting on the group conditions of life calculated to bring about its physical destruction in whole or in part;
> (d) Imposing measures intended to prevent births within the group;
> (e) Forcibly transferring children of the group to another group.

Genocide is not the only term that often suffers from being defined in various ways by different individuals and organizations for vastly different reasons (some good, some not). Others, by way of example, include *ethnic cleansing, intent to commit genocide,* and *humanitarian intervention.*

Once the team of authors had been assembled, Totten drew up an initial list of 600 terms. Each author was assigned 150 that most closely complemented his area(s) of interest and expertise. Each of the authors also agreed to add additional terms that he considered essential to include in such a dictionary.

The terms included in the dictionary address an eclectic and broad array of topics, issues, and events. Those terms that have the most direct relationship to genocide deal with such issues as the following: the definition of genocide; theories of genocide; the history of genocide; specific cases of genocide; the prevention of genocide; the intervention of genocide; and the denial of genocide.

An attempt has been made to be as inclusive and comprehensive as possible in regard to the inclusion of terms herein. Be that as it may, the authors realize that various readers will wonder why certain terms were not included and/or why certain terms were not addressed in greater detail. Just as the authors needed to appreciate the following, so do readers: First, space constraints naturally limited the breadth and depth of the entries. Second, the dictionary is just that, a dictionary, not an encyclopedia. Third, the field is rapidly evolving, and new terms are constantly being coined. Even as the dictionary enters publication, there are certain to be new terms in use previously unknown to the authors. That said, the authors have been intent on including as many entries as possible while still providing a solid overview to each and every term, thus making the dictionary as useful as possible for scholars and practitioners in the field.

The authors wrestled constantly over which entries should be included and, more vitally, those that would be omitted—and how such decisions were to be made. In view of the conceptual breadth encompassed by genocide studies, the authors believe that the inclusion of *every* entry is herein justified. It is this commitment to defensible incorporation that in our opinion renders the dictionary an important research resource that will be beneficial for many years to a wide array of users.

Intent on being as comprehensive and as detailed as possible in the selection and write-up of the definitions, respectively, the authors quickly exceeded the number of pages the publisher had allocated for this project. Kindly and generously, when approached about the latter situation, our editor, Debra Adams, and her superiors at Greenwood Publishing, graciously, and without hesitation, suggested that the dictionary be published as a two-volume set. The authors greatly appreciate such outstanding support for this scholarly endeavor.

A genuine effort has been made to provide definitions that are generally most accepted by the international community. Where germane, any debates or disagreements over a term are duly noted and commented upon. In certain cases, alternative definitions are provided, especially when the latter are definitions that are becoming more commonly accepted among scholars and practitioners.

In order to be as accurate as possible in defining the terms, the authors agreed to consult only the most authoritative sources for developing the definitions and to use at least two sources in working up the definition. The rationale for the latter was to prod each of the authors to cross-check the accuracy of the definitions they developed. In fact, it was not unusual for an author to consult four or more sources prior to developing a definition. Furthermore, each of the authors aimed at conceptual and narrative consistency in the writing of their entries. Still, the authors felt it necessary to constantly circulate entries to each other for critique and commentary. As a result of this process, over time a stylistic mean was achieved and maintained.

Despite the Herculean efforts by the authors to be as inclusive, comprehensive, and accurate as possible, they fully realize and appreciate, as previously mentioned, that certain oversights may remain. In that regard, the authors welcome—indeed, encourage—scholars, practitioners, and others to notify them of any oversights or inaccuracies, and every effort will be made to correct such in any forthcoming editions of the dictionary.

An issue to be confronted by all scholars of genocide studies—or for that matter, of any subject that has the word *studies* in its title—is that there is no single and unitary discipline base embedded within it to which one can turn for guidance. Genocide studies, being a subject dealing with the most basic of social, political, economic, religious, intellectual, historical, military, ethical, and cultural issues, is by its very nature broad; almost anything, conceivably, can be included within its ambit. Consequently, it is important to draw attention to the fact that the authors of this dictionary, while each in his own way an internationally recognized authority on specific genocides and/or on general themes pertaining to genocide, are nonetheless not experts on all facets of humanity's genocidal encounter. No one is nor could be. To be so would be akin to being an expert on nothing less than all elements of the human experience, in all countries, at all times, and in all its manifestations. We, of course, do not claim such authority, though we have attempted, using the most conscientious methods possible, to compile a dictionary that will be the first port of call for students, instructors, and researchers involved in the contemplation of the phenomenon of genocide. It is not intended that the entries in the dictionary will be the final word on a subject; indeed, it is strongly counseled that the entries should *never* be employed as a substitute for solid scholarly research.

Although there are various dictionaries available on the Holocaust, human rights, and war, not a single dictionary, until now, has addressed the issue of genocide directly. It is the hope of the authors that this work complements the two major encyclopedias that now exist on the topic of genocide: *Encyclopedia of Genocide* (Santa Barbara, CA: ABC Clio Publishers, 1999) and *Encyclopedia of Genocide and Crimes against Humanity* (New York: Macmillan, 2004).

Having said that, it should be pointed out that we hold the dictionary to be a valuable resource for those seeking to ascertain meanings of terms with which they are unfamiliar. It also provides the rudimentary details of the lives of key individuals as they relate to genocide and establishes a useful context into which concepts and events can be understood.

A project of this nature cannot be undertaken without additional assistance from others. A vast number of colleagues and contacts, too numerous to mention here, have been consulted on individual points of detail over the course of the research phase of this dictionary. Although we cannot name them all, we are certain that they will recognize their input as they read over the entries of their specific interest.

In the early stages of preparing this dictionary, another genocide studies scholar, Henry Huttenbach of City University, New York, participated as an author. Unfortunately, personal circumstances saw Henry withdraw from the project after having drafted a number of entries. The authors would like to place on record their acknowledgment of Henry's initial involvement in the project and recognize the efforts he made while a member of the team. The authors also wish to acknowledge the contribution of Steven Leonard Jacobs, Department of Religion at the University of Alabama at Tuscaloosa, for his hard work and assistance in regard to suggesting potential terms to define, initial work on a wide range of terms, and drafting of numerous terms.

A

Abdul Hamid II (1842–1918). Sultan of the Ottoman Empire (1876–1909). During his reign, a series of massacres of Armenians took place throughout the empire, most notably between 1894 and 1896. These massacres were ordered by the sultan for the purpose of intimidating the Armenian population into acquiescing to Turkish demands that they cease agitating for special status and that they dampen their national aspirations. For these (and other) atrocities within the empire, Abdul Hamid was often described as the "Red Sultan," due to the bloodshed he was responsible for having unleashed. As sultan, Abdul Hamid was conscious of the need for Turkey to modernize, but he sensed that by doing so the inhabitants of the Ottoman Empire would see new opportunities through education, technology, and commerce that could destabilize his autocratic rule. Consequently, he was resistant to reform on a broad scale, notwithstanding his encouragement of higher education for certain levels of society—though as a force for regime reinforcement rather than public enlightenment. Abdul Hamid's rule became renowned for its harshness, even despotism, and his often reactionary approach to developments within his realm led to a stifling of all initiative from those who might have been his chief supporters. In 1908, a group led by educated military officers, colloquially known as the Young Turks, staged a coup d'état in which power passed from the absolutism of the sultan to rule by a military clique. He was succeeded in 1909 by Mohammed V (1844–1918; reigned 1908–1918), whose rule was henceforth overseen by the Young Turks.

ABiH (Bosnian, ARBiH; *Armija Republike Bosne i Hercegovine* or The Army of the Republic of Bosnia and Herzegovina). The Muslim-led army of Bosnia and Herzegovina during the conflict in the former Yugoslavia between 1992 and 1995.

Absolutism. A style of monarchy in which the monarch wields power to an almost unlimited degree. It is important to realize that an absolute monarch does not possess the same power as a despot, in that his or her authority is limited by age-old convention, often unwritten constitutional constraints, and an aristocracy (or nobility) that can keep the unrestrained power of the monarch in check should the exercise of that power descend into arbitrary—and, therefore, unstable—behavior. Absolute power is most frequently a highly centralized form of power, with the reins of government and administration often embodied directly in the person of the monarch. The most famous example of absolutist rule is to be found in the France of King Louis XIV (1643–1715), during whose reign the notion of an all-powerful absolute ruler—in which the sovereign was the representative of God on earth and thus above the affairs of all other human beings—reached its zenith. In its purest form, royal absolutism is resistant to the arbitrary temptations of tyranny, as an absolutist ruler is invested with an aura of paternal responsibility toward the people over whom he or she rules. In view of this, the system, though undemocratic, is one in which the protection of the population from the excesses of government, at least in theory, is the primary duty of the monarch.

Accelerator. The term *accelerator* refers to the worsening of a situation or grievance(s) between or among groups, which, in turn, increases the probability of an event or incident that could trigger the outbreak of violence or precipitate the start of a violent conflict.

Aché. In 1974, the International League for the Rights of Man and the Inter-American Association for Democracy and Freedom issued the charge that the government of Paraguay was complicit in genocide against the Guayaki Indians (Aché). In doing so, the two organizations filed a complaint with the United Nations secretary-general in which they listed a series of alleged violations that they claimed would ultimately lead to the disappearance of the Guayaki ethnic group. Most of the killings—as well as the forcible transfer of Aché children—had been committed by Paraguayan ranchers, farmers, and laborers and not by members of the Paraguayan army or police forces. Some scholars and activists argued at the time that de facto genocide had occurred and that the Paraguayan government was responsible due to the fact that it had failed to adequately protect its citizens. It was also argued that the Paraguayan government purposely disregarded the actions against the Aché because it favored the opening up of lands for ranching, farming, and other uses. During the debate that ensued over the plight and fate of the Aché, it was argued by some that the issue of the "intent" to commit genocide was difficult, if not impossible, to establish in a clear and decisive manner. Leo Kuper (1908–1994), an early and noted genocide scholar, countered (in his book, *Genocide: Its Political Use in the Twentieth Century*. New Haven, CT: Yale University, 1981) that intent could be imputed when such killings and kidnapping had become an established practice, and, he continued, the latter is exactly what the Aché had faced.

Actors. In international relations, an actor is any entity possessed of a distinctive individual character (or "personality"), sufficient to enable it to play a role within the international community. Most frequently, actors take the form of states, though actors can also be intergovernmental or nongovernmental organizations, transnational corporate companies, heads of state, or heads of global institutions. In the modern world, dominated by the Westphalian states system (established in 1648 as a result of the Treaty of Westphalia at the end of the Thirty Years' War), it is still the state that serves as the primary actor in international relations. Diplomatic recognition, and the relations that come from this, form the foundation of interstate action today. Increasingly, however, nonstate actors— ranging from movements for national independence such as the Kosovo Liberation Army and the African National Congress, to alliance systems such as the North Atlantic Treaty Organization, to terrorist organizations such as Al-Qaeda or Jema'ah Islamiya, to international bodies like the World Health Organization or the International Committee of the Red Cross—are also considered as actors within international relations, though they do not possess the same status as do states and are consequently often frozen out of negotiations (or accorded only observer status) in multilateral dialogues. The roles of actors in international relations are as multifaceted as the types of actors themselves, and it is anticipated that the number of such roles will increase as the twenty-first century unfolds.

Adana. Region and city on the Mediterranean coast of the Ottoman Empire, situated in approximately the same location as the former province of Cilicia. In April 1909, widespread massacres of Armenians took place in Adana, masked by civil strife accompanying the Young Turk revolution and involving attempts by defenders of the deposed Sultan Abdul Hamid II (1842–1918; reigned 1876–1909) to reestablish his autocratic rule. Taken as a whole, the massacres throughout the city of Adana and its hinterland numbered up to thirty thousand Armenians and can be seen both as an afterword to the Hamidian Massacres of 1894–1896 and as a precursor of the more extensive Armenian genocide that began in April 1915. First-person accounts and other documentation have variously implicated supporters both of the sultan and of the Young Turks for the massacres, and it can be said that this outbreak of destructive anti-Armenian savagery was perpetrated by elements on both sides. Despite this, the most important legacy of the massacres was the further reinforcement of murderous violence as a means of action toward the Armenian population of the empire. The socialization of the Turkish population into an acceptance of mass killing authorized by the state, which began at the end of the nineteenth century, was maintained and extended as a result of the Adana massacres, preparing for the much greater cataclysm that was to come in the form of the infamous Ottoman Turk-perpetrated Armenian genocide between 1915 and 1923. Certain Armenians, for their part, realized henceforward that the new Turkey inaugurated by the Young Turks had only a limited role for them to play and that this role was not likely to embrace full and equal participation in the future of the empire.

Administrative Measures. The term *administrative measures* was a euphemism used by the Soviet authorities during the 1932–1933 man-made Ukraine famine and was "used to mean brute force applied in an arbitrary fashion" (Commission on the Ukraine Famine, 1988, p. 229).

Advisory Committee on Genocide Prevention. The Advisory Committee on Genocide Prevention, which was formed in May 2006, was the brainchild of UN Secretary-General Kofi Annan (b. 1938). The committee was established in order to provide support to the secretary general's special adviser on the prevention of genocide, Juan Mendez (b. 1944). Its mandate is to meet at least twice a year. It initially comprised a wide range of experts, including those on conflict prevention, human rights, peacekeeping, diplomacy, and mediation. Among the members of the initial Advisory Committee were: Senator Romeo Dallaire (b. 1946) of Canada (who served as head of the United Nations Assistance Mission for Rwanda [UNAMIR] prior to and during the 1994 Rwandan genocide); Nobel Peace Prize recipient Bishop Desmond Tutu; Gareth Evans of Australia, president of the International Crisis Group and former minister for foreign affairs of Australia; and Sadako Ogata of Japan, cochair of the Commission on Human Security and former high commissioner for refugees.

Aegis Trust for the Prevention of Genocide. Aegis Trust is a nonsectarian, nongovernmental organization genocide prevention initiative that aims to promote a fundamental change in the response to genocidal situations, moving away from reactive measures to policies of prevention. It is based in Nottinghamshire, England.

Afghanistan, Genocide in. In April 1978, a communist government seized power in Afghanistan and immediately set about the task of remaking society in order to entrench its rule. During the first eighteen months of the regime, the precommunist intelligentsia was wiped out in the tens of thousands, and scores of thousands more fled to countries in the West. As Afghanistan seemed to be sliding toward chaos, troops from the USSR invaded in

December 1979 in order to prop up the communist regime and install politicians better disposed toward the Soviet Union. Once the occupation of the country was an established fact, the Soviets were faced with constant guerrilla war from armed Afghan opponents of the Soviet occupation, who called themselves Mujahideen (fundamentalist Islamic freedom fighters). Afghanistan, a country that is essentially rural and agrarian, possessed a society that offered natural cover for the Mujahideen, and the Soviet strategy to combat their effectiveness took two forms. First, Soviet troops launched a systematic operation to depopulate certain regions so that the Mujahideen would be deprived of an environment from which to launch their attacks on the occupiers; second, they initiated a military campaign in which they hoped their more modern and superior firepower would shatter the ability of the insurgents to fight back. It was intended through this that so much destruction would take place that the civilian population would be deprived of the will to continue sheltering the Mujahideen. Such military strategies were effective over large parts of the country, and the toll on the Afghani people was catastrophic. It has been estimated that the military conflict claimed 180,000 casualties overall, with 90,000 killed. But civilian deaths numbered more than 1.5 million, representing 10 percent of the total population (and 13.5% of the male population). Some 6 million refugees fled to surrounding countries; Afghanistan was laid waste, with agricultural production and livestock numbers halved. The Soviet strategy of "rubblization" returned the country to the Dark Ages, paving the way for a radicalization of the survivors (many of whom joined the now infamous Taliban movement) that would be realized in the decade after the Soviet departure in 1988.

African Union (AU). The AU was established in September 1999 as the result of an extraordinary session of the Organization of African Unity (OAU), in which African heads of state and government leaders issued a declaration (the Sirte Declaration) calling for its establishment. The AU's main objective, building on those of the OAU, is to accelerate the process of continental integration for member states by addressing the multifaceted social, economic, and political problems prevailing throughout Africa. The major rubric under which the AU operates is the unity of African peoples and states; given this, it is deeply committed to removing the last vestiges of colonialism and assisting all its members to develop their full potential in a truly African context. It rejects foreign exploitation and seeks to build a strong economic environment from within Africa itself. Further, it is committed to peace, security, and stability for the continent and thus serves as the principal body through which African states and peoples can promote democracy and the guarantee of fundamental human and civil rights. The AU's most pressing concern, since its establishment, has been the ongoing humanitarian crisis and genocide in Darfur, Sudan, an issue still requiring (as of late 2007) resolution. Much of the AU's activity in this regard has been directed toward the attainment of a settlement without external intervention from the United Nations. Darfur has thus served as an important testing ground for the African Union; such gains as it has made have not always been appreciated by the international community, individual nation-states, and scholars, all of whom have often held that Darfur is a bigger problem than the fledgling AU can handle by itself. As things stand, the AU is in danger of becoming another multi-nation "talking shop" unless it can achieve the unity its founding documents proclaim.

African Union, Constitutive Act. In Article 4 of this act, it notes "the right of the Union to intervene in a Member State pursuant to a decision of the Assembly in respect of grave circumstances, namely: war crimes, genocide, and crimes against humanity."

"Agenda for Peace." On January 31, 1992, then secretary-general of the United Nations Boutros Boutros-Ghali (b. 1922) was tasked by the UN Security Council to prepare for circulation to the entire membership of the UN "an analysis and recommendations on ways of strengthening and making more efficient within the framework of the [U.N.] Charter the capacity of the United Nations for preventive diplomacy, for peacemaking and for peace-keeping" and to do so no later than July 1, 1992. That report, dated June 17, 1992, was entitled "An Agenda for Peace: Preventive Diplomacy, Peacemaking and Peace-keeping," and it addressed the following topics: (1) the changing context; (2) definitions; (3) preventive diplomacy—measures to build confidence, fact-finding, early warning, preventive deployment, demilitarized zones; (4) peacemaking—the World Court, amelioration through assistance, sanctions and special economic problems, use of military force, peace-enforcement units; (5) peacekeeping—increasing demands, new departures in peacekeeping, personnel, logistics; (6) postconflict peace-building; (7) cooperation with regional arrangements and organizations; (8) safety of personnel; (9) financing; and (10) an Agenda for Peace (which also addressed the questions of power, democracy, trust, reform, and dialogue among nations).

The lengthier "Supplement to an Agenda for Peace: Position Paper of the Secretary-General on the Occasion of the Fiftieth Anniversary of the United Nations," dated January 3, 1995, comprised the following: (1) introduction; (2) quantitative and qualitative changes; (3) instruments for peace and security—preventive diplomacy and peacemaking, peacekeeping, postconflict peace-building, disarmament, sanctions, enforcement action; (4) coordination; (5) financial resources; and (6) conclusion.

Both documents are comprehensive in nature and thoroughly address the issues with which they are concerned. Tragically, as is evidenced by the 1994 Rwandan genocide, the 1995 genocide in Srebrenica, and the ongoing genocide in Darfur (which ignited in 2003 and is ongoing as of today, late 2007), the oft-used cliché "the spirit is willing but the body is weak" seems applicable here: the right words have been said, but the lack of action, all too often the result of bitter political infighting and rivalries, continues to prevent the UN from acting in a decisive manner to halt crimes against humanity and genocide.

Akashi, Yasushi (b. 1931). Japanese diplomat and officer of the United Nations Secretariat (the first Japanese national to be employed in this role). In his long career of over forty years with the United Nations, he served in numerous posts, rising to under-secretary-general (USG) for humanitarian affairs and emergency relief coordinator. One of his postings, during 1995, was as Special Representative of the Secretary-General (SRSG) to the former Yugoslavia. His major approach in this undertaking was an avowed stance of emphasizing UN impartiality with regard to all sides involved in the fighting during the Bosnian War (1992–1995). This attracted controversy from many critics around the world, who claimed that a policy of impartiality aided the Serbs by enabling them to aggress against the Bosnian Muslims with impunity, while not permitting the Muslims to defend themselves—and the latter was exacerbated by retaining the declared UN arms embargo on all sides, which prevented the Muslims from purchasing weapons to protect themselves with from the ongoing barrage of Serbian attacks. Some detractors implicated Akashi in the success of the Bosnian Serb assault on the eastern Bosnian city of Srebrenica in July 1995; his evenhandedness, it was argued, led to a reluctance to authorize UN military action against the Serb forces commanded by General Ratko Mladic (b. 1942), resulting in the victory of the Serbs and their subsequent massacre of between seven thousand and eight thousand Muslim boys and men from the city. The UN leadership did not see any such complicity, and after his tour of duty in Bosnia, Akashi received very senior postings: as SRSG for Cambodia, USG for disarmament affairs, and USG for public information. He had previously served as Japanese ambassador to the United Nations in 1974.

Akayesu, Jean-Paul (b. 1953). The trial of Jean-Paul Akayesu at the International Criminal Court for Rwanda (ICTR) was the first genocide trial in an international court in history. (Many are under the misconception that the Nuremberg Tribunal conducted the first trials of genocide, but they, in fact, tried the defendants on charges of crimes against humanity, crimes against peace, and war crimes, but not genocide.) Richard Goldstone, the chief prosecutor of the ICTR and the International Criminal Tribunal of the former Yugoslavia (ICTY), charged Akayesu with twelve counts of genocide, crimes against humanity, and violations of Article II of the 1949 Geneva Conventions. Ultimately, three additional counts of genocide and crimes against humanity were added to the charges, which alleged that he had ordered and condoned the rape and sexual mutilation—and then, the murder—of hundreds of Tutsi women.

Akayesu had been a schoolteacher, then a school district inspector, prior to his election to the office of *bourgmestre*, or mayor, of the small Rwandan town of Taba in April 1993. He was a member of the Hutu political party known as the *Mouvement Démocratique Républicain* (MDR), the Democratic Republican Movement, which he joined in 1991 and of which he soon thereafter became the local branch president. In his capacity as mayor, Akayesu had control of the communal police and was responsible for the maintenance of order, but his authority extended beyond these formal limits. In Rwanda, a considerable degree of informal dominion devolved upon the role of mayor, who acted as a kind of father figure within the commune. During the genocide that began in April 1994, it has been estimated that some two thousand Tutsi were massacred in Taba, many of whom had sought refuge in the Bureau Communale (approximating a city hall and a community center)—the heart of Akayesu's domain. It has been alleged that Akayesu did not provide support or succor for those his position had entrusted him to protect; it has also been alleged that he actively encouraged the *Interahamwe* militias who had come to Taba, as well as the local Hutu population, to participate in the mass murder, rape, and torture of the Tutsi. In the aftermath of the conquest of Rwanda in July 1994 by the forces of the Tutsi-led Rwandan Patriotic Front (RPF), Akayesu fled the country. He was arrested in Lusaka, Zambia, on October 10, 1995, and transferred to the jurisdiction of the ICTR, in Arusha, Tanzania, on May 15, 1996. His trial began on January 9, 1997. The trial prosecutor for the Akayesu case was Pierre-Richard Prosper (b. 1963), a U.S. citizen and an attorney, who mounted a successful case in which Akayesu was found guilty, on September 2, 1998, of nine of the fifteen counts—including all of those that related to genocide (inciting genocide, rape as a case of genocide, and genocide). Not only did this make Jean-Paul Akayesu the first person convicted of the specific crime of genocide in an internationally accredited courtroom, but it marked the first occasion on which the UN Genocide Convention of 1948 was upheld as law. The trial and conviction of Akayesu was also notable due to the fact that the verdict/conviction was the first to find rape to be a crime of genocide.

Akayesu was sentenced, on October 2, 1998, to life imprisonment, and, though he appealed, his conviction was confirmed on June 1, 2001. Akayesu is currently serving out his life sentence in Bamako Central Prison, Mali.

Akazu (**Kinyarwanda, "Little House"**). Euphemism given to the heart of the political structure of the Rwandan ruling party, the *Mouvement Révolutionnaire Nationale pour le Développement* (National Revolutionary Movement for Development), or MRND, from 1975 to 1994. The party was begun by Major General Juvenal Habyarimana (1937–1994) as a means of centralizing radical Hutu ideologies across all of Rwanda and taking control of the bureaucracy, the church, and the military—all within the structure of a one-party state, with Habyarimana at its center as president. The major locus of power within this structure was the so-called Akazu, an informal but tight-knit (and highly corrupt) network of Habyarimana's closest family members, friends, and party associates. It was said to be so thoroughly dominated by Habyarimana's wife Agathe (née Kazinga) that, at times, even her husband was often frozen out of the decision-making process. (It was for this essential reason that the Akazu was known in some circles as Le Clan de Madame, a direct reference to the dominance she wielded over those in the circle.) The name Akazu was originally, in precolonial times, a term given to the inner circle of courtiers to the royal family; under the MRND regime, and particularly Agathe Habyarimana's dominance, it developed such awesome power that it even instituted its own death squad, recruited from members of the Presidential Guard. The Akazu was, in reality, an oligarchy that not only held back any possibility of Rwanda returning to democracy but also worked assiduously to promote the interests of northern Rwanda (the Akazu base) over those of the south, to further destabilize the position of the minority Tutsi throughout the country, and, through its extensive network of supporters in the bureaucracy, the financial sector, and society generally, to skim off vast amounts of public money for the sole good of the extended Habyarimana family. The Akazu is the focus of most accusations concerning the planning of the Rwandan genocide of the Tutsi in 1994, with some even suggesting that it was Akazu members who arranged for Juvenal Habyarimana's plane to be shot down on April 6, 1994—the spark that triggered the genocide that took place over the next hundred days and resulted in the murder of between five hundred thousand and one million Tutsis and moderate Hutus.

Aktion(en) (**German, operation[s]**). Best understood as a term used predominantly by the SS (*Schutzstaffel* or "Security Police") and their allies to describe the nonmilitary campaign of roundups and deportations of Jews and other "undesirables" in the eastern territories under German occupation. The two most significant of these *aktionen* were (1) *Aktion Reinhard*, after the assassination of RHSA (*Reichssicherheitshauptamt*, "Reich Security Main Office") chief Reinhard Heydrich on May 27, 1942, in Prague, Czechoslovakia, whose purpose was to murder all the Jews in the five districts of the *Generalgouvernement* (General Government) encompassing Krakow, Warsaw, Radom, Lublin, and Galicia, and later expanded to include all Jews deported to occupied Poland; and (2) *Aktion 1005*, which was developed in the summer of 1942 to obliterate all traces of the Nazi *Endlösung* (Final Solution) by the use of slave laborers, including Jews who were subsequently murdered, to both exhume and burn the bodies of the Nazis' victims. Nearly 400 anti-Jewish *aktionen* took place between November 1939 and October 1944.

Aktion Reinhard (**German, Operation Reinhard**). Code name given to the Nazi implementation of the "Final Solution of the Jewish Question" from 1942 onward. The name was conferred on the operation as a memorial to the head of the Reich Security Main Office and the Gestapo, Reinhard Heydrich (1904–1942), who was assassinated by Czech partisans in June 1942. At first, the plan was to inaugurate measures that would lead to the eradication of the Jewish population of the area known as the *Generalgouvernement* (the Nazi reconstruction of Nazi-occupied Poland, part of which was designated as the area where the extermination of Jews and other "undesirables" would be undertaken), but the scope of the plan broadened to include Jews transferred to Poland from throughout Nazi-occupied Europe. *Aktion Reinhard* was thus an undertaking embracing the resettlement and mass murder of millions of Jews, accompanied by the plunder and transmission of Jewish property back to the Reich. The reach of the operation was so extensive that its realization "necessitated" the creation of three extermination camps in eastern Poland: Sobibor, Belzec, and Treblinka. These became known as the *Aktion Reinhard* Camps and were established with the specific task of murdering Jews. By the time of their termination in 1943, the three camps had resulted in the murders of nearly two million Jews: 250,000 at Sobibor, 600,000 at Belzec, and 870,000 at Treblinka. *Aktion Reinhard* was such a major part of the Holocaust that its contours have come to characterize the popular image of the Nazi destruction of Europe's Jews.

al Anfal Campaign. *See* Anfal.

al-Bashir, Omar Hassan Ahmed (b. 1944). Omar Hassan al-Bashir has been the leader of Sudan since 1989. Born into a peasant family of farming laborers in the tiny village of Hosh Bannaga, north of Khartoum, al-Bashir joined the army as a young man, studied at a military college in Cairo, Egypt, became a paratrooper, and participated in Egypt's war against Israel in 1973. Returning to Sudan, and four years after having been promoted to the rank of general by the democratically elected President Sadeq al-Mahdi (b. 1936), al-Bashir participated in the June 30, 1989, military coup. With the support of Hassan al-Turabi (b. 1932), the fundamentalist leader of the National Islamic Front (NIF), al-Bashir immediately set out to "islamicize" the state. He then dissolved parliament, banned all political parties, and forced all free presses to shut down. He also named himself chief of state, prime minister, chief of the armed forces, and minister of defense. In 1991, al-Bashir instituted sharia (strict adherence to Islamic religious law) and intensified a scorched-earth campaign in which Muslim Arabs from the north had long been engaged in a hard-fought battle with Christian and animist black Africans in the south. (As far back as 1983, the southern-based Sudan People's Liberation Army [SPLA] had begun fighting the Sudanese government in an effort to gain self-determination and establish a secular democracy. From that point onward, the Sudanese government had undertaken a brutal war to suppress the effort. For close to twenty years, al-Bashir's regime carried out military attacks in the south of Sudan, during which time it is estimated some 2 million people lost their lives. Finally, in 2002, following a prolonged peace process, the war in the south came to an end.)

Beginning in 2003, al-Bashir's regime undertook a scorched-earth campaign against the black Africans of Darfur in western Sudan. Beginning in the 1990s, Arabs and black Africans in the Darfur region began to clash over land and water use, primarily as a result of a severe drought and increasing desertification. Over time, the clashes became increasingly violent, but when the clashes were adjudicated by courts, the black Africans often found themselves being treated less fairly than the Arab population. For many years (beginning in the early 1990s and continuing through the early 2000s), in fact, black Africans of Darfur complained bitterly that the Arabs in the region were given preferential treatment over black Africans by the Sudanese government. For example, black Africans asserted that although the Sudanese government taxed them, the government did little to nothing to enhance the infrastructure of Darfur (i.e., the development of roads and schools). They also called for better treatment of black Africans at the hands of the police and court system.

When the black Africans felt that their complaints were falling on deaf ears, a rebel group, the Sudanese Liberation Army (SLA), formed and, in early 2003, began carrying out attacks against government and military installations. Shorthanded due to the war in the south, al-Bashir hired nomadic Arabs to join forces with government of Sudan (GOS) troops to fight the rebels. However, instead of focusing their attacks solely on the rebels, the GOS and the Arab militia (referred to as the *Janjaweed*, or horsemen with guns) carried out a scorched-earth policy against all black Africans in the three-state region of Darfur. Supporting the desire of the al-Bashir's government to allow only Arabs to reside in Sudan, the GOS troops and the *Janjaweed* were bent on either forcing the black Africans to flee Sudan or killing them. Within a short period of time, hundreds of villages had been utterly destroyed by the GOS and the *Janjaweed*, thousands of black Africans had been killed and raped, and hundreds of thousands had fled, seeking sanctuary elsewhere. By late 2004, it was estimated that close to 2 million refugees had sought sanctuary in internally displaced camps (IDP) within Sudan and almost 200,000 others had fled to refugee camps just over the border in Chad. Estimates of the dead ranged from 250,000 to 400,000. By mid-2007, it was estimated that up to 2.5 million black Africans were in IDP camps and over 250,000 were in refugee camps in Chad. Beginning in late 2006 and continuing into 2007, GOS troops and the *Janjaweed* began carrying out attacks on the IDP camps and even on the refugee camps in Chad, where the two groups continued to kill people and rape girls and women at will.

Albigensian Crusade. Between the twelfth and the fourteenth centuries CE, a situation arose in southern France whereby the Cathars, or Albigensians, were accused by the Roman Catholic Church of heresy. In its drive to wipe out all traces of dissent, the French Church fell upon the freethinking people of the Languedoc region, destroying them utterly. The campaign to crush the Cathars was considered by the Church to be a Crusade in that the Cathars were not held to be Christian in the accepted sense but rather a race of apostates. This Crusade was directed by the French monarchy and executed by the French nobility, particularly from the northern parts of the country; the campaign had an added political character in that the northerners were able to conquer the south, thereby assisting the process of French unification. The means employed to suppress the Cathars were denunciations, torture, and, frequently, mass execution through burning at the stake or in open pits. Although some have questioned the applicability of the term *genocide* to describe the fate of the Cathars—*religious persecution* being a preferred expression—there can be little doubt that the Cathars formed an identifiable group (which would have been recognized as such [e.g., a religious group] under the terms of the 1948 UN Convention on the Prevention and Punishment of the Crime of Genocide [UNCG]) and that the measures instituted against them by the Church fit under the terms laid down by the UNCG. When all was said and done, cities with populations numbering in the tens of thousands were wiped out; areas were depopulated, and the crusaders took literally the command attributed to the Cistercian bishop who led the Crusade, Arnold Amaury (d. 1225), during the final assault on the city of Beziers, to "Kill them all; God will know His own!" By the end of the process, at the beginning of the fourteenth century, Catharism was no more, its existence as a major alternative Christian movement in France snuffed out by sword and fire.

Allied Force. The official operation name of NATO's controversial bombing of Kosovo in 1999 that was undertaken in order to force the Serbs from "cleansing" and killing the Albanian residents.

al-Majid, Ali Hassan (b. 1941). Ali Hassan al-Majid, commonly referred to as "Chemical Ali" by Western journalists, was minister of defense in the Baath Party regime of Iraqi dictator Saddam Hussein (1937–2006). A first cousin of Hussein, al-Majid was also one of his senior advisers and was a brutal "enforcer" for the regime. Renowned for his ability to mobilize state resources in order to repress dissent, al-Majid was appointed as Hussein's military governor after the occupation of Kuwait in 1990–1991 and played an important role in extending Iraqi control over the conquered country. Earlier, between 1986 and 1989, he had already achieved a fearsome reputation during the Anfal Campaign against Iraq's Kurdish population in the north, where his willingness to use mustard gas and nerve gas against Kurdish civilians led to international accusations of genocide leveled at Hussein's government—accusations that were subsequently verified by numerous independent organizations (e.g., Human Rights Watch) in the West. After Iraq's defeat in the Gulf War of 1991, Kurds in the north and Shiites in the south (specifically, the Ma'dan people, or "Marsh Arabs"), encouraged by U.S. president George H. W. Bush (b. 1924), rebelled against Baath Party rule. Again, al-Majid was in the forefront of the suppression of this resistance. Throughout the 1990s, al-Majid continued to act as Hussein's chief intimidator, subduing another attempt at Shiite insurgency in 1999—resulting, again, in substantial loss of life. Following the final defeat of the Hussein government in the spring of 2003 by the U.S.-led "Coalition of the Willing," doubt existed as to al-Majid's fate; initial reports about his death gave way to later reports that he was missing, though presumed dead. When finally, on August 21, 2003, he was captured by U.S. forces, he became one of the highest-profile of all alleged Iraqi war criminals. Along with Saddam Hussein and other leading members of his government, al-Majid was placed on trial before the Iraq Special Tribunal for Crimes Against Humanity (IST), an ad hoc court established by the Iraqi Governing Council in December 2003. As of September 2007, al-Majid's trial is continuing.

AMAR Appeal. The AMAR Appeal was established in Britain in 1991 to deliver emergency humanitarian aid for refugees and other vulnerable people in the region of the Persian Gulf. It is essentially a worldwide appeal on behalf of the Shia of southern Iraq, the so-called Marsh Arabs, or Ma'dan people. The AMAR Appeal was founded by a British member of Parliament, the Conservative politician Emma Nicholson (b. 1941)—now Baroness Nicholson of Winterbourne, a Liberal Democrat and member of the European Parliament. The main work of the AMAR Appeal has focused on providing basic health care, clean water, and essential educational services for those Ma'dan who were made homeless by the military campaign waged against them by the armed forces of Iraqi dictator Saddam Hussein (1937–2006) after the Gulf War of 1991. Up to 95,000 still live in refugee camps in Iran, unable to return to their previous way of life owing to Hussein's policy of draining the marshland environment in which their ancestors had lived for thousands of years—an act of retribution after the Ma'dan had risen in revolt following the Gulf War. AMAR has received funding from the British and other governments, from international agencies, and from corporate and private donations. The AMAR philosophy rests on restoring hope to those who were brutalized under the former Hussein regime; its key principle is to build local capacity, keeping its overhead to a minimum and employing local staff as much as possible. The AMAR mission statement clearly delineates the aims of the organization: "to recover and to sustain professional services in medicine, public health, education and basic need provision within refugee and other communities living under stress in war zones or in areas of civil disorder and disruption." In order to achieve these objectives, AMAR engages in a wide variety of activities locally while raising consciousness about the ongoing plight of the Ma'dan externally. Since 1991, AMAR has raised over £8 million to assist its relief operations.

Amaury, Arnold (d. 1225). A French Cistercian bishop of the twelfth and thirteenth centuries, also known as Arnald Amalric. The papal plenipotentiary in Languedoc, he was later appointed archbishop of Narbonne. Instrumental in the campaign of the Roman Catholic Church to wipe out the alleged heresy of the Cathars, or Albigensians, who were practicing their version of Christianity in southern France between the twelfth and the fourteenth centuries CE, Amaury led his followers in what was considered by the Church to be a Crusade. The Cathars were not held to be Christian in the accepted sense but rather were considered a race of apostates. The means employed to suppress the Cathars were denunciations, torture, and, frequently, mass execution through burning at the stake or in open pits. The final assault against the major Cathar stronghold, the city of Beziers, took place in July 1209. As the troops were looking to Amaury for advice on to how to distinguish Cathars from Catholics, he is reputed to have said, in Latin, "Caedite eos. Novit enim Dominus qui sunt eius," or "Kill them all. God will know His own!" Though there is some dispute as to whether Amaury actually did utter these infamous words—they are attributed to him but undocumented—there is no doubt that they clearly encapsulate the attitude prevailing at the time. What is certain is that the sack of the city and the utter annihilation of its inhabitants—Catholic as well as Cathar—formed part of Church policy, as the wider campaign of Cathar suppression saw them completely destroyed as a major alternative Christian movement in France by the beginning of the fourteenth century.

Ambassador Morgenthau's Story. The title of a memoir produced by the U.S. ambassador to the Ottoman Empire between 1913 and 1916, Henry Morgenthau, Sr. (1856–1946). The account pertains primarily to his observations of the Young Turk genocide of the Armenians, beginning in April 1915. The book was published in 1918 by Doubleday, Page and Co., New York, and had the approval of the U.S. State Department. It brought to a wide reading audience the devastation wrought by the Turks on the Armenian people during 1915–1916 and was written in a style that inflamed much American opinion against the Turks. A preliminary rendering of *Ambassador Morgenthau's Story* appeared in the monthly magazine *The World's Work* in November 1918 and thus received some measure of wider circulation just as the book was gaining currency. Among Morgenthau's conclusions regarding the genocide is the very important one that the killing of Armenians was a premeditated policy on the part of the Turks and that, in his numerous meetings with Young Turk leaders—principally, Mehemet Talaat Pasha (1874–1921)—damning statements of culpability in the killings were made frequently. Critics of Morgenthau's memoir, many of whom adopt a denial position regarding the Armenian genocide, contend that the book is a distortion of the truth; was wartime propaganda; and was produced for the purpose of stirring up hatred of Turkey, which its continued appearance still does today. *Ambassador Morgenthau's Story* has gone through many reprintings and is still currently available, published most recently by Wayne State University Press in Detroit, Michigan.

Amin, Idi (c. 1925–2003). Idi Amin Dada Oumee ruled Uganda as military dictator between January 25, 1971, and April 13, 1979. It is not certain when he was born; a range of dates between 1923 and 1928 has been discussed, with 1925 being the most commonly cited. After a very basic education, Amin joined the King's African Rifles of the British colonial army as a private in 1946 and rose through the ranks to become sergeant major before obtaining a commission as lieutenant. Amin expressed himself best physically, at first as an athlete—he was both a champion swimmer and Uganda's light-heavyweight boxing titleholder between 1951 and 1960—and then as a tough military disciplinarian. After Uganda's independence in 1962, the country's first prime minister, Milton Obote (1924–2005), promoted Amin to captain (1963); then to deputy commander of the army (1964); and then to general and chief of staff of the armed services (1965). Amin's rise had been spectacular, but it was possibly because of that very success that, after a while, Obote began to have second thoughts about his protégé. Relations between the two became increasingly acrimonious until, in January 1971, Amin launched a coup against Obote's government while the prime minister was attending a Commonwealth Heads of Government Meeting in Singapore. Amin declared himself president and began a reign of terror throughout the country. Shortly after taking power, he established "killer squads" for the purpose of rooting out and murdering Obote's supporters; these squads were responsible for scores of thousands of deaths and for perpetrating state-sponsored rape and torture. On August 9, 1972, Amin ordered the expulsion of all Asians (mainly Indians or descendants of Indians, a great many possessing Ugandan citizenship) within ninety days. In conditions of great hardship, most managed to obtain urgently needed sanctuary before the deadline expired. All in all, the Amin regime was responsible for up to 300,000 deaths, though some estimates reach as high as half a million. In June 1976, an Air France passenger plane flying from Tel Aviv to Paris was hijacked by Arab terrorists, who separated the Jews on board from the non-Jews (the latter of whom they released in Benghazi, Libya). The ninety-eight Jews on the plane were taken to Entebbe, Uganda, and held hostage at the airport there. The Israeli government launched a successful commando raid to rescue the hostages—effectively an incursion into sovereign Ugandan territory—in which Amin was a bit player pushed aside by bigger events. There was little doubt that the terrorists found their way to Uganda because of their expectation of a positive reception from Amin, a Muslim. In October 1978, Amin overreached himself when he attacked neighboring Tanzania; not only did that country's troops launch a successful counterattack, but they took the fight into Uganda itself, forcing Amin out of office in 1979 and restoring Obote in 1980. Amin, who became more and more devout religiously, found sanctuary first in Libya and then in Saudi Arabia. He died in Saudi Arabia on August 16, 2003, never having been called to account for the crimes against humanity committed under his rule and in his name.

Amnesty. A legal guarantee that a person or group will not be charged or held.

Amnesty International (AI). AI is a worldwide human rights movement of people acting on the conviction that governments must not deny individuals their basic human rights. Founded in 1961 in London by Peter Benenson (1921–2005), a barrister, it was the recipient of the Nobel Peace Prize in 1977. AI bases its work on the United Nations Universal Declaration of Human Rights. As part of its campaign to protect fundamental human rights, AI regularly publishes country reports and other documents on human rights issues around the world. It also issues "urgent action bulletins" for the purpose of alerting its membership of the dire need to contact government officials where particularly serious or egregious human rights infractions are taking place. Although AI does not focus on genocide per se, its efforts to address "extrajudicial killings" (or political killings) and crimes against humanity are undoubtedly germane to the issue of genocide. Indeed, much of its work has focused on major human rights abuses in countries where, ultimately, the government has been found to have committed genocide (e.g., Guatemala in the 1980s and 1990s, Rwanda in the early 1990s, the former Yugoslavia throughout the 1990s, and Darfur throughout the early 2000s). It is also noteworthy that AI was involved in pushing for the establishment of the International Criminal Court (ICC).

Anfal (also referred to as al Anfal and the Anfal Campaign). The al Anfal (the spoils of war) campaign was the name of a series of military campaigns undertaken by Saddam Hussein's (1932–2006) Iraqi Baathist regime against the Kurdish population residing in northern Iraq. The campaign was named after the eighth chapter of the Koran, which is titled Surat al-Anfal and is about a battle against "unbelievers" and the need to cut off the roots of the unbelievers. It was an odd choice of terms, for the Kurds, themselves, are Muslim and Iraq, at the time, was a secular state.

In early 1987, shortly after Iraqi president Saddam Hussein named his cousin Ali Hassan al-Majid (a.k.a. "Chemical Ali"; b. 1938 or 1941 [undetermined]) as secretary-general of the administrative zone called the "Northern Bureau" (the location of Iraqi Kurdistan), al-Majid promised "to solve the Kurdish problem and slaughter the saboteurs." The Kurds were perceived to be a problem by Iraq as they desired their own autonomous area, were hard to control, often engaged in battle with Iraqi military forces based in northern Iraq, and some were known to have fought with Iran during the Iran-Iraq War. Indeed, a true understanding of the campaign cannot be divorced from the protracted Iraq-Iran War, fought between 1980 and 1988.

The prelude to the Anfal began in spring 1987 when al-Majid oversaw the initial destruction of villages and the resettlement of thousands of Kurds against their will. The Kurds, whose ancestors had lived in theses villages for centuries, were forcibly moved into relocation centers where the Iraqi government could easily monitor their movements. During this same period, the first order to carry out mass killing was made. More specifically, those Kurds who refused to leave the so-called prohibited zones and relocate in the newly designated areas were deemed traitors and automatically became targets of extermination. From that point forward, a series of sieges or Anfals were carried out: (1) the First Anfal: February 23–March 19, 1988, including a chemical attack on Halabja; (2) the Second Anfal: March 22–April 1, 1988; (3) the Third Anfal: April 7–20, 1988; (4) the Fourth Anfal: May 3–8, 1988, including chemical attacks on Goktapa and Askar; (5) the Fifth, Sixth, and Seventh Anfals: May 15–August 26, 1988; and (6) the Eighth (and final) Anfal: August 25–September 6, 1988, which also included chemical attacks (Human Rights Watch, *Genocide in Iraq*, 1993). An area comprising over one thousand villages (possibly as many as two thousand) was designated a "killing zone" by the Iraqi minister of defense, and, subsequently, thousands of Iraqi Kurd homes were destroyed and close to one hundred thousand Kurds—men, women, and children—were, variously, machine-gunned and gassed to death. Generally, the survivors were forced into areas bereft of water, food, housing, or medical care.

Over 4 million pages (some fourteen tons) of Iraqi government documents have been gathered by investigators of the Anfal, and such evidence supports the fact that there was the intent on the part of the Iraqi regime to destroy the village population of Kurds as such, thus constituting a genocidal process. With the fall of Hussein in 2003, the ongoing struggles for democracy in Iraq, and the incessant resistance incursions, the volatility of the region has not yet ended. The question of whether the Kurds will have a voice in the new Iraq or a sovereign nation-state of their own remains open-ended.

Anfal Campaign. *See* Anfal.

Angkar Loeu. Angkar Loeu, which literally means the "high organization" in the Khmer language, was, in reality, Pol Pot's (1925–1998) Communist Party that was responsible for the genocide of the Cambodian people between 1975 and 1979. Angkar Loeu served as the top leadership echelon in Democratic Kampuchea (the latter a bizarrely ironic name for what was, in actuality, a totalitarian dictatorship).

Angkar's Eight-Point Agenda. Pol Pot (1925–1998), the leader of the Cambodian communist revolutionaries known as the Khmer Rouge, which overthrew the Cambodian government in 1975 and established the totalitarian state of Democratic Kampuchea, created an eight-point agenda for *Angkar Loeu* (the "high organization," or the leadership of Kampuchea's communist dictatorship) to follow as it set out to create what it perceived as a utopian state. The eight-point agenda comprised the following: (1) evacuate the people from the cities; (2) abolish all markets; (3) abolish all currency; (4) defrock all Buddhist monks; (5) execute the leaders of Lon Nol's government and army; (6) establish cooperatives across Cambodia, with communal eating; (7) expel the entire ethnic Vietnamese population; and (8) dispatch Khmer Rouge troops to the Thai and Vietnamese borders to secure the integrity of the revolution from encroachment from Cambodia's traditional rivals.

Annan, Kofi (b. 1938). UN undersecretary-general for peacekeeping (1993–1997) and UN secretary-general (1997–2006). Annan was undersecretary-general for peacekeeping during the UN's incompetent handling of the crisis in Rwanda prior to, during, and following the 1994 Rwandan genocide and the extremely complex and murderous crisis in the former Yugoslavia. He was the UN secretary-general during the relatively successful containment of violence in East Timor (1999), the controversial NATO bombing of Kosovo (1999), and the first four years (2003–2006) of the genocidal crisis in Darfur, Sudan, during which the UN did little to nothing to stanch the killing. In the latter two cases, the UN Security Council largely tied his hands, though many assert that he could have used his post as a bully pulpit much more than he did to generate attention and concern over both genocidal crises.

Anschluss. German-language term usually understood to mean "linkage," "connection," "union," or "annexation" and referring specifically to the annexation of Austria by Germany on May 13, 1938, which was met with no significant resistance either governmentally or militarily. Shortly thereafter, the Nazi racial laws were instituted against Austria's Jewish population of approximately 185,000 persons.

Antecedents to the Holocaust. Historians do not always agree on all of the antecedents that have been cited as leading up to the Holocaust. For many years, historians were roughly grouped as being either *intentionalists* (who argued that the Nazis' intent, early on, was to exterminate the Jews) or *functionalists* (that the unfolding of events—setbacks and opportunities—resulted in the decision to establish the death factories in Poland). More recently, though, there is a group of historians that fall somewhere in the middle of the two camps, acknowledging and building their own interpretations on the strengths (while winnowing the weaknesses) of each of the aforementioned groups' positions—in addition to their own analysis of documents that were unearthed in the archives of the former Soviet Union in the 1990s. That said, some of the many antecedents that many historians can and do agree on are as follows: the long, sordid history of antisemitism by Christians; the advent of political antisemitism; the racial antisemitism of the Nazis; social Darwinism; extreme nationalism; totalitarianism; industrialism; and the nature of modern war.

Anti-Jewish Legislation Implemented by the Nazis. Between 1933 and 1939, the Third Reich passed four hundred pieces of legislation whose express purpose was to "define, isolate, exclude, segregate, and impoverish German Jews" (Berenbaum, 1993, p. 22). A week after the National Socialists (Nazis) gained power in Germany, the government passed its first series of laws that targeted the Jews: the Civil Service Law of April 7, 1933, whose express purpose was the dismissal of all so-called non-Aryans from the civil service, including all educators working in state schools.

Antiquity, Genocide During. *Genocide* is a new word for an ancient practice, and it has taken many forms in the past. In the Ancient World, the destruction of entire groups was common enough that we can identify a pattern within the literature of total extermination appearing regularly. The Hebrew Bible contains a number of important passages that refer to mass destruction which today would be identified as genocide (see, e.g., Deuteronomy 7). The Greeks engaged in the practice widely; one well-known example, among many chronicled, is that of Thucydides (c. 471–399 BCE), in the case of the island inhabitants of Melos. The Romans, too, committed genocide, in numerous locations—most notably in the fate that befell the inhabitants of Rome's archenemy Carthage in 146 BCE, where both the people were destroyed and the land upon which they lived was despoiled. In the aftermath of the Roman victories over the Jews of Palestine (Judaea) during the first and second centuries CE, at which time the Temple was destroyed (70 CE), the Jews were a devastated people. After the final confrontation between Roman and Jewish forces at Betar (135 CE), over half a million Jews had been killed, and the survivors were dispersed through slave markets across the known world. War was the most common facilitator of genocidal destruction, and, after a victory (or a defeat, depending on one's perspective), it was frequently a given that the wholesale massacre of those defeated might take place as a means of cementing in place one's conquest of the opposing army. It might just as easily not have taken place, depending on the disposition of the king or general in charge at the scene; thus, genocides in the Ancient World were not always predictable. One thing is certain, though: a consciousness for genocidal activities existed in the Ancient World, and Western civilizations were far from tentative at invoking it when circumstances (as their leaders viewed it) required such action to take place.

Antisemitism (German, *Antisemitismus*). Hatred of the Jews as a people and/or Judaism as the religious/cultural/social traditions of the Jewish people. The term was coined by the German antisemite Wilhelm Marr (1818–1904), who used it to describe the Jews as a racial group, and then used the term in a political context. The origins of such antipathy toward Jews and Judaism can be traced back to the Hebrew Bible, where the Jews are described by the pharaoh of Egypt (Exodus 1) and the prime minister of Persia (Esther 3) as an alien, disloyal, overly numerous group. Such antisemitism may best be labeled as social-cultural and political antisemitism. With the birth and success of Christianity, and the New Testament's orientation of the Jews as primarily responsible for the murder of its Christ (i.e., deicide) rather than the Romans, antisemitism takes on a religious or theological expression, as does the early Christian understanding that the Jews and Judaism's relationship with their God had now been superseded. Particularly pernicious during the Middle Ages was the false charge that Jews needed to murder innocent Christian children to drain their blood for the preparation of the unleavened cakes (matzo) used in the celebration of the Passover, as well as the charge that the Jews poisoned the wells, resulting in the Black Death (bubonic plague) that ravaged Europe. During the evolution of Western civilization, specifically the rise of mercantilism and capitalism, at which time Jews were outsiders to the guilds and thus prevented from many craft occupations as well as owning and farming land, antisemitism took on an economic coloration. With the rise of the Enlightenment in Europe, the severing of power from the Church, and the refusal of the Jews to surrender their identity and merge into the larger societies, social and cultural forms of antisemitism, again, came to the fore, accompanied by variations of political antisemitism. Marr's transmutation of antisemitism into a racial category ultimately set the stage for the most virulent and violent expression of antisemitism: that of the racial or biological antisemitism of the Nazis during World War II and the Holocaust, which, at its end, saw the murder of almost 6 million Jewish men, women, and children (1 million below the age of twelve and half a million between the ages of twelve and eighteen). In the aftermath of World War II, and the revelations of the Holocaust, antisemitism as such, in all its permutations, saw a dramatic decrease throughout the world. However, with the beginnings of the twenty-first century, most especially as a result of the ongoing tensions in the Middle East between Israel and her Arab neighbors, falsely described as "anti-Zionism" rather than antisemitism, violent expressions of antisemitism continue to rear their ugliness both on the continent of Europe (e.g., France and Germany) and throughout the Middle East.

Arabism. The belief system held by certain Arab groups that Arab values and norms are superior to all others. A classic case of Arabism is the conflict in Darfur, Sudan (2003–2008), in which the Arab-run government of Sudan has disparaged the black Africans of Darfur as less than human (e.g., "dogs," "slave dogs," and "Nuba" or "slave") and have made it clear in their ongoing attacks (2003–2008) against the black Africans that they are not welcome in Sudan as they are not Arabs. During the process of their attacks, Sudanese government troops and the *Janjaweed* (Arab militia) have carried out a scorched-earth policy that has resulted in the utter destruction of black African villages and the mass rape and genocide of the black African people.

Ararat. A major motion picture produced in 2001 by Canadian film director Atom Egoyan, *Ararat*, which premiered at the Cannes Film Festival, is based on the 1915–1923 genocide of the Armenians by the Ottoman Turks. The latter resulted in the murders of more than 1 million Armenian men, women, and children.

The somewhat convoluted plot of this almost two-hour film involves a series of intertwining subplots, the unifying theme revolving around a studio making a movie about the genocide. The various characters (Ani, the art historian hired as consultant; her son Raffi; an actor hired to play a Turkish officer; and a customs officer) in the movie-within-the-movie work through the historical and moral elements of the parts they are to play, while the production staff wrestles with the most appropriate way(s) to bring the story of the Armenian defense of the city of Van, within the overall texture of the genocide, to the screen.

Produced by Robert Lantos (b. 1949) and Atom Egoyan (b. 1960) and directed by Egoyan, *Ararat* is one of only a very few major motion pictures taking the Armenian genocide as its theme, and, as such, it is controversial. It has been condemned by many Turks and Turkish sympathizers, who deny the veracity of the Armenian genocide and assert that *Ararat* is nothing but anti-Turkish propaganda. When the film was released, many cinemas in the English-speaking world would not screen it for fear of attracting pro- and anti-Armenian demonstrations, and the film was given only a limited release in the United States, the United Kingdom, and Australia. In Canada, on the other hand, *Ararat* was the recipient of Best Picture, Best Actress, and Best Supporting Actor (to Arsinée Khanjian [b. 1958] and Elias Koteas [b. 1961], respectively) at the Canadian Genie Awards, as well as awards from other bodies. In 2006, an edited version of *Ararat* was shown on Turkish television, to mixed responses.

Though it received mixed reviews, this film has kept the issue of the Armenian genocide before a wide audience that is largely unfamiliar with the events contained therein.

Arbour, Louise (b. 1947). Louise Arbour received her BA from the Collége Régina Assumpta in 1967 and her law degree in civil law from the Université de Montréal in 1970 and was admitted to the Ontario bar in 1977. Between 1974 and 1987, she taught at and was associate dean of the Osgoode Hall Law School at York University and continued to publish extensively in the fields of criminal procedure, criminal law, human rights, civil liberties, and gender issues. Appointed to the Supreme Court of Ontario in 1987, she was later appointed to the Court of Appeals for Ontario in 1990, and in 1996 she was appointed chief prosecutor of war crimes for the International Criminal Tribunal for Rwanda (ICTR) in Arusha, Tanzania, and the International Criminal Tribunal for the former Yugoslavia (ICTY) in The Hague. In May 1999, at the ICTY, she presented the indictment against Slobodan Milosevic, the president of the Federal Republic of Yugoslavia. In 1999, she was also appointed to the Supreme Court of Canada. On February 10, 2004, she accepted the position of high commissioner for human rights of the United Nations, taking her oath of office on July 1, 2004.

Area Bombing. Area bombing is a military air strategy that targets a city in its totality as a single military objective, rather than by identifying specific military objectives and attacking them. This can disrupt an enemy's lines of communication, weaken civilian morale, sap a nation's willingness to continue military operations, and even sow discord toward a government that could allow its citizens to be attacked this way—and any of these, for military planners, can be considered legitimate objectives. But the upshot of area bombing has traditionally been the killing of vast numbers of innocent civilians. Some authors, such as Eric Markusen and David Kopf in their 1995 book *The Holocaust and Strategic Bombing: Genocide and Total War in the Twentieth Century*, have suggested that such bombing borders on the genocidal (where it is not an act of genocide outright), as the people were killed for no other reason than by virtue of their nationality as the air planners sought a way to destroy the enemy's capacity to continue waging war through killing substantial numbers of civilians. Examples of area bombing abounded in the twentieth century, including the bombing of the following cities prior to and during World War II: Guernica, Rotterdam, Coventry, and London by the Germans; Dresden by the Allies; and Tokyo (and arguably Hiroshima and Nagasaki) by the United States. Later, in the late 1960s and early 1970s, the United States also dropped a huge tonnage of bombs on North Vietnam during the Vietnam War.

Area bombing is not to be confused with the air bombardment of military targets in urban areas, from which it is distinguished by carpet bombing's declared illegality under international law. Additionally, Protocol 1 of the Fourth Geneva Convention, signed in 1977, declared area bombing to be a war crime, though an imprecision in the Protocol's language has made it possible for states to find loopholes to help them avoid the stigma of international condemnation.

Argentina and "Disappearances." During the period 1976–1983, at which time Argentina suffered under harsh military rule, between 11,000 and 15,000 people were killed in what has become known as the "Dirty War" (in Spanish, *La Guerra Sucia*; more colloquially, *El Proceso* or "The Process"). The victims were murdered by the military authorities not because they had transgressed the law but because of their known or suspected political beliefs. The victims were most frequently arrested, tortured, and then "disappeared," the practice of detention without trial and murder without due visible process giving its name to the victims as *Los Desaparecidos* (the disappeared ones). Often, as documented cases show, military helicopters would take the victims far out to sea, where they would be dumped. Military officers justified such acts as necessary to stop what they referred to as acts of terrorism, but, without any form of open trial, the *desaparecidos* were more than likely to have been only political opponents or those on the political left—trade unionists, students, priests of liberal opinion, and the like. Although not constituting genocide according to the terms of the 1948 UN Convention on the Prevention and Punishment of the Crime of Genocide, Argentina's Dirty War undoubtedly amounted to a series of politically inspired mass killings. The purpose of the killings was to destroy a vague and perpetrator-defined group, the right wing Argentinian government's opposition on the left.

Arierparagraph. This term refers to the Nazi definition of a person who was of "non-Aryan descent." On April 11, 1933, the Nazis issued a regulation that a person of non-Aryan descent was any person who had a Jewish parent or grandparent; the parent or grandparent was presumed to be Jewish if he (or she) belonged to the Jewish religion.

Arkan (Nickname of Zeljko Raznatovic; [1952–2000]). A former criminal who became one of the most infamous, vociferous, and violent paramilitary leaders/warlords of the Serbs in 1990s. He led the so-called Arkan's Tigers.

Arkan's Tigers. Arkan's Tigers was the popular name of the Serbian Volunteer Guard headed by the paramilitary leader Zeljko Raznatovic (1952–2000), who went by the nickname of Arkan. The Tigers were notorious for the atrocities they committed on the behalf of the regime of Slobodan Milosevic (1941–2006). They were a huge force, and by 1994 the group had, according to its own claims, trained some ten thousand men. It is suspected that many of the members of the group had been seconded from both police and army units. Despite claims by Milosevic that Arkan ran an independent operation, there were scores of signs that the Tigers operated with Milosevic's imprimatur and assistance. For example, during the massacre at Prijedor in May 1992, Arkan's Tigers, along with other Serb paramilitary groups, perpetrated the atrocities not only with the full knowledge of the Yugoslav People's Army (JNA) but also with its full support. In addition, when Arkan's men committed atrocities in Zvornik, they were allowed to do as they wished in the center of the city while Yugoslav army units held down the perimeter areas.

Armageddon. Corruption of the Hebrew term *Har Megiddo* (Mount Megiddo), a rocky outcrop in northern Israel. A number of biblical and extrabiblical accounts align Armageddon with the Last Days, a time during which the final divine revelation will reportedly take place and ultimate heavenly redemption will begin under the direction of a God-sent messiah (Hebrew, *moshiach*). A precondition for this, in both the Jewish and the Christian religious traditions, will be a massive human catastrophe (Hebrew, *chevlei ha-mashiach*, "the birth pangs of the Messiah"). In ancient times, two events seemed to fit this precondition; both, interestingly, took place following the death of Jesus. In 70 CE, the Romans completed their subjugation of the Jews with the capture and sacking of Jerusalem. In the last battle, one hundred thousand Roman troops stormed the city, destroyed the holy temple, and turned their swords on the people. At least 600,000 Jews were slaughtered. Then, during the Bar Kochba Revolt of 132–35 CE, another 580,000 Jews were massacred, and nearly a thousand towns and villages were destroyed. The emperor Hadrian (76–138 CE) then rebuilt Jerusalem, renamed it Aelia Capitolina, and dedicated it to pagan gods. On the site of the Temple Mount, a column in honor of Hadrian was erected alongside a shrine to Jupiter Capitolinus. All Jewish rites were forbidden on pain of crucifixion, as were Jewish religious days and the weekly observance of the Sabbath. It was said that, in the final battle between the Roman legions and Simeon Bar Kochba's (d. 135 CE) warriors at Megiddo, the number of dead on both sides was piled so high as to form a mountain of corpses. This may have been the origin of Mount Megiddo's association with massive human carnage that comes to us today as Armageddon. The concept was revived again in Christian scripture as the location of the final struggle between good and evil (Revelation 16:14, 16:16, 19:19), again, imbued with strong messianic prophecy.

Armenia: The Betrayed. This 2003 BBC-produced video provides a historical overview of the Ottoman-Turk genocide of the Armenians (1915–1923) as well as contemporary footage and interviews (with noted historians and various contemporary politicians) about the ongoing effort by the current Turkish government to deny the fact of the genocide and how the Armenians are responding to such denial.

Armenian Atrocities Committee. The Armenian Atrocities Committee was a nongovernmental organization formed in the United States to draw public attention to the mass murder of fellow Christians (e.g., the Armenians citizens) by the Ottoman Turks (1915–1923). The group was successful in drawing broad public attention to the massacres (actually a genocide, but the term had not been coined yet), raising money for humanitarian purposes but also calling for a pacifist approach that "put safety first" and thus advocating against military intervention by the United States.

Armenian Genocide. A genocide committed against Armenians by the regime of the Committee of Union and Progress (*Ittihad ve Terakki Jemyeti*), also known as the Young Turks, in the Ottoman Empire in the period following April 24, 1915 (1915–1923). According to most accounts, at least 1 million—though, on the balance of probabilities, closer to 1.5 million—Armenians were slaughtered as a direct result of deliberate Turkish policies seeking their permanent eradication from the empire. At the time the genocide began, well after the outbreak of World War I, the Turkish military forces were waging war against the Russians in the northeast and the British, French, and Australian and New Zealand Army Corps (ANZAC) forces at Gallipoli, but resources were diverted to the campaign of murdering the Armenian population within the empire. The genocidal measures were far more extensive than any previous anti-Armenian massacres (such as those in 1894–1896 or at Adana in 1909) and saw all the relevant agencies of government directed toward the singular aim of totally destroying the Armenian population.

That the genocide took place under cover of war was more than just a matter of interest; the war was in reality a crucial part of the genocide's success. By conducting deportations of Armenians in places far off the beaten track, forcing many victims (primarily women and children, including babies) into harsh, scorching-hot underpopulated regions of the empire, the Turks were able to exploit the war situation for the purpose of achieving their genocidal aims. Technology, in the form of modern telecommunications and transportation, was employed to coordinate the killing activities and speed up the process, while other minorities supportive of the Turks' aims, in particular Kurdish and Arab allies, assisted in carrying out the murders. The eventual result was a loss of life—in a relatively short span of time—of what had hitherto been unimagined proportions. The worst of the killing was over within a year, but only because the ferocity of the Turks' campaign led to a shortage of potential victims. This did not, however, stop the killing, and Armenian communities in various parts of the empire, where they were found, continued to be attacked up through the early 1920s.

Armenian Genocide, British Response to. Throughout the nineteenth century, British governments had taken careful note of anti-Christian developments within the Ottoman Empire, which ultimately culminated in the large-scale massacres of Armenians on order of Sultan Abdul Hamid II (1842–1918; reigned 1876–1909) between 1894 and 1896. Foremost in his condemnation of these actions was the senior British statesman and former prime minister William Ewart Gladstone (1809–1898), who had been highly critical of the Turks throughout his prime ministerships in the 1870s and 1880s. In the period immediately prior to the outbreak of World War I in July–August 1914, British concern was voiced about the fate of the Christian populations of the Ottoman Empire in the face of Young Turk nationalist campaigns, but it was not until news of the genocide of the Armenians began to circulate during the spring and summer of 1915 that serious British attention was directed specifically toward their plight. In that year, the government assigned to Viscount James Bryce (1838–1922) the task of gathering whatever information could be found on the then-developing genocide. Bryce took on as his researcher a young historian, Arnold J. Toynbee (1889–1975), who edited and arranged a vast range of documents into a blue book, or official documentary collection. It was a devastating indictment of the deportation and extermination of the Armenians.

On May 24, 1915, the British joined with their French and Russian allies in publicly warning the Young Turk regime that they would hold all the members of the Ottoman government personally responsible for the massacres. Unable to do anything concrete to stop the genocide outside of winning the war, Britain could not ease the plight of the Armenians while the killing was taking place. In 1917, the British prime minister, David Lloyd George (1863–1945), promised the Armenian population that Britain would not support any postwar settlement that allowed the Turks to retain control over Armenian territory. This promise was reaffirmed in 1918 and formed part of the Treaty of Versailles at the end of the war. Power politics intruded into these sentiments, however, and Britain found itself forced—by circumstances and by preference—to back away from its stated commitments to the Armenians. This found its clearest expression in the half-hearted attempts by the British authorities to bring arrested Young Turk leaders before a military or criminal tribunal after the war; most of those in British custody were ultimately released, with only a few trials of minor figures having taken place (resulting in few convictions).

Armenian Genocide, Denial of. Arguments questioning the veracity of claims of a Turkish genocide of the Armenians during and after World War I have usually taken one of four basic forms: the destruction of the Armenians at the hands of the Ottoman Turks never happened; Turkey is not responsible for the vast number of Armenian deaths, which inadvertently resulted from disease and starvation during the deportation of Armenians out of war zones; the term *genocide* is inapplicable owing to the fact that there was no intent on the part of the Young Turk government to destroy the Armenian population; and, finally, any deaths that did occur were the result of a destructive civil war in the Ottoman Empire, during which at least as many—for some, more—Turks died as did Armenians. These assertions, individually and collectively, have been made by successive Turkish governments and their supporters since the 1920s and are still prevalent today. The most recent areas in which issue has been taken with claims of an Armenian genocide have been in academia (through the establishment of Turkish-funded chairs of Turkish studies dedicated to a "no-genocide" position) and in political campaigns lobbying national legislatures against voting on propositions recognizing the genocide. Because denial of the Armenian genocide is Turkish state policy, it differs from most other forms of genocide denial, which are, for the most part, conducted by individuals or organizations acting in a private capacity. For several decades, Turkish governments were in some ways successful in their worldwide advocacy of a "no-genocide" position, but in recent years various states (e.g., France) and international organizations (e.g., the United Nations) have rejected Turkish denialism and passed resolutions acknowledging the genocide. Moreover, the European Union has made oblique references to Turkish accession being dependent on a public recognition of the genocide and a departure from the long-held denialist policy.

Armenian Genocide Institute-Museum. The Armenian Genocide Institute-Museum was opened in Yerevan, Armenia, in 1995, as part of the events commemorating the eightieth anniversary of the beginning of the Armenian genocide (1915–1923) at the hands of the Young Turk regime. One of its architects, Sashur Kalashian, also designed the nearby Armenian Genocide Memorial. Both the museum and the memorial are situated on the same hilltop overlooking Yerevan, Tsitesrnakaberd (Swallow's Fort), though the presence of the one had been designed so that it does not detract attention from the other. The museum contains an impressive collection of historical documentary material, archival documents, photographs, and other artifacts from the time of the genocide. The principal activities of the institute-museum are both to gather together historical documents and to conduct tours for the public. In this sense, it serves primarily an educational function; in addition, however, its ongoing brief is to collect new data whenever it emerges. International activities undertaken under the institute-museum's aegis include academic conferences, liaison with scholarly institutions around the world, and translation of Armenian and Turkish documents into other languages so as to help broaden the range of scholarship on the Armenian genocide.

Armenian Genocide, Role of Turkish Physicians in. For many in Ottoman Turkish society, the racial necessity of the Armenian genocide required a justification that transcended ideology or abstract propaganda. Consequently, biological reasons were often raised for the need to remove Armenians from Turkish society; such reasons looked to medical science for support. Early statements referred to the Armenians as "dangerous microbes," and Dr. Mehemet Reshid (1873–1919), in particular, formulated ways to bring home to the Armenians their less-than-human status. Reducing them to the level of animals, Reshid pioneered the technique of nailing horseshoes to the feet of living men and marching them through the streets and of nailing Armenians to crosses in emulation of that which happened to Jesus Christ. This conception of his role placed his Turkish identity above that of his calling as a medical practitioner. In other instances, Turkish physicians were known to have killed Armenian children by injecting them with morphine prior to dumping them in the Black Sea, and Red Crescent hospitals were known to have poisoned Armenian children. Ultimately, Turkish physicians played a role in the Armenian genocide in several ways similar to that of the medical profession during the Nazi genocide of the Jews two decades later. Indeed, the perversion of medical science to the cause of genocide pointed to a major failure of the ethical underpinnings of medicine in Turkey early in the twentieth century, a perversion taken up by others later. After World War I, a trial was held of those apprehended for the massacres that took place at Trebizond during the genocide; the doctors arraigned were for the most part acquitted.

Armenian Genocide, United States' Response to. News of the Armenian genocide of 1915 at the hands of the Young Turk regime almost immediately appeared in the press in the United States. Accounts from Armenian missionaries and journalists in Turkey, particularly in Constantinople, were filled with strong detail describing Turkish atrocities. At an official level, U.S. consuls in the provinces, as well as the U.S. ambassador, Henry Morgenthau, Sr. (1856–1946), sent back thorough reports of what they had themselves seen or been told by eyewitnesses. The response of the U.S. public was one of shock and anger. Although the United States had not yet entered the Great War, the news of what was happening to the Armenians turned the American public against the Turks. Specifically as a reaction to news of the genocide, a charity named Near East Relief was created in order to raise funds for the alleviation of Armenian distress. The transfer of monies was authorized by the U.S. Department of State, and any additional attempts at humanitarian relief received the earnest support of U.S. president Woodrow Wilson (1856–1924). The amount of relief money collected was enormous; at its height, Near East Relief administered a budget of $117,000,000, the majority of it having been raised through donations from U.S. citizens. This generosity was replicated politically by the Wilson administration, and his idea of self-determination for the peoples of Europe found a healthy audience among those who thought the Armenians' only hope of freedom from continued persecution lay in the creation of an independent Armenia. By 1920, this had crystallized around a movement to create an American League of Nations mandate for Armenia. This did not eventuate. In the chaotic environment of the postwar years, U.S. oil interests, fearful they might lose access to the oil fields of the Middle East, pressured the U.S. government to soften its stance on Turkey and Armenia. The mandate proposal was dropped, and, in the decades that followed, right through to the end of the twentieth century, every U.S. administration fell into line behind a Turkey committed to denying the Armenian genocide. The Armenians were effectively abandoned by successive U.S. governments, which were held hostage by big business, the strategic interests generated by the Cold War, and the biases of individual politicians. The response of the United States to the Armenian genocide has thus undergone a number of changes, from full support of the victims to their near-total abandonment.

Armenian Massacres. Massacres were carried out against Armenians by different regimes within the Ottoman Empire during two time frames—between 1894 and 1896 and in 1909. In the first, from 1894 to 1896, Sultan Abdul Hamid II (1842–1918; reigned 1876–1909) carried out a series of massacres, the worst occurring in 1895. Estimates of those killed range widely, anywhere between 100,000 and 300,000, with thousands more maimed or rendered homeless. Most of those killed were men; the killings took place in open areas, in the full sight of the community, and seemed to be designed for the purpose of intimidating the Armenian population rather than its wholesale destruction. The massacres were, in fact, an attempt to quash talk of independence and the spread of a distinctive nationalist (perceived to be anti-Ottoman) identity. The massacre of 1909, by contrast, which took place in the region surrounding the city of Adana, was largely the result of civil strife between the supporters of the sultan and the Young Turk reformers, in which the Armenians appeared to be scapegoats for both sides. The Adana massacres claimed possibly up to thirty thousand victims. Both persecutions—the 1894–1896 massacres (also referred to as the Hamidian Massacres, after the sultan) and the 1909 Adana massacres—seemingly prepared the Turkish population to accept the much greater genocidal measures that were undertaken from 1915 onward and must be seen as physical and psychological precursors to that tragedy.

Armenian Question, The. Term used to describe the issue of how to bring about reforms in the condition of the Armenian population of the Ottoman Empire during the reign of Sultan Abdul Hamid II (1842–1918; reigned 1876–1909). In the latter part of the nineteenth century, the Ottoman reform movement known as Tanzimat attempted to restructure society on constitutional and social lines, trying to bring the Ottoman Empire closer to modern European standards. The Armenians of the empire, encouraged by this development, hoped that an alteration to their status as second-class citizens might follow; consequently, a number of petitions were sent to the grand vizier's office in Constantinople requesting protection from Turkish violence and ill-treatment in the provinces. Such requests were viewed by Abdul Hamid and his government as an affront to the sultan's authority. As the problem of how to treat the Armenians (and by extension, other non-Muslim minorities in the empire) began to attract the attention of Europe's Christian nations, the sultan's thoughts turned to the most efficient way to solve it. His decision, by 1894, was that the only viable way to get rid of the "Armenian Question" would be for the Armenians themselves to be eradicated. The Hamidian Massacres of 1894–1896, in which at least 100,000 (and possibly double that number or even more) people were murdered on the royal command, were the direct result of Abdul Hamid's "solution" to the "Armenian Question."

Arms Embargo. The embargo of weapons is a form of sanctions. The United Nations, a regional organization such as NATO, or a coalition of nations may impose an arms embargo (prohibition on the purchase and/or shipment of military armaments) against a nation that is threatening and/or actually carrying out threats against one component or another of its citizens. An arms embargo represents an effort to bring such a conflict to a political—rather than military—solution. Under Chapter VII of the Charter of the United Nations, such an embargo can be imposed in response to "a threat of peace, breach of peace or act of aggression" and, although not explicitly stated, may also be invoked under Article 41. Such embargoes are understood to be binding upon all member states. Only the UN Security Council itself has the power to invoke mandatory embargoes. Once an embargo is implemented by the UN, the UN, in turn, must establish a Sanction Committee to monitor the effectiveness of an embargo, gather information regarding its effectiveness, address humanitarian exceptions, and keep the international community informed of the progress of such efforts. Individual nation-states themselves have also sanctioned such embargoes, usually through their own control and limiting of exports to warring countries.

Arusha Accords. A set of five agreements signed by the Hutu-dominated government of Rwanda and the Rwandan Patriotic Front (RPF) in Arusha, Tanzania, on August 4, 1993. It was intended that the Arusha Accords would end the civil war between the two parties. The talks leading to Arusha were cosponsored by the United States, France, and the Organization of African Unity and ranged over a wide variety of topics: refugee resettlement, power sharing between Hutu and Tutsi, the introduction of an all-embracing democratic regime, the dismantling of the military dictatorship of President Juvenal Habyarimana (1937–1994), and the encouragement of a transparent rule of law throughout Rwanda. In the months that followed the signing of the accords, a number of meetings took place for the purpose of negotiating their implementation. These meetings required the parties to travel to and from Arusha, sometimes by road and at other times by plane. It was after one of these meetings, on April 6, 1994, that the plane carrying Habyarimana and the president of Burundi, Cyprien Ntaryamira (1955–1994), was shot down—it has never been proven conclusively by whom—by a missile fired from the outskirts of the Kigali Airport. All on board were killed, triggering the genocide of Rwanda's Tutsi population and the murder of moderate Hutu over the next 100 days.

Aryan. Originally a Sanskrit term understood to mean "noble" or "superior." Ironically, the term Aryan was, originally, a reference to a group of people who lived in a region now divided into India, Afghanistan, and Iran. The people were hardly, as the term now suggests, blond-haired and blue-eyed.

Via a rather tortured and twisting road of numerous interpretations and conflations of Sanskrit, Indo-Iranian, and German words by various scholars and nonscholars, the term was eventually adopted by nineteenth-century European and U.S. "race specialists" who came to understand the word to mean something along the lines of "the honorable people." Many of these same individuals came to believe and tout their descendants as being Nordic. Physical characteristics such as blond hair, blue eyes, above-average height, a particular shape of the skull, muscularity, and athletic prowess were later characterized by the Nazis as evidence of membership in the "true Aryan race," distinct from such "lesser forms" as Jews and blacks. Although other so-called white Europeans, such as Poles, may have shared some of these characteristics, they were, according to the Nazis, ineligible for membership in their "master race" and were referred as *untermenschen* (subhuman).

Ironically, other than SS Chief of the Reich Security Main Office Reinhard Heydrich (1908–1942), none of the other Nazi leaders (e.g., Hitler, Bormann, Goering, Goebbels) met their own criteria of Aryan Nordicness.

Aryan Myth. Though the root meaning of the word Aryan comes from the Sanskrit in which it means something akin to either "nobleman" or "gentleman," a nineteenth-century misreading of history suggested an invasion of the Indian continent and peoples by a fair-skinned Central Asian migratory superior warrior race. Ultimately, Hitler and the Nazis drew upon that misunderstanding to divide the world between themselves (Aryans)—insisting that the Germanic peoples were themselves the descendants of that original conquering force—and their enemies (Jews). In this way they created a dichotomy that they perceived as constituting a battle between superior and inferior peoples. Thinking such as this, though fictitious, thus made the adaptation of the Hindu swastika (i.e., the wheel in motion, though the position of the feet is different) a powerful visual and graphic reminder of the connection and furthered the Nazi philosophy, drawing upon Charles Darwin (1809–1882) and others, as a biological conflict between two different orders ("races") of human beings, with disastrous consequences for the Jews.

ASEAN. An international organization whose focus is the region of Southeast Asia. The Association of South-East Asian Nations was established on August 8, 1967, in Bangkok, Thailand, by five states: Indonesia, Malaysia, the Philippines, Singapore, and Thailand. Subsequently, five additional states joined ASEAN: Brunei Darussalam (January 8, 1984); Vietnam (July 28, 1995); Laos and Myanmar/Burma (both July 23, 1997); and Cambodia (April 30, 1999). The association's founding document, the ASEAN Declaration, states that the assembled states "represent the collective will of the nations to bind themselves together in friendship and cooperation and, through joint efforts and sacrifices, secure for their peoples and for posterity, the blessings of peace, freedom and prosperity." The key elements by which this is to be realized include nonintervention in the affairs of member states; settlement of disputes in a peaceful manner; renunciation of the use of force; and "mutual respect for the independence, sovereignty, equality, territorial integrity, and national identity of all nations." Pursuant to ASEAN's promotion of peace and stability, it has overseen the establishment of a number of international accords pertaining to a variety of regional issues. In 1992 ASEAN leaders declared that the association should intensify the level of its dialogue on political and security issues with other states in the Asia-Pacific region, and consequently, in 1994, the ASEAN Regional Forum (ARF) was established as a means to reach out to such states (which include Australia, Japan, South Korea, India, the United States, China, Canada, and Russia, among others). In 1997 ASEAN adopted a program called ASEAN Vision 2020, which aimed at creating closer economic integration within the region. The ambition is to transform the area covered by the ASEAN states into a single economic powerhouse by the end of the first quarter of the twenty-first century. In its external relations, too, ASEAN sees itself playing an increasingly important role in the future, though the earthquake and tsunami that devastated much of the region on and after December 26, 2004, are likely to result in some of ASEAN's activities being cut back, perhaps for several years.

Asocials, Nazis' Designation as. *Asocials* was the general Nazi term for those persons declared outside the community of the *Volk*, the latter of which was used to indicate a highly mystical understanding of membership. Asocials included criminals, prostitutes, drug addicts, juvenile delinquents, homosexuals, vagrants, and the Roma peoples. The Nazi orientation toward such persons was that their behaviors were genetically and racially determined and, therefore, beyond correction. Once inside the concentration and death camps, asocials were forced to wear black triangles on their clothing, whereas pink triangles designated homosexuals and brown triangles designated Romas.

Association of Southeast Asian Nations. *See* ASEAN.

Assyrian Genocide. The Assyrian genocide took place at the hands of the Young Turk regime in the Ottoman Empire, alongside the Armenian genocide and the Pontic Greek genocide that the Turks carried out during and after World War I. The Assyrians, an ancient people inhabiting modern-day southeastern Iraq and northwestern Iran, refer to their experience as having taken place between 1915 and 1918. By 1922, in a memorandum from the Assyro-Chaldean National Council, an estimate of approximately 275,000 was given as the total number of deaths caused by the Turks and their Kurdish collaborators. As with the Armenian genocide, a large proportion of the deaths occurred as a result of death marches from victims' homelands into the Syrian Desert. Most of those who died were the victims of heat, starvation and thirst, exposure, and incessant brutality at the hands of their captors. Although no official national or international recognition of the Assyrian genocide has been made, acknowledgment at lower levels of government has taken place. Perhaps the most significant of these came in April 2001, when New York governor George Pataki (b. 1945), in a statement also embracing the Armenian and Pontic Greek genocides, made specific reference to the Assyrian tragedy. Other individuals, notably American Pontic Greek scholar and activist Thea Halo, have referred to the Turkish campaign more broadly, calling it a genocide against the Christian population of the Ottoman Empire; the preference in this case is not to divide the three national experiences into their constituent parts but rather to categorize all of the deaths and atrocities as being of a single cloth. There is, certainly, a remarkable similarity between them, at least on the surface. The Assyrian population throughout the empire was subjected to massacre, deportation, dismemberment, torture, and other atrocities. Whole cities were depopulated, and, when not killed outright, the inhabitants were sent on the aforementioned death marches. The question of whether they were the victims of anti-Christian persecution, as both the Assyrians and the Pontic Greeks claim, or were caught up in necessary relocations by the Turkish army caused by World War I brings up issues of authenticity and denial—as with the Armenian situation, another case of Turkish refusal to consider the reality of their nation's history. The genocide of the Assyrians has largely been written out of history; this small people's past as a victim of genocide has been largely subsumed by that of the Armenians (and, to a lesser extent, the Pontic Greeks), a situation that must be addressed by scholars of genocide if the final act of the Assyrian genocide—historical amnesia—is not to occur.

Asylum. An act by a nation to grant protection within its boundaries to individuals in flight from persecution, the threat of death, or other types of serious harm resulting from, for example, violent conflict due to ethnic cleansing, religious persecution, abject racism, crimes against humanity, and/or genocide. An individual granted asylum is known as a refugee. Asylum involves numerous components, including non-*refoulement* or the permission to remain indefinitely in the country of asylum.

Asymmetrical Killing. *See* One-Sided Killing.

Atatürk, Mustafa Kemal (1881–1938). Turkish general and statesman, founder of the Republic of Turkey, and the man recognized by his people as the father of the nation. Mustafa Kemal, called Atatürk (Father of the Turks), had dabbled in a small way in Young Turk politics prior to World War I but was never a major figure in any capacity until his defense of Gallipoli in 1915. The invasion of the Dardanelles by British, French, Indian, and ANZAC (Australian and New Zealand Army Corps) troops on April 25, 1915, saw Kemal's absence from Constantinople and Anatolia at exactly the time that the Turkish genocide of the Armenians got under way. As a result, he was spared the opprobrium of being linked to the killing and was able to concentrate solely on the military side of saving his country from invasion and defeat. After the war, in the aftermath of the collapse of the Ottoman Empire, Kemal was able to rally the forces of Turkish nationalism and reclaim Turkish pride. Mobilizing the remnants of the old Ottoman armies into a new fighting force, he negotiated the withdrawal of the occupying French and Italians, beat back the Greeks amid a campaign of massive destruction and killing on both sides, and browbeat the British into relinquishing their foothold at Chanak in September 1922. As part of his campaign to reclaim Turkey from the Allies, however, remaining pockets of the Armenian population were wiped out, in a continuation of the Young Turk genocide. Two areas were hit particularly hard: the French occupation zone of Cilicia, in southern Anatolia, and the area on the Turkish-Soviet border, in what was left of historic Armenia. Under Kemal's orders, Nationalist troops occupied substantial areas of what had been slated as independent Armenia (a proposal that was watered down into a U.S.-controlled League of Nations mandate, though this, too, failed to see the light of day), and in a last outbreak of extreme violence the city of Smyrna, with a large Greek and Armenian population, was razed in 1922 and its population massacred by advancing Turkish Nationalist troops. Subsequently, Kemal turned his attention to the modernization, militarization, and industrialization of Turkey—all goals that had been sought by the Young Turks. The one thing that had stood in their way was an obsession with racial issues, primarily with regard to the Armenians and the Pontic Greeks. With those populations gone, Kemal was able to pick up where the Young Turks had left off and, in so doing, both distance himself from the Young Turks' actions and, at the same time, suppress national awareness of what they had done. It was from this foundation that a Turkish culture of denial surrounding the Armenian genocide developed, a culture of denial that has to this day been reinforced by successive Turkish governments.

Atrocities Documentation Project (ADP). In July and August of 2004, the U.S. State Department and the U.S. Agency for International Development (USAID) sponsored an investigation into the ongoing killing of black Africans in Darfur, Sudan. Twenty-four investigators from around the globe interviewed over 1,100 black African refugees in some nineteen refugee camps inside Chad, along the Chad-Sudan border. In an analysis of the data collected, it was reported that the following percentage of interviewees ($n = 1,136$) witnessed or experienced the following: killing of a family member, 61 percent; the killing of a non—family member, 67 percent; shooting, 44 percent; death from displacement, 28 percent; abduction, 25 percent; rape (which was believed to be underreported), 16 percent; hearing racial epithets, 33 percent; village destruction, 81 percent; and aerial bombing, 67 percent. Based on the analysis of the findings, U.S. Secretary of State Colin Powell (b. 1937) declared, in a report to the U.S. Senate Foreign Relations Committee, on September 9, 2004, that Sudan had committed genocide (and possibly still was committing genocide) against the black Africans of Darfur.

Powell's announcement was historic in that it was the first time one sovereign nation had formally accused another sovereign nation of genocide. During his testimony, the United States, via Powell's declaration, also invoked for the first time ever by any government, Chapter VIII of the UN Convention on the Prevention and Punishment of the Crime of Genocide (UNCG), calling on the UN Security Council to take action "appropriate for the prevention and suppression of acts of genocide." The ADP, itself, was historic in that it was the first official investigation by a sovereign nation of an ongoing case of mass violence for the express purpose of determining whether the violence amounted to genocide.

Ultimately, the U.S. government referred its findings and concerns to the UN Security Council, which, in turn, conducted its own study in December 2004 and January 2005.

Upon analysis of the data collected by its Commission of Inquiry (COI), the UN declared, in late January 2005, that it had found ample evidence of crimes against humanity but not genocide (though, it said, the collection and analysis of additional evidence could possibly result in the finding of genocide). Subsequently, the UN referred the matter to the International Criminal Court (ICC), which then began its own investigation with an eye toward prosecuting the alleged perpetrators.

Two genocide scholars (Dr. Eric Markusen [1946–2007] and Dr. Samuel Totten [b. 1949–]) served as members of the ADP, along with a host of lawyers (including a prosecutor with the U.S. Justice Department), high-ranking police investigators from Canada, Great Britain , and the United States, and humanitarian specialists. Totten and Markusen edited a book, *Genocide in Darfur: Investigating Atrocities in the Sudan* (New York: Routledge, 2006), that provides a description, discussion, and analysis of the ADP, its findings, and the ramifications of the latter.

Auschwitz-Birkenau. In 1940 SS Chief Heinrich Himmler ordered the establishment of what would later become the largest extermination site under Nazi hegemony, thirty-seven miles west of Krakow in southern Poland. Auschwitz I, primarily for Polish political prisoners, already held almost 11,000 prisoners by 1941 when Auschwitz II, or Birkenau, was constructed less than two miles away. Birkenau held the primary instruments of extermination, the gas chambers, and, ultimately, realized the murders of the majority of Jews, Poles, Roma, and others, not only due to gassings but also due to so-called medical experiments, starvation, torture, beatings, and so on. Close to 1.5 million Jews, the primary victims, including children, met their deaths there, as well as almost 16,000 Soviet POWs; between 200,000 and 500,000 Roma (definitive figures are difficult to ascertain); and as many as 2 million others, including Poles, "asocials," and political dissidents. Auschwitz III, or Monowitz (Polish *Monowice*) was used to demarcate a number of additional camps throughout the area; it was mainly a slave-labor operation, which, in 1943, began producing large quantities of synthetic rubber (German *Buna*) under the auspices of the German industrial conglomerate I. G. Farben, as well as other products. In 1944 an unsuccessful uprising-rebellion took place which saw both the destruction of one of the gas chambers and crematoria and the deaths of the leaders of the rebellion and a number of the other participants. Toward the end of that same year, Himmler ordered the dismantling of both Auschwitz I and Auschwitz II. On January 27, 1945, representatives of the Soviet army entered Auschwitz and liberated those still alive.

Australia, Genocide in. The situation concerning the Aborigines of mainland Australia during the time of colonial settlement by Britain poses a number of questions relative to genocide. The most important of these is also the most straightforward: did the destruction of Aboriginal society in the century following the arrival of the First Fleet in 1788 constitute genocide? For some, the answer is an unequivocal yes; for others, the answer is nowhere near as obvious. There was no definite state-initiated plan of mass extermination; indeed, it was frequently the case that colonial governments tried to maintain Aboriginal security in the face of settler and pastoralist encroachments and meted out punishments (even hangings) of those found guilty of the murder of Aborigines. Despite this, there were immense and very intensive periods of killing in the bush, accompanied by enormous population losses as a result of disease and starvation. The result saw the effective destruction of Aboriginal society by European settlement during the nineteenth century. Where genocide is concerned, however, this must be understood against two essential facts. In the first place, there was no unified stance on Aborigines throughout the century, as the Australian continent was divided into six separate British colonies (mostly self-governing from the middle of the century) until federation in 1901. Second, no government at any time displayed the necessary intent, in word or in deed, that would prove the existence of a genocidal policy. This in no way mitigates the catastrophe that destroyed the Aborigines, but neither does the history show that the tragedy was the result of what might be termed genocide. In the twentieth century, however, a policy of the independent Commonwealth of Australia did constitute genocide as defined under the 1948 UN Convention on the Prevention and Punishment of the Crime of Genocide (i.e., Article II [e], which refers to the forcible transference of children from a group to another group for the purpose of permanently transforming the group's identity). This relates to the forcible removal of children of part-Aboriginal descent from their parents and subsequent placement in a non-Aboriginal environment for the purpose of "breeding out the color." The policy, which was set in place by state and federal governments, was to last in various forms until the 1970s. It decimated at least two generations of Aborigines of mixed descent, and, in a major federal government inquiry (*Bringing Them Home: National Inquiry into the Separation of Aboriginal and Torres Strait Islander Children from their Families*) in 1997, the allegation of genocide of these "Stolen Generations" was for the first time raised in an official capacity. The inquiry concluded that a case for genocide, according to this policy of forced child removal, could be made.

Australian Institute for Holocaust and Genocide Studies (AIHGS). Formerly known as the Centre for Comparative Genocide Studies (which was founded by genocide scholar Colin Tatz), the official objectives of the AIHGS are research; consultancy work; education of and supervision of research by undergraduate, graduate, and postgraduate students; and conducting community and public education programs. Among its occasional publications are *International Holocaust and Genocide Network* (ITNetwork) and *Genocide Perspectives*. It also offers courses across the globe over the Internet through the Online University. The AIHGS is based at the Shalom Institute, Shalom College, University of New South Wales, Sydney.

Authoritarianism. A type of control—whether in government, in the workplace, or within formal institutions—that is characterized by rigid forms of authority and an expectation on the part of the managing executive that such authority will be closely adhered to by an acquiescent or servile population. At the state level, in an authoritarian regime, citizens are subjected to a vast number of governmental intrusions upon their lives and often have their personal liberties controlled by the state from the cradle to the grave. It is important to note that there are a number of shades of authoritarianism, which can range from severely repressive dictatorial (e.g., Nazi Germany or Soviet Russia) or absolutist rule (e.g., royalist France or tsarist Russia) right through to milder forms in democratic countries (e.g., Britain under the prime ministership of Winston Churchill [1874–1965] during World War II or France under the rule of Charles de Gaulle [1890–1970] during the 1960s). Authoritarian rule need not, therefore, be synonymous with dictatorship, with which it is sometimes confused, though an authoritarian government, once set in place, can lead to this under certain circumstances—for example, if the economy deteriorates severely, the nation becomes involved in a foreign war, or civil strife breaks out within the country.

Autocracy. A form of government, usually located in the person of a single ruler invested with supreme political power. A notable feature of an autocracy is that the autocrat is in exclusive possession of executive, legislative, and judicial power or has the authority to delegate and rescind such powers according to his or her individual decree. Historically, autocracy is associated with monarchy, particularly royal absolutism, though even in an absolutist system the monarch needs the active assistance (or, at the least, the compliance) of an aristocracy that serves as an enforcement arm of the royal will. In the modern world, an autocrat can also be a totalitarian political leader such as Josef Stalin (1879–1953) of the Soviet Union or a military dictator such as Idi Amin (c. 1925–2003); under such regimes, power concentrated in the hands of a single leader can be corrupted such that the unimpeded persecution of political, ethnic, racial, or religious minorities can take place with impunity and without recourse to constitutional or democratic forms of redress.

Autogenocide. A term used to describe the genocidal events that took place in Cambodia between 1975 and 1979, under the Khmer Rouge regime of Pol Pot (1925–1998). It looked as if the regime was practicing genocide on its own people—indeed, as if the population was killing its own in a kind of genocidal self-imposed civil war. This was before the various group identities of the victims—ethnic Vietnamese, Chinese, Chams, and others—had become known. The killing of Cambodians by Cambodians seemed unprecedented, hence the forging of a neologism—autogenocide (or self-genocide)—to pinpoint the singularity of the genocidal events in what was now called the Democratic Republic of Kampuchea. Later, this proved to be an oversimplification, as it became apparent that the lethal policies of the Khmer Rouge were far more complex than originally thought. All manner of issues were involved. It was a civil war but also much more: there was anticolonialism, a Marxist revolution, monoethnic nationalism, the autonomy of ethnic minorities, and romantic utopianism, among others. None of these is conveyed by the term *autogenocide*.

AVEGA-AGAHOZO. AVEGA, a name derived from *Association des Veuves du Génocide* (Association of Genocide Widows), is a nonprofit organization conceived and created by fifty widows of the1994 Rwandan genocide. The founders, themselves all genocide survivors, established the association on January 15, 1995; it received ministerial approval from the Rwandan government on October 30, 1995. AVEGA-AGAHOZO was initiated to assist the scores of thousands of widows and orphans produced by the genocide and to alleviate their sufferings as they struggle to adapt to their postgenocide situation. Since its inception, AVEGA has expanded its areas of concern to include not just widows and orphans but also children who have become heads of households as a result of the genocide; parents who have lost some or all of their children; the elderly; and the handicapped. After 1997, given the increasing number of individuals who benefit from AVEGA, the organization adopted a policy of administrative decentralization. This enables AVEGA to support its client group across the country, avoiding the possibility of a recurrence of the tribal or regional biases that led to the genocide in 1994. AVEGA sees its mission as the following: to promote the general welfare of the genocide victims, to promote solidarity among members of the association, to carry out activities aimed at helping the widows, to cooperate with like organizations, to uphold the memory of the genocide victims, to fight for justice, and to participate in the national reconstruction and reconciliation process of Rwanda. AVEGA is a good example of the determination of many in Rwanda to act in a positive way—of coping with the past, in order to build the future.

Awami League. Founded in 1949 as an oppositional party in what was then East Pakistan, prior to the creation of Bangladesh, the Awami League was conceived out of a moderate socialist ideology that had a specific concern for students, workers, laborers, peasants, young people, and women. In 1970, because of its electoral successes, the government of Pakistan banned the Awami League, but with the outbreak of war in 1971, and the breakaway of Bangladesh (during which Pakistan perpetrated genocide against the Bangladeshis), it, initially, became the dominant political party of the new nation-state, though, in the years succeeding independence, it lost elections to the Bangladesh National Party (BNP) in 1981, 1991, and 2001. The political successes and failures of the Awami League must be viewed in the context of violent upheaval both within Pakistan and within Bangladesh itself.

Awlad Al-Beled. This Arabic term literally means "children of the country." A self-given sobriquet of the riverine Arabs living in Sudan, it denotes that they are "the true Sudanese" within Sudan. It is a term, then, that separates them from, for example, the black Africans of Darfur, who are not considered to be "true Sudanese" by the riverine Arabs.

Axis Rule in Occupied Europe. Authored by Dr. Raphael Lemkin (1900–1959), this massive 674-page text was published in 1944 by the Carnegie Endowment for International Peace in Washington, D.C. Subtitled "Laws of Occupation, Analysis of Government, Proposals for Redress," it is, according to its author's preface, "an analysis, based on objective information and evidence, of the rule imposed upon the occupied countries of Europe by the Axis Powers—Germany, Italy, Hungary, Bulgaria, and Rumania" (p. ix). Significantly, chapter 9 introduces its readers to the concept of genocide, discussing the meaning and concept of the term and techniques of its use in various fields (political, social, cultural, economic, biological, physical, religious, and moral), and includes recommendations for the future (e.g., prohibitions and international controls; pp. 79–95). *Axis Rule in Occupied Europe* would later become a primary document in Lemkin's ongoing successful crusade to cajole the United Nations to adopt the 1948 Convention for the Prevention and Punishment of the Crime of Genocide, which remains the only such legal document and definition in effect.

B

Babi Yar. A ravine located northwest of the Ukrainian city of Kiev. On September 29 and September 30, 1941, somewhere between 33,000 and 50,000 Jews were brutally murdered after they were forced to line up in groups of ten at the edge of a ravine, strip naked, and surrender both clothing and valuables, all in reprisal for a Soviet partisan attack on the German command center in Kiev. They were then shot by Einsatzgruppe 4A (mobile death squad) of the Nazi SS. Subsequent to the initial slaughter, the murders continued and included Soviet non-Jewish citizens, Ukrainians, and Roma. Estimated additional deaths between 1941 and 1943 range from 100,000 to 133,000.

In 1961 the Russian poet Yevgeni Yevtushenko commemorated these murders with his now-famous poem "Babi Yar," which begins "No gravestones stand on Babi Yar; / Only coarse earth heaped roughly on the gash: / Such dread comes over me." In 1962 the Russian musical composer Dimitri Shostakovich set it to music in his Thirteenth Symphony. In 1974 a monument was erected to the victims; unconscionably, no mention of the Jews was included.

Back to Ararat. This documentary (1993) provides a chronicle of the Ottoman-Turk genocide of the Armenians between 1915 and 1923. In doing so, it traces the generations of people who were driven from their homeland—as well as the generations who dream of someday returning to Mount Ararat—through interviews with people living in various parts of the world.

Bagosora, Théoneste (b. 1941). Chief of cabinet in the Rwandan Ministry of Defense in the administration of President Juvenal Habyarimana (1937–1994), Bagosora assumed effective control of Rwanda after April 6, 1994. Most accounts consider Bagosora as being the man responsible for coordinating the genocide of Rwanda's Tutsi population following the assassination of Habyarimana on that date.

A colonel in the *Forces Armées Rwandaises* (FAR), the Rwandan military forces, Bagosora was one of the Hutu extremists in a government of hard-liners and had visions of himself as presidential material at some time in the future. He was a highly placed associate of the *Akazu*, the inner circle of the ruling *Mouvement Révolutionnaire National pour le Développement*, or National Revolutionary Movement for Development (MRND) party, dominated by members of Habyarimana's family.

Bagosora had a history of planning and engaging in violent anti-Tutsi activities long before the 1994 genocide. By 1990, Bagosora reportedly had developed a plan to exterminate the

Tutsi in Rwanda. As early as 1992, Bagosora reportedly had the Rwandan army's general staff draw up lists of all those persons who were thought to be associated in any way with the Rwandan Patriotic Front (RPF). Ultimately, such lists were used by the military and the *Interahamwe* to locate, capture, and kill Tutsi and moderate Hutu during the period of the genocide. Beginning in early 1993, Bagosora is known to have distributed weapons to militias and other extremist Hutu.

Bagosora was a vehement opponent of the Arusha Agreements (signed in 1993), as he wanted nothing to do with the RPF or, for that matter, shared governance of Rwanda with the Tutsi, let alone coexistence with the Tutsi. Bagosora publicly stated that the Tutsi would be wiped out if the RPF continued its fight against Rwanda or if the Arusha Accords were enforced. Bagosora is said to have been the individual who gave the order on April 7, 1994, to the military to begin the mass killing and who issued the order that roadblocks be set up all across Rwanda so as to capture and kill fleeing Tutsi and moderate Hutu.

After the conclusion of the genocide and the victory of the antigovernment RPF, Bagosora disappeared. On September 3, 1996, he was apprehended in Cameroon and subsequently transferred for trial to Arusha, Tanzania.

At the hearing before the International Criminal Tribunal for Rwanda (ICTR) in March 1997, he pleaded not guilty to the charge of genocide. His trial began on April 2, 2002, simultaneously with the trials of three others—Brigadier-General Gratien Kabiligi (b. 1951), former chief of military operations in the FAR; Lieutenant-Colonel Anatole Nsengiyumva (b. 1950), former military commander of Gisenyi Military Camp; and Major Aloys Ntabakuze (b. 1954), former commander of the Kanombe Paracommando Battalion, Kigali. At the time of this writing, the trial is continuing.

Baha'is in Iran. The Baha'i faith originated in Iran in 1844. Almost from the first proclamation of the new faith by the Bab (1819–1850), and its development by Bahaullah (1817–1892), Baha'is have been persecuted as Muslim heretics. In the 1850s and 1860s, over twenty thousand Baha'is were put to death, with thousands more imprisoned, often for life. Persecution and massacres continued throughout the nineteenth and twentieth centuries. When the Islamic revolution began in Iran in 1978, discrimination, harassment, persecution, torture, and killings increased dramatically. Baha'is were hounded from their jobs, denied entry to colleges and universities, and forbidden employment in government service. Pensions for the elderly were cut off completely, and Baha'is were denied the right to own businesses. Baha'i cemeteries were confiscated and vandalized. International travel was forbidden to Baha'is. Baha'is were also routinely killed in small groups numbered in the tens and hundreds by the revolutionary authorities. The Bahai'is' persecution by the fundamentalist Islamic regime in Iran is based on their status as a breakaway movement from Islam, certainly, but it is just as much the modernity and dynamism of the Baha'i religion that drives fundamentalist Islam to wage its ongoing campaign of persecution within Iran. Baha'i beliefs gravitate naturally toward pacifism, parliamentary democracy, religious toleration with regard to other faiths, and the compatibility of science with religion. Against this, a hard-line intolerance within Islam, born of the belief that there is but one way to salvation, has meant the Baha'is have been a ready target for persecution. Although this has not resulted in wholesale mass killing of the Baha'is in Iran, there can be little doubt that Iranian revolutionary actions against the Baha'i community are aimed at its long-term destruction.

Bahutu Manifesto (March 1957). On March 24, 1957, Gregoire Kayibanda (1924–1976), the chief editor of Rwanda's Roman Catholic newspaper *Kinyamateka*, together with the archbishop of Kabgayi, André Perraudin (1914–2003), published the now-infamous *Bahutu Manifesto*, which, for the first time in Rwandan history, explained the political problems of the country in racial terms as a clash between Hutu and Tutsi. It demanded the emancipation of the Hutu and the establishment of a racial quota system in both education and employment (which favored the Hutu, the larger population of the two). The implications of the *Bahutu Manifesto* were to provide an ideological foundation and justification for various genocidal massacres and, ultimately, the 1994 genocide, which were to follow, by further dividing Hutu and Tutsi, providing a false intellectual argument, and supposedly addressing the highly questionable superiority of the former and the dubious inferiority of the latter.

"Banality of Evil." A term introduced by German Jewish philosopher and refugee émigré Hannah Arendt (1906–1975) in her 1963 book, *Eichmann in Jerusalem: A Report on the Banality of Evil*, about the trial in Israel of Nazi bureaucrat Adolf Eichmann (1906–1962). The book originally appeared as a series of articles in *New Yorker* magazine and took the form of a report on the trial, the circumstances leading up to it, and the nature of Eichmann's testimony throughout. Arendt's major conclusions were that there was, in fact, little that was special about Eichmann and that he was simply a career bureaucrat working within a totalitarian system that condoned mass murder. His own "evil" was neither outside the human experience nor anything other than normal within its time-and-place setting. She argues that he was, in fact, a petty civil servant who did not question his orders because it was not within his professional competence to do so. In short, he simply got on with his job and made the best possible use of it that he could. In that regard, Arendt asserts, there was nothing demonic about Eichmann, one of the major architects of the Nazi "Final Solution of the Jewish Question"; rather, he was the epitome of how the phenomenon of evil can in fact be quite banal or ordinary. In view of her thesis—which by implication took the actions of Eichmann out of the realm of the supernatural and made them very, very human—Arendt was criticized by many who could not bring themselves to believe that the radical evil expressed by the Nazis could, in fact, be anything other than superhuman, not of this world, "monstrous," and the like. Arendt's thesis regarding "the banality of evil" went quite the other way, exposing, through Eichmann, that, if the conditions are "right," anyone could permit themselves to be carried along by the momentum of a murderous totalitarian regime—and to become willing accomplices in its crimes.

Bangladesh Genocide. The year 1971 saw an independence struggle take place on the Indian subcontinent, in which East Pakistan sought to secede from West Pakistan. It was a move that was resisted by West Pakistan with staggering violence. The Pakistani army was dominated by West Pakistanis, who saw any possibility of an Eastern departure as being essentially a weakening of their own position. When the East Pakistani Awami League won a majority of seats in a new Constitutional Assembly that seemed likely to give the Easterners political control of the country, the army moved in on East Pakistan with the intention of destroying the Awami League's ascendancy. Along the way, it was envisaged that the army could also rid East Pakistan of its large Hindu minority and terrorize the East Pakistani people into accepting what was in reality a colonial status. In a short period of time, a massive explosion of violence resulted in the murder of 3 million people, a quarter of a million women and girls raped, 10 million refugees who fled to India, and 30 million displaced from their homes. Ultimately, a calculated policy of genocide initiated by the government of West Pakistan was unleashed on the people of East Pakistan for what seemed to be the singular purpose of coercing the people into accepting a continuance of Pakistani rule over the region. In the end, the strategy did not work. From the ruins arose the independent country of Bangladesh, supported by intervention from the army of neighboring India and the consequent defeat of the Pakistani forces. But the human cost was staggering, and an argument can be made that, to this day, the war of 1971, and an unsettled political situation, have still not enabled Bangladesh to settle into a confident nation-building environment.

Bangladesh Genocide, U.S. Response to. The independence struggle that took place in 1971 on the Indian subcontinent, in which East Pakistan seceded from West Pakistan, resulted in an paroxysm of violence in which the army of Pakistan, dominated by West Pakistanis, engaged in extreme acts of terror. In a short span of time, some 3 million Bangladeshis (a term the East Pakistanis preferred to be called) lost their lives, an estimated 250,000 women and girls were raped, and approximately 10 million fled to India. It was a calculated policy of genocide initiated by the government of West Pakistan for what seemed to be the singular purpose of coercing the people into accepting a continuance of Pakistani rule over the region. Observing this, the U.S. administration of President Richard M. Nixon (1913–1994) seemed little concerned to intervene. Cold War politics featured as an important determinant of how the U.S. government approached third world developments. Because Pakistan enjoyed a close positive relationship with the United States as a counter to Soviet influence in India, Nixon did not wish to upset that delicate balance by issuing a protest over Pakistani actions in East Pakistan. Added to his concerns about the Soviet Union, Nixon knew that Pakistan was a useful conduit to opening and maintaining contacts with Communist China. The Chinese enjoyed good relations with Pakistan owing to their mutual enmity of India, and Nixon saw that this could be played on provided there was no boat-rocking over Pakistani excesses in Bengal. Though it was reported that some U.S. diplomats and other members of the U.S. State Department expressed their disgust and distress over Washington's adoption of a realpolitik perspective at a time of immense human catastrophe, the Nixon administration's path was set—a path that would lead to the opening of a dialogue between the United States and China later that year and pave the way for Communist China to take its seat at the United Nations.

Barayagwiza, Jean-Bosco (b. 1950). Anti-Tutsi media executive in Rwanda, active before and during the genocide of 1994. Barayagwiza was born in Mutura commune, in Gisenyi, western Rwanda. He was a cofounder, with Jean Shyirambere Barahinura (b. 1956), of the extremist *Coalition pour la Défense de la République* (CDR) party and presided over the party's affairs in Gisenyi Prefecture from February 6, 1994, up to and including the period of the genocide. Barayagwiza, with Dr. Ferdinand Nahimana (b. 1950), also founded the anti-Tutsi radio station, *Radio-Télévision Libre des Mille Collines* (RTLM), which was largely responsible for sustaining the Hutu public's focus on the extermination of the Tutsi both before and after the start of the genocide on April 6, 1994.

Prior to the genocide, Barayagwiza was director of political affairs in the Rwandan Ministry of Foreign Affairs, having studied law in the Soviet Union. As Rwanda was progressively overrun by troops of the Rwandan Patriotic Front (RPF) during the genocide in June and July 1994, Barayagwiza, along with most other high-ranking génocidaires, left the country. He was arrested in Cameroon on March 27, 1996, and—after incarceration for 330 days without being informed of the charges against him—was transferred to the jurisdiction of the International Criminal Tribunal for Rwanda (ICTR) in Arusha, Tanzania, on November 19, 1997. The delay was contrary to ICTR standing orders, which stipulate that charges must be laid within ninety days of an arrest being made. Because of this infraction, the ICTR was obliged to release him. However, on March 31, 2000, the ICTR Appeals Chamber overturned its earlier decision and directed that he stand trial. This, in turn, was consolidated into a larger proceeding, along with two other media personalities involved in the genocide, Nahimana and Hassan Ngeze (b. 1961). According to the ICTR indictment against him, in addition to his actions vis-à-vis RTLM, Barayagwiza allegedly presided over several meetings to plan the murder of Tutsi and moderate Hutu in Mutura commune, Gisenyi prefecture. He is also alleged to have assisted in the distribution of weapons and funds to the *Interahamwe* militia and to have ordered murders and violent acts against people of Tutsi origin. Furthermore, it was alleged that he knew or had reason to know that members of the CDR party had participated in the killings of Tutsi and moderate Hutu in Gisenyi prefecture. In spite of his position and responsibilities in the CDR, he allegedly did nothing to prevent those acts or to punish those responsible.

During what became known as the "Media Trial," the three were found responsible for creating a climate that implanted the idea of Tutsi annihilation onto the Hutu worldview long before the killing actually began. In a decision handed down in December 2003, all three defendants were found guilty by the ICTR. Barayagwiza was declared guilty of crimes against humanity and incitement to genocide and given a sentence of thirty-five years; with credit for time served, this was later reduced to twenty-seven years.

Barmen Declaration of the Confessional Church. In Germany, on May 31, 1934, a group of dissident Protestant Evangelical Church pastors and theologians, in what would later become the Confessing or Confessional Church, issued the "Theological Declaration of Barmen," disassociating themselves from their own denomination by refusing to acknowledge the primacy of the state over the Church, concepts of racial superiority, and the dismissal of non-Aryans in church positions. The document itself was written by Reformed theologian Karl Barth and Lutheran theologian Hans Asmussen and consisted of two sections: (1) "An Appeal to the Evangelical Congregations and Christians in Germany," and (2) "Theological Declaration Concerning the Present Situation of the German Evangelical Church." Its condemnations included the following:

> We reject the false doctrine that beyond its special commission the State should and could become the sole and total order of human life and so fulfill the vocation of the Church as well. We reject the false doctrine that beyond its special commission the Church should and could take on the nature, tasks and dignity which belong to the State and thus become itself an organ of the State. We reject the false doctrine that the Church could and should recognize as a source of its proclamation, beyond and besides this one World of God, yet other events, powers, historic figures and truths as God's revelations. We reject the false doctrine that the Church could have permission to hand over the forms of its message and of its order to whatever itself might wish or to the vicissitudes of the prevailing ideological and political convictions of the day. We reject the false doctrine that there could be areas in our life in which we would not belong to Jesus Christ but to other lords, areas in which we would not need justification and sanctification through him. We reject the false doctrine that with human vainglory the Church could place the Word and work of the Lord in the service of self-chosen desires, purposes, and plans. We reject the false doctrine that, apart from this ministry, the Church could, and could have permission to, give itself or allow itself to be given special leaders (Führer) vested with ruling authority.

Bassiouni, M. Cherif (b. 1937). A visionary in the field of international law, Bassiouni, professor of law at DePaul University in Chicago, Illinois, and president of DePaul's International Human Rights Law Institute, was an early and strong advocate—through his writings and speeches—of the establishment of an international criminal court. Ultimately, Bassiouni played a major role in the establishment of both the International Criminal Tribunal for the former Yugoslavia (ICTY) and the International Criminal Court (ICC). In 1992 he was appointed a member, and later chairman, of the UN Commission to Investigate Violations of International Humanitarian Law in the former Yugoslavia. From 1995 to 1998 he served as the vice chair of the UN General Assembly Committee for the Establishment of an International Criminal Court, and in 1998 he was elected chairman of the Drafting Committee of the UN Diplomatic Conference on the Establishment of an International Criminal Court. His writings (well over two hundred law review articles published in Arabic, English, French, German, Italian, and Spanish and over sixty books of which he was the author and/or editor) are considered to be seminal works in the field of international law, particularly as they apply to the issues of human rights, crimes against humanity, and genocide.

BBTG. *See* Broad-Based Transitional Government.

Belzec. Located in southeastern Poland, the Nazi death camp at Belzec was established on November 1, 1941, began operating on March 17, 1942, and ceased operations in December 1942. By that time, upwards of six hundred thousand persons had been murdered, primarily Jews but also Roma and Poles. Only two Jews are known to have survived. Belzec was part of the overall plan of "Operation Reinhard" for the extermination of all the Jews within the *Generalgouvernement* of Poland under the administration of Governor-General Hans Frank (1900–1946) and was the initial camp for testing the mass extermination of Jews. The camp itself was divided into three separate areas: administration, a storage area for plundered goods, and the extermination area, which initially contained three gas chambers but which were later replaced by six. SS Colonel General Christian Wirth (1885–1944) served as its first commander, and SS Master Sergeant Lorentz Hackenholt (1914–?) was responsible for both extermination procedures and the use of Zyklon B Gas in the crematoria. The camp's second commander was Gottlieb Hering (1887–1945). At the direct order of SS Chief Heinrich Himmler (1900–1945), the camp—after being dismantled, the bodies cremated and buried, the plunder relocated—was turned into a farm for a Ukrainian family. In the summer of 1994, the entire region was overrun by Soviet troops.

Benenson, Peter (1921–2005). Peter Benenson, a British lawyer, founded Amnesty International (AI), the now renowned international human rights organization, in 1961. The founding of AI resulted from a newspaper article, "The Forgotten Prisoners," Benenson wrote and had published on May 28, 1961, in the *Observer* (London) and that was reported on in *Le Monde* (Paris). In announcing an impartial campaign to assist victims of political persecution, Benenson wrote: "Open your newspaper any day of the week and you will find a report from somewhere in the world of someone being imprisoned, tortured or executed because his opinions or religion are unacceptable to his government. . . . The newspaper reader feels a sickening sense of impotence. Yet if these feelings of disgust all over the world could be united into common action, something effective could be done." In a matter of a week, Benenson received over a thousand letters offering help, thus laying the foundation for the human rights organization that ultimately became known as Amnesty International.

Beothuk People, Genocide of. The indigenous people of Newfoundland, the Beothuks, were termed "Red Indians" by the earliest English travelers at the beginning of the sixteenth century owing to their practice of painting their bodies with red ocher. In June 1829 a young Beothuk woman, Shanawdithit (c. 1803–1829), died of tuberculosis in St. John's; she is generally regarded as "the last Beothuk." A people numbering anywhere between five hundred and two thousand at the time of first European contact (the higher figure is the more likely), the Beothuk population collapsed steadily after the middle of the eighteenth century. It has been estimated that by 1820 the Beothuk population had been reduced by 92 percent of its approximate total at first contact; by 1823, it reached 96 percent. The pitiable few Beothuks left by the end of the decade could probably be counted on the fingers of two hands, if they could be found. The major reasons behind the demise of the Beothuk population of Newfoundland can be attributed to settler depredations and murders, a decline in Beothuk hunting areas, kidnapping of Beothuk women and a consequent decline in reproductive potential, and—above all—diseases, particularly tuberculosis. Applying the definition of the 1948 UN Genocide Convention, none of this amounts to genocide because the critical component of intent is absent. The British colonial government did not pursue a policy aimed at the destruction of the Beothuk; in 1769 there was, instead, a clear statement that the murder of the Beothuk was a capital crime, and, during the first two decades of the nineteenth century—by which time it was far too late—there were a number of serious official attempts undertaken to rescue the last Beothuks from what was regarded as an inevitable fate. Modern-day claims that the Beothuks were "murdered for fun" by the English settlers, who hunted them for "sport," do the historical record less than justice and sow an unfortunate confusion in the mind of an unsuspecting public. Extinction came to the Beothuks of Newfoundland, but it did not come through genocide.

Bermuda Conference. Convened by Britain and the United States in Bermuda on April 19, 1943, the Bermuda Conference's avowed purpose was to discuss the plight of Jewish refugees under Nazi rule. The fact is, the knowledge that Germany was exterminating Jews was already well established.

Held at the relatively remote site of Bermuda for the express purpose of controlling the flow of information by the news media, no official representatives of Jewish organizations were permitted to attend. The agenda of discussion was also severely curtailed; that is, the particularity of specifically Jewish tribulations was masked by use of the term *political refugees*. Further to this, more attention was placed on prisoners of war than on refugees. The possibility of Palestine, then under British control, as a site for refugees and the issue of direct negotiations between Britain and Germany were not even discussed. Even discussion concerning the possibility of sending food parcels to those already incarcerated in the concentration camps was curtailed.

At its conclusion, on May 1, 1943, the Bermuda Conference was, in truth, more of a public relations ploy on the part of both Britain and the United States than a serious attempt to address the issue. Other than the establishment of a small refugee camp in North Africa, no real attempt was made to save those who could have been saved.

Ironically, April 19, 1943, the first day of the Bermuda Conference, was also the first day of the Warsaw Ghetto Revolt. No statement during the conference, however, was issued concerning the revolt, nor did the revolt have any impact on the deliberations regarding the plight or fate of the refugees.

Bettelheim, Bruno (1903–1990). A professor of psychoanalysis who was born in Vienna, Austria, and was incarcerated in Nazi concentration camps during 1938 and 1939. He emigrated from the Third Reich to the United States and became best known for his educational methods in addressing the needs of emotionally disturbed children as well as for his theories regarding prisoner behavior in Nazi concentration camps. In the latter regard, the principal theory he advanced and developed over four decades was trailblazing, though it was challenged by some in the decades following owing to its oversimplification of highly complex issues.

He pursued a degree in psychology at the University of Vienna, which awarded him a PhD in 1938. With the *Anschluss* (literally, union; which, in reality, was a forced union) by Germany of Austria in March 1938, Bettelheim, a Jew, became subject to Nazi antisemitic policies, and, in May of that year he was arrested. First incarcerated in Dachau in September 1938, he was transferred to Buchenwald but through good fortune and friends on the outside, he managed to be released in April 1939. He arrived in the United States on May 11, 1939, where he began a new life during which he became one of the world's leading psychotherapists. In October 1943, he published his first study of prisoner behavior in the Nazi concentration camps, based largely on his own experiences in Dachau and Buchenwald. Arguing that the Nazis had instituted a highly complex camp regime designed to break the prisoners' will to resist their (the Nazis') directives, Bettelheim noted that the major effect of this was to produce changes in the prisoners' own psychological perceptions of themselves, such that the longer they remained incarcerated the more they came to identify with the goals of their persecutors, along the way regressing to a state of childlike helplessness and dependence. It was a highly controversial position, which he would be required to defend increasingly throughout succeeding decades. But as the first major attempt to analyze and explain the behavior of individuals living under the stresses imposed by life in the Nazi concentration camps, Bettelheim's work was nonetheless influential on a generation of younger scholars. Other Bettelheim theories were less so, such as his views on Jews who went passively to their deaths in the concentration camps, in ghettos, or at the hands of the *Einsatzgruppen* in which he basically argued that the Jews were suicidal or his suggestion that Anne Frank's family cooperated with the Nazi war machine by not resisting it. Never one to shy away from a fight, Bettelheim took on his critics vigorously, especially (though not exclusively) Colgate University English professor Terrence Des Pres (1939–1987), the latter primarily over the nature of survivorship. Despite his success, influence, and authority, throughout his life Bettelheim fell into deep depressions; during one such bout, on March 13, 1990, he committed suicide.

Beyond Borders. A motion picture released in 2003, focusing on the work of humanitarian aid workers during the 1980s and 1990s. The film locates its story in Ethiopia, Cambodia, and Chechnya and provides a dramatic perspective of the dangers and difficulties faced by aid workers in situations of war, genocide, and natural disasters. The movie stars U.S. actress Angelina Jolie (b. 1975) and British actor Clive Owen (b. 1964) and was directed by Martin Campbell (b. 1940). In the United States, it received an R rating for language and war-related violence, the latter of which is recreated with impressive effectiveness. Although the film was received suspiciously by critics, who responded negatively to what was perceived as a moralizing "issues movie," the passion for the cause it attempts to portray shines through. In fact, *Beyond Borders* can on one level be viewed as Jolie's elegy for a world in danger: at the same time as the film's release, she published a book, *Notes from My Travels* (2003), based on her work in 2001–2002 as a United Nations Higher Commission for Refugees (UNHCR) Goodwill Ambassador. Despite a budget of US$35 million, *Beyond Borders* was financially unsuccessful, reinforcing, in the view of some, that movies dealing with complex humanitarian problems are unwelcome at the box office.

Biafra, Genocide in. Biafra was a breakaway state formed out of the Eastern State of the Federal Republic of Nigeria in 1967. For those who were teenagers or adults during the crisis, the name Biafra conjures up images of babies with large staring eyes and bloated bodies, little sticklike limbs, and a helplessness preceding death which only starvation can bring. The Nigerian Civil War of 1967–1970, which was fought as a war of independence for the Biafrans and a war of national reunification for the Nigerians, was the first occasion in which scenes of mass starvation were brought home to a television-dominated West; resulting in millions throughout Europe, North America, and elsewhere being horrified by what they saw. Less apparent was the reality that lay behind this case of a brutal and bloody secessionist conflict; that is, in the Nigerian determination to defeat Biafran separatism, a deliberately designed genocidal policy of enforced famine was perpetrated against the population of the newly formed country. The conflict led to an eventual death toll of up to a million people, mostly of the largely Christian Igbo ethnic group. The Nigerian Federal Army, and the government that supported it, was a perpetrator of genocide through a premeditated and strictly enforced policy of starvation, as well as the military targeting of civilians. The Biafran state lasted only two and a half years, until its final military collapse in January of 1970. In the 1990s, discussion began to take place on the extent to which the countries of the West (particularly Britain) and the United Nations chose to turn a blind eye to events in Biafra and how Cold War concerns rather than humanitarian considerations clouded their judgment as they framed their policies toward the breakaway state.

Bibliographies of Genocide. The bibliographies available on genocide are extremely eclectic and are located in single articles, books, and CD-ROMs. They range from single bibliographies on particular acts of genocide (e.g., the Armenian genocide, the Holocaust, the fate of the Roma and Sinti during the Holocaust period, the Cambodian genocide) and/or specialized subjects (e.g., literature of the Holocaust, first-person accounts of genocide, and the prevention and intervention of genocide) to an entire bibliographical series (*Genocide: A Critical Bibliographic Review*) founded by Israel W. Charny (b. 1931) and edited by Charny and Samuel Totten (b. 1949).

Bikindi, Simon (b. 1954). A Rwandan singer and a propagandist for the extremist Hutu. He recorded songs with anti-Tutsi lyrics that were in turn broadcast repeatedly on *Radio Télévision Libre des Mille Collines* (RTLM). One of his most popular songs, "Bene Sebahinzi" (The Descendants of Sebahinzi), praised the significance and value of the 1959 Hutu revolution. When groups of extremist Hutu went out to search for Tutsi to kill during the 1994 Rwandan genocide, they often sang songs they had heard on RTLM, and Bikindi's were especially popular. Bikindi was indicted by the International Criminal Tribunal for Rwanda (ICTR) for using music to help incite the genocide. He pleaded not guilty to six charges: conspiracy to commit genocide; genocide, or alternatively, complicity in genocide; direct and public incitement to commit genocide; murder as a crime against humanity; and persecution as a crime against humanity. The prosecutor trying the case alleged not only that Bikindi helped to incite the genocide through his music but also that he took an active part in the mass murder of Tutsi and moderate Hutu and did so through the recruitment and training of *Interahamwe* members. As of this writing (February 2007), the trial is still ongoing.

Bilateral Aid. In common usage, the word *bilateral* means something that is of, on, or with two sides. In relation to the provision of international aid (as between states), the term refers to instances where aid is imparted from one country to another. This implies a relationship, if not of dominance, then at least of influence, by the donor state over the recipient. Such a notion is often expressed in the form of what is referred to as "tied aid," whereby the donor benefits economically from its aid provision; an example could be where the donor state insists that the recipient purchase goods, services, or expertise from the donor in order to receive the aid being offered. In circumstances such as these, the economic instrument can be turned on and off like a tap, depending on the degree of control the donor wishes to exercise. When dealing with a poor or nondemocratic state as the recipient, bilateral aid donors sometimes find themselves supporting governments that oppress, exploit, or, in other ways, violate the human rights of their citizens for purposes of aggrandizement or profit, as they take advantage of aid donations intended for the population of their countries.

Birkenau. Also known as Auschwitz II, Birkenau was one of the three primary camps in the Auschwitz complex and was designed to "process" (mass murder) more than six thousand persons on a daily basis, especially Jews and Roma. It began its operations in October 1943. Over 1 million persons are estimated to have been murdered there in its four gas chambers and two crematoria. For a more complete understanding of this subcamp, see the entry entitled "Auschwitz."

Bisengimana, Paul (b. 1945). Paul Bisengimana was mayor of Gikoro commune in the prefecture of Kigali-rural prior to and during the 1994 Rwandan genocide. According to the International Criminal Tribunal's (ICTR) indictment of Bisengimana, he, from late 1990 through July 1994, reportedly took part in the planning and execution of the genocide of the Tutsi in Gikoro. In doing so, he helped to train and distribute weapons to militias and other extremist Hutu, drew up lists of individuals to be murdered, and took part in carrying out the massacres. After pleading guilty to the charges lodged against him, the ICTR, on April 15, 2006, sentenced Bisengimana to fifteen years imprisonment.

Bitburg Cemetery. Site of a German military cemetery where both Wehrmacht (military) and Waffen-SS are buried. In 1985, U.S. president Ronald Reagan visited the site and created an international furor by doing so. Elie Wiesel, a Holocaust survivor and acclaimed author, responded directly to him, "I am convinced . . . that you were not aware of the presence of SS graves in the Bitburg cemetery. Of course you didn't know. But now we are all aware. May I . . . implore you to do something else, to find another way, another site. That place, Mr. President, is not your place." According to *The New York Times*, "President Reagan's regret at having promised such a cemetery tribute was palpable. He walked through it with dignity but little reverence. He gave the cameras no emotional angles. All day long he talked of Hell and Nazi evil, to submerge the event. . . . Not even Mr. Reagan's eloquent words before the mass graves of Bergen-Belsen, [though,] could erase the fact that his visit there was an afterthought, to atone for the inadvertent salute to those SS graves." In a speech later that same afternoon at the Bitburg Air Force Base, where he was accompanied by German Chancellor Helmut Kohl, Reagan stated, "There are over two thousand buried in Bitburg cemetery. Among them are forty-eight members of the SS—the crimes of the SS must rank among the most heinous in human history—but others buried there were simply soldiers in the German army."

Bizimungu, Augustin (b. 1952). The former chief of staff of the Rwandan Armed Forces (*Forces Armées Rwandaises*, or FAR) at the time of the genocide in 1994, Bizimungu was born in Byumba in northern Rwanda on August 28, 1952, and was a career soldier. His climb through the Rwandan military was a steady one and was crowned by his promotion to the rank of major-general and chief of staff on the same day, April 16, 1994—ten days after the beginning of the genocide. An extremist Hutu, Bizimungu was reputedly one of a number of senior officers opposed to the Arusha peace accords signed between the government of Rwanda and the Rwandan Patriotic Front (RPF) in August 1993. Allegedly, his view was that any attack on Rwanda, for whatever reason, by the RPF would result in the extermination of the Tutsi population in his area of operations. Earlier, he worked closely in the supervision and training of members of the *Interahamwe* youth militia, a body established expressly for the purpose of persecuting the Tutsi. Throughout the genocide, from April to July 1994, Bizimungu was the leading military figure involved in negotiations with the United Nations Mission for Rwanda (UNAMIR) and its force commander, Lieutenant-General Romeo Dallaire (b. 1946). With the victory of the RPF in July 1994, Bizimungu fled Rwanda. Ultimately, he was arrested in Luena, northeastern Angola, on August 2, 2002. Within three weeks he was transferred to the jurisdiction of the International Criminal Tribunal for Rwanda (ICTR) in Arusha, Tanzania, and made his first court appearance. Charged with genocide, crimes against humanity, and war crimes, Bizimungu was also charged with additional crimes and command responsibility for crimes committed by his subordinates. The prosecution alleged that Bizimungu conspired with other army officers to plan the extermination of the Tutsi; but from the first, Bizimungu pleaded not guilty on all counts. Bizimungu's trial, in which he is standing alongside of three other senior military officers accused on the same counts, is still (as of mid-2007) proceeding.

Black Africans, of Darfur. The term *black Africans* is the name by which non-Arab Africans in Darfur, Sudan, refer to themselves. It is also the way in which the government of Sudan (GOS) refers to the non-Arab African peoples of Darfur. The main black African groups attacked by GOS troops and the *Janjaweed* (Arab militia) from early 2003 through today (September 2007) were the Massaliet, Zaghawa, and Fur peoples. The attacks of the GOS and *Janjaweed* were carried out as a scorched earth policy that the United States government, among others, deemed to be genocidal in intent.

Black and Tans. The nickname given to a British military unit, the Royal Irish Constabulary Reserve Force, deployed to subdue the Irish independence movement during 1920 and 1921. Its primary focus was the suppression of the Irish nationalistic revolutionary movement Sinn Féin (Ourselves Alone) and its military arm, the Irish Republican Army (IRA). The force was recruited for the purpose of assisting the Royal Irish Constabulary (RIC) and comprised, for the most part, former soldiers who had recently been demobilized after World War I. By late 1921, it was a force nearly ten thousand strong. Their name came from the hastily assembled uniform that was issued to recruits: khaki trousers and surplus tunics and caps from the RIC (which were dark green) or British police (which were dark navy blue). The first of the "Tans," as they rapidly became known, arrived in Britain on March 25, 1920, and, with another armed body of British ex-military officers, the Auxiliary Division of the RIC—known colloquially as the "Auxies"—launched an intensive campaign of brutal counterinsurgency throughout Ireland. This took the form of besieging and burning villages and small towns, shooting civilians suspected of having links with the IRA, abduction, murder, and other random acts of violence and human rights abuse. On the night of December 11, 1920, large numbers of Black and Tans attacked the major city of Cork, in southern Ireland, sacked it, and put it to the torch. The central city area sustained significant damage from this action. Many additional atrocities were committed by the Auxiliaries and the RIC and were blamed on the Black and Tans, but this is not to exonerate the Tans themselves; they were as brutal an occupation force as any seen in other places during the twentieth century, and they carried out their reign of terror with the assent of the British authorities. Quite legitimately, the Black and Tans could be fitted into a category of state-sponsored terror. During their term in Ireland, this violent force was responsible for hundreds of civilian deaths, for large-scale destruction throughout many parts of Ireland, and for the deprivation of civil rights and normal justice mechanisms guaranteed to all British subjects. The existence and activities of this unit, raised and endorsed by a thoroughly democratic government such as that of Britain, is testament to the fragility of civil society in a time of stress and shows that no society is immune to harsh and draconian methods of repression when such methods are considered or deemed necessary.

Black Deeds of the Kremlin, The. Title of a two-volume work edited by S. O. Pidhainy (1907–1965), published between 1953 (Volume 1) and 1955 (Volume 2) by the Democratic Organization of Ukrainians Formerly Persecuted by the Soviet Regime. The second volume is devoted exclusively to the Soviet man-made Ukrainian terror-famine of 1932–1933 and contains hundreds of eyewitness accounts of conditions prevailing at that time. In many cases, those providing their testimonies used their initials rather than their full names for fear of reprisal that might take place against family members then still living under Soviet occupation. Some of those relating their accounts had been able to travel outside of Ukraine itself in their regular duties as technicians, skilled workers, and the like; their stories show no evidence of famine in Russia or other Soviet republics save nearby Byelorussia (now Belarus). During the Cold War, supporters of the Soviet Union routinely denounced *The Black Deeds of the Kremlin* as a capitalist-inspired forgery that had no basis in fact; their cause has been taken up more recently by genocide deniers (particularly on the Internet) who consider the publication to be nothing other than anti-communist propaganda. Others, by contrast, have looked to *The Black Deeds* in order to confirm their opposition toward communism, Jews, and the Soviet Union.

Black Legend. A frequently raised issue in discussions of the Roman Catholic Church and its past regarding apostates and heretics concerns the institution known as the Holy Office, commonly called the Inquisition. This had been established in the thirteenth century as a special ecclesiastical court to investigate heresy and to try heretics. Its membership comprised monks appointed by the pope or by local bishops, and it conducted its proceedings in secret—using torture to obtain "confessions" both from those who had been accused and, often, from those called as witnesses. Heretics adjudged guilty were sentenced to fasting and prayer; sometimes fines or imprisonment was added to this. The Church drew the line at executions, however, preferring instead to hand convicted heretics over to the "the secular arm," that is, to the civilian authorities. The civilian authorities, in turn, were expected to punish heretics by burning them at the stake. On occasion, local kings or lords anticipated the Inquisition by taking the task on themselves to suppress heresy and condemned heretics prior to the Inquisition's arrival. The relationship between the Inquisition, the civil authorities, and capital punishment was an intimate one, leading to the growth in imperial Spain of a belief that the Inquisition was responsible for all judicial and extrajudicial killings carried out in the name of the state. This was referred to as the "Black Legend," from the robes worn by the monks of the Inquisition. The Black Legend spread beyond Spain, giving rise to a reputation painting the Church as barbaric sadists whose clerics delighted in committing sexual crimes against women and young boys and whose bloodthirsty ways led directly to the deaths of thousands. The Black Legend was incorporated into accounts of Spanish ecclesiastical and lay cruelty in the New World and was even employed as an explanation for the mass extermination of the native populations there in the sixteenth and seventeenth centuries. The Black Legend stirred up considerable debate over the centuries since then, particularly within the Catholic Church: supporters say it is wildly exaggerated, but critics of the Church consider it to be an accurate portrayal of the Church's brutality as it responded to major challenges to its authority during the period of the Reformation.

Blackbirding. Term applied in nineteenth-century Australia to describe the practice of kidnapping Melanesians to work in the sugarcane fields of Queensland as slave labor. It was generally reckoned that the work was too hard and the heat too debilitating for Europeans to undertake cane harvesting, so ships set forth to the islands north of Australia ostensibly to "recruit" workers who would be indentured for a specific period of time—after which they would be returned to the islands from which they originated. In reality, the situation was far from this labor relations ideal. Ships plied the waters around the New Hebrides, Solomon Islands, and Fiji searching for local men (and, less frequently, women) to whom they would sometimes offer contracts that were for the most part meaningless documents to those the whites referred to derisively as "Kanakas" (from the Polynesian word for "man"). In the last four decades of the nineteenth century, it has been calculated, more than eight hundred ships searched the South Pacific for Kanaka labor. Over 62,000 contracts were "arranged" with Melanesians, but, in many cases, young islanders were simply kidnapped, thrown into the holds of the ships, and transported by means reminiscent of the Middle Passage taking slaves from west Africa to the Americas. Whole islands were depopulated, either outright or piecemeal, so that the survivors were deprived of a male population from which to breed. Once in northern Australia, the Kanakas were put to work in slavelike conditions. Foremen watched over them from on horseback, often forcing them to work harder by means of whips. Harsh corporal punishment was common, but the Melanesians had no recourse to the law; by the terms of the contracts into which they had supposedly entered voluntarily, such punishments were permitted. Of course, the white farm owners and those directing the blackbirding trade were engaging in actions that were little different from outright slavery, but, given the fact that slavery had been abolished throughout the British Empire in 1833, the contract system had been devised as a legal cloak for their actions. By the late 1890s, the system had outlived its usefulness, as had the Kanakas their presence in Queensland. As the movement for a white Australia gathered momentum, a push came for the remnants of the Kanakas to be repatriated to the islands of the South Pacific. This opened up another element of white brutality, as people were often simply dumped on the first island ships' captains saw—all too frequently, not the place from which the workers had originated. Many more perished in these foreign conditions. A small population of Melanesian descent remained in Australia, mostly in Queensland and northern New South Wales, where they live today—a minority within the minority black population of Australia.

Blaskic, Tihomir (b. 1960). A colonel in the army of the Bosnian Croats, and later a general in the regular Army of Croatia, who was convicted by the International Criminal Tribunal for the Former Yugoslavia (ICTY) in March 2000 in connection with a massacre in the Bosnian village of Ahmici, in which approximately one hundred Muslims were killed by Croat forces. In 1996 Blaskic was indicted by the ICTY for a variety of crimes committed by troops under his command. These included murder, attacks on noncombatants, the taking of civilians as hostages, racial and religious persecution, and destruction of property for nonmilitary reasons. Later, in 1996, he surrendered voluntarily to the court. His trial began in July 1997, and, in March 2000, his conviction was handed down. He was sentenced to forty-five years in prison. An appeal was launched immediately, on the ground that not all documentation had been forthcoming from the Croatian government regarding the chain of command. The former president of Croatia, Franjo Tudjman (1922–1999), had opposed cooperation with the ICTY and did little to assist defense attorneys who sought access to government archives. The appeal stipulated that Blaskic was not in charge of the forces who committed the war crimes for which he was convicted. A strong campaign for his release was waged in Croatia, and on July 29, 2004, it was successful. The appellate court of the ICTY reduced his sentence from forty-five years to nine years, and he was released on August 2, 2005.

Blood Libel. The accusation that Jews engaged in ritual murder of Christians for religiously prescribed reasons seems to have first emerged in England during the twelfth century. The story of the events in 1144, in which a twelve-year-old Christian boy from Norwich named William was allegedly tortured, crucified, and murdered during Passover week, was the first of many in which Christian children were said to have been ritually murdered by Jews at the time of Easter and/or Passover. The core of the accusation was that Jews murdered Christian children at Easter in emulation of the crucifixion of Jesus; over many centuries, widely spread folktales throughout Europe added that Jews also used the blood of these murdered children for their Passover rituals, most often through mixing the blood into matzo (the correct transliteration from the Heb. is *matzah*; the term matzo is an Ashkenazic rendering that is becoming increasingly archaic) dough so that the Jews would literally devour the Christian life force throughout the Passover festival. The libel of a Jewish quest for Christian blood—oftentimes focusing on infants or small children, at other times on virgin girls—became a central charge motivating peasant reprisals in the form of pogroms and other acts of persecution. Given the proximity of Easter and Passover, March and April became months in which anti-Jewish violence often peaked in European countries. As Christians observed the death of Jesus (at the hands of the Jews, as the Church taught) and his resurrection, stories that Jews were "still" engaging in horrific practices against the innocent stirred up intense antagonism toward them. (A practice emerged in some Jewish communities, as a result of these apocryphal stories, to abstain from drinking red wine at their Passover meals so as to avoid the impression that they were actually drinking blood.) In the modern era, blood libels took on an added dimension; although the influence of the religious struggle between Christians and Jews had begun to recede, racial antisemites built on the blood libel tradition in Europe in order to harass, kill, and uproot a Jewish presence in lands developing modern forms of national identity and expression. The Austro-Hungarian, Russian, and Ottoman empires saw the most frequent expressions of the blood libel. Well-known examples of these included the Damascus blood libel of 1840, in which the murders of a Capuchin friar and his servant were blamed on Jews; and the Beilis affair in Russia in 1911, in which Mendel Beilis (1874–1934), the Jewish manager of a brick factory in Kiev, Ukraine, was accused of murdering a boy for ritual purposes. (After a trial and appeal process lasting two years, Beilis was acquitted.) Even into the twentieth century, successor states of the old central and eastern European empires experienced violence "justified" on account of ritual murder accusations.

"Blue Helmets" or "Blue Berets." A colloquial term that refers to United Nations peacekeeping operations; the term is derived from the powder blue helmets or berets worn by the peacekeepers. It is a term used by the UN staff, as well as most scholars, in referring to both UN peacekeeping operations and the individuals deployed with them.

Blue Scarf. The Khmer Rouge leadership of Communist Kampuchea (1975–1979) reportedly issued a blue scarf to each cadre member from the country's Eastern Zone whom they forcibly relocated to the northwest province of Pursat. The blue scarf marked them—and ostracized them—as "impure Khmers" who were destined to be murdered.

Body Bag Effect or Syndrome. In relation to the issue of genocide intervention, the body bag effect (syndrome) refers to the potential, and/or actual, number of casualties suffered by a nation's troops and the impact this number has on the political will of a nation's citizens and/or leaders to commit troops to a potential or ongoing intervention. Put another way, the body bag syndrome refers to the hypothesis that the support for military action "diminishes in proportion to the number of expected or real casualties" (Everts, 2003, p. 226).

Bonhoeffer, Dietrich (1906–1945). Dietrich Bonhoeffer, a conservative German Protestant pastor and theologian, was, early in his career, of a mind-set whereby Jews could realize their ultimate salvation only by their acceptance of Jesus Christ. Shortly after the Nazis came to power in 1933, however, he came to appreciate the inherent evils in National Socialism, and the failure of Christianity in its relationship with Judaism, and thus became one of the founders of what would later be called the "Confessing Church." His opposition both to Nazism and to the attempted German Christian validation of it, as well as the ill treatment of German Jews, prompted him to reassess the relationship between church and synagogue. His 1933 essay, "The Church and the Jewish Question," was an initial attempt to rethink the position of the Church and was a source of his uncompleted work on Christian ethics. His opposition to the collusion of the Protestant Evangelical Church with the government of Nazi Germany led to his temporary reassignment in the United Kingdom between 1933 and 1935, after which he returned to Germany to work with an opposition seminary that was, in 1938, shut down by the Nazis.

Later, Admiral Wilhelm Canaris (1887–1945) of the Wehrmacht Intelligence Service (*Abwehr*) recruited Bonhoeffer as a secret contact and liaison with foreign churches. By 1942, he was involved in resistance efforts that resulted in the successful smuggling of fifteen Jews to Switzerland, for which he was arrested and taken to Buchenwald concentration camp in 1943. His involvement in the July 1944 bomb plot against Adolf Hitler (1889–1945) led to his transfer to Flossenburg concentration camp, where he was hanged on April 9, 1945.

Among Bonhoeffer's more well-known writings were his smuggled-out *Letters from Prison* and *The Cost of Discipleship*. These and other writings continue to be regarded as playing an important role in Christian rethinking of the relationship with Judaism in the aftermath of the horrors of World War II and the Holocaust (Shoah). His student, Eberhard Bethge (1909–2000), later published the definitive biography of his teacher in 1977, titled *Dietrich Bonhoeffer: A Biography*. Unresolved is whether Bonhoeffer should be accorded the status of a "Righteous Gentile" by Yad Vashem, the State of Israel's Holocaust Memorial Authority, as a question continues to linger as to whether he was directly involved in the saving of Jewish lives. A recent (2004) assessment of Bonhoeffer is found in Stephen Haynes's book *The Bonhoeffer Phenomenon: Portrait of a Protestant Saint*.

Booh-Booh, Jacques-Roger (b. 1938). Special representative of the UN secretary-general in Rwanda (November 1993 to June 1994). In the aftermath of a series of murders of Tutsi in late February 2004, Booh-Booh reported to UN headquarters that there was no evidence that the killings had been "ethnically motivated." When genocide broke out in Rwanda in April 1994, Booh-Booh played down the seriousness of the killing by pooh-poohing its systematic nature as well as how widespread it was. Many in the international community voiced concern about just how impartial Booh-Booh really was for someone in his position. Not only was he a close friend of Rwandan president Juvenal Habyarimana (1937–1994), but he was also close with the leadership of the extremist Hutu-dominated MRNDD (*Mouvement Républicain National pour Démocratie et le Développement* or the Republican Movement for National Democracy and for Development) and associated with some who became the most notorious leaders of the 1994 Rwandan genocide, including Jean-Paul Bagosora (b. 1955).

Bophana, a Cambodian Tragedy. This 1996 film, which was produced by Rithy Panh, who, as a teenager, fled the Khmer Rouge takeover in Cambodia, portrays the true and tragic story of two young intellectuals, Bophana and her husband. Disgusted by the corruption of the Sihanouk regime, Bophana's husband joined the Khmer Rouge, the Communist underground movement. During their separation, the pair stayed in contact through the love letters they wrote one another and, eventually, they were reunited after the fall of Phnom Penh. Ultimately, however, they were denounced, arrested, tortured, and forced to make false confessions. In 1976 both of them were executed by the Khmer Rouge.

Bosnia-Herzegovina. Bosnia-Herzegovina was, and remains, a much-disputed region at the crossroad of empires, dating back to Roman times. The Romans, Byzantines, Ottomans, and Hapsburgs all sought to gain control of this strategic Balkan territory, and all left their mark, especially in the form of a multiethnic population consisting of Croats (Catholics), Serbs (Christian Orthodox), and Bosnians (Muslims). Under Josip Broz Tito (1892–1980), the region became the heartland of the former state of Yugoslavia's military industries, whose engineers and managers were largely drawn from the urban Muslim population, not from the more rural Croats and Serbs. During World War II, some Bosnian Muslims collaborated with the Croatian *Ustashe* in the formation of a Nazi puppet state called Greater Croatia. The memory of this was not lost on future generations of Serbs, especially when Yugoslavia began to disintegrate in the early 1990s. During the Tito decades, between 1945 and 1980, Bosnia's population became the most ethnically integrated and assimilated, via intermarriage and economic growth. This was not, however, enough to stem the tide of hostile ethno-nationalism that was revived following Tito's death, especially when it was whipped up by Serbia's and Croatia's leaders, Slobodan Milosevic (1941–2006) and Franjo Tudjman (1922–1999). The war for the partition of Bosnia was fought so ferociously that it became a three-way war of atrocities and counteratrocities, involving troops and militia led by Milosevic, Tudjman, and Bosnian president Alija Izetbegovic (1925–2003). Bosnia was hardest hit by this vicious warfare, resulting in the deaths of up to 250,000 Bosnian civilians and the worst massacres in Europe since the end of World War II (most notoriously, the Serb massacre of between seven thousand and eight thousand Bosnian Muslim men and boys at Srebrenica, in July 1995). The fighting lasted for three years, until, in November 1995, a settlement was negotiated through the U.S.-sponsored and UN-supported Dayton Agreement (November 21, 1995). In effect, this treaty, which was to be supervised by NATO, segmented Bosnia into three ethnic enclaves, while still referring to Bosnia as a unitary state. The fiction prevails to this day. Only a handful of the scores of thousands of refugees have returned to their original homes. Some observers optimistically look to a bright future for Bosnia; others see a renewal of ethnic violence between the two administrative regions of the country (a unified Muslim-Croat confederacy and a separate Serbian sector named Republika Srpska), especially when outside restraints (such as the UN-sanctioned NATO forces currently stationed in Bosnia) are removed. Much will depend on Bosnia's future integration into the European Union, though membership lies many years away. As Bosnia-Herzegovina struggles to recover from the physical destruction wrought by its disastrous experiences in the 1990s, its still-divided condition, and the emotional legacies that now prevail throughout the country, hope for a healthy future would seem to be a long way off, though the people themselves, possibly owing to these difficulties, are optimistic that the state can be viable and prosperous.

Bosnian Safe Areas. Various regions were declared "safe areas" by the United Nations during the ongoing conflict in the former Yugoslavia (1991–1999) in order to provide protection for civilian populations. Such safe areas, though, often came under attack— indeed, some were shelled mercilessly, while others were overrun and some even suffered genocidal massacres. Bosnian Serb troops were notorious for their vicious and repeated attacks on such areas, which included the expulsion of both Croats and Muslims and the indiscriminate bombing of towns and cities such as Sarajevo, Tuzla, and Gorazde. Genocidal ethnic cleansing of non-Serbian populations through forced population transfers became the norm rather than the exception, coupled with the physical destruction of both cultural sites (e.g., libraries) and religious sites (e.g., mosques). In various instances, Croatian military troops and Muslim rebels also carried out such attacks in Bihac and Banja-Luka, in both 1994 and 1995.

In May 1995, in response to Bosnian president Alija Izetbegovic's (1925–2003) declaration that he would not agree to extend a cease-fire beyond April 1995, along with the fact that the Muslim and Croat forces continued fighting their Serbian foes, Bosnian Serb forces captured 370 UN peacekeepers. Then, in July 1995, the UN-declared safe areas of Srebrenica and Zepa were overrun by Bosnian Serb forces. Subsequently, the Serb forces proceeded to commit genocidal massacres and ethnic cleansing.

Complicating the process was the Bosnian Serbs' continuous restriction of international human rights monitoring by such human rights groups as Human Rights Watch. The restrictions were primarily due to the fact that the Serbs did not want their practices of ethnic cleansing to be exposed to the international community.

Air strikes by NATO forces in response to increasing harassment of peacekeepers and others by Bosnian Serb forces, including continuing violent attacks on the safe areas, began at the end of August 1995 and increased in September 1995. Though peace negotiations were ultimately resumed toward the end of 1995, human rights abuses continued until President Slobodan Milosevic (1941–2006) was arrested on April 1, 2001, and turned over to the International Criminal Tribunal for the former Yugoslavia (ICTY) on June 28th of that year. Milosevic was charged with violations of the laws and customs of war, crimes against humanity, grave breaches of the 1949 Geneva Conventions, complicity in genocide, and genocide.

Boutros-Ghali, Boutros (b. 1922). An Egyptian national, Boutros-Ghali was UN secretary-general from January 1, 1992, to December 31, 1997. Most notably, he was the architect and author of the UN's "Agenda for Peace" (1992), which, at the time, was considered to be one of the most comprehensive statements in the post–Cold War period vis-à-vis the role of the United Nations in peacekeeping operations. Ironically, he was also the secretary-general that oversaw the totally inadequate UN response to the events leading up to and culminating in the 1994 Rwandan genocide.

In 1995 Boutros-Ghali issued his "Supplement to An Agenda for Peace" in which he discussed the dramatic increase in UN peace operations since 1991, and made recommendations regarding changes needed in how the UN dealt with violent crises across the globe. Also, in 1995, when a reporter at a news conference asked Boutros-Ghali whether the July collapse of the "safe area" in Srebrenica (during which some seven thousand to eight thousand Muslim boys and men were slain by Serb forces, constituting the largest massacre in Europe in fifty years) was the UN's greatest failure in Bosnia, the secretary-general said: "No, I don't believe that this represents a failure. You have to see if the glass is half full or half empty. We are still offering assistance to the refugees . . . and we have been able to maintain the dispute within the borders of the former Yugoslavia."

Brahimi Report. Issued in August 1999, the *Brahimi Report* is based on a UN study of UN peacekeeping, which was conducted following the UN's inept response to the 1994 Rwandan genocide. Basically the report called for a complete overhaul of UN peacekeeping operations and made a series of recommendations for doing so. The report was named after Lakhdar Brahimi (b. 1934), the Algerian diplomat and UN official, who headed the commission that issued the report.

Brand, Joel (1906–1964). Born in Transylvania, Hungary, Joel Brand grew up and was educated in Germany, where he became a communist and was arrested in 1934 by the Nazis. After his release, he relocated to Budapest and became an ardent Zionist. He is most noted for playing a role in trying to save Hungarian Jews from deportation to Auschwitz at the hands of the Nazis in 1944. After Germany invaded Hungary in 1944, Brand was informed by SS Colonel Adolf Eichmann (1906–1962) that he (Eichmann) was prepared to release up to 1 million Jews in exchange for ten thousand trucks and vast quantities of tea, coffee, and soap to be supplied by the United States. The transaction was to be made using Brand as the intermediary, but the exchange was never consummated, much to Brand's frustration, because both the British government and the Jewish Agency in Palestine saw it as a ruse on Eichmann's part, who they believed had no intention whatsoever of bringing the deal to fruition. In May 1944, after his last meeting with Eichmann, Brand (together with fellow Jew Bandi Grosz, about whom nothing is known), supposedly representing SS Chief Heinrich Himmler (1900–1945) and other top SS officials, left for Vienna and a secret meeting with U.S. intelligence officers, to negotiate a secret peace treaty with the Allies which was to take place in Istanbul, Turkey. Due to a series of unfortunate circumstances, Brand, who was using a false passport, was never given an entrance visa into Turkey. Along with representatives of the Jewish Agency, Brand proceeded to Aleppo, where he was arrested by British intelligence operatives. Prior to leaving Budapest, Eichmann had insisted upon Brand's return. Brand's unavoidable inability to do so proved disastrous both for the Aid and Rescue Committee, which he helped found, and for Hungarian Jewry in general. Knowing that his failure to return to Budapest spelled death for those Jews who remained in Hungary, he attempted to persuade Moshe Sharett (1894–1965) of the Jewish Agency, as well as British intelligence, to allow him to return. This effort was to no avail. Ultimately, Brand was transferred to Cairo, Egypt, where he went on a hunger strike. In the summer of 1944, British intelligence leaked details of Brand's mission to save the Hungarian Jews, thus ending whatever possibilities for its success remained. Brand was released by the British in October 1944 but was allowed to travel to only Palestine. Once there, he tried, without success, to contact Chaim Weizmann (1874–1952), then head of the World Zionist Organization, again to no avail. After the war, Brand remained bitterly contemptuous and condemnatory of the Jewish leadership of the period. He died in 1964 of cirrhosis of the liver brought about by his bouts of intense drinking. He was, in all probability, according to historian Yehuda Bauer of Hebrew University, the most maligned figure of the period, a Jew who attempted to help save his people but was denied the chance to do so.

Brazil, Genocide of Indigenous Peoples. Indigenous Brazilians, prior to the arrival of Europeans in the early sixteenth century, were divided into four main language groups—the Tupi-Gurani, the Ge, the Carib, and the Arawak. Most lived in temporary villages, inhabiting a broad region and moved nomadically in a cyclical fashion every few years. After the arrival of the Portuguese in 1500, colonial settlement saw the start of a process of expropriation of indigenous land. A favored land use was cultivation of sugar cane on sugar plantations, and indigenous labor was used for land clearance. Often, this land was simply occupied, and entire tribes were either pushed off or killed if they offered resistance (and, all too often, regardless of whether there was any resistance). For those captured and impressed into forced servitude, European diseases—particularly in the more closely settled environments of the plantations—took a fearsome toll on the previously unexposed indigenous populations. As Portuguese rule became more established across the entire country, and settlement patterns saw the building of cities and towns, regulations relating to the indigenous population sought to minimize harm and enhance protection. Opposition to this came from settlers and was reinforced by mixed messages as governments changed and Indians periodically rose in rebellion. This tended to mute the preferred tendency, which was to try to ensure that the Indians would be accorded decent treatment. At the back of the push to take care of the indigenous population was the Catholic Church, which was keen to convert as many of the natives as possible, rather than furthering their demise. Intermarriage was encouraged, and the mixed-descent progeny of such unions were to be accepted rather than stigmatized. By the latter part of the twentieth century, such a perspective had to a large degree been forgotten. Development in all fields of endeavor had long been viewed as the ideal to which Brazil should be aspiring, and government ministers were often dogmatic in their statements that such development not be held up because Indians were standing in the way. Absorption and assimilation were hence the ideal goals at which Indian policy should be aimed, not ethnic separateness. In the 1980s, road construction was seen as one way to achieve this; as a network of roads was built across the country, Indian communities were either dispersed or forcibly brought into the mainstream of Brazilian society. Where there was opposition, it was put down harshly. And road-building is just one example within a large array of efforts to dispossess the Indians of their land and way of life. Development destructive of indigenous lifestyles (and all too frequently, of lives) also came from oil interests, airport construction, plantation growth, and urban expansion. The best-known example of such measures designed to drag an indigenous people into the modern world concerns the Yanomami of the jungles of northern Brazil, whose engagement with Brazilian society began in only the 1980s. Within a very short space of time, charges of genocide had emerged. It is an engagement that continues.

Bringing Them Home. The title of an Australian report produced by the National Inquiry into the Separation of Aboriginal and Torres Strait Islander Children from Their Families. The inquiry was commissioned by the government of the Commonwealth of Australia in 1995 and undertaken by the Australian Human Rights and Equal Opportunity Commission under the direction of former High Court judge Sir Ronald Wilson (1922–2005). The report, handed down in 1997, concluded that the forcible removal of children of part-Aboriginal descent from their parents during the twentieth century, and their subsequent placement with white families with the intention of eventually "breeding out the color" after several generations, was a case of genocide in accordance with Article II (e) of the 1948 United Nations Convention on the Prevention and Punishment of the Crime of Genocide. The report further concluded that this constituted a crime against humanity for which due reparation would have to be made to the so-called Stolen Generations. In its findings, the authors of the report asserted that anywhere between one in three and one in ten Aboriginal children were taken under the policy of forcible removal, numbering tens of thousands of children. *Bringing Them Home* provoked a storm of controversy in Australia, with the charge of genocide vehemently rejected by many who had previously viewed genocide only from the perspective of killing. Others agreed that removals had taken place but argued that the report was unfair in labeling the policy as genocide (with the negative connotations attached to the term) in view of the fact that those carrying it out were acting from good intentions that were in the best interests of the children. The upshot of the report was that, although it brought the fullest details of the forcible-removal policy into public view for the first time, no action was taken by the right-of-center government of Prime Minister John Howard (b. 1939) that was in office when the report was released.

Broad-Based Transitional Government (BBTG). A term given to a negotiated administration agreed to by former warring parties in conjunction with an arbitrating body at the conclusion of a conflict. Sometimes the term "of national unity" is added, reinforcing the "broad-based" dimension of such an administration. A BBTG is always intended to be temporary in nature and to serve as a bridge between a former government that has been defeated in external war, civil war, insurrection, coup d'état, or revolution and a new administration based on a multiparty democratic system. As a broad-based structure involving a number of political parties or factions, a BBTG is, in most cases, overseen by an occupation force from outside, usually (though not always) authorized by the United Nations. The intention is to nurse a country's political and governmental arrangements back to robust health or, if such health had never existed, to nurture its development. As a temporary compromise measure, the formation of a BBTG is, by definition, established on the basis of power sharing, with ministerial posts being allocated across the range of all parties participating in the effort. (The latter are, in most cases, determined by the victors of the conflict that led to the establishment of the BBTG in the first place, though, in a spirit of reconciliation, preconflict parties shorn of their radical elements may also be invited to join under controlled conditions.) A BBTG is, most frequently, established only at the conclusion of a conflict, as part of some sort of peace agreement, which is why third-party involvement in the form of an occupation or monitoring force is now the norm. The duration of the force's stay depends on the success of the BBTG in achieving its transitional objectives. Recent examples of states in which a BBTG has been either imposed or recommended include Bosnia-Herzegovina, Burundi, Cambodia, East Timor, and Rwanda.

Bryce, Viscount James (1838–1922). British intellectual, ambassador, and politician with an authoritative knowledge of Armenia and the Turkish genocide perpetrated from 1915 onward. Lord Bryce had a lengthy association with Armenia that began in the 1870s. At the time of the Hamidian Massacres in 1895, he wrote a seminal essay on the "Armenian Question," which attracted widespread attention on both sides of the Atlantic. In 1904, he became active in the International Pro-Armenia Movement, an organization established to raise consciousness about the need to do something to assist the Armenians who had long suffered persecution under the sultan's rule. In 1907, in recognition of his professional work in Britain's Foreign Office, he was appointed British ambassador to the United States; later, in 1914, he was elevated to the Hague Tribunal. With the onset of World War I in 1914, Lord Bryce busied himself collecting evidence of enemy contraventions of international law, and, in 1915, the British government assigned him the task of gathering whatever evidence could be found on the mass murder of the Armenians. Through his contacts in the U.S. State Department, he was able to tap into American dispatches emanating from Constantinople, both formal and informal, and these, together with other documents, Bryce entrusted to a young historian, Arnold Toynbee (1889–1975), to edit into a government blue book, or official documentary collection. It was a devastating indictment of the deportation and extermination of the Armenian people at the hands of the Young Turk regime. Lord Bryce's collection was published as *The Treatment of Armenians in the Ottoman Empire, 1915–1916*, and was presented to the British parliament by the foreign secretary, Viscount Grey of Fallodon (1862–1933). Although by now elderly, Bryce spent the rest of his life in active pursuit of the ideals that came to be enshrined in the League of Nations, whose appearance in 1919 he embraced enthusiastically.

Buchenwald. A Nazi concentration camp located near Weimar, Thuringia, Germany, Buchenwald was established in 1937 to house male slave laborers for use in the armaments industry. Women were not imprisoned there until 1944. Its first commandant, from 1937 to 1941, was Karl Otto Koch (1897–1945), whose wife was Ilse Koch (1906–1967), the notorious "Bitch of Buchenwald," known for her sadistic cruelty. Sometime during Koch's last year, medical experiments were also performed on prisoners. Both Koch and his wife were brought to trial by the Nazis on charges of corruption stemming from their theft of goods and diversion of camp monies. He was executed in April 1945, and she was given a four-year term, which was reduced to two, and later set free, only to be rearrested and imprisoned by the Allies. It is estimated that as many as 250,000 prisoners were incarcerated during Buchenwald's period of operation (1937–1945), during which some sixty thousand were killed, including Soviet prisoners of war.

Among the many prisoners incarcerated in Buchenwald by the Nazis were Konrad Adenhauer (1876–1967), the first chancellor of Germany after the war; French writers Jean Amery (1912–1978) and Robert Antelme (1917–1990); child psychologist Bruno Bettelheim (1903–1990); Protestant pastor Dietrich Bonhoeffer (1906–1945); French and American actor Robert Clary (b. 1926); 2002 Nobel Prize for Literature winner Imre Kertész (b. 1929); and 1986 Nobel Peace Prize winner Elie Wiesel (b. 1928).

The camp was liberated by U.S. forces on April 11, 1945. From 1945 to 1950, the camp was renamed "Special Camp 2" by Soviet occupation forces and used to house German prisoners, of whom over seven thousand died from conditions there, including overcrowding, diseases such as typhus and dysentery, lack of sanitation, and starvation.

Buddhists, Destruction of by Khmer Rouge. As part of its genocidal campaign, the Khmer Rouge purposely set out to destroy the country's Buddhist community and way of life. It is estimated that 80 percent of Cambodian citizens were Buddhists; as part of its destructive policies, the Khmer Rouge immediately murdered Buddhist religious leaders and destroyed Buddhist temples. It is also estimated that in 1975, at the beginning of the genocide, there were some seventy thousand Buddhist monks living in Cambodia, and less than fours years later, in 1979, or the point at which the Khmer Rouge were routed by the Vietnamese, less than two thousand monks had survived. In September 1975, approximately five months after the outset of the genocide, the Kampuchean Communist Party (CPK), in stark testimony vis-à-vis their goals, issued a document that asserted, "The monks have disappeared . . . 90 to 95 percent [killed]."

Bund Deutscher Mädel **(BdM; League of German Girls).** The female division of the German youth movement during the Nazi regime from 1933 to 1945. This complemented the male Hitler Youth (*Hitlerjugend*), and, although an important socializing agency among young females, it nonetheless did not rank on an equal footing in the Nazi state with its male counterpart. The organization was formed in 1930 (prior to the Nazi accession to power) and was structured on parallel lines to the *Hitlerjugend*. Girls aged ten to fourteen years were enrolled in the *Jungmädel* and graduated at fifteen to the higher levels of the BdM. At age seventeen, the girls became eligible for entry to the *Glaube und Schönheit* (Faith and Beauty) organization, where they were taught domestic science and received advanced training in preparation for marriage. The BdM constantly taught that women in the Third Reich had but a singular function, the bearing and raising of children. In advance of marriage, they were required to serve a year of national labor service to the state. In line with the militaristic regimentation undertaken by the male organization, BdM girls were continually instructed in the areas of service to the state, physical fitness, comradeship, and the raising of families. As with the *Hitlerjugend*, the leader of the BdM was the high-ranking Nazi Baldur von Schirach (1907–1974).

Bund Report(s). In May 1942, and again in November 1942, Szmul Zygielbojm (1895–1943), a leading member of the Polish National Committee in London, received two reports from a group still active in Poland, The Jewish Labor Organization called the Bund, specifically detailing the ongoing annihilation of Polish Jewry from inside Poland. Zygielbojm's inability to enlist any support from either the Polish-Government-in-Exile, the Allies, or major Jewish organizations resulted in abject frustration, depression and, ultimately, his suicide on May 12, 1943. Prior to killing himself, he wrote letters condemning all of the latter for their failure to act.

"Burning Times, The." Euphemism employed by some scholars when referring to the period of witch persecutions in Europe between the fifteenth and eighteenth centuries. The spread of the witch craze at the end of the fifteenth and throughout the sixteenth century was in large part a response to two stimuli: a desire on the part of the Roman Catholic Church to reestablish its control in light of the Protestant Reformation; and an urgent need for the mass of the European population to explain a series of climatic changes that led to famine, crop damage, and livestock losses across certain parts of the continent. Women (and in some areas of northern Europe, significant numbers of men) were frequently accused of witchcraft, of being in league with the Devil, and of possessing secret conspiratorial knowledge designed to enslave humanity. For this, across the three centuries in question, at least one hundred thousand heresy and other trials were conducted, often at the direction of the Inquisition. Tens of thousands of innocent women were executed, many by burning at the stake, others by hanging or drowning.

Approximate numbers of those killed have fluctuated wildly over the years, from a high of 9 million posited in the 1970s to a more plausible recent figure of between forty thousand and sixty thousand (of whom perhaps a quarter were men). Though most of the killing took place in the sixteenth century, persecution, trials, and executions were still relatively common even up to the middle of the eighteenth century; by this time, however, public burning had diminished drastically as a preferred means of execution.

Burundi, Genocide in. Burundi, a small country in the Great Lakes region of central Africa, is generally regarded as the "twin" of its neighbor, Rwanda. Like Rwanda, Burundi has a population that is dominated by a large Hutu majority (85%), with a much smaller Tutsi minority. At the time of independence from Belgium in 1962, the Tutsi, who had been the traditional rulers before and during Belgian colonialism, retained their ascendancy—largely by force of arms and a tightly controlled bureaucracy. In 1965 legislative elections gave Hutu parties a resounding victory, winning twenty-three out of thirty-three seats in the National Assembly. This victory was overthrown, however, when the *mwaami* (king)—a Tutsi—appointed a Tutsi from the royal family as prime minister. Soon thereafter, on October 19, 1965, an attempted coup was suppressed ruthlessly, but this served only to intensify Hutu anger at their second-class status. Against this background, an uprising of Hutu in the southern provinces of Burundi broke out in April 1972. This was viewed as a final challenge for Hutu supremacy by many Tutsi leaders, in particular President Michel Micombero (1940–1983), an army officer who had been installed as the result of a military takeover in 1966. In what appears to have been a series of deliberate campaigns against specific categories of Hutu—for example, Hutu in government employ, intellectuals (which could include any Hutu with a university education, whether completed or in the process of completion, secondary school students, and teachers), and the Hutu middle and upper classes (the latter designation was based on wealth or Tutsi perceptions of wealth)—a series of massacres were carried out. Estimates of the number killed between April and October 1972 vary, but most settle at somewhere between 100,000 and 150,000. And the killing did not end there. Subsequent large-scale massacres of Hutu by Tutsi government forces took place in 1988, and massacres of Tutsi by Hutu forces occurred in 1993. Accompanying all these savage deaths was the wholesale exodus of scores of thousands of refugees to neighboring countries, leading to an intensifying destabilization of the region.

Bushnell, Prudence (b. 1946). A senior U.S. diplomat who took a prominent role in attempting to keep the Rwandan genocide of 1994 at the forefront of her government's attention while it was in progress. Born in Washington, D.C., herself the daughter of American diplomat Gerald Bushnell (1914–2005), Prudence Bushnell joined the U.S. Foreign Service in 1981 and served in Dakar (Senegal) and Mumbai (India) prior to entering the Bureau of African Affairs. Ultimately, she rose to the position of principal deputy assistant secretary of state. Prior to the Rwandan genocide, Bushnell was sent to Rwanda to try to impress upon President Juvenal Habyarimana (1937–1994) the importance of seeing the Arusha Accords implemented successfully, warning him that failure could cost Rwanda support from the United States in the future. Then, after the missile attack on the president's plane that took Habyarimana's life on April 6, 1994, Bushnell was the first U.S. official to warn—on the same day—of the likelihood of widespread violence if word got out that Habyarimana had been assassinated. During the crisis weeks that followed, Bushnell was the U.S. official most closely connected to developments in Rwanda. On numerous occasions, she spoke directly by phone to the chief of staff of the Rwandan Armed Forces (*Forces Armées Rwandaises*, or FAR), Major General Augustin Bizimungu (b. 1952), warning him that U.S. president Bill Clinton (b. 1946) was holding him personally responsible for the killings that were then taking place in Rwanda. On April 28, Bushnell rang the presumptive head of the interim Hutu Power government, Théoneste Bagosora (b. 1941), ordering him on behalf of the United States to stop the killing and to immediately arrange a cease-fire. Although this was clearly a case of foreign intervention in the domestic affairs of a sovereign state, Bushnell was unrepentant about exceeding her authority in this instance. Elsewhere, Bushnell planned to reduce the effectiveness of the Hutu killers by jamming their major anti-Tutsi propaganda arm, *Radio-Télévision Libre des Mille Collines* (RTLM), but permission to do this was denied on the grounds that it was both too expensive and contrary to international (as well as U.S.) law. Overall, Prudence Bushnell was the only high-ranking American official to keep attention focused on the killing in Rwanda. Although derided for this by many in the U.S. government in 1994, she has since been applauded for her efforts, both in and outside the corridors of government in the United States.

Butz, Arthur (b. 1945). Associate professor in the Department of Electrical and Computer Engineering at Northwestern University, in Illinois, Butz is the author of a notorious Holocaust-denial text, *The Hoax of the Twentieth Century*, which was originally published by the Holocaust-denial Institute of Historical Review, Torrance, California, in 1976. This work remains one of the so-called classic works of anti-Holocaust literature. Because of his academic credentials (MS and PhD from the University of Minnesota), his book presents the appearance of a scholarly publication with copious footnotes and an extensive bibliography. Be that as it may, his work is accorded absolutely no scholarly credibility whatsoever. Butz is, thus, considered little more than a Nazi apologist and antisemite.

Bystanders. In relation to the act of genocide, the term *bystanders* refers to those who are cognizant of the perpetration of crimes against humanity and genocide but do nothing to halt such. In that regard, bystanders are neither the perpetrators of genocide, collaborators with the perpetrators, nor the victims of genocide. Individuals and organizations (e.g., churches, nongovernmental organizations on the ground, other—uninvolved—states) become bystanders for various reasons, not all of which can be cast in black-and-white terms. Some bystanders, for example, may harbor animus against the victim population but not necessarily be inclined to carry out harmful actions against them. Some may simply be apathetic to what is happening to "the other." Still other individuals may fear for their lives or loved ones should there be repercussions for their speaking out against the genocide and/or attempting to halt it. There are many other reasons as to why individuals may choose not to speak out or act on the behalf of others; these reasons do not excuse their behavior, but they do help to explain individuals' motives, decisions, and inaction.

C

Caedite eos. Novit enim Dominus qui sunt eius. *See* Amaury, Arnold.

Calling the Ghosts: A Story about Rape, War and Women. Produced in the 1996, this extremely powerful and Emmy Award–winning documentary is the first-person account of two women who became victims in a war (the 1992–1995 Bosnian war) where rape was used as a weapon. Jadranka Cigelj and Nusreta Sivac, childhood friends and lawyers, were imprisoned at the notorious Serb concentration camp of Omarska, where they, along with hundreds of other Muslim and Croat women interned therein, were systematically raped by their Serb overseers. Upon their release and as they fought to regain a modicum of stability in their lives, they undertook a Herculean effort to have rape tried as a major war crime by the International Criminal Tribunal for the Former Yugoslavia.

Cambodian Documentation Commission (CDC). Based in New York City, the CDC was founded in 1982 by David Hawk, Dith Pran, Haing Ngor, Kassie Neou, Yang Sam, and Arn Chorn. All but Hawk were survivors of the Cambodian genocide. The CDC's focus is fourfold: to document the genocide that was perpetrated in Cambodia between 1975 and 1979; to seek accountability (through either an international or a domestic tribunal) for those responsible for planning and carrying out the genocide; to prevent the Khmer Rouge from returning to power; and to promote human rights in Cambodia. In an effort to carry out its mandate, CDC has worked along the following lines: presented petitions and appeals to states that are parties to the UN Convention on the Prevention and Punishment of the Crime of Genocide, member states of the United Nations, and Cambodian political leaders; presented testimony to the UN Commission on Human Rights as well as at U.S. congressional hearings; and produced translations of archives that document repression of the Cambodian people under the Khmer Rouge. Hawk, an indefatigable human rights activist, along with Hurst Hannum, also wrote "The Case against Democratic Kampuchea," a model legal brief for an Article IX complaint, and submitted it to the International Court of Justice.

Cambodian Genocide. Between April 1975 and January 1979, the communist Khmer Rouge, under the rule of Pol Pot (1925–1998), perpetrated a genocide in Cambodia that resulted in the deaths of an estimated 1.7 million (and perhaps up to 2 million) Cambodian citizens. The Khmer Rouge carried out a policy that aimed to totally erase all signs of French colonial rule and restore Cambodia to what it viewed as the pristine condition that prevailed before the foreigners had stamped their cultural traits on the land, its people, and their society. For nearly four years, Cambodia was brutally eradicated of any evidence of "alien" ways. The primary targets were the cities, in particular the capital of Phnom Penh. The city's population of nearly 2 million was uprooted and "resettled" in the countryside, so as to purge them of their exposure to "bourgeois" ways. The express purpose was to indoctrinate them to rural, traditional Khmer (or Cambodian) culture, ostensibly unspoiled by colonialism and capitalism—the purported twin enemies of the anticolonialist, communist, and monoethnic nationalist Khmer Rouge. Millions were forced to undergo "reeducation," which included public confessions. Throughout the period, hundreds of thousands perished from exposure and lethal violence. The Khmer Rouge's fanaticism led to executions of "enemies" that covered the full spectrum of society: intellectuals, artists, professionals, those who had traveled abroad, and those who spoke a foreign language. In short, all who embodied "foreignness"—that is, anticommunist or non-Khmer ideals—were systematically killed as having been too "contaminated" to participate in building the new society under Pol Pot's rule. The Khmer Rouge was so committed to destroying the old society and creating a new one that it completely obliterated even the most fundamental of social forms, the family. It also included the destruction of such expressions of modernity as transportation, education, technology, administration, and governance. Henceforth, the national project was to be dedicated to serving *Angka*, the "Organization," from which all was to emanate in the new Democratic Republic of Kampuchea. When the carnage was over, stopped by an invasion from Vietnam in January 1979, it is estimated that the equivalent of one in four Cambodians had been killed, worked, and/or starved to death. Among the dead, and targeted for extinction, were the non-Khmer minorities, including the Muslim Chams, ethnic Chinese and ethnic Vietnamese, and Buddhist monks. With the Vietnamese invasion, the Pol Pot government fell, and the Khmer Rouge fled into the jungles of western Cambodia. Since then, over the past thirty years or so, the country has struggled to reestablish itself as a stable political and economic entity, founded on democracy and the rule of law. Most disturbing, in this context, is that in all this time, the principal actors of the Cambodian genocide, who one by one have been dying off, have not been brought to justice, despite ongoing calls from Cambodians and foreign nongovernmental organizations for some form of accountability and redress to take place.

Cambodian Genocide Justice Act. This was an act the U.S. Congress passed in 1994, fifteen years after the toppling of the regime of Cambodia's Khmer Rouge dictator Pol Pot (1925–1998) by Vietnamese forces. Between the end of the dictatorship and the passing of the U.S. act, no concrete steps (neither inside nor outside of Cambodia) had been taken to hold anyone accountable for the deaths of at least 1.7 million Cambodian citizens at the hands of the Khmer Rouge between 1975 and 1979. The purpose of the act was to establish a tribunal to deal with Khmer Rouge–era crimes against the Cambodian people. The campaign for such a tribunal came from various U.S.-based nongovernmental organizations working in Cambodia that had firsthand experience with many former victims of Pol Pot's genocidal campaign. Before the legislation could be set in place, however, there had to be a proper body of evidence to justify indictments of the Khmer Rouge perpetrators of the Cambodian genocide. Spearheading the move was a U.S. specialist on Cambodian history and politics, Craig Etcheson (b. 1955). He and others managed to gain the ear of several sympathetic members of Congress, who, in turn, persuaded the government of U.S. president Bill Clinton (b. 1946) to appoint Charles Twining (b. 1940)—a former U.S.

ambassador to Cambodia—to coordinate efforts to bring about justice. The U.S. Congress passed the Cambodian Genocide Justice Act, allotting $400,000 to the U.S. State Department's budget for the purpose of assembling evidence against the Khmer Rouge génocidaires. This led to the establishment of Yale University's Cambodian Genocide Program (CGP), under the supervision of Professor Ben Kiernan (b. 1953), in December 1994. Both he and Etcheson, and the team of researchers based at the CGP, have since gathered millions of documents incriminating both the leadership and the lower ranks of the Khmer Rouge for their perpetration of horrific crimes before, during, and after their four-year rule over the people of Cambodia.

Cambodian Genocide, the United States' Response to. The response of the United States to the Cambodian genocide (1975–1979) must be seen in the context of the Vietnam War (1962–1975). In the latter years of that conflict, the United States had to cope with North Vietnamese supplies being sent to the Vietcong via Cambodia. The United States' response—in order to disrupt the flow of men and matériel through what was, in reality, neutral territory—was one of heavy U.S. bombing of the jungle trails employed to smuggle these supplies. The air war over Cambodia strengthened the radical elements of Cambodia's Khmer Rouge, whose rise to power in 1975 coincided with the retreat of the United States from Vietnam.

The end of the Vietnam conflict, which the United States lost, coincided with the start of the genocidal killings in Cambodia. At the time, the United States was led by President Gerald Ford (1913–2007), an interim president following the resignation, in disgrace, of President Richard Nixon (1913–1994) in 1974. Politically, the Ford administration, following the Vietnam debacle, was not inclined to get involved in the crisis in Cambodia. In 1976 Jimmy Carter (b. 1924), a Democrat, was elected president of the United States, and he did not want to risk another Vietnam-style engagement in Cambodia. In fact, his administration's general tendency was to support the Khmer Rouge so as not to offend China, a staunch ally of Khmer Rouge leader Pol Pot's (1925–1998) regime. It is also true that many of the early accounts of the brutality by the Khmer Rouge in Democratic Kampuchea (the new name the Khmer Rouge gave Cambodia) were deemed "inconclusive accounts" and/or "unconfirmed reports." Some, both inside and outside of the U.S. government, could simply not force themselves to believe the accuracy of the reports that they heard or read about. Essentially, the brutality described was seemingly all but unimaginable to them. But, then again, as Morton Abramowitz (b. 1933), an Asia specialist at the Pentagon at the time, said: "There could have been two genocides in Cambodia and nobody would have cared. . . . People just wanted to forget about the place. They wanted it off the radar."

Later, Carter was also forced to choose between the Khmer Rouge regime and its former enemy—Communist Vietnam, a government backed by the United States' Cold War adversary, the Soviet Union. Thus, Carter, who entered office speaking of the significance of the universal protection of human rights, did not speak up about the Khmer Rouge–perpetrated killings—and this was despite the fact that ever-increasing evidence corroborated the truth of the Khmer Rouge's atrocities. Again, for many, if not most, the dark cloud of Vietnam hovered over U.S. foreign affairs matters, especially those that pertained to issues involving Southeast Asia. By the time Carter's term came to an end, his administration was bogged down by the Iranian crisis and the taking of U.S. diplomats as hostages. In short, by 1979, when Pol Pot's genocidal regime was overthrown by Vietnam, the United States had done nothing to stem the tide of genocide in Cambodia.

In the aftermath of the Pol Pot years, none of the Khmer Rouge génocidaires were indicted, let alone convicted, in the absence of a tribunal.

Canada, Genocide in. In the nineteenth century, the indigenous peoples of Canada were, to a large degree, spared much of the violence committed against Native Americans in the United States. This is not to say that the First Nations, as they are termed in Canada, escaped persecution, dispossession, or measures introduced to weaken their position as European settlement took place. Indeed, the Beothuk of Newfoundland were completely destroyed (as a result of starvation, disease, and settler-perpetrated murder), and the situation in other parts of Maritime Canada were little better; large-scale population collapse was widespread among certain peoples, such as the Miqmaq. The first sweeping legislation covering First Nations peoples in nineteenth-century Canada came in 1850, with the passage of the Statute for Lower Canada in which the term *Indian* was first defined legally. In 1870, after Confederation, the Act to Encourage the Gradual Civilization of the Indian Tribes in the Province and to Amend the Laws Respecting Indians was passed. The act raised the issue of assimilation, by which male Indians could "enfranchise" by renouncing their First Nations status and living as Europeans did. Measures introduced to encourage or force assimilation included inducements of land, lump-sum payments of money, the taking of land, exposure to alcohol, debility caused by disease or starvation, destruction of religious and cultural practices, and the enforcement of government orders through police coercion. Although it cannot be argued successfully as a whole that Canadian governments engaged in genocide against the First Nations as policy, a great deal of cultural destruction took place over a lengthy period of time. In many parts of the country, racism still exists, and provincial policies sometimes threaten to disrupt further the lives of First Nations peoples. Nonetheless, this cannot be termed genocide—discriminatory and racist though it frequently has been.

Carlsson Report. This December 1999 report, which was chaired by former Swedish prime minister Ingvar Carlsson (b. 1934), is officially entitled "Report of the Independent Inquiry into the Actions of the United Nations during the 1994 Genocide in Rwanda." In part, it addresses descriptions of key events associated with the genocide, including but not limited to the following: the Arusha Peace Agreement; the establishment of UNAMIR; the cable of January 11, 1994, sent by Lt. General Romeo Dallaire (b. 1946) titled "Request for Protection for Informant"; the shooting down of the Rwandan presidential plane on April 6, 1994; the outbreak of the genocide; and the withdrawal of Belgian troops shortly after the genocide began. It also comprised a lengthy list of conclusions, which cite the following failures, among others: UN headquarters' reaction to the various warnings that mass murder was on the horizon; the inadequacy of UNAMIR's mandates; the lack of political will on the part of the United Nations member states to adequately address the growing crisis in Rwanda in the early 1990s, as well as the outbreak of the genocide; and impediments to the flow of information between the UN departments and its field operations. Most important, with an eye to the future, fourteen strongly worded recommendations were included in the report: (1) an action plan to prevent genocide; (2) the need to improve the capacity of the UN to conduct peacekeeping operations; (3) the need for military preparation on the part of contributing member states to "prevent acts of genocide or gross violations of human rights wherever they may take place";

(4) the need to improve the early-warning capacity of the UN; (5) the need to improve the protection of civilians; (6) the need to improve protection of UN personnel and staff; (7) the need to improve cooperation of UN personnel; (8)/(9) the need to improve the flow of information in both the United Nations system and the Security Council; (10) the need to improve the flow of information on human rights issues; (11) the need to improve the coordination of evacuation operations; (12) the need to readdress what membership in the Security Council means (this was particularly relevant in light of the fact that Rwanda itself was a member of the Security Council during the period of the genocide); (13) the need to support efforts to rebuild Rwanda; and (14) the need for the UN to acknowledge of its own responsibility (i.e., its failure) for not having done more to prevent or stop the genocide. The report concludes with a lengthy appendix titled "Chronology of Events (October 1993 to July 1994)."

Carnegie Commission on Preventing Deadly Violence. Established in 1994 by the Carnegie Corporation of New York, the express purpose of the Carnegie Commission on Preventing Deadly Violence is to address the various and dire threats to world peace of intergroup violence and to advance new ideas and methods vis-à-vis the prevention and resolution of deadly conflict. A key part of its mandate is to examine the principal causes of deadly ethnic, nationalist, and religious conflict within and between states and the circumstances that foster or deter their outbreak. "Taking a long-term, worldwide view of violent conflicts that are likely to emerge, the Commission seeks to determine the functional requirements of an effective system for preventing mass violence and to identify the ways in which such a system would be implemented." The Commission has also undertaken an examination of the strengths and weaknesses of various international bodies in regard to conflict prevention and is considering ways in which international organizations could possibly contribute toward developing an effective international system of nonviolent problem solving. The Commission issues three basic types of publications: reports of the Commission, reports to the Commission, and discussion papers.

Carpet Bombing. *See* Area Bombing.

Carthage, Genocide in. Carthage was an ancient city-state in North Africa, the major protagonist of Rome during the Punic Wars of 264–241 BCE and 218–201 BCE. A third Punic War, lasting from 149 to 146 BCE, would see the final confrontation between the two Mediterranean powers. The bitter hatred existing between Rome and Carthage was at its most powerful during the Second Punic War, when the Carthaginian general Hannibal (c. 247–182 BCE) invaded Italy and threatened Rome itself, winning a crushing victory at Cannae (216 BCE). The war subsequently settled into a period of stalemate and small-scale guerrilla tactics, until, many years later, the Romans gathered their forces under the generalship of Scipio Aemilianus (185–129 BCE), invaded the city, and, in the spring of 146, conquered it after several days of savage street fighting. As the historian Polybius (c. 200–118 BCE) recorded, Scipio surveyed the burning ruins and wept as he reflected on the fate of great cities, fearing that the same destiny might one day befall Rome. He then ordered that the city be completely destroyed. Carthage was looted, stripped of anything that could be reused as building materials, and the soldiers of Rome went on a killing spree that saw the deaths of tens of thousands of people. Tens of thousands more were sold into slavery, and the city was razed. Earlier, during the Second Punic War, the Roman statesman Cato the Elder (234–149 BCE) had ended every speech in the Senate—regardless of the topic—with the words *Ceteram censeo Carthaginem esse* *delendam!* ("I declare that Carthage must be destroyed!"). By 146 BCE, that rallying cry had become a reality. A story spread that the Romans even salted the earth around the city so as to ensure no possibility of a Carthaginian revival; although believed by many for generations, the story has not been proven beyond doubt. The destruction of Carthage, though a confirmed reality, has led to debates among historians regarding the charge of genocide. Although for many the city's fate as a victim of genocide is obvious (especially given the fact that the survivors of the city were deliberately split up and dispersed throughout the empire so that all traces of a distinct Carthaginian identity would disappear after a few generations), for others the destruction of Carthage was a military issue in which the victims were casualties of war as practiced at that time—and not the targets of a genocide as it is understood today.

Carthago delenda est! (Latin, Carthage is destroyed!). A Latin term frequently attributed, wrongly, to the Roman statesman Cato the Elder (234–149 BCE), in relation to the destruction by Rome of the Carthaginian Empire at the end of the Third Punic War (149–146 BCE). The bitterness created in Rome by the first two Punic Wars (264–241 BCE and 218–202 BCE) was so intense that Cato was moved, on every occasion in which he spoke to the Senate, to end with the words *"Ceteram censeo Carthaginem esse delendam!"* (I declare that Carthage must be destroyed!). Convinced that the security of Rome depended on the annihilation of Carthage, he used every opportunity to sound the tocsin about the Carthaginian threat and repeated his message whenever he could. By 146 BCE, his rallying cry had become a reality, as the Romans defeated Carthage, invaded the city, and put the population to the sword. Throughout the centuries, Cato's message has been corrupted to read, *"Carthago delenda est,"* which translates as "Carthage is destroyed." This, however, is an incorrect rendering of the original, as his entreaty was always intended to be a call to action, rather than a triumphant proclamation.

Catholic Church, and the Holocaust. There is, perhaps, no more complicated and contentious issue surrounding the Holocaust than the role of the Roman Catholic Church during the years associated with World War II (1939–1945); its role immediately preceding the war (1933–1939), paralleling Adolf Hitler's rise to power; or its papal leadership, specifically Pope Pius XI (Achille Ratti, 1857–1939) and Pope Pius XII (Eugenio Pacelli, 1876–1958). Questions include the following: (1) How much or how little did the Church know about the attempted extermination of European Jewry? (2) What could the Church, including its leadership, have done with that knowledge? (3) How much or how little did the Church do to save Europe's Jews? (4) How forcefully, both publicly and privately, did the popes address the fate of the Jews? (5) After World War II, did the Church play a significant role in aiding Nazis to escape punishment by arranging or assisting in their safe passage out of Europe? (6) What role did the historical religious-theological antisemitism of Christianity play in the decision-making process of the Church? These and other questions remain subject to continuous scrutiny and scholarly investigation; no definitive conclusions have thus far been reached. In 1933 the Vatican under Pius XI signed a concordat with Nazi Germany, supportive of the new regime and seemingly acknowledging its national emphases. The Catholic secretary of state at the time was Cardinal Pacelli, who would later become pope. Different in temperament from his predecessor, Pope Benedict XV (1914–1922), who, in 1938, said publicly, "Antisemitism is inadmissible. We are all spiritually Semites," Pacelli was shy by nature, committed to the survival and protection of the institutional Roman Catholic Church, isolated from contact with both the

Italian Jewish community or the German Jewish community where he had served as Papal Nuncio (ambassador or emissary) during the 1920s. Ultimately, he saw the conflict from the Church's perspective as that between the godless communism of the East and the fascisms and democracies of the West. Thus, any number of the above-mentioned questions can be understood from this perspective. To complicate matters even further, during World War II itself, the hierarchy of the Church (priests, nuns, monsignors, bishops, archbishops, cardinals, and laypeople, as well as churches, convents, and monasteries) did aid Jews, especially children, often at the expense of their own lives and the lives of their families. How much of this was done with the full support and acknowledgment of superiors, their ignorance of such activities, or their "blind eye" toward these rescue efforts is, equally, a fully unanswered question. In the aftermath of World War II, and the fuller revelations of the Holocaust, the Roman Catholic Church began an intense reevaluation of its attitude toward the Jews, primarily under Pope John XXIII (Angelo Roncalli, 1881–1963), resulting in the very welcome Declaration Nostre Aetate of 1965, beginning a thorough rapprochement with the Jewish community which continues to the present day.

Center for International Development and Conflict Management (CIDCM). The CIDCM, which is based at the University of Maryland in College Park, brings together faculty, students, researchers, and practitioners to investigate the relationships among economic, social, and political development and the conflicts that frequently arise from them. As part of its work, the CIDCM also conducts early-warning research. While its Minorities at Risk Project tracks and analyzes the status and political activities of some three hundred politically active communal groups throughout the world, its Global Event Data System identifies and codes conflictual and cooperative political events as reported in a variety of news sources.

Centre for Comparative Genocide Studies. *See* Australian Institute for Holocaust and Genocide Studies.

Century of Genocide. The phrase *century of genocide* was coined by genocide scholar Roger Smith (b. 1936) to describe the twentieth century in recognition of the fact that the century was plagued with one genocide after another (e.g., the 1904 genocide of the Hereros in Southwest Africa; the 1915–1923 Armenian genocide; the 1932–1933 Soviet man-made famine in Ukraine; the Holocaust [1933–1945]; the 1971 Bangladesh genocide; the Cambodian genocide [1975–1979], the Iraqi gassing of its northern Kurd population [1988]). Tellingly, he coined the term prior to the 1994 Rwandan genocide and the genocide perpetrated in the former Yugoslavia in the 1990s.

Century of Genocide: Critical Essays and Eyewitness Accounts. *Century of Genocide: Critical Essays and Eyewitness Accounts*, coedited by Samuel Totten, William S. Parsons, and Israel W. Charny (New York: Routledge, 2004), comprises essays on a wide range of genocides (thirteen in all), including but not limited to the following: the German genocide of the Hereros in Southwest Africa in 1904; the Ottoman Turk genocide of the Armenians between 1915 and 1923; the Soviet man-made famine in Ukraine in 1933; the Nazi-perpetrated Holocaust of Jews, Roma, and Sinti and the physically and mentally handicapped (1933–1945); the 1971 genocide in Bangladesh; the Indonesian-perpetrated genocide of the East Timorese (1975–1990s); the Khmer Rouge–perpetrated Cambodian genocide (1975–1979); the Iraqi gassing of its Kurd population in the north (1988); the 1994 Rwandan genocide; and genocide in the former Yugoslavia (early to mid-1990s). It concludes with a chapter on genocide in the Sudan at the turn of the century (from the twentieth to the twenty-first) and an essay on the prevention and intervention of genocide. Each essay, written by a specialist on a specific genocide, is accompanied by first-person accounts of the particular genocide.

Cham People, Genocide of. The Chams are a Muslim people located in Indochina, the majority of whom live in Cambodia. Originally of Hindu and Buddhist extraction, they are the descendants of the Champa, a kingdom extant between the second century CE and the year 1720. During the seventeenth century, the Champa king converted to Islam, and soon thereafter the Chams became a Muslim people. (The exact date of when Islam first arrived in the region is unknown, though Muslim grave markers dating to the eleventh century CE have been located.) By the middle of the twentieth century, the Chams enjoyed a high birthrate, outpacing both the ethnic Vietnamese (also a minority) and the dominant Khmer majority. With the coming of communism under the Khmer Rouge regime of Pol Pot (1925–1998), the Chams were viewed as separatist nationalists possessed of a different identity to that of the Cambodians. For this, it was held, they had to be integrated forcefully into the Cambodian mainstream. The fact that they were Muslim merely aggravated relations between the state and the Cham minority, as Islam was seen as an alien, foreign, culture that had no place in the new communist order. Whereas ethnic nationalism was viewed as a bourgeois aberration, Islam was seen as an alien import that had to be excised along with other foreign elements, if Cambodia were to become a "healthy" nation as the Khmer Rouge claimed it had been in precolonial times. Given this, the Khmer Rouge became determined to expunge the Cham presence from revolutionary Cambodia. The government's plan was to dislodge Chams from their villages and scatter them across the country in the hope of forcing assimilation by thinning their ranks. As the Chams resisted, Pol Pot tried intimidation, by killing village elders and prominent families. Finally, the regime opted for mass killing, which, in the end, led to massacres of entire Cham village populations. Were it not for the end of the Khmer Rouge regime in January 1979, the Chams may very well have been annihilated except for those few who collaborated with the government. As it was, at least half of the Cham population was killed during the Pol Pot years, the victims of a mentality that would not tolerate pluralism and actively sought to eliminate difference through violence and massive slaughter.

Chamberlain, Neville (1869–1940). Born into a political family (his father, Joseph Chamberlain [1836–1914], was a former cabinet minister under Queen Victoria [1819–1901], and his half brother Austen Chamberlain [1863–1937] was a chancellor of the exchequer), Neville Chamberlain was elected lord mayor of Birmingham in 1915 and a member of Parliament in 1918. He became postmaster general in 1922, minister of health that same year, and chancellor of the exchequer (finance minister) in 1923. In May 1937 he became prime minister of Great Britain. In September 1938, in Munich, he and Adolf Hitler (1889–1945) signed an agreement stating that their two nations would never go to war again. Upon his return to London, Chamberlain delivered his now-famous speech entitled "Peace in Our Time."

Chamberlain was the most powerful of a group of British politicians and civil servants known to history as the appeasers, that is, those who preferred to back down in the face of what they considered to be Hitler's legitimate claims. It was noted by some in Britain that Chamberlain's visit to Munich was negligent in that, at the Munich meeting, he referred neither to Nazi human rights abuses against Jews nor to the city's close proximity to the

Dachau concentration camp, just seven kilometers away. This was, however, never likely to happen: in the first place, because to do so would have been unseemly in light of diplomatic practice of the day; and second, because Chamberlain—a "closet" antisemite—would never have thought to do so.

With Germany's invasion of Poland (with whom Great Britain already had a treaty of mutual defense assistance negotiated during Chamberlain's tenure) on September 1, 1939, and the start of World War II, Chamberlain's hand was forced. He declared war against Germany on September 3. As continuing criticism of his prosecution of the war mounted in light of Germany's initial military successes, and his inability to restructure and form a government of national unity, Chamberlain resigned from office in May 1940 and was succeeded by Winston Churchill (1874–1965). Chamberlain died of bowel cancer later that same year, 1940.

Chap Teuv. *Chap teuv* is the Cambodian phrase for "taken away, never to be seen again." In the context of the Khmer Rouge–perpetrated genocide (1975–1979), it referred to those individuals who disappeared abruptly, were taken somewhere—for no apparent reason—by the Khmer Rouge, and were never to return. Such disappearances served the purpose of instilling chilling fear in people of not following the exact orders they were given by the Khmer Rouge and/or doing something "wrong" or "incorrectly."

Chapter Six and a Half. "Chapter six and a half" is an unofficial term used by military officials to refer to those peacekeeping missions that either result in or need to constitute (and thus allow for) actions somewhere between a Chapter VI (traditional peacekeeping) and a Chapter VII (peace enforcement) mission under the United Nations Charter. For example, several months prior to the outbreak of the 1994 Rwandan genocide, UN Force Commander Lt. General Romeo Dallaire (b. 1946) of the UN Assistance Mission for Rwanda (UNAMIR) noted that

> I knew that given the ethnic nature of the conflict, the presence of some who opposed the [Arusha peace] agreement and the potential for banditry or ethnic killings by demobilized soldiers, I needed to be able to confront such challenges with military force. Therefore, in the rules of engagement (ROE) that I promised for this mission (largely cribbed from the Cambodian rules), we inserted paragraph seventeen, which authorized us to use force up to and including the use of deadly force to prevent "crimes against humanity." We were breaking new ground, though we didn't really understand it at the time. We were moving toward what would later be called "Chapter six and a half," a whole new approach to conflict resolution. (Quoted in Dallaire's *Shake Hands with the Devil: The Failure of Humanity in Rwanda* [New York: Carroll & Graf Publishers, 2005, p. 72])

Chapter VI of the UN Charter. Chapter VI specifically reads as follows: "Pacific Settlement of Disputes." Article 33 under Chapter VI states:

> (1) The parties to any dispute, the continuance of which is likely to endanger the maintenance of international peace and security, shall, first of all, seek a solution by negotiation, enquiry, mediation, conciliation, arbitration, judicial settlement, resort to regional agencies or arrangements, or other peaceful means of their own choice; and (2) the Security Council shall, when it deems necessary, call upon the parties to settle their dispute by such means.

In the recent past, the UN has placed Chapter VI missions in untenable situations (e.g., where full-blown war or genocide is under way—such as in Rwanda in 1994 and Darfur, Sudan, 2003 through today, late 2007). Due to their limited mandate under Chapter VI, missions were not able to provide the type of protection and/or undertake the action needed to prevent the violence that was being perpetrated. What was needed in place of the Chapter VI mission was a Chapter VII (or peace enforcement) mission.

Chapter VII of the UN Charter. Chapter VII specifically reads as follows: "Action with Respect to Threats to the Peace, Breaches of the Peace, and Acts of Aggression." Article 39 under Chapter VII states the following: "The [UN] Security Council shall determine the existence of any threat to the peace, breach of the peace, or act of aggression and shall make recommendations, or decide what measures shall be taken in accordance with Articles 41 and 42, to maintain or restore international peace and security." Article 41 says: "The Security Council may decide what measures not involving the use of armed force are to be employed to give effect to its decisions, and it may call upon the Members of the United Nations to apply such measures. These may include complete or partial interruption of economic relations and of rail, sea, air, postal, telegraphic, radio, and other means of communication, and the severance of diplomatic relations." Article 42 reads states that: "Should the Security Council consider that measures provided for in Article 41 would be inadequate or have proved to be inadequate, it may take such action by air, sea, or land forces as may be necessary to maintain or restore international peace and security. Such action may include demonstrations, blockade, and other operations by air, sea, or land forces of Members of the United Nations."

What is essential is the need to determine if, in fact, massive human rights violations and/or armed internal conflicts can be considered threats to international peace and security and therefore justify the adoption of humanitarian resolutions by the Security Council.

Charny, Israel W. (b. 1931). Israel Charny, who was born and educated in the United States and then immigrated to Israel in the 1960s, is a noted psychologist and genocide scholar. In fact, Charny is considered by many to be one of the early pioneers of the field of genocide studies.

In 1982, Charny coplanned and coimplemented the first international conference on genocide, the "International Conference on the Holocaust and Genocide." During the course of the planning phase, Charny became a cause célèbre of sorts when the Turkish government placed pressure on the Israeli government to prevent him from including a discussion of the Armenian genocide, which was perpetrated by Ottoman Turks between 1915 and 1923. Charny refused to capitulate even though he received threats both from the Israeli government and from his own academic institution, Tel Aviv University. Although some individuals chose not to attend the conference due to the uproar over the conference, most notable of whom was Holocaust survivor/author Elie Wiesel (b. 1928), the conference was a resounding success and basically set the stage for the development of the field of genocide studies.

Charny wrote an early and important book, *How Can We Commit the Unthinkable? Genocide: A Human Cancer* (1982), in which he not only examined the causes of genocide but also notably delineated his now famous effort to develop what he deemed the Genocide Early Warning System (GEWS). Following his founding of the Institute on the Holocaust and Genocide (Jerusalem, Israel), Charny undertook one innovative project after another in an attempt to attract attention to the fact of genocide and to draw together scholars from various fields to work collaboratively on genocide-related projects. Among some of the more notable efforts of Charny are the following: the development of the now acclaimed Genocide: A Critical Bibliographic Series; the editing and publication of the *Internet on the Holocaust and Genocide* (one of the first newsletters on the topic of genocide); the creation and publication of the first encyclopedia on genocide (*Encyclopedia of Genocide* [Santa Barbara, CA: ABC CLIO Press, 1999]); cofounding the International Association of Genocide Scholars (IAGS); and creating and cofounding a scholarly journal, *Genocide Studies and Prevention: An International Journal* (University of Toronto Press). For IAGS, he served as vice president (2003–2005) and president (2005–2007).

Beginning in the early 1980s, Charny served with great verve and support as the mentor to a large group of then young genocide scholars, including Samuel Totten (b. 1949), the late Eric Markusen (1946–2007), and Yair Auron (b. 1945), among others.

Chelmno. The Polish name for the Nazi extermination camp known as "Kulmhof" in German. Chelmno was the first camp set up for extermination. It was a relatively isolated camp, fifty miles from Lodz; estimates of murder victims include more than two hundred and fifty thousand Jews and five thousand Roma. Chelmno was established at the end of 1941, and its primary method of killing was carbon monoxide asphyxiation from the motorized exhausts of large-capacity "killing wagons" (i.e., trucks); its secondary method of killing was execution by firing squad. The exterminations themselves took place at the *Schloss* or "castle," with the crematoria and mass-grave site some two and one-half miles away. Its victims were initially brought to the central rail station and then transported either on a subtrack or directly by truck. Told, at first, they were being sent to a work camp, the inmates were ordered to undress and then taken to the supposed "washrooms" (i.e., the passageways attached to the gas vans). Fifty to seventy people were then forced into two smaller and one larger van. Approximately ten minutes later, all inside were dead. Closed from December 1942 until May 1944, Chelmno was permanently shut down by the Nazis in January of 1945 as Russian soldiers began to approach the area. Only fourteen of those who participated in the murderous work at Chelmno were ever brought to trial at war's end: two were sentenced to death, three to imprisonment from seven to thirteen years, and the remaining eight to lighter sentences.

"Chemical Ali." The nickname given to the cousin of former Iraqi leader Saddam Hussein (1937–2006), Lieutenant General and presidential adviser Ali Hassan al-Majid (b. 1941). The latter was captured by Allied forces after the invasion of Iraq on August 21, 2003. A member of Hussein's inner circle, he was a member of the Revolutionary Command Council and Baath Party regional commander as well as the head of the Central Workers Bureau. From 1991 to 1995, he served as defense minister under Hussein, serving the previous year as interior minister. He earned his sobriquet because he was allegedly the figure most responsible for the use of chemical weapons as a "solution" to the Kurdish rebellion, which resulted in the murders of fifty thousand to one hundred thousand Kurds during the 1988 campaign against them. In the town of Halabja, for example, the Iraqi air force dropped chemical bombs that killed five thousand people and left ten thousand others seriously affected. On June 24, 2007, Ali Hassan al-Majid was sentenced to death for genocide and war crimes committed against Iraqi Kurds during the *Anfal* or "spoils of war" in which an estimated 180,000 Kurds were killed. (For a more detailed discussion, see al-Majid, Ali Hassan.)

Chetniks. In Serbo-Croatian, the word *četa* translates as "military unit." One who is a member of such a unit, in colloquial usage, is thus a *četnik*, or, in English transliteration, a Chetnik. Traditionally, the Chetniks were a Serbian military force with close royalist and nationalist allegiances. Starting in the nineteenth century, when they were opposed to continued Ottoman Turkish rule over the Serb-speaking areas of the Balkans, the

Chetniks later became a major fighting force opposed to the Nazis during World War II. Their early successes were neutralized, however, when a split in the force saw half continuing to fight the Nazi occupation and half moving on to a different area of battle, fighting Yugoslav communist partisans. During World War II, Chetnik bands, in fighting for the old royal order, engaged in fierce battles with the Croatian *Ustashe* and communist partisans under the command of Josip Broz Tito (1892–1980). In the latter endeavor, they collaborated openly with the Nazis and the Italian Fascists. The fighting with the Croats had the added dimension of savage interethnic hostility. By 1946, the last Chetnik units, under the command of Dragoljub ("Draža") Mihailovic (1893–1946), were captured, and the organization was suppressed. When Slobodan Milosevic (1941–2006) assumed office in Serbia in 1989, Chetnik groups made something of a comeback. Many Serb paramilitary units during the wars of Yugoslav disintegration (1991–1995) styled themselves after the fashion of the Chetniks of old, growing long hair and beards, which began as a symbol of grief over the state of Serbia—first, in being occupied by the Nazis, and then by the communists. After the reappearance of the Chetniks in the 1990s, verified accounts of massacre and war crimes identified them as facilitators of ethnic cleansing, particularly in Croatia and Bosnia-Herzegovina. One of the most notorious of these self-styled new Chetniks was Zeljko Raznatovic (1952–2000), known as "Arkan," whose paramilitary force, the Tigers, was responsible for numerous atrocities. Other Chetnik forces contributed to genocidal mass murder in Vukovar and Srebrenica (where another Chetnik unit, the Scorpions, committed a number of well-publicized murders). Within Serbia today, there have been attempts at rehabilitating the image of the Chetniks as loyal patriots fighting for the defense of their country, but their reputation for arbitrary violence, brutality, and murder has done little to foster a positive image outside of Serbia itself.

Chile. On September 11, 1973, the democratically elected socialist government of President Salvador Allende (1908–1973) was deposed from office in a military coup led by General Augusto Jose Ramon Pinochet Ugarte (1915–2006). The junta thereby established was to remain in power until Pinochet restored Chile to democracy in 1990, after which Patrico Aylwin (b. 1918) took office following national elections. (Pinochet retained his position under the new government as commander in chief of the armed forces and senator, which he relinquished when forced to do so only in 2002.) Under Pinochet's rule, Chile became a military dictatorship. Immediately after he seized power, all left-wing political parties and movements were crushed by decree and by force. Freedom of speech, multiparty democracy, trade unions, and open courts of justice were all suppressed. Pinochet established an office called the DINA (*Dirección Nacional de Inteligencia*), or National Intelligence Directorate, which served as a secret police force. Tens of thousands believed by Pinochet to be threats to his new order were arrested and tortured; at least two thousand became *Desaparecidos*, "those who have disappeared," their fate officially unknown, though almost certainly they were murdered. The junta justified both its existence and the need for a harsh and controlling regime on the perceived danger posed by communism against Chile. After the restoration of democracy in 1990, Pinochet kept a careful eye on the government that succeeded him, always with a veiled threat of himself making a comeback as dictator if the democratic system veered too far to the left. His influence collapsed in 1998 when he was arrested in London under an international arrest warrant issued by Spain charging him with the torture of some of its citizens in Chile and conspiring to commit torture and genocide. After a lengthy appeals process, and then hearings regarding his extradition to Spain to stand trial, Pinochet was not extradited from Britain. On March 2, 2000, he returned to Chile. Within the country, a Truth and Reconciliation Commission was established to try to heal the rifts caused by the Pinochet years, and upon his return Pinochet himself was placed under house arrest pursuant to various charges.

China, Genocide in. China experienced significant episodes of genocidal destruction during the course of the twentieth century. It would be a mistake to think that its people have suffered only under communism, even though killing has predominated over the course of communist rule since 1949. Under the rule of warlords and the pre-1949 Nationalist government, millions were killed, both deliberately, for political reasons, and, as innocent victims, who were swept up in the course of the many wars and rebellions that beset China during the first half of the twentieth century. The precommunist atrocities visited upon the Chinese people were not only caused by internal upheaval, however; China's experience at the hands of its Japanese occupiers throughout the 1930s led to a low estimate of 4 million deaths, and possibly even up to 6 million. In 1937 the Japanese treatment of China's then capital city, Nanking (now Nanjing), became a paradigm for genocidal massacre, as the Japanese, in an orgy of murder, rape, torture, and looting, killed more than three hundred thousand of the city's residents. After the communist victory in October 1949, millions of Chinese citizens were killed as the party sought to develop its revolutionary platform and shape society according to the teachings of the party chairman, Mao Zedong (1893–1976). The Chinese communists employed brutal repression in order to terrorize the population into following the new ways. They executed all those who had represented the former Nationalist government or its ideals, those of whom the communists deemed to be counterrevolutionaries opposed to the revolution, and anyone else considered to be an "enemy" of the people. In the communist drive to institutionalize the revolution through schemes of social engineering such as the Great Leap Forward (1958–1962) and the Cultural Revolution (1966–1976) perhaps up to 30 million lost their lives owing to starvation and more political killing. Under communism, China has had a record of unrelenting state-imposed death on a genocidal scale, and to this should be added a clear-cut case of genocide against the people of Tibet, invaded by China in 1949, in which about one-quarter of the preinvasion population has been wiped out in order to make way for Han Chinese transmigrants. In addition there has been an ongoing and intensive campaign of ethnocide carried out by successive Chinese governments against the culture and religion of the Tibetans. More recently, Chinese communist attempts at suppressing the quasi-religious movement known as Falun Gong have also been considered by some to fit the 1948 UN Genocide Convention's criteria of what constitutes genocide.

Chittagong Hill Tracts, Genocide in. The Chittagong Hill Tracts (CHT) occupies a land area of 5,093 square miles (13,295 square kilometers), constituting some 10 percent of the total area of the country of Bangladesh. The land is hilly and covered with dense vegetation, in marked contrast to the rest of the low-lying country. The majority of the population of CHT, a people known as the Jummas, had been the target of massive human rights abuses since before the inception of the state in 1971, but increasingly so since Bangladesh's independence. In March 1972, M. N. Larma (d. 1983) formed a Jumma political party, Jana Samhati Samiti (JSS), to seek better living conditions for the Jummas; a military wing of the JSS, the Shanti Bahini, emerged soon thereafter. This intensified the persecution of the Jummas by the Bangladeshi authorities. In the name of "counterinsurgency," Jummas have often been detained and tortured by the army; thousands have been killed in combat and in executions, and many have also suffered rape and torture. Massacres have been frequent since 1980. Mass detention has taken place, and thousands have been placed in so-called cluster villages—effectively a form of concentration camp under the direct jurisdiction of the army. In addition to all this, it has been alleged that the state supports the forcible conversion of the Jummas (who include among their number Buddhists and Hindus) to Islam, together with the destruction of Jumma temples and shrines. One of the fundamental reasons for the persecution of the Jummas has been a desire on the part of the central authorities to force the Jummas off their land in order to make way for large-scale resettlement of Bangladeshis. Settlers have been able to take over land and even whole villages from the Jummas; it has been estimated that the settlers now make up nearly one-third of the total population of the CHT. Despite all this, on December 2, 1997, the JSS managed to sign a treaty with the Bangladeshi government, though this has failed to guarantee the necessary safeguards to the Jummas as it has not addressed the core issues of settler encroachment and the ongoing militarization of the region.

Chmielnicki, Bogdan (c. 1595–1657). Antisemitic Cossack Ukrainian nationalist leader, and rebel against Polish overlordship of Ukraine. In Ukrainian his name can be transliterated as "Bohdan Khmelnytsky," whereas in Russian it becomes "Bogdan Khmel'nitski." Reference to "Bogdan Chmielnicki" is thus a synthesis of the Ukrainian or Russian version of his first name and the Polish variation of his surname, and it is that combination that has most commonly entered general usage. Chmielnicki does not seem to have come from a Cossack background, though he embraced both the Cossack cause and Orthodox Christianity as he grew to maturity. Ultimately, he became leader of the Zaporozhian Cossacks and hetman, or supreme leader, of Ukraine. The Polish-Lithuanian Commonwealth, a vast state incorporating Ukraine among its domains, experienced a number of rebellions against its rule during the early seventeenth century, with the worst being led by Chmielnicki himself between 1648 and 1654. The attempt to overthrow Polish rule became a civil war between forces loyal to the Commonwealth and Chmielnicki's Cossacks. The most obvious representatives of Polish rule in many parts of Ukraine were Jewish Arendas, leaseholders of estates, farmland, or mills, with hunting and fishing rights, who were given authority to collect taxes from the Ukrainian peasantry on behalf of the Polish aristocracy and crown. It was the Jewish Arendas who thus bore the full brunt of Cossack fury, and, as Chmielnicki's Cossacks swept through Ukraine, widespread destruction of Jewish towns and farms became commonplace. Large-scale massacres of Jews occurred, with perhaps as many as one hundred thousand Jewish deaths during the uprising. At least three hundred Jewish communities were completely destroyed, as the Jews were deliberately targeted, first, because of their identification with Polish rule and, second, because of their Jewishness. In 1654, Chmielnicki's Cossacks allied themselves with tsarist Russia, and the full weight of the combined Cossack and Russian forces became too great for the Commonwealth to hold back. By the Treaty of Pereyaslav (1654), Ukraine became a Russian territory.

The Chmielnicki massacres made a deep impression on the Jews of eastern Europe. The despair generated by the massacres led indirectly to a rise in the number of messianic pretenders over the course of the next hundred years—the most notable of whom, Shabbetai Zvi (1626–1676), failed to deliver the Jews from their desolation and cast them into a despondency that was relieved by only the appearance of the Ba'al Shem Tov (c. 1700–1760) in the eighteenth century.

Chmielnicki Pogroms. In 1648, mainly between May and November, Jews by the thousands were slaughtered by Ukrainian Cossacks under the leadership of Bogdan Chmielnicki (1595–1657) in the context of the larger peasant uprising against Polish rule, which would, ultimately, under his leadership, result in a realignment and unification with Russia. The savagery and violence with which Jews were slaughtered remains a "dark stain" in Jewish history, caught, as they were, in a political cross fire where antisemitism was already rampant. Although it is impossible to establish the actual numbers of Jewish dead as a result of these pogroms (massacres), Jewish chroniclers of the times put the toll as high as one hundred thousand with approximately three hundred Jewish communities destroyed, most noticeably the communities of Nemirov, Tulchin, Polonnoye, Bar, Narol, and Lvov. Two giants of modern Hebrew literature composed laments to mark the event: "Daughter of the Rabbi" by Saul Tchernichovski (1875–1943) and "The Burden of Nemirov" by Chaim Nahman Bialik (1873–1934).

Choeung Ek. Choeung Ek is the site of the best-known complex of mass graves in Cambodia, containing the bodies of tens of thousands of victims of the Khmer Rouge regime (1975–1979), under the communist dictatorship of Pol Pot (1925–1998). Choeung Ek is located about seventeen kilometers south of Phnom Penh and was a preferred dumping ground for those executed at the nearby Tuol Sleng prison, commanded by Khang Khak Iev (b. 1942), known as "Comrade Duch." The image of Choeung Ek—of large burial mounds scattered over a broad landscape—has given rise to the term "the killing fields" as a way of describing all such places, and it was from this that a Hollywood movie, *The Killing Fields* (director, Roland Joffe, 1984), derived its title. Choeung Ek today is a memorial to the Cambodian genocide. The featured centerpiece of the memorial is a Buddhist stupa, a shrine containing some five thousand skulls of victims. Choeung Ek is a place of pilgrimage and quiet contemplation, and those of the current generation can visit the site as a way of learning valuable lessons about Cambodia's past.

Christian X, King of Denmark (1870–1947). King Christian became the symbol of Danish resistance to Nazism in his occupied country when he himself refused to implement their anti-Jewish legislation, yet he was forced to leave his throne in August 1943. Many believe he served as the inspiration for his own people in their heroic rescue and successful efforts to save the vast majority of Danish Jews—approximately 7,500 Jewish Danes from a total Jewish population of nearly 8,000—from their ultimate extermination at the hands of the Nazis.

Contrary to popular belief, King Christian did not appear in public wearing a yellow star in support of the Jewish population of Denmark, though a legend quickly sprang up that he did. The legend was reinforced by novelist Leon Uris (1924–2003) in his 1958 novel, *Exodus*, and popularized in the film version of the novel in 1960 directed by Otto Preminger (1906–1986).

Churban. A Hebrew term best translated by the English word *destruction*. It is used mainly within the traditional religious Orthodox Jewish communities and references not one but three past tragedies: the destruction of the First Temple by the Babylonians in 586 BCE (Before the Common Era), the destruction of the Second Temple by the Romans in the year 70, and the Holocaust of 1933–1945. For the Orthodox (or traditional religious thinkers), the Holocaust is not seen as a uniquely distinctive event, but yet another in a series of tragedies, accepted as part of God's divine plan, which limited humanity cannot fully understand or comprehend. Among the possible attempts at such understanding, however, has been that of liberal rabbi Ignaz Maybaum (1897–1976) (the Holocaust as the sacrificial victimization of the Jewish people in preparation for the creative destruction of the old world and an ushering in of a new order); orthodox rabbi Menahem Hartom (the Holocaust as punishment for sin for a Jewish people living in exile); and orthodox rabbis Isaac Hutner (1906–1980) (the Holocaust as the burden of Jewish chosenness and the truth of Judaism's religious claims), Menachem Mendel Schneersohn (1902–1994) (the Holocaust as punishment for the sin of assimilation), and Joel Teitelbaum (1887–1979) (the Holocaust as punishment for the "sin" of Zionism, i.e., forcing God's hand prior to the messianic redemption).

CIA and Genocide. The U.S. Central Intelligence Agency (CIA) was formed in 1947 from a number of predecessor organizations that had been established during World War II. Its major tasks include providing accurate, comprehensive, and timely foreign intelligence to government departments on domestic security issues and conducting counterintelligence activities and other functions related to foreign intelligence and national security. The CIA is an independent arm of government, responsible to the president of the United States through the director of central intelligence. It is accountable to the people of the United States through the intelligence oversight committees of the U.S. Congress. Although the CIA is primarily engaged in intelligence gathering and ongoing research activities, it has frequently come under close scrutiny by critics around the world owing to its secrecy and reputation for covert actions involving intervention in the affairs of foreign governments. In fact, the CIA has been vilified and/or implicated in a very wide range of issues relating to genocide. These include allegations concerning both the nature of the hunt for Nazi war criminals after World War II and the provision of shelter to these criminals in order to employ their skills against communism during the Cold War; supporting genocidal regimes conducting counterinsurgency campaigns, such as in Guatemala in the 1970s and 1980s; and facilitating the overthrow of governments that have views or policies inimical to the United States, such as in Chile in 1973. From time to time, allegations have been made by journalists and other commentators that the CIA has engaged in covert operations that have led some U.S.-supported regimes to commit actions that could be deemed genocide (e.g., in Indonesia in 1965–1966, in East Timor after 1975, and in Guatemala in the 1980s). As with so many areas relating to genocide, there is a great need for care to be taken in ascribing responsibility for the development of specific events, and this is even more the case when considering an organization that conducts much of its work in an essentially secretive manner for reasons of national security.

Civil War. A state of civil war exists when competing factions, groups, or parties vie for power in physical confrontation within the same polity—usually, though not always, a state. By their nature, civil wars are highly destructive and deadly and can be accompanied by the commission of war crimes, atrocities, and, in recent times, genocide. In the civil conflicts that have taken place since the 1980s in Africa—for example, in Burundi, Rwanda, Congo, and Sudan—the loss of life has been enormously high. The same was true in the case of Biafra, the short-lived West African state that seceded from Nigeria between 1967 and 1970. Elsewhere—for example, in Russia between 1918 and 1921, China in the 1930s and 1940s, or in the former Yugoslavia between 1991 and 1995—civil war led to a massive number of deaths. One of the reasons for such mayhem, especially in the last quarter of the twentieth century and into the twenty-first century, lies in the fact that many of those doing the fighting have not been professional soldiers but irregulars, members of militia groups who possess neither the training and behavioral restraints of professional soldiers nor an accompanying sense of military honor. Modern civil war has been the most frequent setting for genocide, as it remains today. This would appear to be an evolutionary phenomenon: earlier civil wars, such as in England (1642–1645 and 1648) and the United States (1861–1865), though bloody and destructive, were not accompanied by a genocidal level of violence (though France's revolutionary experience in the Vendée during the period 1793–1795 would tend to suggest that the establishment of clear rules around this is a task fraught with inconsistency). The aftermath of a destructive civil war can be just as traumatic for a state as the war itself, particularly if it has been accompanied by genocidal destruction, as postgenocide agendas are frequently difficult to achieve owing to the divisions—often reinforced or entrenched—wrought by the conflict.

Class. Social rank; a group sharing basically the same economic and social status; common status with others in a particular economic or social level of society; those who have approximately the same level of education, resources, wealth, and ability and/or opportunity to gain certain types of employment and obtain economic resources and power.

Classification of Genocides in Multiple Categories. According to the 1948 United Nations Convention on the Prevention and Punishment of the Crime of Genocide (UNCG), Article 2, "genocide means any of the following acts committed with intent to destroy, in whole or in part, a national, ethnical, racial, or religious group, as such: (a) causing serious bodily or mental harm to members of the group; (b) deliberately inflicting on the group conditions of life calculated to bring about its physical destruction in whole or in part; (c) forcibly transferring children of the group to another group; (d) imposing measures intended to prevent births within the group; and (e) killing members of the group." The two main groups omitted from the above are political and social groups, which was the result of compromise between various states developing the convention in the post–World War II years, leading up to the final version of the UNCG resolved by the UN General Assembly. (Other groups not addressed, for example, include sexual and sexual preference groups.) Much scholarly debate has taken place since 1948 in an attempt to, paradoxically, both expand and limit the definition of genocide, all in an attempt to clarify what the world community understands by the term *genocide*.

"Clearing the Bush." A euphemism used by extremist Hutu prior to and during the 1994 Rwandan genocide to denote the murdering of Tutsi and the destruction of their homes.

Clinton's Apology, Rwandan Genocide. In 1998, four years after the world community passively watched as 500,000 to 1 million Tutsi and moderate Hutu were slain in a hundred-day period, former U.S. president Bill Clinton flew to Rwanda and, never leaving the airport, offered a typical Clintonesque statement that presented a torturously perverse sense of the facts as he offered an "apology" to the Rwandan people for the international community's lack of action during the course of the genocide. More specifically, he said: "We in the United States and the world community did not do as much as we could have and should have done to try to limit what occurred. It may seem strange to you here, but all over the world there were people like me sitting in offices, day after day, who did not fully appreciate the depth and the speed with which you were being engulfed by this unimaginable terror." The truth, however, is that from the outset of the genocide, newspapers that Clinton, his staff, and his appointees must have read reported the mass killing that was taking place in Rwanda. For example, three days into the killing, "[an] April 9 front-page

Washington Post story quoted reports that the Rwandan employees of the major international relief agencies had been executed 'in front of horrified expatriate staffers.' On April 10, a *New York Times* front-page article quoted the Red Cross claim that 'tens of thousands were dead, 8,000 in Kigali alone and that corpses were in the houses, in the streets, everywhere.' The *Post*, the same day, led its front-page story with a description of 'a pile of corpses six feet high' outside the main hospital" (Power, 2002, p. 356). There were also, of course, the regular updates that any U.S. president receives on a daily basis from a variety of intelligence sources.

"CNN Effect" (also commonly referred to as "CNN Factor"). The "CNN effect" refers to the impact of the media (and particularly twenty-four-hour news covering all parts of the globe) to both inform and ostensibly influence public opinion about major conflicts and/or humanitarian disasters. It also refers to the debatable issue as to whether the CNN effect provides the public with the leverage to prod the international community to address and ameliorate, in some way, the conflict/disaster. The term itself refers to the first television station, CNN, to provide twenty-four-hour coverage of global events.

Coalition for an International Criminal Court (CICC). The CICC was formed by the more than one hundred nongovernmental organizations (NGOs) that were officially represented at the Rome Conference (June and July 1998), which was held to finalize the International Criminal Court Statute. Though the NGOs lacked the rights and privileges of the individual nations (some 162) represented at the conference (meaning that they had no vote and were not even allowed to observe the major informal negotiations that were taking place), their presence was significant in that they carefully followed the many and intense negotiations, provided technical expertise to national delegates, and wrote and distributed papers on major issues. Ultimately, the various NGOs worked together through the CICC in order to maximize their impact, reach, and effectiveness.

Coalition for International Justice (CIJ). CIJ, which had offices in Washington, D.C., and The Hague, was an international, nonprofit nongovernmental organization (NGO) that supported the international war crimes tribunals for Rwanda (ICTR) and the former Yugoslavia (ICTY) and justice initiatives in East Timor, Cambodia, and elsewhere. CIJ initiated and conducted advocacy and public education campaigns, targeting decision makers in Washington and other capitals, the media, and the public. Working with other NGOs in Washington and elsewhere, CIJ helped to focus and maximize the impact of individual and collective advocacy. In the field, CIJ provided practical assistance on legal, technical, and outreach matters to the tribunals and/or justice initiatives. During the summer of 2004, CIJ headed up the Darfur Atrocities Documentation Project, which collected evidence for the U.S. State Department in order to ascertain whether genocide had been perpetrated in Darfur, Sudan, against the Massaleit, Fur, and Zagahawa peoples. Using the outcomes of the analysis of the data, U.S. Secretary of State Colin Powell declared that genocide had been perpetrated by the government of Sudan and the *Janjaweed* (Arab militia). CIJ shut down in 2006, having completed the tasks it initially set out to do.

Coalition Pour la Défense de la République (CDR) (French, Coalition for the Defense of the Republic). A Rwandan political party established in February 1992. Composed of radical members of the *Mouvement Révolutionnaire Nationale pour le Développement* (MRND), the CDR has been described as "Rwanda's version of the Ku Klux Klan" (i.e., racist, extremist, and hateful). The party was founded by three extreme anti-Tutsi

Hutu ideologues: a former member of the Rwandan Patriotic Front (RPF) who had defected, Jean Shyirambere Barahinura (b. 1956); Jean-Bosco Barayagwiza (b. 1950), who was a senior executive at *Radio-Télévision Libre des Mille Collines* (RTLM), Rwanda's anti-Tutsi hate radio station; and founder-owner of the radical newspaper *Kangura*, Hassan Ngeze (b. 1961). The latter two were later tried before the International Criminal Tribunal for Rwanda owing to their anti-Tutsi hate pronouncements through the media arms they controlled. The party was exclusively Hutu, to the extent that a person with even one Tutsi grandparent was denied membership. It was also extremely violent; a party militia movement, the *Impuzamugambi* (those with a single purpose), was established expressly for the purpose of harassing, assaulting, and, ultimately, murdering Tutsi wherever they could be found. The viciousness of this movement was acknowledged by many as being more extreme than that of its much larger partner-in-genocide, the *Interahamwe*. Initially supportive of Rwandan president Juvenal Habyarimana (1937–1994), CDR became an opposition party when it decided that he was too moderate. Ultimately, the CDR became fervently opposed to Habyarimana's rapprochement with the RPF during 1993 and early 1994 and was in the forefront of those undermining his authority after the signing of the Arusha Accords on August 4, 1993. In fact, the leaders of the CDR adamantly refused to sign, and thus abide by both the Arusha Peace Agreement and Statement of Ethics, and as a result were denied the right to join the transitional government composed of representatives of the three main factions: President Habyarimana's *Mouvement Révolutionnaire National pour le Développement* (MRND) and its allies, the internal opposition parties, and the RPF. Essentially, the CDR wanted no part in a multiethnic and multiparty democracy in Rwanda. Unsurprisingly, after Habyarimana's assassination on April 6, 1994, the CDR entered into a coalition with the MRND interim government that was formed to "deal" with the "emergency" that, it was claimed by Hutu extremists across the country, had been instigated by the Tutsi. Through the *Impuzamugambi*, the CDR became a major participant in the Rwandan tragedy, a criminal organization that played a key role in the fastest genocide in the twentieth century.

Coercive Diplomacy (also referred to as Coercive Inducement). Coercive diplomacy refers to the concept of diplomacy that places pressure on the leaders in a targeted state to rethink the costs and benefits of policies that have been deemed illegal or highly questionable by the international community. The concept of coercive diplomacy is predicated on a "carrots and sticks" approach to diplomacy or one that comprises a commixture of inducements for compliance as well as punitive measures for noncompliance. Such an approach assumes that a "targeted state" is more likely to comply with sanctions if it receives positive incentives as it proceeds along the road to full compliance. Ultimately, the approach of coercive diplomacy is to persuade versus using overwhelming force. It may make use of diverse means—including but not limited to politico-diplomatic, economic, and military—to bring about the desired behavior.

Cold War. Subsequent to World War II, the victorious Allies divided into two "armed camps" based on ideological, economic, and political differences, with the United States, Britain, and their allies (the so-called Western bloc) on one side and the Soviet Union and its allies (the so-called Eastern bloc) on the other. While the Western bloc espoused democracy and capitalism, the Eastern bloc practiced totalitarianism and socialism. The term *Cold War* was itself first used by U.S. presidential adviser Bernard Baruch (1870–1965) in 1947, its "coldness" referring to the lack of open military conflict. The

Cold War was a reality for over fifty years, up until the breakup of the Soviet Union in the early 1990s.

Periodically, tensions heated up—for example, the Korean War (1950–1953), the Vietnamese conflict (1962–1975), the Soviet invasion of Afghanistan (1979–1988)—but they never escalated into full-scale armed conflict between the two blocs. In various situations, one or the other, and sometimes both, used proxies to fight their battles against one another.

The Cold War was further fueled by mutual distrust and suspicion, coupled with aggressive intelligence-gathering activities; overt propaganda praising one's own position while deprecating the other's; and the race for space and military (particularly, nuclear) technological supremacy. At that time, the world was confronted by an enormous number of bewildering stresses and strains: economic boom and bust, decolonization and wars of liberation, social protest and sweeping calls for change. And, as each became a major nuclear power and developed ever more sophisticated nuclear weapons, the tension between the two nations grew, risking the gravest threat of all, mutually assured total nuclear destruction. Scholars of the Cold War tend to view it in three phases: 1947–1953, 1953–1962, and 1962–1991.

At the same time, both nations were embroiled in a fierce competition to sway other states to their policies, particularly in the Third World or those new nations that were spawned as a result of the end of colonialism. Throughout the Third World, the United States and the Soviet Union supported different states (by supplying the latter with weapons, training, and even manpower) in proxy wars.

The Cold War may also be perceived on an ideological level as a political conflict between the leaders of the two superpowers, the United States and Soviet Russia. That is to say, Presidents Harry S. Truman (1884–1972), Dwight D. Eisenhower (1890–1969), and John F. Kennedy (1917–1963) saw themselves in staunch opposition to the expansionist policies of Joseph Stalin (1878–1953) and Nikita Khrushchev (1894–1971). With the rise to Soviet leadership of Leonid Brezhnev (1907–1982), Mikhail Gorbachev (b. 1931), and Boris Yeltsin (1931–2007), an "East-West thaw" began to surface, a new openness began to set in, and capitalism began to assert itself in Russia coupled with the diminishing of the political and military stranglehold of the Communist Party, all of which led to the ultimate demise of the Soviet Union. Although such quasi-democratic policies remain in effect under the leadership of Vladimir Putin (b. 1952), a former KGB secret police official who became president of Russia in 1999, there are troubling hints of a creeping return to the right and a certain nostalgia, not yet widespread, for the so-called glory days of Soviet power and strength.

At the United Nations, the fact of the Cold War often resulted in the two superpowers waging their Cold War via their votes within the UN Security Council. One result was that there was often a stalemate in regard to taking action to stave off a potential genocidal situation or to staunch one that had broken out. Put another way, the objectives of those who had shaped the post-1945 agenda to reduce or prevent genocide became diluted at this time, as the major powers and the United Nations found that other issues (primarily their own survival) became more of a priority. In turning a blind eye here and there for the purpose of accommodating allies or potential allies, the great powers allowed dictatorial or authoritarian rulers literally to get away with mass murder on the domestic scene. The second half of the twentieth century, as a result, began to appear as nothing other than a continual period of massacres and genocidal killing—in large wars, small wars, civil wars, and sometimes where there was no war at all. A number of these, such as in Biafra, Bangladesh, Burundi, Cambodia, and East Timor, stand out as models of what the world became during the period of the Cold War. Indeed, the Cold War was a period that had a devastating effect on post-1945 hopes that a new, nongenocidal regime could be created throughout the world. It showed with great clarity that the world's major players only paid lip service to their postwar commitment to "never again" stand by while genocide took place. With the breakup of the Soviet Union between 1989 and 1991, the Cold War came to an end. Although some believed that the world would be a safer place in the aftermath of the Cold War, they were quickly dispelled of that notion when both civil war and genocide quickly became regular features of the 1990s and early 2000s.

Collaborators. The term *collaborators* refers not to those individuals who are the primary perpetrators of a genocide but rather to those who willfully aid the perpetrators in one way or another—including providing political, economic, administrative, or military support to the perpetrator group and/or through such actions as spying on, reporting on, locating, and/or killing the "target" or victim population.

Collective Intervention. Collective intervention is the intrusion by more than one outside power (two or more countries or an intergovernmental organization such as the United Nations and a regional organization such as NATO) into a sovereign nation's so-called internal or territorial matters. The intrusion or intervention can take various forms, from the issuing of sanctions on the country (e.g., arms embargoes, trade embargoes, the freezing of financial assets overseas) to the insertion of peacekeeping troops and from the imposition of "no-fly zones" over part of the country to carrying out battle operations.

Collective Responsibility, Imposition of by Nazis. Once the Nazis were in control of various jurisdictions (e.g., towns, ghettos, villages, nations) throughout occupied Europe in the late 1930s and early to mid-1940s, they imposed severe restrictions and punishments against those who sought to resist. Acts of sabotage, military strikes by partisans, and the like against the Nazis oftentimes resulted in retaliatory deaths of disproportionate numbers of those who bore no direct responsibility for such acts. An example of such treatment occurred on June 10, 1942, when the Nazis razed the village of Lidice, killing most of the male population and deporting the women and children to concentration camps, as a reprisal for the assassination, just days before, of the Reich Protector of Bohemia, Reinhard Heydrich (1904–1942). The people of Lidice had nothing to do with the assassination but suffered the brunt of the Nazis' rage and retributive actions.

Collectivization. The term *collectivization* refers to

> the process used by Soviet authorities prior to and during the 1932–33 Soviet man-made famine of Ukraine to consolidate individual peasant holdings into centralized collective farms, theoretically owned by the peasant-members, but actually controlled by the state. It constituted total collectivization of agriculture on the basis of the liquidation of the kulaks as a class … [The] peasants were forced to sign up voluntarily as members of the new collective farms, which seemed to many to be indistinguishable from the pre-emancipation serf states (U.S. Commission on the Ukraine Famine, 1988, p. 229).

As for the term *kulak*, it was officially used by Soviet officials "to refer to a rural capitalist who hired labor, a generic rural class enemy, or a member of the upper socio-economic stratum of the village" (U.S. Commission on the Ukraine Famine, 1988, p. 230). During the 1932–1933 Soviet man-made famine in Ukraine, the term *kulak*, however, was used to refer to anyone, no matter how poor, that the Soviet officials wished to disenfranchise. In fact, if the "'class enemy' marked for 'liquidation' was too poor for the term *kulak* to be used, he would be disenfranchised as a subkulak" (U.S. Commission on the Ukraine Famine, 1988, p. 230).

Colonial Genocide. The process of colonization of a territory or nation by another, especially involving incursions of European states into the Americas, Asia, Africa, and Australasia, has often been characterized by violent confrontation, deliberate massacre, wholesale annihilation, and, in several instances, genocide. Many indigenous peoples in these continents have been completely, or almost completely, wiped out since the expansion of Europe began in the sixteenth century—among such, for example, were the Yuki of California, the Beothuk of Newfoundland, the Pallawah (indigenous peoples) of Tasmania, and the Hereros of Namibia. Most countries throughout the world today have been involved with or impacted by colonialism in way or another, either as Western imperialists or as First World or Third World actors who were the object of the imperialists' incursions. It is vitally important, therefore, that care is taken when employing the term *genocide* relative to colonial expansion: each and every claim must be assessed individually and on its merits. In some instances, genocide might be unequivocal; in others, despite a sudden or enormous population collapse, an intent on the part of the colonizers for this to happen might not have been present. Often, populations declined as a result of diseases that arrived with the colonizers, but the deaths that occurred were not anticipated. Elsewhere, lethal diseases were deliberately introduced for the purpose of wiping out a population. In most cases, if we were to generalize (not an easy task over five centuries and spanning most of the globe), it could be said that colonial expansion saw attempts at clearing the land of indigenous populations (which could result in genocidal episodes); of forcibly assimilating the indigenous populations for racial, religious, or ethnic reasons; or of intimidating indigenous populations such that they would seek to retreat before the advance of the colonizers. It is through the need for terminological precision that many aggrieved former colonial populations today are dissatisfied with existing definitions of *genocide* and reject the term as a Western construct that excludes their national subjugation and attendant suffering.

Colonialism. A form of political control by one state over another, frequently characterized by the establishment of settler communities that can result in the displacement, absorption, or destruction of preexisting indigenous communities. Colonialism was largely responsible for reshaping the demographic composition of vast areas of the world's surface from the sixteenth to the twentieth centuries, particularly in North and South America, southern Africa, and Australasia. On these continents, huge numbers of settlers from European states left their homelands to start new outgrowth communities or to reinforce those of their kin already there. In so doing, they took over the land (sometimes quite brutally) already occupied by indigenous populations. Genocidal massacres of the latter were not infrequent, and ongoing oppression or neglect has, in numerous cases, persisted up to the present day.

Colonialism, as it impacts upon indigenous populations, has also led to the suppression of local languages, religions, and folkways, as the settlers look for ways to consolidate their rule and ward off perceived threats to the physical expansion of their territory in the new land. Colonialism is different from imperialism (with which it is often confused), primarily because in the latter case state control may exist without a physical presence (such as a permanent settler population) needing to be present. In both instances, however, the human cost can be devastating and long-lasting for the indigenous populations being taken over by the colonizing or imperialist power.

Command Responsibility. Command responsibility refers to the fact that a person who gives the order to commit war crimes, crimes against humanity, or genocide is as responsible as the person actually committing the crime(s). This principle applies both to military superiors (within regular and irregular armed forces) and to civilian authorities. A superior is, moreover, individually responsible for war crimes, crimes against humanity, and genocide committed by his or her subordinates if he or she (the superior) knew, or had information at the time which should have enabled him or her to conclude, that his or her subordinates were about to commit or were committing such an act and (the superior) neglected to take all feasible measures to prevent or repress the act. Military commanders, though, are not absolutely responsible for all offenses committed by their subordinates. Isolated offenses may be committed over which the commanding officer has no knowledge or control.

Commission for Historical Clarification. The Commission for Historical Clarification (more commonly referred to as the Truth Commission) is the United Nations–sponsored commission that was developed and implemented to provide a forum for the victims of the thirty-six-year Guatemalan conflict to tell their stories in order to finally break the curtain of silence that had smothered any discussion about the massacres perpetrated by the military and army-sponsored death squads throughout the 1980s and 1990s. In February 1999, the Truth Commission issued a report that concluded, in part, that

> these massacres and the so-called scorched earth operations, as planned by the State, resulted in the complete extermination of many Mayan communities, along with their homes, cattle, crops and other elements essential to survival. The CEH registered 626 massacres attributable to these forces.
>
> . . . The CEH concludes that the events referred to herein are grave violations of international human rights law whose precepts the Guatemalan State has been committed to respect since it approved the Universal Declaration of Human Rights and the American Declaration of the Rights and Obligations of Man in 1948. The fundamental principles of human rights have achieved the category of international customary law.
>
> The gravity of this conclusion is accentuated by the fact that some of these violations, especially arbitrary executions, forced disappearances and torture, were repeated throughout the entire internal armed confrontation, at some stages becoming systematic. This obliges the authorities of the Guatemalan State to accept historical responsibility for these violations before the Guatemalan people and the international community.
>
> . . . The legal framework adopted by the CEH to analyse the possibility that acts of genocide were committed in Guatemala during the internal armed confrontation is the Convention on the Prevention and Punishment of the Crime of Genocide, adopted by the United Nations General Assembly on 9 December 1948 and ratified by the Guatemalan State by Decree 704 on 30 November 1949.
>
> Considering the series of criminal acts and human rights violations which occurred in the regions and periods indicated and which were analysed for the purpose of determining whether they constituted the crime of genocide, the CEH concludes that the reiteration of destructive acts, directed systematically against groups of the Mayan population, within which can be mentioned the elimination of leaders and criminal acts against minors who could not possibly have been military targets, demonstrates that the only common denominator for all the victims was the fact that they belonged to a specific ethnic group and makes it evident that these acts were committed "with intent to destroy, in whole or in part" these groups (Article II, first paragraph of the Convention).

Among acts aimed at the destruction of Mayan groups, identified by the Army as the enemy, "killings" deserve special mention (Article II.a of the Convention), the most significant of which were the massacres. The CEH has verified that in the four regions studied, between 1981 and 1983, agents of the State committed killings which were the most serious acts in a series of military operations directed against the non-combatant civilian population. In accordance with the testimonies and other elements of evidence collected, the CEH has established that, both regular and special Army forces, as well as Civil Patrols and military commissioners, participated in those killings characterised as massacres. In many cases, the survivors identified those responsible for directing these operations as being the commanders of the nearest municipal military outposts.

Committee of Jurists. In 1920 the Committee of Jurists, which was appointed by the League of Nations, proposed the establishment of an International Criminal Court "to try crimes constituting a breach of international public order or against the universal law of nations." This suggestion by international lawyers was dismissed by professional diplomats of the day. The concept of an International Criminal Court (ICC) was revived at the end of the twentieth century and became a reality at the beginning of the twenty-first century. The ICC is based at The Hague.

Committee of Union and Progress (CUP). In Turkish, *Ittihad ve Terakki Jemiyeti*. This was a political movement formed in 1895 in the Ottoman Empire. From its Turkish name, members of the committee became known as *Ittihadists* (Unionists). The movement was dedicated to the radical development of a new Turkish nationalism that was effectively based on a model of racial exclusion that did not permit the possibility of an ethnically or religiously pluralistic state. The CUP was the most powerful of a loose coalition of Ottoman progressives known as the Young Turks, which seized power from Sultan Abdul Hamid II (1842–1918; reigned 1876–1909) in a coup d'état in 1908. Following the disastrous Balkan War of 1912, the CUP staged a coup of its own in 1913 in which it assumed complete power and began the process of modernizing the empire. With the onset of the Great War or World War I (which Turkey entered in 1914 on the side of Germany and Austria-Hungary), the CUP leaders saw an opportunity to unite the Turks of the empire by waging the military war and simultaneously engaging in a racial and religious conflict against the empire's Christian population. The subsequent Armenian genocide (1915–1923) claimed the lives of up to 1.5 million Armenians and a further 350,000 Pontic Greeks and 275,000 Assyrians. The ancient Christian communities in Turkey were destroyed forever. With the Allied military defeat of the Ottoman Empire in October 1918, the leading Ittihadists either fled into exile or were arrested and put on trial by Allied-directed tribunals. With the exception of some minor officials of the CUP, almost all of the leadership escaped formal justice at the end of the war, though several— including Mehemet Talaat Pasha (1874–1921), Ismail Enver Bey (1881–1922), and Ahmed Djemal Pasha (1872–1922)—were assassinated by Armenians-in-exile soon after they (the former CUP leaders) had fled Turkey prior to its occupation by the allies. The death knell of the movement came in 1926, when a new republican nationalist government suppressed the last vestiges of the existing party structure and executed its leaders for treason.

Committee on Conscience (COC). The COC was conceptualized in the mid-1980s, at the same time that the United States Holocaust Memorial Museum (USHMM) was being planned. The COC began operation in 1999, as an arm of the USHMM, for the express purpose of alerting the national conscience, influencing policy makers, and stimulating worldwide action to confront and work to halt acts of genocide or related crimes against humanity. In 2000, the COC issued a genocide warning in regard to a situation in Sudan, where, the committee asserted, "starvation was being used as a weapon of destruction," which, in part, with other offenses, was "threatening the existence of entire groups." In 2004, the COC declared that the plight of the black Africans of Darfur and the attacks being carried out against them by government of Sudan troops and the *Janjaweed* (Arab militia) constituted a genocide emergency.

Communism. A political ideology and economic system that advocates a society devoid of social classes, or differences based on wealth or possessions. The communist ideal sees the withering away of states, such that all people live in a harmonious world where national boundaries no longer exist. The most fundamental identifying feature of communism is its advocacy of worker (i.e., proletarian) control of the means of production, within an urban-industrialized social environment, and a forced repression of those who either stand in the way of the realization of such an ideal or come from a class seen as holding back those who seek it (most specifically, the industrial bourgeoisie, or middle class). Communism is thus an extreme form of the broader socialist movement. Although the term was first introduced by Karl Marx (1818–1883) and Friedrich Engels (1820–1885) in the aftermath of the failed 1848 revolutions in Europe in their pamphlet *The Communist Manifesto*, issued in 1848, it was the Russian revolutionary leader Vladimir Ilyich Ulyanov, known as Lenin (1870–1924), who gave the ideology its modern expression as an intolerant, repressive, and potentially (when not actually) genocidal political force in the modern world. Whereas in many states classical socialism evolved into social democracy, working within a democratic political structure, in others it took on a revolutionary form of communism, first in Russia (1917) and then in many other countries supported by a Russia reconstituted as the Union of Soviet Socialist Republics (USSR); after World War II (1939–1945), these nations included Poland, Hungary, Romania, Czechoslovakia, Bulgaria, and East Germany. Other states that were successful in imposing a more distinctive, indigenous but still totalitarian form of communist regime were Yugoslavia, Albania, North Korea, China, Cambodia, Vietnam, and Cuba, among others. In most cases, the revolutionary nature of communism saw the new regimes tear down existing socioeconomic structures using brutal, even exterminatory, methods.

Compassion Fatigue. Compassion fatigue (which is also referred to as donor fatigue) is a concept that some use to explain a lack of interest in or concern about humanitarian emergencies, including genocide. More specifically, it suggests that the international community, regional organizations, and/or individual states are hesitant, tentative, or unwilling to effectively address a conflict or humanitarian crisis. The tentativeness and/or unwillingness to provide such assistance is due to numerous factors, including but not limited to the sheer number of crises erupting across the globe; the endless, and ultimately overwhelming, expectation to address each and every crisis; along with the sense that not every single one can be addressed adequately and thus some sort of "triage" must be undertaken.

Conversely, both terms are also used to attempt to explain why individuals and/or nations over time seem to care less and provide less assistance when such emergencies crop up. The terms also suggest that donors may have become so overwhelmed by the ever-increasing humanitarian emergencies in the world and their concomitant needs that they either cut back their giving or cut out giving entirely.

Complementarity Principle. The complementarity principle refers to the notion that political leaders and military officers who perpetrate crimes that are universally condemned as war crimes, crimes against humanity, or genocide must, upon capture, be tried for their crimes in a national court, and if they are not tried therein, no what matter the reason is, then the defendant must be tried before an international court. Inherent in the complementarity principle is the notion of comity or the informal and voluntary recognition by courts of one jurisdiction of the laws and judicial decisions of another. Essentially, this means that the international community gives priority to national courts to respond to, for example, a case of genocide within its purview, but it also means that if the nation's justice system does not act, then the international system can step in and try the defendants.

Complex Humanitarian Emergency (CHE). CHE refers to a multidimensional conflict or crisis that involves, in one form or another, economic, political, and/or social destabilization. It often involves some combination of forced dispersal of people, intrastate violent conflict (if not outright war), and hunger (if not outright starvation).

"Comrade Duch" (b. 1942). Comrade Duch (sometimes spelled *Deuch*) was the revolutionary nickname of Khang Khek Iev, a communist leader of Cambodia during the regime of Pol Pot (1925–1998) and the Khmer Rouge, between 1975 and 1979. A teacher of mathematics, he joined the Communist Party of Kampuchea (CPK) in 1967; in 1970 he became a revolutionary fighter in the Khmer Rouge, opposing the rule of Cambodian military strongman Lon Nol (1913–1985). His immediate superior, Vorn Vet (c. 1934–1978), saw the potential for Khang/Duch to serve as a committed warden over political prisoners captured by the Khmer Rouge during the civil war (1970–1975). He was appointed as deputy head of the Santebal, the special branch of the security police, under the leadership of Son Sen (1930–1997), and later became head of the Santebal in his own right. Ultimately, Khang/Duch became commander of a number of prisons but is best known as the director of the notorious Tuol Sleng prison, code-named S-21, in Phnom Penh. Under his direction, Tuol Sleng became a byword for Khmer Rouge brutality; at least sixteen thousand prisoners were incarcerated there between 1975 and 1979, and all—save seven, who outlived the regime—perished by torture or execution. Comrade Duch's viciousness extended to party members considered to have been disloyal; to male and female civilians denounced by party cadres for not being supportive enough of the communist revolution; and even to small children, the family members of those already apprehended. After the fall of the Khmer Rouge government to invading Vietnamese forces in January 1979, Duch (who was the last high-ranking Khmer Rouge leader to leave Phnom Penh in the face of the invasion) made his way to Cambodia's western border region with Thailand and from there moved on to China. In Beijing he worked as a broadcaster with Radio China International. In 1991 he returned to Cambodia, and in 1995 he converted to Christianity. In 1999 he surrendered to Cambodian authorities in Phnom Penh, and he has been in detention ever since, awaiting trial.

Concentration Camps, Bosnian War. During the Bosnian War of 1992–1995, a network of what can only be described as concentration camps was established by the Bosnian Serbs. Their purpose was literally to concentrate in designated areas large numbers of Bosnian Muslims, in particular, but also Bosnian Croats. The camps varied in size and style: some were rudimentary, temporary affairs such as guarded warehouses, schools, or factories that had been pressed into service; others were more developed and ranged across a number of buildings surrounded by barbed wire, displaying what are now normally accepted characteristics of all such camps. The best-known camps, whose infamy and notoriety became widespread throughout the region, were Omarska, Keraterm, Trnopolje, Partizan Sports Hall, Manjaca, Brcko-Luka, and Susica. There were many others. Several of the camp commandants were indicted by the International Criminal Tribunal for the Former Yugoslavia (ICTY) for genocide, crimes against humanity, and war crimes. The latter included Zeljko Meakic (b. 1964) from the Omarska camp; Dragan Nikolic (b. 1957), known as "Jenki," from the Susica camp; and Simo Drljaca (b. 1947) and Milan Kovacevic (b. 1941), known as "Miko," who were charged with having "planned, organized and implemented the creation of Omarska, Keraterm and Trnopolje" camps. Most of those held in the Serb concentration camps were civilians (though at Manjaca and Brcko, the latter were mixed in with military prisoners) who were subjected regularly to killings and torture (and frequently the two were combined). In camps set up specifically to house women, mass rape was the primary purpose behind their concentration in these locations. When the first news stories about these places were brought to a stunned world by trailblazing Western journalists such as British *Guardian* reporter Ed Vulliamy and *New York Newsday* journalist Roy Gutman, analogies were made immediately with the Nazi camps of a previous era, particularly when newsreel footage and photographs were published showing starved, emaciated men—walking skeletons—staring back at the cameras from haunted eyes. The camps were not, however, extermination camps in the Nazi sense, as there was no intention on the Serbs' part to annihilate every Bosnian Muslim or Croat. Nonetheless, at least ten thousand prisoners lost their lives in these camps, innumerable injuries were inflicted in various ways, and mass rape was both frequent and deliberately carried out for reasons that can be termed genocidal. Some of the camps had an informal status and were run by local militias, but most were staffed and operated by military and police personnel. The chain of command stretched back, through the army, to military commander Ratko Mladic (b. 1942) and the president of the Bosnian Serbs, Radovan Karadzic (b. 1945).

Concentration Camps, Holocaust. Penal institutions employed in German and German-occupied territories for the incarceration of real and perceived opponents of the Nazi regime (1933–1945). The Nazi concentration camp system began at the very start of the Third Reich with the establishment of Dachau, in March 1933, and many more followed in the ensuing months and years. In mid-1934, an Inspectorate of Concentration Camps was created to coordinate the diverse camps throughout the Reich, with Theodor Eicke (1892–1943) as first inspector. He selected Dachau as the model by which all concentration camps were to be run, resulting in many of the earlier, more haphazardly built camps ("Wilde-KZ") being closed down. By early 1938, only three camps were operating: Dachau, Buchenwald, and Sachsenhausen. After the Anschluss (union) of Germany with Austria in March 1938, a camp in Austria, Mauthausen, was added. The onset of war in September 1939 saw the expansion of the concentration camp system to levels hitherto never before contemplated. Originally, the Nazis intended the concentration camp system to be a device for the suppression of political dissent. As the Third Reich expanded physically, the rationale for retention of the camps was broadened to include religious prisoners of conscience (Roman Catholic priests, Protestant clergy, Jehovah's Witnesses); "racial" prisoners (Jews, Roma, and Sinti); "antisocial elements" (vagrants, itinerant merchants, and "work-shy individuals"); prisoners based on sexual preference (male homosexuals); foreign opponents of the Nazis (resistance fighters, political opponents); and prisoners of war (in particular, prisoners from the Soviet Union). In almost all cases, the

Nazis exploited the labor of their prisoners, often working them to death in conditions of utmost privation. In many of the camps, a separate compound for women was also built. In one case, an entire camp, Ravensbrück, exclusively housed women until almost the very end of the Third Reich.

Significantly, the concentration camp system underwent huge transformations over the twelve-year course of the Third Reich (1933–1945), until the camps were liberated by British, U.S., Canadian, and Soviet forces during 1944 and 1945. Literally millions had been incarcerated in the concentration camps, and hundreds of thousands (at least) had lost their lives at Nazi hands.

The image of the Nazi concentration camps has been confused in the popular consciousness by reference to the so-called *Vernichtungslager*, or extermination camps, created for the "Final Solution of the Jewish Question" (*Die Endlösung des Judenfrage*): Auschwitz-Birkenau, Lublin-Majdanek, Treblinka, Sobibor, Belzec, and Chelmno. It should be remembered, however, that the last four of these camps were not, strictly speaking, concentration camps in the accepted sense of the term, as they were not intended to house large numbers of people for any length of time: their sole purpose was factorylike annihilation, in which millions were murdered.

Concentration Camps, South African War. In October 1899 the British Empire found itself at war with the two Afrikaner republics of southern Africa, the South African Republic and the Orange Free State, known collectively as the Boer Republics. In December 1900 a strategy to win the war was introduced by the British military authorities. Henceforth, enemy sources of supply would be targeted along with the Boer forces themselves. As by this stage Boer towns had been captured, the only remaining foci of operations were Boer farmhouses and estates, which were often used as bases for the Boer guerrilla units. Responding to this situation, British Commander in Chief Lord Horatio Herbert Kitchener (1850–1916) ordered that Boer farms be destroyed and their inhabitants—for the most part women and children, owing to the fact that most men were then fighting in the field—be herded together and interned in what were termed "concentration camps." These camps were an unmitigated humanitarian disaster from the first. Unsuitable locations, huge overcrowding, a thorough inadequacy of sanitary conditions and medical personnel, and unsatisfactory supply and poor quality of foodstuffs were just a few of the problems. These institutions were an amalgam of refugee and internment camps, but in concentrating together families from widely distant farms and towns they brought people into close contact who were often devoid of the necessary immunities from disease that urban living can promote. The upshot saw an unprecedented death rate. By the end of October 1901, it had risen to an average of 344 per 1,000 inmates across forty-six camps, though in some locations, at certain periods, it was nearly twice that number. At its height, the camp network confined 117,000 Boer women and children, but, by war's end in 1902, some 27,000, mostly children, had died. Protests about this state of affairs were noisy in Britain and elsewhere, and efforts were made late in the war to alleviate the situation. The legacy of bitterness the camps created, however, lasts to this day, with some extremist Afrikaners (*Boerevolk*) claiming that the British actions were genocidal in that a projection of up to 3 million Afrikaners were not born in the century following the end of the South African War because of the population losses incurred by the concentration camps. It is also claimed that this was a deliberate policy on the part of the British government in order to depopulate the Afrikaner areas of South Africa and replace them with English settlers. Though extreme and unfounded owing to the fact that the British strategy was military and not genocidal in intention, these allegations point to a deep and lasting existential anger that has not yet been reconciled.

Concordat (Latin, Agreement). Term used by the Roman Catholic Vatican and its papal leader for those treaties entered into with foreign governments. Prior to World War II, Pope Pius XI (1857–1939) signed one in 1929 with Italy under Benito Mussolini (1883–1945) and one in 1933 with Germany under Hitler (1889–1945). The purpose of these agreements was to guarantee the rights of their Roman Catholic citizens and the right of the Church itself to administer its own affairs and administrate its own properties. Neither the Nazis nor the Fascists upheld their end of these agreements as World War II began to drag on. Hitler's attack on Rome in 1943 and the unrealized plot to kidnap the incumbent pope, as well as Mussolini's own disregard for the papacy, are callous evidence of such disregard.

Conference on Security and Cooperation in Europe (OSCE). The OSCE, whose headquarters are located in Vienna, Austria, is the largest regional security organization in the world, with fifty-five participating states from Europe, Central Asia, and North America. It is active in early warning, conflict prevention, conflict management, and postconflict rehabilitation. The OSCE approach to security is comprehensive and cooperative: comprehensive in that it deals with a wide range of security-related issues, including arms control, preventive diplomacy, confidence- and security-building measures, human rights, democratization, election monitoring, and economic and environmental security; cooperative in the sense that all OSCE participating states have equal status, and decisions are based on consensus.

Confessional or Confessing Churches. Primarily organized by traditional Protestant clergy, these churches broke away from the German Protestant Evangelical Church because they refused—unlike the Evangelical Church itself—to accede to the primacy of the Nazi state over the Church and, equally, refused to accept the dominance of the racial laws instituted by the Nazis. In 1934 the Confessional Churches issued the Barmen Declaration, wherein they accused the state of bowing to idolatrous practices, yet they did not overtly condemn the antisemitic practices against the Jews. Among the more well-known leaders of the Confessing Church were Karl Barth, Dietrich Bonhoeffer, and Martin Niemoeller. Throughout the Nazi period of political, military, economic, and social hegemony in Germany, the religious communities, of all denominations, found themselves increasingly disenfranchised, and their leadership cadres removed, oftentimes to the point of imprisonment and/or death.

Conflict Prevention Network (CPN). CPN provides the European Commission and the European Parliament with analyses and policy options vis-à-vis potential conflicts. CPN, which was established in January 1997, consists of a network of research institutes, nongovernmental organizations, and individual experts. Because CPN is part of the European Union's policy-making structure, its policy advice is confidential. However, CPN also organizes public seminars. It executes its task in cooperation with the *Stiftung Wissenschaft und Politik* (SWP) in Ebenhausen, Germany.

Conflict Resolution and Genocide. Conflict resolution is a process whereby differences, disputes, disagreements, or conflicts are arbitrated in such a way that a settlement acceptable to all parties is arrived at. The ideal of those engaging in conflict resolution processes is to stop conflict before it leads to an escalation into physical engagement or, at worst, combat. The process thus involves some form of negotiation (or, at the state-to-state level, diplomacy) via a mediating third party (or parties). In order for conflicting parties to engage in conflict resolution processes, both need to see that their goals can be realized without recourse to combat or physical confrontation. There must also be a willingness by the disputants to abide by the decisions rendered, including the acceptance of sanctions if appropriate. If conflict resolution is to be successful, the process must also take into account, as a first step, that each side is capable of renegotiating its relationship with the other in a peaceful manner. All too frequently in the past, ignoring this fundamental principle has been a major stumbling block to the attainment of conflict resolution (and hence, conflict avoidance). The International Court of Justice in The Hague, Netherlands, and the United Nations in New York (either the Security Council or General Assembly) are the most common venues for such deliberations.

In the specific case of genocide, however, the situation is complicated by the internal nature of the conflict and the unwillingness of sovereign nation-states to allow others, either individually or collectively, to intervene either prior to the actual genocide or early on in the mass killing. Thus, in order to bring the dominating power (i.e., government) and the victim group to the bargaining table, the United Nations and/or other regional organizations must bring to bear the spotlight of world opinion, economic or other sanctions, and limited military intervention, all in an attempt to speedily defuse a potentially escalating genocidal tragedy. In the cases of Bosnia (early to mid-1990s), Rwanda (early to mid-1990s), and Darfur, Sudan (2003 through today, 2007), such nonmilitary attempts at conflict resolution did not prove effective and, as a result, massive numbers of people were killed by the perpetrators.

Conquistadores (Spanish, conquerors). Term given to Spanish military adventurers and mercenaries who invaded and subdued large areas of Central and South America in the sixteenth century, overpowering indigenous nations and cultures in order to enrich themselves and the Spanish monarchy. The best known of the conquistadores were men such as Vasco Núñez de Balboa (1475–1519), Hernán Cortés (1485–1547), Francisco Pizarro (c. 1478–1541), Francisco de Orellana (c. 1511–1546), Francisco Vázquez de Coronado (1510–1554), and Fernando de Soto (c. 1496–1542). Military conquest of highly advanced peoples such as the Aztecs and the Incas was accompanied by massacre, physical destruction of native property (particularly livestock and crops), widespread use of terror, and, often, a resultant loss of the will to survive. The freebooting conquistadores were essentially hirelings of the Spanish king, equipped with commissions to conquer new territories, exploit their wealth, and enrich both the royal family and the entrepreneurs who backed them financially, back in Spain. While abroad and in the field, the conquistadores and their armies acted as a law unto themselves, suppressing all feelings of Christian humanity toward those they encountered. Wherever they went—and their range traversed thousands of miles throughout the Americas—they left carnage and slaughter in their wake, determined to maximize their opportunities for plunder and loot. Moreover, the conquistadores fought as religious fanatics in a holy war for the Roman Catholic Church, for which they sometimes received the blessing of priests in Spain and those based throughout the New World. The conquistadores were not agents of the Church, however; the priests and friars who often accompanied them did the work of converting the indigenous peoples conquered by the soldiers, but they could do so only after the military work of breaking the survivors' spirits had been completed. In short, the conquistadores rampaged across the Americas, laying waste to all those they encountered, killing inno-cents by the tens and hundreds of thousands, and paving the road for subsequent conver-sion and colonization. Along the way, they enriched Spain to unsurpassed levels at the time, catapulting it into the first rank of European (and, through its overseas empire, world) powers.

Conspiracy. A made-for-television film jointly produced by the BBC and HBO in 2001. *Conspiracy* is a movie that dramatically brings to the screen the Wannsee Conference of January 20, 1942, in which leading Nazi bureaucrats and department heads in the Third Reich met to coordinate the details that put into practice the "Final Solution of the Jewish Question" (*Die Endlösung des Judenfrage*). Chaired by SS General Reinhard Heydrich (1904–1942), with minutes taken by SS Lieutenant Colonel Adolf Eichmann (1906–1962) and with many senior Nazis in attendance (such as Dr. Wilhelm Stuckart [1902–1952] and Dr. Roland Freisler [1893–1945], among others), the meeting revealed a plan for the complete industrialized mass murder of every Jew in Europe. *Conspiracy*, taking as its foundation the sole surviving record of the meeting, is an intimate movie in which nearly every scene takes place in the meeting room itself. The movie provides a psychological, cultural, and ideological profile of the Nazi thinking that contemplated the mass extermination of millions of people, and this is clearly the film's greatest strength. The director, Frank Pierson (b. 1925), is positively clinical in permitting as little subjec-tive emotion as possible to show through. His preferred strategy is to allow the words of the participants themselves to provoke the audience's revulsion he seeks. As a penetrat-ing snapshot into this definitive moment in the Nazi annihilation of the Jews of Europe, *Conspiracy* is an important work of cinematography. It won numerous awards, notably an Emmy for Kenneth Branagh (b. 1960) as Best Actor for his portrayal of Heydrich and a Golden Globe for Stanley Tucci (b. 1960) as Best Supporting Actor for his portrayal of Eichmann.

Contact Group. The Contact Group, which is composed of representatives from France, Germany, Russia, Italy, Great Britain, and the United States, was formed in April 1994. It was created when both the United States and Russia became major actors in the Bosnia peace-negotiating process, during which it was obvious that the previous efforts (beginning in late 1991) of the European Union (EU) and United Nations had not been effective.

The Contact Group met regularly in the 1990s, though informally (it had neither a sec-retariat nor staff personnel), to discuss its concerns and progress in peace-building efforts. It also addressed policies proffered by each nation regarding the Balkans and whether such efforts could be politically coordinated.

On July 24, 2006, representatives of various nations of the Contact Group met with the presidents of both Kosovo and Bosnia to discuss Kosovo's future. A statement released on September 20, 2006, through the U.S. State Department, read as follows: "Ministers urge Kosovo's provisional institutions of self-government and leaders of all of Kosovo's com-munities to accelerate efforts to implement UN-endorsed standards, promote reconcilia-tion and build trust among ethnic communities. . . . They renew their call on Belgrade to cease its obstruction of Kosovo Serb participation in the Kosovo's instructions." Contin-uing, the ministers stated that they "welcome efforts to prepare for the implementation of a settlement, including through a continued military presence to provide a safe and secure environment, and an international civilian presence to supervise implementation of and ensure compliance with the settlement." As of late 2007, the future of Kosovo remains unresolved.

Control Council Law No. 10. Appended to the Nuremberg Trials Final Report at the International Military Tribunal (IMT), which tried Nazi leaders and others for both war crimes and the waging of aggressive war at the conclusion of World War II, this document was entitled "Punishment of Persons Guilty of War Crimes, Crimes against Peace and against Humanity" and had as its stated purpose the following: "to establish a uniform legal basis in Germany for the prosecution of war criminals and other similar offenders other than those dealt with by the International Military Tribunal." It consisted of five articles: (1) reaffirmation of the Moscow Declaration of October 30, 1943 ("Concerning Responsibility of Hitlerites for Committed Atrocities"), and the London Agreement of August 8, 1945 ("Concerning Prosecution and Punishment of Major War Criminals of European Axis"); (2) definition of "crimes against peace," "war crimes," "crimes against humanity," and membership in criminal groups and organizations, and consequent punishments; (3) the responsibilities of the authorities in the various Zones of Occupation to bring such persons to trial; (4) the responsibilities of the authorities in the various Zones of Occupation regarding those residents in their zones whose crimes were committed outside of Germany; and (5) the necessity of speedy trials within a six-month period after incarceration of such persons. The document itself was signed in Berlin, Germany, on December 20, 1945, by representatives of the United States, Britain, France, and Soviet Russia.

Convention. The general term in international law for a formal written and legally binding international agreement vis-à-vis a specific matter of shared concern among states that creates legal obligations to which the actors/parties agree to adhere to and support. When used as a proper noun (*Convention*), the term is often used by genocide scholars to refer to the UN Convention on the Prevention and Punishment of the Crime of Genocide (UNCG), though in this regard *Convention* is generally used only after the complete title is first used.

Cordon Sanitaire. Cordon sanitaires are safe places established by regional organizations such as NATO or intergovernmental organizations such as the United Nations in order to provide sanctuary for civilians in areas of violent conflict. In certain cases, such places of safety work quite well (as in the case of the safe area established for the Kurds in northern Iraq following the Gulf War), but at other times they prove to be anything but safe and can result in an absolute disaster, particularly when they are not well guarded by troops with a strong mandate, as in the case of Srebrenica in July 1995 where an estimated seven thousand to eight thousand Muslim boys and men were rounded up and murdered by Serbian forces.

Cossacks, Genocide of. The Cossacks, a people from the area surrounding a broad expanse between the Don and Kuban rivers, first appeared as a settled and identifiable community in the sixteenth century. Owing to a generally held belief that the Cossacks were unswervingly loyal to the tsarist monarchy and the royal family, the Bolshevik regime of Vladimir Ilyich Lenin (1870–1924) saw the Cossack lands as a region likely to be conservative, even reactionary, and definitely opposed to the new government installed as a result of the Bolshevik Revolution of October 1917. To some extent, this was true in certain Cossack territories (though not in all), prompting the view in Bolshevik circles that the Cossacks would have to be physically suppressed or otherwise a threat to the government would continue to exist in Russia's south. This was exacerbated by active Cossack support of the White Armies in the Russian Civil War. Resulting from the fall of the tsarist regime in February–March of 1917, the Cossacks had already lost both prestige and state protection; by December 1917 they were also classified by the Bolsheviks as *kulaks*, or wealthy peasants—and thus, as class enemies. On January 24, 1919, a secret resolution of the Bolshevik Party's Central Committee approved a program of "de-Cossackization": "we must recognize as the only politically correct measure massive terror and a merciless fight against the rich Cossacks, who must be exterminated and physically disposed of, down to the last man." Victims were to be selected in accordance with very broad, and often quite arbitrary, categories by Bolshevik police or other officials; in less than three months well over ten thousand individuals had been summarily executed. Rising up against this murderous policy, a Cossack army of thirty thousand men was formed and now joined the White Armies for their very survival. By February 1920 the Bolsheviks hit back in force. Tens of thousands of civilians lost their lives as Bolshevik divisions swept through the countryside burning villages, destroying houses, and gathering local inhabitants together in concentration camps. The so-called Red Terror, which the Bolsheviks applied throughout Russia, then hit the Cossacks especially hard, with a combination of scorched earth, starvation, collectivization, and "dekulakization" activities taking a huge toll. In short, the "de-Cossackization" campaigns of 1919 and 1920 claimed somewhere between three hundred thousand and five hundred thousand lives. The genocidal treatment meted out to the Cossacks—in part class-based, in part ethnic, and in part political—was an initial foretaste of what the rest of the country would experience under the Bolsheviks as they stabilized and centralized their rule and then began to remake society in accordance with their vision of the communist ideal.

Coughlin, Father Charles E. Roman (1891–1979). U.S. Roman Catholic priest from Little Flower Parish, Detroit, Michigan, notorious for his antisemitic invective throughout the 1930s and early 1940s. Dubbed "the radio priest" because of his weekly broadcasts of sermons on the radio (which he began as early as 1926), Coughlin was an early and enthusiastic supporter of U.S. president Franklin Delano Roosevelt (1882–1945) but turned against him when Roosevelt's sweeping reforms during the New Deal ostensibly went "too far." Although Coughlin's major interest during the Depression years was economic rehabilitation and the amelioration of the conditions of unemployed Americans, his sermons increasingly adopted an antisemitic tone as the 1930s progressed. A populist, he inspired his listeners toward a hatred for Jews by attacking prominent Jewish figures and condemning Roosevelt for failing to drive "the money changers from the temple" and for "overstating" the extent to which Jews were being harassed in Germany. In 1936 he began publishing a weekly newspaper, *Social Justice*, in which he reprinted excerpts from the notorious antisemitic forgery *The Protocols of the Learned Elders of Zion*. In 1938 he created an organization called the Christian Front, which won approving support from Irish Catholic Americans in considerable numbers. Christian Fronters, once the movement developed properly, were in the forefront of antisemitic activities in the United States and frequently conducted meetings at which Nazi and Fascist sympathizers were also present. Often such meetings would end with the Nazi salute. At such rallies, Christian Fronters were often called upon to "liquidate the Jews in America." Above all this, Coughlin was lauded as the man of the moment, and he received support from diocese after diocese in New York, Boston, Chicago, and many other cities with large Irish and/or

Catholic populations. He was, at no time, publicly criticized by the archbishops in Brooklyn (which was a particularly influential diocese in the 1940s), Boston, or Chicago. At its height, Coughlin's radio program had a weekly listening audience of nearly 16 million, of whom 67 percent, in a poll, said they agreed strongly with his major claims. With the United States' entry into World War II, Coughlin was ordered by Attorney General Francis Biddle (1886–1968) to cease broadcasting, and he returned to his work as a parish priest in Detroit until his retirement and death in 1979.

Crimes against Humanity. A legal category within international law that identifies punishable offenses for gross violations of human rights, atrocities, and mass murder of noncombatant civilians. Such offenses are a relatively new category, largely the product of international human rights legislation enacted during the twentieth century. Often, crimes against humanity are bracketed alongside of war crimes, though they differ from war crimes in that they are not, for the most part, violations of the laws of war; indeed, crimes against humanity need not occur in wartime at all. A lengthy list of acts that can be considered as crimes against humanity include, but are not confined to, the following: murder, extermination, enslavement, deportation, imprisonment, torture, rape, and persecutions on political, racial, and religious grounds. Other inhumane acts not listed above can also be included, rendering crimes against humanity as an evolutionary category over which international (or, less likely, national) courts have some degree of discretion. There is no generally accepted definition of crimes against humanity, and, to date, no universal international legislation covering such crimes exists. Several groundbreaking initiatives have, however, placed the category of crimes against humanity in the forefront of major international humanitarian concern. For example, important case law precedents were created through the International Military Tribunal (IMT) at Nuremberg in 1946, when the category of crimes against humanity was actually listed as one of the four counts faced by the accused Nazi leaders. Since then, the category has been included in the articles establishing the International Criminal Tribunals for the Former Yugoslavia and Rwanda (ICTY and ICTR, respectively). On July 1, 2002, the International Criminal Court (ICC) was established at The Hague, and it incorporated a lengthy list of acts that were to be included as crimes against humanity. The category is, generally speaking, a useful one for covering acts that are not considered as genocide according to the UN Convention on the Prevention and Punishment of the Crime of Genocide (1948). Given that there is no universally recognized or binding definition of crimes against humanity, and that the term is therefore legally imprecise, heinous acts that cannot be prosecuted as genocide can be prosecuted as crimes against humanity. But the two categories are not interchangeable, and genocide is now usually considered to be a crime of greater magnitude.

Crimes of Universal Jurisdiction. Certain crimes—war crimes, crimes against humanity, and genocide—are considered *hostis humani generis* (an enemy of all mankind). In that regard, they are considered crimes of universal jurisdiction, which means that any nation has the right to try any perpetrator of such crimes, no matter where the crimes were committed.

Cromwell, Oliver (1599–1658). Lord Protector of England (1649–1658), parliamentarian, and military commander during and after the English Civil War (1642–1649). After the execution of King Charles I (1600–1649; reigned 1625–1649) on January 30, 1649, Cromwell turned the attention of Parliament to the ongoing and unresolved issue of Ireland. An Irish rebellion against English rule had taken place in 1641, and since then the country had been ruled by Irish Catholic Confederates. In 1649, in the aftermath of Charles's execution, these same Irish Catholics entered into an alliance with English Royalists who had removed themselves to Ireland. In August 1649 Cromwell's Parliamentary forces, under his own command and that of his chief lieutenant, General Henry Ireton (1611–1651), invaded Ireland, with two major objectives in mind: defeating the Catholic and Royalist forces in the field and exacting lasting punishment against the Irish for the rebellion of 1641. Cromwell's invasion—in effect, a reconquest of Ireland—was accompanied by great brutality against both the military and civilian populations. Indeed, allegations in Ireland down to the present time have accused Cromwell's forces of engaging in war crimes and crimes against humanity, such that the invasion period is known informally in Ireland as *An Mallacht Cromail*, or "the curse of Cromwell." Debate over Cromwell's impact on Ireland has been intense over the years, but a broad consensus has been reached which estimates that up to one-third of the preinvasion Irish population was destroyed through killing, hunger, disease, or expulsion under Cromwellian rule. Perhaps as many as half a million (and possibly more) Irish men and women lost their lives. The best known of many instances of unrelenting and total war against the Irish concerned the English siege of the port town of Drogheda, in September 1649. The siege itself was of short duration, Cromwell bringing overwhelming numbers to bear against the Irish— twelve thousand English troops against some three thousand defenders. Giving them the option of surrendering prior to assaulting the city (which was rejected), Cromwell, in accordance with the standard military practice of the day, issued an order to his troops that no quarter would henceforth be given once capture had been achieved. Almost all the defenders were massacred, as were any Catholic clergy that could be taken; many civilian townsfolk were also killed, prior to the town being looted and, in parts, put to the torch. Overall, the siege and fate of Drogheda became a byword for English brutality in Ireland, as it remains to this day. Cromwell remained lord protector—effectively, military dictator—of England until his death on September 3, 1658, having subjugated Ireland so thoroughly that it would take more than two and a half centuries for the country to be able to successfully regain its independence.

Cultural Genocide. A broad term that unavoidably overlaps other explanations for genocide. Even though the UN Convention on the Prevention and Punishment of the Crime of Genocide (1948) explicitly does not recognize a category of "cultural genocide"— thus rendering the term irrelevant in international law—cultural destruction can certainly take place that contributes to genocide as measured by other criteria. The term *culture*, broadly speaking, embraces such factors as language and literature, art, artifacts, and architectural monuments, as well as a common past—in short, all the concrete ingredients that help a group forge a collective identity. Were one to systematically destroy all or part of a group's cultural heritage, one could eventually weaken its group identity. Thus, the destruction of archives, libraries, and art galleries could seriously undermine a sense of a group's past. Similarly, loss of language could endanger a group's collective future. The targeting of ancient churches and libraries could easily weaken group morale and cause other psychological damage. Examples are many and diverse: U.S. Indian policy in the mid-nineteenth century, which forcibly transplanted whole nations from their ancestral lands; Nazis in Germany burning books by Jews in 1934 and synagogues in 1938; Stalin forbidding the use of the Ukrainian and Yiddish languages and generally stamping out religious life throughout the USSR; the Khmer Rouge's utter obliteration of Cambodia's colonial past, together with all schools, temples, and religious practice; Bosnian Serbs consciously shelling the historic library of Sarajevo and destroying its precious collection of books and ancient manuscripts; and Croatians purposely destroying the ancient Turkish bridge in Mostar.

Cultural Revolution. The Great Proletarian Cultural Revolution, a mobilization of youth by Chinese Communist Party (CCP) Chairman Mao Zedong (1893–1976) designed to revitalize the Chinese revolution while rooting out those whom he considered to be a political threat, began in 1966. Various indications had led Mao to sense that China's revolutionary movement had begun to lose its vigor and that, as a result, some in the higher echelons were losing their confidence in his leadership. Mao's tactics to meet this twofold challenge were themselves dual in nature. First, he declared that the vitality of the revolution was ebbing because "counterrevolutionaries" and "bad elements" were "revising" communist doctrine and allowing capitalist influences to penetrate China; second, he cajoled his Red Guards—Chinese youth brought up on Mao's teachings, who were fanatically loyal to Mao himself—to denounce such elements and to purge them completely from the life of the country. This was the high tide (and the realization) of Mao's "personality cult," and for him it worked brilliantly. All over China, millions of Red Guards hastened to their task of renewing the revolution. Anything deemed to be "old" was disposed of. Denunciation of the "four olds"—old customs, old habits, old culture, and old thinking—paved the way for personal and physical destruction of limitless dimensions. Prominent figures, teachers, artists, and intellectuals of all sorts were publicly harangued, ridiculed, and shamed before mass crowds. Often, the latter were beaten, detained, and even executed. Hundreds of thousands of people, on the flimsiest of grounds, were sent to labor camps, where many died owing to maltreatment therein. At Mao's insistence, senior party leaders were dismissed and all state officials had to subject themselves to public "self-criticism" hearings in order to demonstrate their loyalty. Often such hearings descended into ritual humiliation sessions in which young Red Guards would go out of their way to abuse and degrade those who were "confessing" their crimes against the state. At one point, in many areas, it seemed as though Red Guard zealotry had gotten out of hand, as judicial processes were usurped, looting of whole villages (and even towns) became widespread, book burnings took place, normal policing was suspended and extensive killings occurred. Quite simply, Red Guard anarchy became the norm, with untold numbers killed and a new form of revolutionary terror unleashed upon the country. The Cultural Revolution began to subside only in the mid-1970s and was brought to an end with Mao Zedong's death in 1976.

Cultural Survival. Established in 1972, Cultural Survival's main goal is to help indigenous peoples and ethnic groups across the globe deal as equals in their relations with national and international societies. The Cultural Survival Center, the formal research arm of Cultural Survival, and the former Program on Nonviolent Sanctions were formally merged in January 1995 to consider the problems of dictatorship, war, terrorism, genocide, and oppression in the complex context of cultures and events that form the backdrop of many ongoing conflicts. The combined program is organized to address nonviolent alternatives for the preservation of all peoples and their cultures.

Culture of Impunity, Relationship to Genocide. Just after the founding of the United Nations and during the advent of the Cold War, a "culture of impunity" seemingly arose in regard to holding perpetrators responsible for their commission of genocidal crimes and crimes against humanity. Who, for example, among the perpetrators of the Bangladeshi, Cambodian, and Kurdish genocides were ever held responsible? Even with the establishment of the International Criminal Court for the Former Yugoslavia (ICTY) and the International Criminal Court for Rwanda (ICTR) and their numerous trials and convictions, many of the main fomenters of hate and perpetrators of genocidal actions in, for example, the former Yugoslavia are still free (e.g., Radovan Karadzic and Ratko Mladic, being two of the most noteworthy). It has taken the international community over twenty-five years to bring the Khmer Rouge (KR) to trial (trials might commence sometime in late 2007), and as a result many of the leaders of the KR have already died. Many in the international community hope that with the recent establishment of the International Criminal Court (ICC) the culture of impunity will slowly but surely dissolve. It is noteworthy that a major goal in establishing the ICC was to put an end to such impunity. In fact, the Rome Statute's preamble states, in part, that the international community is "determined to put an end to impunity for the perpetrators of these crimes" (meaning, in part, crimes against humanity and genocide).

CUSHRID Net. CUSHRID (an acronym for Canada-U.S. Human Rights Information and Documentation) Net was established in 1994 by Human Rights Information and Documentation Systems International (HURIDOCS), Amnesty International USA, Amnesty International Canada, and the American Association for the Advancement of Science (AAAS). The various purposes of the organization are as follows: facilitate the exchange of ideas and information between human rights organizations; establish uniform standards for human right documentation, information management, and information exchange; develop cooperative projects in the areas of documentation and information management to avoid duplication; provide training in various aspects of documentation and information management; and maintain contacts with information and documentation networks in other parts of the world.

Customary International Law. Customary international law refers to international laws that have evolved out of the constant and consistent practice of states and constitutes a set of conventions, patterns of behavior, and established norms considered binding on a community. Although such forms of conduct, rooted in customary routines, are not founded on legislation, they nevertheless can establish a basis for judicial decision making. In international law, the regulation of relations between states was, for many centuries, based on customary forms, some of which evolved from more formal treaties. The best known of these was the Treaty of Westphalia in 1648, which established and codified the modern states system that still prevails today. Yet, although customary laws in the international sphere can emerge out of previously negotiated treaties, it is just as accurate to say that often the opposite is also the case: formal international agreements, when contracted, are often based on long-held practices or restraints that have always prevailed but never been enacted. Thus, for example, atrocities such as crimes against humanity and genocide were not legislated in international law until the twentieth century, though the kinds of actions that are defined therein were traditionally not permitted in the relationships between nations (particularly in the Western tradition) as acceptable forms of conduct. The norms of customary international law thus derive their authority from their universal acceptance.

Formal international law, usually established through treaties or signed international conventions, differs from customary international law in that the former embodies specific undertakings agreed to in an official prescribed context and binds the signatories into accepting clearly delineated liabilities or responsibilities.

Czechoslovakia and Ethnic Cleansing. At the end of World War II, the restored Czechoslovak government of Eduard Benes (1884–1948) instituted a policy of removing all Germans (with very few exceptions) from its Sudeten districts. As the Nazi armies retreated, the Czech militia and groups of communist cadres moved into German ethnic areas and attacked civilians in their homes and on the streets. Anti-German pogroms were perpetrated in which ethnic Germans were beaten, tortured, and/or shot. It quickly became clear that all of the 3 million Germans in Czechoslovakia would be forced to leave and transferred to German sovereign territory. During 1946 the Czech government established transit camps, often on the sites of former Nazi concentration camps, with the intention of facilitating the transfer of the Germans more systematically. According to Sudeten German sources, some 272,000 Germans, representing about 8 percent of the total German population in Czechoslovakia, died from harsh treatment, hunger, despair, and exposure during the course of the transfers, though this figure has been challenged by Czech and German historians (who claim the figure to have been much smaller). It has been estimated that during the second half of 1947 almost the entire Sudeten German population had been transferred to Germany, and the areas in which the Germans had lived—often for several hundred years—were reoccupied by Czechs. In what was a clear case of ethnic cleansing, Bohemia and Moravia were thoroughly Slavicized; the German ethnic presence, in the space of no more than two and a half years, was eliminated from Czech life forever. In a smaller-scale operation (though still involving hundreds of thousands of people), and at the same time, similar treatment was accorded Czechoslovakia's Hungarian population.

D

Dachau. The model for the concentration camp system used by the Nazis during World War II, Dachau was located near the town with the same name, about seven kilometers from Munich. It was established in 1933 and remained opened until its prisoners were liberated in 1945. At its height, over two hundred thousand prisoners representing more than thirty countries were incarcerated there, of whom more than thirty thousand of them were murdered there or in its more than thirty subcamps that surrounded it. Medical experiments were also performed there, under the direction of Dr. Sigmund Rascher (1909–1945), including those involving high-altitude compression chambers, hypothermia, and injections of experimental medications. Its first commandant was Theodor Eicke (1892–1943), who developed the camp system itself and was later promoted to inspector-general of all concentration and death camps. Dachau was also the main camp for religious prisoners, including Pastor Martin Niemöller (1892–1984), and began to add women to its prison rolls in August 1944. Jehovah's Witnesses, homosexuals, Roman Catholic priests, so-called asocials (e.g., the Roma and Sinti or Gypsies, vagrants, beggars, alcoholics, the homeless), and criminals were also incarcerated there, but very few Jews. From the end of 1944 until its liberation by U.S. troops on April 29, 1945, more than fifteen thousand prisoners died from increasingly deteriorating conditions, including overcrowding and rampant disease such as typhus. In addition to Niemöller, its inmates included Bruno Bettelheim (1903–1990), Polish writer Tadeuscz Borowski (1922–1951), and French writer Robert Antelme (1917–1990).

Daimler-Benz. A German manufacturer of automobiles whose management provided valuable assistance to the National Socialist (Nazi) party prior to Adolf Hitler's accession to office in January 1933. It reaped substantial financial rewards from its association with the Nazi government throughout the 1930s, and exploited captive labor forces in Nazi concentration camps and elsewhere after the outbreak of war in 1939. By 1934, as a result of business provided by Hitler, production at Daimler-Benz had more than doubled; in 1935 military manufacture accounted for 38 percent of production; by 1940 this had risen to 76 percent, and, in 1944, to 93 percent. Daimler-Benz was largely responsible for motorizing the German army and creating the new German air force in the years following Hitler's rise to power. Owing to the enormous growth of Daimler's output during the war years, manpower became a major problem, particularly as men were conscripted into the armed forces and women were brought into new roles within the German workforce.

Consequently, foreign workers were impressed to work in Daimler's factories (they numbered about one-third of all Daimler's workers by September 1942), as were concentration camp inmates. In early 1944 Governor Hans Frank (1900–1946), head of the Polish *Generalgouvernement* (the territorial unit in Poland, created by the Nazis on October 26, 1939, to which was added Eastern Galicia in the summer of 1941, following Nazi Germany's attack on the Soviet Union) visited one of the Daimler-Benz factories in his territory, describing it as "the model factory" of the Generalgouvernement. With the advance of the Allies through Germany in April and May 1945, Daimler-Benz premises were progressively occupied and closed down. The company was reconstituted and rehabilitated during the late 1940s and early 1950s.

Dallaire, Major General Romeo (b. 1946). Born in the Netherlands to a Canadian father and a Dutch mother, Dallaire grew up in Montreal, Canada. Prior to, during, and following the 1994 Rwandan genocide, Dallaire was the force commander of the United Nations Assistance Mission for Rwanda (UNAMIR) (October 1993–March 1996) peacekeeping force in Rwanda. UNAMIR's mandate was to keep the peace in Rwanda after the power-sharing agreement known as the Arusha Accords was signed. As part and parcel of keeping the peace, the UN peacekeepers were mandated to oversee the cease-fire arranged by the Arusha Accords (a set of five agreements signed by the Hutu-dominated government of Rwanda and the Rwandan Patriotic Front [RPF] in Arusha, Tanzania on August 4, 1993, it was intended that the Arusha Accords would end the civil war between the two parties and help to establish both demilitarization and demobilization in the area). What Dallaire was not informed of prior to his posting was that the extremist Hutu were intent on annihilating the Tutsi and had said as much in media broadcasts, newspaper articles, and declarations. In January 1994 a Hutu informant, reportedly a person of influence in the higher echelons of the Rwandan government, contacted Dallaire in order to inform him of the frantic effort by extremist Hutu to arm and train local militias in preparation for the decimation of the Tutsi. In a fax to the United Nations, which has been alternately referred to as "the Dallaire fax" and the "genocide fax," Dallaire asserted that the informant informed him that Hutu extremists "had been ordered to register all the Tutsi in Kigali" and that "he suspects it is for their extermination." Dallaire also informed the powers that be at the United Nations, that he, Dallaire, was planning an arms raid on the Hutu cache of weapons. The UN, however, cabled back ordering him not to carry out the raid out of fear of exacerbating the situation. As the crisis in Rwanda worsened, particularly in early 1994, Dallaire came to the conclusion that the constant stream of murders he and his soldiers were discovering and witnessing was not a result of warfare between the former combatants, but rather crimes against humanity by one group (Hutu) against another (Tutsi). Initially he referred to such killing as "ethnic cleansing." Dallaire continued to fire off one urgent message after another to UN headquarters in New York City requesting more forces, supplies and the broadening of his mandate (from a Chapter VI or peacekeeping mandate to a Chapter VII or peace enforcement mandate) in order to quell the violence perpetrated by the Hutu extremists, but it was to no avail as the UN Security Council would not countenance such a change. Ultimately, in late April (some two weeks after the genocide had actually begun), Dallaire came to the conclusion that what he was witnessing was, in fact, genocide, and reported such to the international press and the United Nations. The international community, though, failed to respond, and within one hundred days between five hundred thousand and 1 million Tutsi and moderate Hutu were killed by the extremist Hutu government and its lackeys. What he and his fellow UN soldiers witnessed and lived through is described in excruciating detail in Dallaire's book, *Shake Hands with the Devil: The Failure of Humanity in Rwanda* (New York: Carroll and Graf, 2004). Today, Dallaire is a Canadian senator.

Darfur (Sudan), Genocide in. Beginning in 2003 Sudanese President Omar al-Bashir's (b. 1944) regime undertook a scorched earth campaign against the black Africans of Darfur in western Sudan. By mid-2007, the estimates of those who had been killed or perished due to genocide by attrition (i.e., due to a lack of water, starvation, or injuries) ranged from a low of 250,000 to over 400,000 individuals.

In the 1990s, Arabs and black Africans in the Darfur region began to clash over land and water use, primarily as a result of a severe drought and increasing desertification. Over time the clashes became increasingly violent (a result, in part, of the fact that outbreaks of violence in that region of Africa had resulted in a flood of weapons surging into the Darfur region). When the clashes were adjudicated by courts, the black Africans often found themselves being treated less fairly than the Arab population. Ultimately, and for many years (beginning in the early 1990s and continuing through the early 2000s), black Africans of Darfur complained bitterly that the Arabs in the region were given preferential treatment over black Africans by the Sudanese government. For example, black Africans asserted that while the Sudanese government taxed them, the government did little to nothing to enhance the infrastructure of Darfur (meaning, the development of road systems and the erection of schools). At the same time, they called for better treatment of black Africans at the hands of the police and court system.

When the black Africans felt that their complaints were falling on deaf ears, a rebel group, the Sudanese Liberation Army (SLA), formed and, in early 2003, it began carrying out attacks against government and military installations. Short-handed due to the war in the south, al-Bashir hired nomadic Arabs to join forces with government of Sudan (GOS) troops to fight the rebels. Instead of focusing their attacks solely on the rebels, the GOS and the Arab militia (referred to as the *Janjaweed*, or horsemen with guns and/or devils on horseback) carried out a scorched earth policy against all black Africans in the three state region of Darfur. In doing so, the GOS and *Janjaweed* indiscriminately killed men, women, and children, raped young girls and women, and, prior to burning down hundreds of villages, plundered what they could. Within a relatively short amount of time, hundreds of villages had been utterly destroyed by the GOS and *Janjaweed*, and hundreds of thousands of black Africans had fled, seeking sanctuary elsewhere. By late 2004, it was estimated that close to 2 million refugees had sought sanctuary in internally displaced camps within Sudan and almost two hundred thousand others had fled to refugee camps just over the border in Chad.

After conducting an investigation (the Atrocities Documentation Project [ADP]) during July and August of 2004 by carrying out a systematic series of over one thousand interviews of Sudanese refugees in Chad, the U.S. State Department reported, "Sixty-one percent of the respondents witnessed the killing of a family member, 16 percent said they had been raped or heard about a rape from a victim. About one third of the refugees heard racial epithets while under attack" (U.S. State Department, 2004, p. 1). In regard to the latter, the ADP found that during the attacks, GOS troops and *Janjaweed* jeered the black Africans, calling them "black slaves" and "slave dogs," both of which are highly derogatory terms in the region. The perpetrators also repeatedly asserted that the black Africans were not true Sudanese and had no right to remain in Sudan. Based on the analysis of the data, U.S. secretary of state Colin Powell (b. 1937), declared, on September 4, 2004, that the killing in Sudan constituted genocide.

Subsequently, the U.S. referred the matter to the United Nations, hoping the UN would halt the mass killing. By this point in time, the UN Security Council had voted on numerous resolutions urging sanctions against the Sudanese government, but realpolitik hindered the Security Council in making any serious headway in confronting Sudan over the mass killing of the black Africans. More specifically, China, which has huge petroleum interests in Sudan, refused to vote in favor of any sanctions. Likewise, Russia, which has a huge arms deal and petroleum interests in Sudan, was against sanctioning Sudan. The United States took an on-again, off-again approach, calling for sanctions but then easing up due to the fact that the Sudanese governments agreed to join the U.S. in its so-called war against terrorism. And thus, as the United Nations dithered, tens and hundreds of thousands of people were brutally murdered, saw their villages and homes destroyed and their loved ones raped and murdered.

That said, the UN decided to carry out an investigation for the express purpose of ascertaining for itself whether, in fact, genocide had been or was being perpetrated in Darfur. Thus, in December 2004 and January 2005 the, UN sent its own team (the UN Commission of Inquiry [COI]) of investigators into Darfur, the refugee camps in Chad, to Khartoum to meet with Sudanese leaders, and other parts of the region. Ultimately, the UN's report concluded that while it found that serious crimes of humanity had been perpetrated it did not find that the GOS and *Janjaweed* had committed genocide. Continuing, it stated that it did not rule out entirely that genocidal acts had been committed and said that the analysis of additional evidence in the future might come to such a conclusion.

Based on the COI's findings, the UN Security Council placed seventeen individuals from the Sudanese government on targeted sanctions. Five other individuals were listed as potential targets of sanctions, including al-Bashir. At one and the same time, the UN referred the matter to the International Criminal Court (ICC) in The Hague. In 2005 the ICC began an investigation into the atrocities committed by the GOS and *Janjaweed* in Darfur in order to collect evidence for potential trials against the perpetrators. As of August 2007 the killing, rapes of women and girls, and destruction of what few villages are left continues unabated, as do GOS and *Janjaweed* attacks on internally displaced camps in Sudan and the refugee camps in Chad. Although the UN Security Council has issued numerous condemnations over the years of the ongoing killing and destruction, it has also chosen to heed Omar al-Bashir's demands that no troops other than the African Union (AU) be allowed in the Darfur region. As a result, the seven thousand African Union troops, on a Chapter VI or peacekeeping mandate (which only allows for engaging in combat to protect their own safety but not that of the refugees) are forced to attempt the impossible—that is, to provide security for some 2.5 million black African refugees in an area roughly the size of France.

Because foreign oil companies and consortiums continue to infuse Sudan's economy with cash, al-Bashir continues to view both the United Nations and the World Bank with open distain and hostility. Whether the pressure brought upon him and his government to stem the genocide by the international community, including neighboring African nation-states, will be successful, remains open to debate.

Dark Tourism. A term coined in 2000 by British academics John Lennon and Malcolm Foley, from Glasgow Caledonian University (Scotland). The term describes the growth and incidence of tourist interest in sites of death, disaster, and atrocity. Lennon and Foley hold that the way in which the tourism industry packages such sites is an expression, in part, of the circumstances of late modernity, in which death, disaster, and atrocity have become defining characteristics of the contemporary world. Lennon and Foley further argue that dark tourism is as much a product of the forces of modernity as the events to which tourists are drawn, and that it is thus an intrinsic aspect of the human experience in present-day society. Most frequently, visits to sites connected with death, such as battlefields, concentration or extermination camps, museums, jails, major crime scenes and places of pilgrimage show a developing fascination with the destructive tendencies of humanity as manifested in the last two centuries of human history, culminating in the vast number of genocides of the twentieth century.

Dayton Agreement. Also known as the Dayton Accords or the Dayton Settlement. The interim peace agreement, signed on November 21, 1995, brought to an end the genocidal violence in the war for control of Bosnia by Serbs, Croats, and Bosnian Muslims (or *Bosniaks*) that had been taking place since April 1992. The settlement took its name from the location of the signing, at the Wright-Patterson Air Force Base near Dayton, Ohio. As a summit meeting involving heads of states and other leading figures, the peace conference was officially hosted by the president of the United States, William Jefferson Clinton (b. 1946), though it was chaired by Clinton's principal Balkans negotiator, Richard Holbrooke (b. 1941). The major negotiators were Serbian president Slobodan Milosevic (1941–2006), Croatian president Franjo Tudjman (1922–1999), and Bosnian president Alija Izetbegovic (1925–2003). Other participants included senior military figures from the United States, the United Kingdom, France, and Germany. The main features of the Dayton Agreement were (1) to determine the political divisions of Bosnia-Herzegovina and establish secure and guaranteed internal and external borders; (2) to mandate a NATO-led armed force, codenamed IFOR (Implementation Force), for the purpose of overseeing and fulfilling the military elements of the disengagement process; and (3) to have the Agreement ratified in a general peace conference, at a later time and place to be determined. The subsequent full and final agreement took place in Paris, on December 14, 1995. This was again signed by Milosevic, Tudjman and Izetbegovic, but not they alone; in a pledge to safeguard the peace thus created, the Paris Protocol was also signed by Clinton, British prime minister John Major (b. 1943), French president Jacques Chirac (b. 1932), German chancellor Helmut Kohl (b. 1930), and Russian prime minister Viktor Chernomyrdin (b. 1938). A major criticism of the Dayton Agreement, even though it brought hostilities to an end, was that it rewarded Serb aggression and ethnic cleansing by allowing the ethnic Serb entity in Bosnia-Herzegovina, known as *Republika Srpska*, to retain formerly Muslim or Croat areas that had been taken forcibly during the war, and from which the previously existing population had been deported or killed.

Death Camps (German, *Vernichtungslager*). Six camps established by the Nazis in Poland for the express purpose of the extermination/annihilation of the Jews. The six camps were Treblinka, Sobibor, Belzec, Chelmno, Auschwitz-Birkenau, and Majdanek. The combined death toll of Jews in all the camps was approximately 3.5 million men, women, and children. Jews and others (e.g., Jehovah's Witnesses, Russian prisoners of war, homosexuals, Sinti, and Roma) were gassed, worked to death, shot, starved, tortured, beaten to death, poisoned, and subjected to gruesome medical experiments of dubious scientific value. Those who were to be gassed were processed along an "assembly line of death." The chambers themselves, the largest of which at Auschwitz could hold upwards of one thousand persons, were hermetically sealed. Once the victims were inside, Zyklon B crystals were poured down chutes and, upon contact with the air, became prussic acid. The victims, in their hunger for one more moment of life, clawed at each other, and, as a result of the abject fear and effects of the poison, urinated and defecated on themselves. Death usually resulted in under thirty minutes, after which the doors were opened by Jews (referred to as *Sonderkommandos* or "special commandos") who were forced to extract the bodies and examine them for gold and other valuables, either hidden in various bodily orifices (anal and/or vaginal) or gold teeth. Any riches located on them were immediately extracted by the Jewish workers. The bodies were then carried to the crematoria for incineration, with the resultant ash either packaged as fertilizer for Germany's agricultural industry, or otherwise disposed. In the last days of World War II the assembly lines broke down, and Allied liberators found the dead on the disembarking platforms, the clothing piled high and unsorted, the gas chambers with victims still inside, and the crematoria with the remains of the dead not yet fully reduced to ashes.

Death Squads. "Death squads" refers to the "security forces" of various governments whose express purpose—in the 1970s, 1980s, 1990s, and early 2000s—was to summarily execute "political enemies." Tens of thousands of people (those suspected of opposing the government, those—such as journalists, church activists, trade unionists, and political activists—calling for reform by the government, and unarmed peasant farmers residing in places where the government was carrying out counter insurgency campaigns) were killed. In the 1970s and 1980s such death squads existed in numerous areas across the globe, particularly in countries located in Central America, South America, Asia, and Africa. In the 1990s and early 2000s such squads have been most prominent in certain countries in Africa, and parts of Asia.

Death Squads in Rwanda. In Kinyarwarda (the language of Rwanda), the *Interahamwe*, or "those who stand together," were the largest militia group organized by the Hutu extremists, and are believed to have been primarily responsible for the majority of genocidal deaths occurring in that country in 1994. With the retaking of the capital Kigali by the Rwandan Patriotic Front (RPF), many *Interahamwe* fled to neighboring Zaire (Democratic Republic of Congo), Uganda, and Burundi, and, because they have never been officially disbanded as such, continue to stage raids back in Rwanda and other locales. Their exact numbers, military strength, and political status remain difficult to determine.

Declaration. a nonbinding international document that suggests the individual and collective intention of states to adhere to and honor the ideals delineated in such a joint promise/statement.

Declaration on Principles of International Law Concerning Friendly Relations and Co-operation (1970). Those who argue that no legal right exists for carrying out unilateral humanitarian intervention point, in part, to the 1970 Declaration on Principles of International Law Concerning Friendly Relations and Co-operation that states that "no State or group of states has the right to intervene, directly or indirectly, for any reason whatever, in the internal or external affairs of any other State." Such individuals and groups also sight the 1965 Declaration on the Inadmissibility of Intervention, which basically declares that there are no legal grounds—or "reason(s) whatever"—for intervention, and the 1987 Declaration on the Enhancement of the International Relations, which states that "no consideration of whatever nature may be invoked to warrant resorting to the threat or use of force in violation of the Charter."

Declaration on the Enhancement of the International Relations (1987). Those who argue that no legal right exists for carrying out unilateral humanitarian intervention often point, in part, to the 1987 Declaration on the Enhancement of the International Relations, which states that "no consideration of whatever nature may be invoked to warrant resorting to the threat or use of force in violation of the Charter." These same individuals and groups also point to the 1965 Declaration on the Inadmissibility of Intervention, which basically declares that there are no legal grounds—or "reason(s) whatever"—for intervention, and the 1970 Declaration on Principles of International Law Concerning Friendly Relations and Co-operation, which confirms that "no State or group of states has the right to intervene, directly or indirectly, for any reason whatever, in the internal or external affairs of any other State."

Declaration on the Inadmissibility of Intervention (1965). Those who argue that no legal right exists for carrying out unilateral humanitarian intervention frequently point to the 1965 Declaration on the Inadmissibility of Intervention, which basically declares that there are no legal grounds—or "reason(s) whatsoever"—for intervention. Such individuals and groups also sight the 1970 Declaration on Principles of International Law Concerning Friendly Relations and Co-operation, which confirms that "no State or group of states has the right to intervene, directly or indirectly, for any reason whatever, in the internal or external affairs of any other State," and the 1987 Declaration on the Enhancement of the International Relations, which states that "no consideration of whatever nature may be invoked to warrant resorting to the threat or use of force in violation of the Charter."

Definition of Genocide, Chalk and Jonassohn's. Historian Frank Chalk (n.d.) and sociologist Curt Jonassohn (b. 1929) define genocide in the following way: "Genocide is a form of one-sided mass killing in which a state or other authority intends to destroy a group, as that group and membership in it are defined by the perpetrators" (cited in Charny, 1988, p. 23).

Definition of Genocide, Charny's. Psychologist and genocide scholar Israel W. Charny (b. 1931) proposed in the 1980s what he deemed a "humanistic" definition of genocide that is more inclusive than most, if not all, other definitions of genocide, and thus, less exclusive: "The wanton murder of human beings on the basis of any identity whatsoever they share—national, ethnic, racial, religious, political, geographical, ideological." In providing a rationale for his definition, Charny asserted that "I reject out of hand that there can ever be any identity process that in itself will justify the murder of men, women, and children 'because' they are 'anti' some 'ism' or because their physical characteristics are high- or low-cheekboned, short- or long-eared" (Charny, 1988, p. 4).

Definition of Genocide, Dadrian's. In 1975, Vahakn Dadrian (b. 1926), an expert on the Ottoman-Turk perpetration of genocide against the Armenians (1915–1923), created the following definition of genocide: "Genocide is the successful attempt by a dominant group, vested with formal authority and/or with preponderant access to the overall resources of power, to reduce by coercion or lethal violence the number of a minority group whose ultimate extermination is held desirable and useful and whose respective vulnerability is a major factor in contributing to the decision for genocide."

Definition of Genocide, Fein's. Sociologist and genocide scholar Helen Fein (b. 1934) developed what she referred to as "a new sociological definition" of genocide: "Genocide is sustained purposeful action by a perpetrator to physically destroy a collectivity directly or indirectly, through interdiction of the biological and social reproduction of group members, sustained regardless of the surrender or lack of threat offered by the victim" (Fein, 1990, p. 24).

Definition of Genocide, Horowitz's. Sociologist Irving Louis Horowitz (b. 1929) defines *genocide* as "a structural and systematic destruction of innocent people by a state bureaucratic apparatus" (Horowitz, 1989, p. 17).

Definition of Genocide, Lemkin's. Raphael Lemkin (1900–1950), the Polish international jurist who coined the term *genocide*, defined genocide in the following way:

> Genocide does not necessarily mean the immediate destruction of a nation, except when accomplished by mass killings of all members of a nation. It is intended rather to signify a coordinated plan of different actions aiming at the destruction of essential foundations of the life of national groups, with the aim of the annihilation of the groups themselves. . . . [It may result in] the disintegration of the political and social institutions of culture, language, national feelings, religion, and the economic existence of national groups, and the destruction of the personal security, liberty, health, dignity, and even the lives of the individuals belonging to such groups (Lemkin, 1944, p. 79).

Definition of Genocide Used in the UN Convention on the Prevention and Punishment of the Crime of Genocide (UNCG). The term *genocide* was coined in 1944 by Raphael Lemkin (1900–1959), a Polish Jewish émigré and noted jurist, who taught law at Yale and Duke universities. To form the new term, Lemkin combined the Greek *genos* (race, tribe) and *cide* (killing). On December 9, 1948, after lengthy and heated debate and ample compromise, the United Nations adopted the UN Convention on the Prevention and Punishment of the Crime of Genocide (UNCG) and in doing so defined genocide in the following manner:

> In the present Convention, genocide means any of the following acts committed with intent to destroy, in whole or in part, a national, ethnical, racial or religious group, as such: (a) Killing members of the group; (b) Causing serious bodily or mental harm to members of the group; (c) Deliberately inflicting on the group conditions of life calculated to bring about its physical destruction in whole or in part; (d) Imposing measures intended to prevent births within the group; (e) Forcibly transferring children of the group to another group.

Degrees of Genocide. Ward Churchill (b. 1947), Professor of American Indian Studies with the Department of Ethnic Studies at the University of Colorado at Boulder, and author of *A Little Matter of Genocide: Holocaust and Denial in the Americas 1492 to the Present*, developed a schema in which he suggested that genocide be broken down into various "degrees," just as murder is broken into first, second and third degrees. The degrees of genocide that he proposed are as follows:

> (a) "*Genocide in the First Degree*, which consists of instances in which evidence of premeditated intent to commit genocide is present; (b) *Genocide in the Second Degree*, which consists of instances in which evidence of premeditation is absent, but in which it can be reasonably argued that the perpetrators(s) acted with reckless disregard for the probability that genocide would result from their actions; (c) *Genocide in the Third Degree*, which consists of instances in which genocide derives, however unintentionally, from other violations of international law engaged in by the perpetrators; and (d) *Genocide in the Fourth Degree*, which consists of instances in which neither evidence of premeditation nor other criminal behavior is present,

but in which the perpetrators(s) acted with depraved indifference to the possibility that genocide would result from their actions and therefore to effect adequate safeguard to prevent it. (italics in the original; Churchill, 1998, pp. 434–35)

Degrelle, Leon (1906–1994). A Belgian fascist leader during the 1930s and 1940s, in 1930 Leon Degrelle founded a Walloon political party, officially called *Christus Rex* (Christ the King), but known informally as the *Parti Rexiste*, or Rexist Party. Degrelle, who came from a devout Catholic family, was a strong advocate of law, order, monarchy, and racial purity. An antisemite, he saw Jews as a negative force in society, not capable of truly becoming members of a nation owing to their internationalist outlook and "cosmopolitanism." He was, in addition, passionately anticommunist, antisocialist, and antibourgeois; he modeled his movement on that of Benito Mussolini (1883–1945), and carried himself in open emulation of his hero, Adolf Hitler (1889–1945)—who is alleged to have commented, when referring to Degrelle, "If I was ever to have had a son, I would wish for him to be like you." As the party of fascist purity, Degrelle took the Rexist Party to the polls in February 1937, only to lose after all other political parties combined to defeat it. Only the onset of World War II, and the defeat of Belgium in May 1940, enabled Degrelle to attain political influence. In 1941 he established a regiment of Walloon volunteers for the German army (*Wehrmacht*), but this unit was transferred to the Waffen-SS (the "armed SS"), and sent to the Eastern Front to fight against the Soviet Union. Degrelle was promoted to the rank of SS-*Obersturmbannführer* (a rank approximating lieutenant colonel), and received a number of military decorations, including the *Ritterkreuz*, or Knight's Cross. His unit, however, was ground to pieces on the Eastern Front, with only three of the original contingent of 850 still alive by the end of the war. In 1945 Degrelle fled to Denmark, then Norway, and finally to the Falangist Spain of General Francisco Franco (1892–1975), which gave him refuge for the rest of his life. Belgium tried him in absentia, found him guilty of treason, and sentenced him to death by firing squad. Successive Spanish governments, even after Franco, refused to extradite Degrelle, and he remained a free man. In a somewhat luxurious exile, he wrote and published actively, speaking out against communism and the Jews, and engaging in Holocaust denial (for which he was tried in a civil suit by a Holocaust survivor, and found guilty of bringing offence to the memory of the victims by a Spanish court). He died of a heart attack in Malaga in 1994, the last major Nazi-era leader from any of the European countries.

Dehumanization. In its most basic form, dehumanization—a psycho-social process—aims at redefining public perceptions of the person in question in such a way that society in general will no longer consider that person to be deserving of the same degree of decency, sympathy, empathy, or sensitivity given other human beings. In other words, the public identity of that person is transformed into something looked upon as lower in the local scheme of social types. The identity transformation process that takes place as a result of dehumanization can take many forms, and has been practiced in numerous settings. In the Nazi concentration camps between 1933 and 1945, for example, the SS systematically applied tactics of personal terror toward their prisoners, ritually degrading them until they no longer felt the dignity required to resist the Nazis' brutal treatment. The nadir of a prisoner's degradation came when he or she ceased resisting it, and allowed its effects to swamp him or her. At that moment it could be said that a person's self-image had literally become dehumanized. Accounts abound of how victims in genocidal environments see themselves no longer as human beings, but as "animals" or "objects."

Assertions and slurs by one group against another are often used to suggest "the other" is less than human. This can be, and often is, accomplished in several ways: the use of demeaning language that suggests "the other" constitutes something dangerously unhealthy (e.g., a virus, diseased microbes, a parasite, a cancer), an animal (e.g., baboons, rats, dogs) and/or insects (e.g., leeches, cockroaches). For example, during the nineteenth century, Native Americans were frequently referred to as "savages," heathens, and infidels by white citizens of the United States. During the Holocaust years (1933–1945), the Nazis frequently referred to Jews as germs, bacilli, cancer, vermin, parasites, and lice. Further, in the Nazi death camps the prisoners were referred to as so many *stücke* ("pieces"), rather than as human beings. (The Nazis, of course, went far beyond referring to Jews by negative names or names with negative connotations. They also systematically classified, collected, transported Jews as if they were cattle, exploited them for purpose of labor, conducted horrific experiments on them as if they were without feelings, killed them in an industrial manner, burned them, and used their remains as fertilizer.) During the 1994 Rwandan genocide, the Hutu commonly referred to the Tutsi as *Inyenzi* or cockroaches. During the genocide in Darfur, Sudan (2003 to present [late 2007]), the black Africans of Darfur have been referred to as "dogs" and "slave dogs." In that region of the world dogs are seen as some of the lowliest creatures on earth and the term "slave" is the worst slur that can be used against another human being.

When one is considered as less than human and/or as dangerous to humanity, then, ostensibly, it is easier to mistreat, abuse, and exterminate "the other." Indeed, from the perpetrators' perspective the latter portrays the target/victim group as "not worthy of living." This can be further reinforced by reference to victims no longer having names, but numbers (as happened in Auschwitz), or of having other trappings of their individual humanity taken away.

The process of dehumanization in a genocidal environment is not restricted only to the victims; both the perpetrators and the general public (where the two are not the same) will, in most cases, undergo some sort of psychological or behavioral modification regarding their image of the targeted population.

Dehumanization, then, is generally a necessary process in the preparation of a population that is going to commit genocide, as a person is transformed from being seen as equal in their humanity to one who is less than human. The process does not of itself cause genocide, but is certainly one of a number of steps on the road to it.

Deir ez Zor. Today the town of Deir ez Zor (population 133,000), located along the Euphrates River, is the capital of the Dayr az Zawr governorate in eastern Syria. The town was originally established by the Ottoman Empire in 1867. During the period of the Armenian genocide (1915–1923), tens of thousands of Armenians forced from their homes and villages were herded into the vast, burning desolation of Deir ez Zor. As they were forced into this wasteland, they were beaten, raped, and killed. Still others were herded into roughshod camps where they were starved to death, brutalized, and murdered. When they attempted to drink from the Euphrates they were slain. Still others jumped to their deaths as they sought freedom from the brutality meted out by Ottoman troops, Kurdish brigands, and others. It was also in the area of Deir ez Zor that certain groups of Bedouin chieftains and their tribal members reached out to the forlorn Armenian remnant and offered them water, food, shelter, and protection from their abusers. To this day, bones of the Armenian victims can be found in the desert sands of Deir ez Zor. And to this day, the relatives of those Bedouins who reached out to help the Armenians are recognized for their altruism each year by the Armenian community of Syria, Lebanon, and those from further afield during the commemoration of the Armenian genocide.

Dekulakization. Applied to independent, landowning peasants (who were commonly referred to as kulaks) by the Bolsheviks, dekulakization referred to the stripping of economic power from such peasants. From the start of the Bolshevik regime in October–November 1917, the government of Vladimir Ilyich Lenin (1870–1924) signaled its intention to destroy the kulaks as a class and to replace their independent status with a collectivized, communist structure. Kulak populations in several parts of central Russia were reduced substantially in the years that followed, but it was only after December 1927 that a wholesale state program of kulak destruction was launched by Lenin's successor, Josef Stalin (1879–1953). In the drive to collectivize agriculture, the independence of agricultural producers—even of smallholders who made a modest profit from their harvests—was to be totally destroyed. The systematic nature of this destruction was massive. The kulaks were targeted in two major campaigns: one in 1930, the other in 1931. These saw the rounding up of about 1.8 million kulaks, and, by the end of 1933 another four hundred thousand had been apprehended. The key aspect of the communist strategy was the resettlement of the kulaks; by removing them from the land and placing them on communal farms at a substantial distance from their original districts, a transformation could be effected both in agricultural practices and demography. Privation, cold, disease, and violent treatment by the communists during these forced population transfers produced a death toll in the hundreds of thousands, but at no time did this cause the government to waver from their dekulakization program, even when it caused a massive disruption in agricultural production. Perhaps up to 6 million peasants starved to death due to Stalin's forced collectivization campaigns. By the middle of the 1930s the full collectivization of agriculture had taken place throughout the Soviet Union, and the rural peasantry was no longer identifiable in the form it had been just two decades earlier.

Del Ponte, Carla (b. 1947). An international criminal lawyer, best known for her role as chief prosecutor for the International Criminal Tribunal for the Former Yugoslavia (ICTY) and the International Criminal Tribunal for Rwanda (ICTR). Born in Lugano, Switzerland, Del Ponte studied law in Bern, Geneva, and the United Kingdom. In 1981 she was appointed as a public prosecutor in Lugano, prosecuting cases of fraud, drug trafficking, arms dealing, terrorism, and espionage. She also pursued, and thus antagonized, the Italian mafia, which attempted to assassinate her in 1992. In 1994 Del Ponte became attorney general for Switzerland.

In 1999, Del Ponte was appointed chief prosecutor at the ICTY in The Hague, and the ICTR in Arusha, replacing Louise Arbour (b. 1947). In 2003 she was relieved of her responsibility as prosecutor for the ICTR, in order to focus exclusively on prosecutions involving the former Yugoslavia. Renowned for her intensity in pursuing justice, she does not favor one side or the other when bringing cases to the ICTY; it matters not whether an alleged criminal is Serb, Croatian, Bosnian, or Kosovar Albanian. (Because of her dogged determination and concern with the victims of such genocides and other illegal criminal activities, her detractors have labeled her "the whore," "the new Gestapo," "the unguided missile," and "the personification of stubbornness.") That said, the majority of those against whom a case has been brought or is pending have been Serbs. Consequently, she has been condemned by many Serbs for having transformed the ICTY into an anti-Serb tribunal. Although Del Ponte has successfully prosecuted a number of high-profile cases at the ICTY, her three most important actions to date have not borne results. One of them, against former president Slobodan Milosevic (1941–2006), will never be resolved—while his trial was proceeding he died in custody before a determination of his guilt or innocence could be made. The other two cases—against Radovan Karadzic (b. 1945) and Ratko Mladic (b. 1942)—cannot currently proceed due to the fact that they have not yet been apprehended, though Del Ponte has been steadily building strong cases against both men in absentia. Carla Del Ponte's standing at the ICTY has been an important one, sending a clear message to the perpetrators of grave human rights abuses that they will not be safe from prosecution during her term as chief prosecutor.

Democide. A concept coined by U.S. political scientist Rudolph J. Rummel (b. 1932) to designate the murder of any person, or group of people, by a government. This can include genocide, mass murder, or what Rummel refers to as "politicide," that is, government-sponsored killings for political reasons. Rummel also considers any deaths caused through intentional governmental neglect or disregard for the lives of its citizens, with some kind of ultimate destructive objective in mind, as a case of democide. Capital punishment, civilian deaths in a war zone, and military deaths in combat are, though, excluded from his definition of democide.

As for mass killing Rummel has two kinds in mind. The first is the product of nuclear warfare, which entirely eliminates the distinction between combatant and civilian by the scope of the destructive violence it unleashes. The same can be said of the potential in chemical and biological weaponry. Any future war resorting to these weapons would claim untold millions of casualties. In this scenario democide has the potential of thoroughly disrupting urban and rural life to the point that the survivors would be left with no basic society and culture to salvage. It is destruction well beyond that wreaked by genocide or other forms of political, social and cultural devastation.

A second application of the term *democide* characterizes the massive collective destruction that took place throughout the twentieth century. Between 1900 and 2000 there was a quantum increase in what Rummel refers to as megadeaths by human hands. Colonial wars, World War I and World War II, civil wars, and revolutions collectively killed hundreds of millions, as if the human race were at war with itself. Although these events all had genocidal attributes they need not, in every situation, be considered genocide per se, but are more accurately transgenocidal, that is, something more than genocide. The 1994 Rwanda genocide had certain aspects of this phenomenon: not only were Tutsi targeted for annihilation, but so were moderate Hutu who belonged to the political opposition. Hence, democide considers the idea of "genocide plus"—genocide with an additional dimension to mass killing.

Democide, in Rummel's view, is far less likely to occur in democratic states than in those that are authoritarian, totalitarian, or absolute. He argues strongly that political power and democide are intimately connected: the more absolute a regime, the greater its propensity for democide. Thus, he concludes that truly democratic regimes should be strongly encouraged and supported if democide is to be reduced (and, hopefully, eradicated).

Rummel's work on democide and its consequences are spelled out in a series of books he wrote, including *Lethal Politics: Soviet Genocides and Mass Murders 1917–1987; China's*

Bloody Century: Genocide and Mass Murder since 1900; Democide: Nazi Genocide and Mass Murder; Death by Government: Genocide and Mass Murder in the Twentieth Century; Statistics of Democide; and *Power Kills.*

Democracies. Such entities guarantee both civil and political rights for all citizens, provide for constitutional limitations on the power of the executive branch of government, have two or more legitimate and active parties that compete for influence in governmental affairs, and transfer governmental power between parties via constitutionally indicated means.

Democracy and Genocide. The notion of democracy as an effective force for deterring the emergence of genocidal situations has been most thoroughly developed by U.S. political scientist Rudolph J. Rummel (b. 1932). Rummel's hypothesis, cultivated over nearly four decades of research, is summarized in five essential points: (1) well-established democracies do not make war on, and rarely commit lesser violence against, each other; (2) the more two nations are democratic, the less likely it will be that war or lesser violence will occur between them; (3) the more democratic a nation, the less severe its overall foreign violence; (4) the more democratic a nation, the less likely it will have domestic collective violence; and (5) the more democratic a nation, the less will be its democide (murders committed by official agencies when acting under state instructions).

By confining his analysis to "well-established democracies," Rummel was able to dismiss regimes which are either: (a) simply those which refer to themselves as democracies by name, but are in fact dictatorships (e.g., the so-called communist "People's Democracies" of the Cold War era); or (b) polities that are yet in the process of becoming democratic, in which sectional aggression and violence still plays a part in the public culture of the state. The idea of "democratic peace," therefore, feeds directly into concepts concerning genocide prevention; put succinctly, the more democracies exist, the less likely both war and genocide are to occur.

Attractive as this theory is—and for many scholars, it is quite convincing—it has its detractors. Two basic arguments are posited by critics of the "democratic peace notion." The first is that democracies such as the United States, Canada, Australia, and others are founded on genocidal dispossession of indigenous populations. The second is that so-called first world nations, such as those previously mentioned (as well as many European states), have engaged (and still engage) in genocidal practices against other, less-developed nations. Two of the most notable critics along these lines are U.S. professor of linguistics Noam Chomsky (b. 1928) and British-based Australian journalist John Pilger (b. 1939), among many others, principally from the political left. What such critics miss, however, is the fact that the relationship in such instances is not between two democratic states, as the "democratic peace" idea requires in order to be effective. That said, as of the late 1990s and early 2000s, critics of this theory are no longer primarily from the left; others, many of whom could be deemed "moderates," have also called into question the validity of Rummel's arguments vis-à-vis the issue of democracy and genocide.

Democracy Promotion. *Democracy promotion* is a concept and term that became popular in the 1990s, as a result of U.S. efforts to link aid to failed states, and/or states emerging from authoritarian rule, with a move toward the establishment of democracy. Democracy promotion involves a combination of the following: institution building (e.g., the strengthening of judicial systems, the development of an effective legislature); the education of journalists to work in a free society; the establishment of a free press; the development and implementation of election policies and actual elections; and the involvement of nongovernmental organizations in various human rights projects germane to various facets of society.

Democratic Kampuchea. Immediately upon its take-over of Cambodia in 1975, the revolutionary communist Khmer Rouge renamed the country Democratic Kampuchea. The use of the word "democratic" was both ironic and cynical, as there was nothing democratic about the ironclad, totalitarian state that eventually became infamous for its genocidal policies and "killing fields."

Denazification. The term applied by the Allied victors (Great Britain, the United States, and the Soviet Union) to the eradication of Nazism in Germany as well as the punishment of those responsible for the implementation of National Socialism and its various agendas (e.g., waging aggressive war, and crimes against humanity).

The initial agreement regarding denazification took place between Franklin Roosevelt (USA), Winston Churchill (Great Britain), and Joseph Stalin (the Soviet Union) at a meeting in Yalta in the Crimea in February 1945, and later reaffirmed at Potsdam, Germany, in August of that same year. The Potsdam Agreement called for the removal from public office and other positions of responsibility those associated with National Socialism, though specific guidelines were not addressed at that time. Thus, each of the victorious Allies in their own zones of responsibility addressed the process differently. France, whose representatives played no significant role at either Yalta or Potsdam, was later brought into the discussion, and thus a fourth zone of occupation was created. In an attempt to standardize the process somewhat, several organizations were created, including the Allied Control Commission for Italy, the Allied Control Council, the Central Registry for War Criminals and Security Suspects, the Counter-Intelligence Corps, the Office of the Military Government of the United States, the United Nations War Crimes Commission, and the War Crimes Groups. According to the West German Government, by 1949 more than 3.5 million persons had undergone the process of denazification, including those who had been punished for their crimes. With a change in the international political climate, and the onset of the Cold War between East and West, enthusiasm for this agenda waned, as Germany herself, now a split nation (East Germany and West Germany) began its own rebuilding.

Deportations, in USSR. The communist regime in the Soviet Union of Josef Stalin (1879–1953) recognized early on that a distinctive sense of nationhood was a factor militating against the creation of a proletarian state. In the multiethnic Soviet Union, the existence of so many separate national groups posed a threat which Stalin could not ignore. As a way to constrain their aspirations, his dictatorial government introduced measures to exile entire national groups to the interior of the USSR. Deported to places vast distances from their historic homelands, disoriented and removed from familiar networks, the intention was that they would more readily be able to embrace the communist way of life, rather than one in which their (often) nascent nationalism could take hold. Accordingly, in 1937, Soviet Koreans were removed from the Far East to Kazakhstan and Uzbekistan; in 1941 and 1942 the Volga Germans and other *Volksdeutsche* (German communities living outside of Germany proper) were rounded up and sent to Kazakhstan and Siberia; in May 1942, Greeks living in the Crimea were deported to Uzbekistan; in late 1943 the Karachays and Kalmyks were sent to Siberia, Kazakhstan, and Kirghizia; and, at various times in 1944, the Chechens and Ingush, Balkars, Crimean Tartars, Meskhetian

Turks, Kurds, and Khemshils were deported to Kurdistan, Siberia, and Uzbekistan. Between 1937 and 1944 it is estimated that some 2 million people from fourteen distinct nationalities were deported because of their membership in these national groups. The conditions during and after the deportations were so bad that over four hundred thousand people (and probably more) lost their lives, which, in some cases, cut deeply into the population size of the smaller nations.

According to the 1948 United Nations Convention on the Prevention and Punishment of the Crime of Genocide, the deportations can be interpreted as a case of genocide in that the Soviet government inflicted conditions of life on the deported groups that were intended (where possible) to bring about their physical destruction in whole or in part—through harsh treatment involving murder, privation, disease, hunger, social dislocation, and exposure to the elements. The physical annihilation of individuals within the national groups was not Stalin's intention; rather, it was the destruction of the nationalities themselves that was his goal. It was only in the late 1980s and the 1990s, with the downfall of communism, that the process of repatriating many of the survivors and subsequent generations to their original homelands began to take place.

Der Stürmer (German, the Attacker). Weekly Nazi Party newspaper founded by Julius Streicher (1885–1946), the slogan of which was *Die Juden sind unser Unglück!* (The Jews are our misfortune). The focus of its content was on the Jews and their supposed "evil ways," including the murder of Jesus Christ, the ritual blood murder of innocent children, the rape of young German girls, financial thievery, and political wheeling and dealing. Written in an easily readable format, the cartoons, which accompanied the articles and were drawn by Phillip Rupprecht (n.d.), depicted stereotypic distortions of Jewish males as ugly, overweight, bloated, thick-lipped, slovenly, hairy, and sexually perverted. The Jewish women portrayed in the cartoons were not any better. In 1933 twenty-five thousand copies a week were sold; by 1938 the number had risen to five hundred thousand.

Des Pres, Terrence (1939–1987). A U.S. professor of English, Des Pres was best known for his theories on the survival of concentration camp prisoners under the Nazis and Soviets. He was born in Illinois and raised in Missouri, and, for fifteen years prior to his early death at the age of forty-eight, he held the Crawshaw Chair in English Literature at Colgate University, Hamilton, New York. In 1976, Des Pres, an author, poet, and political activist, published *The Survivor: An Anatomy of Life in the Death Camps*. He examined the question of survival from the point of view of the survivors themselves by conducting an in-depth investigation into the accounts written by former concentration camp prisoners. Until this time, analysis of prisoner behavior had largely been dominated by the writings of psychologist (and former prisoner of Buchenwald and Dachau) Bruno Bettelheim (1903–1990), and those who agreed with him. Their view was that survival in the concentration camp was essentially a random occurrence, in which the actions of prisoners counted for little. Des Pres, to the contrary, held that prisoners struggled at every turn to find ways of staying alive in the camps, despite the conditions under which they were compelled to exist. His message was one of positive affirmation of the human spirit, regardless of the degradation and violence to which the prisoners were subjected on a daily basis. The book called into question the negative arguments of Bettelheim, though most of its content, dependent as it was on the rich documentation to be found in survivor accounts, contained little direct reference to Bettelheim himself. In the years that followed, acrimony between those advocating the two positions, as personified in Des Pres and Bettelheim, dominated the discussion, but the debate breathed new life into questions about survivorship. Indeed, Des Pres was thus responsible for stimulating a major transformation in the nature of scholarship in this area, and, since the appearance of *The Survivor*, an entire literature addressing issues of survival in extremity—in which both Bettelheim and Des Pres are acknowledged—has emerged. Des Pres died suddenly in November 1987.

Desecration of the Host. In the Christian Mass (also referred to as the Eucharist, or Holy Communion), the central act of remembrance of Christ's sacrifice is the partaking of bread and wine that has been blessed, in accordance with the divine instruction issued in Matthew 26:26–28 ("do this in remembrance of me"). In Roman Catholic tradition, this consecration changes the bread and wine literally into the flesh and blood of Jesus Christ, through a process called transubstantiation. The consecrated bread (usually in the form of wafers) is commonly known as the Host (from the Old French *oiste*, derived from Latin *hostia*, a sacrificial victim). Since medieval times a false charge was often heard in Christian Europe that Jews broke into churches, stole pieces of the Host, and "tortured" the bread by sticking pins in it or stabbing it with knives. In this way, the Jews continued to kill Jesus, as Christian scripture had recorded in the story of the crucifixion (see, for example, Matthew 27:25), through the desecration of communion bread which became the living flesh of Christ. It was sometimes alleged that such bread began miraculously to "bleed" with the blood of Jesus, when stabbed by the Jews. When allegations like this were spread, violent attacks on Jewish communities would frequently take place. Often, allegations of Host desecration took place around Easter time, accompanied by blood libel accusations.

Desensitization. The psychosocial process whereby individuals are introduced gradually to the performance or acceptance of behaviors they would otherwise reject or be unaccustomed to performing. A process of desensitization can be initiated by a state authority or an individual authority figure, and involves a series of actions aimed at behavior modification. This can take place through assisting a person to confront an issue in which he or she will not usually be engaged, by exposing him or her to the least threatening elements of the issue, and building steadily toward more challenging elements—by which time the original behavior of the subject toward the issue in question will have become transformed sufficiently to ensure the subject's acceptance or compliance. Under normal circumstances, modifications to behavior brought about through the desensitization process require some measure of volunteerism on the part of the subject. In areas of genocide and other extreme behaviors, however, desensitization must take place in order for communities to become willing (or at least, acquiescent) participants in the destructive tasks demanded by their government. In a similar vein, desensitization rituals and activities are usually undertaken in the area of military training, particularly during the early transition period whereby a civilian is transformed into a soldier. In the vast majority of cases of genocide, state-driven desensitization programs take place well before the killing itself begins, so that the perpetrator population, incrementally, will be prepared to commit or permit later destruction of targeted victims.

Desk Killing. Term sometimes given to the process whereby bureaucrats administer policies of genocide that have been devised by politicians or military leaders. The most infamous desk killer was the Nazi civil servant Adolf Eichmann (1906–1962), who was given responsibility by his superior Reinhard Heydrich (1904–1942) for devising the means and coordinating the process of deporting and transporting Jews to ghettos, labor camps and, ultimately, to the Nazi death camps situated in Poland. As policy is a response to a perceived administrative challenge, Eichmann threw himself into his work with enthusiasm and efficiency. He saw himself as an effective administrator, dealing with a major policy issue that had been entrusted for resolution to his care. That it involved the murder of millions of people was of little concern; the important thing for him, in his bureaucratic capacity, was to deal with the task assigned to him. Desk killers have typically addressed their tasks in a vein similar to Eichmann, regardless of their national or ideological background. They have been detached, deliberate, speedy, and highly focused on meeting their objectives, without succumbing to the temptation of human morality that might deflect their attention. It is because of their detachment that desk killers often fail to see the criminal nature of their work—but it is that work that facilitates modern genocide—the more so in highly developed states. In fact, it could be said that the more modern a society, the greater the reliance on desk killers in planning and carrying out policies of genocide.

Despotic Genocide. Despotic genocide, a category coined by sociologist and genocide scholar Helen Fein (b. 1934), constitutes a situation where the perpetrators annihilate those groups it considers to be opposed to its power and in opposition to its policies and goals. The Soviet Union's genocide of its people falls under this category (Fein, 1990, p. 86).

Despotism. A style of government in which an individual leader or small political clique rules with unlimited power over the whole population, who are reduced to little more than personal possessions, vassals, or slaves. Traditionally, despots held royal status, and thus often passed their authority from one generation to the next; royal despots were therefore an accepted part of Western tradition right down to the dawn of the democratic age at the end of the eighteenth century. Given the onset and advance of democracy after this, the arbitrary nature of despotic rule, particularly as it was understood to have occurred in non-Western societies, came to be associated with tyranny, or the cruel exercise of absolute rule. In such manner, some early Asian despots—for example, Genghis Khan (c. 1167–1227) and Amir Timur, or Tamerlane (1336–1405)—came to be recognized as models of brutal, bloodthirsty, and tyrannical despots.

Destruction Process of the Jews by the Nazis. In *The Destruction of the European Jews*, historian Raul Hilberg (b. 1926) argues that while the destruction process of the Jews may seem as if it was monolithic and/or impenetrable, it, in fact, "unfolded in a definite pattern. . . . The steps of the destruction process were introduced in the following order: At first, the concept of Jew was defined; then the expropriatory operations were inaugurated; third, the Jews were concentrated in ghettos; finally, the decision was made to annihilate European Jewry" (Hilberg, 1985, p. 53).

Developmental Genocide. Developmental genocide constitutes a situation in which the perpetrators push indigenous people off their land and/or systematically kill the members of the group for purposes of colonization or extraction of riches (e.g., wood, minerals, oils) from the land.

Diary of Anne Frank. Along with Elie Wiesel's (b. 1928) *Night*, the *Diary of Anne Frank* is the most internationally well-known and well-received book, addressing the reality of the Holocaust (or, Shoah) from the viewpoint of a young person's trauma. Born in 1929 in Germany, Anne Frank and her family—mother, father, and sister—went into hiding in a "Secret Annex" in a factory in Amsterdam, Holland, to escape the Nazis. A talented writer, the years encompassed by her diary were 1942–1944, when she was ages thirteen to fifteen. In the diary, she records not only her thoughts, dreams, aspirations, and growing awareness of her own sexuality but also details of life in hiding, for this Jewish family and the others who would join them, along with the daily tensions among them. Though befriended by non-Jews, she, her family, and the other inhabitants were betrayed by a Dutch policeman and transported to Bergen-Belsen, where she died of typhus three months shy of her sixteenth birthday in 1945. The diary itself was retrieved after the war by her father, Otto Frank (1889–1980), the only member of the family to survive. The diary was edited by him, and subsequently published in numerous languages beginning in 1952. In the United States it was turned into a stage version, originally by Meyer Levin (1905–1981), and later into a movie starring Susan Strasberg (1938–1999), daughter of famed director Lee Strassberg (1901–1982); both versions provoked controversy, particularly over the universalization of her experiences versus the parochiality of her Jewish identity.

The *Diary* has become a standard in both middle school and high school language arts curricula in many nations around the globe. In the Netherlands itself, the *Diary* remains akin to a "book above reproach" (though a critical edition of the original manuscript was published there), and Anne herself has become something of an icon.

International Holocaust deniers continue to attack the authenticity of the diary, but to no avail. Objectively speaking, while acknowledging both its merit and popularity, the *Diary of Anne Frank* must not be equated with the whole of the Holocaust; it is a window of insight into one small part of the spectrum of the victims' experiences, specifically, those who went into hiding but, tragically, did not survive.

Diary of Dawid Sierakowiak, The: Five Notebooks from the Lódz Ghetto. This is a remarkably detailed diary by a teenage Jew who lived, suffered, and died in the Lódz Ghetto. The diary describes the horrors faced by the ghettos' hundred thousand-plus Jews—their endless struggle to obtain food, the physical and emotional pain of watching loved ones waste away and die, and the constant threats posed by starvation, disease, deportation, and death. It also provides unique insights into the mind and life of a single individual and his family, and the torment they lived through (including the fact that his father stole bread from his loved ones in order to attempt to stanch his own hunger). This document is invaluable in that it that relates new and important information about life and death within the Lódz Ghetto, including information about the underground resistance of ghetto youths. Ultimately, Dawid Sierakowiak (1924–1943) died of tuberculosis, exhaustion and starvation, the combination of which was known as the "ghetto disease."

Dictatorship. An autocratic style of government in which a single leader or small cabal rules over a polity without restriction, or any form of redress on the part of those over whom they wield a seemingly absolute form of power. Dictatorship has a long history, and was an institutionalized office during the time of the Roman Republic (between the third and first century BCE). It has been argued in some quarters that the prototypes of the modern military dictator were England's Oliver Cromwell (1599–1658) and France's Napoleon Bonaparte (1769–1821). In modern times, dictators have characterized many of the most repressive and genocidal regimes, including, but not limited to: the governments of the Young Turks (1908–1918), Communist Russia/Union of Soviet Socialist

Republics (1918–1989), Nazi Germany (1933–1945), Fascist Italy (1922–1943), Communist China (1949 to the present), Cambodia under the Khmer Rouge (1975–1979), Rwanda under Hutu Power (1973–1994), and the Sudan (1993–currently). The dictators of these regimes were, respectively: the triumvirate of Mehemet Talaat Pasha (1874–1921), Ismail Enver Bey (1881–1922), and Ahmed Djemal Pasha (1872–1922); Vladimir Ilyich Lenin (1870–1924) and Josef Stalin (1879–1953); Adolf Hitler (1889–1945); Benito Mussolini (1883–1945); Mao Zedong (1893–1976); Pol Pot (1925–1998); Juvenal Habyarimana (1937–1994), and Omar Hasan Ahmad al-Bashir (b, 1944).

After the massive genocidal upheavals of World War II (1939–1945), dictatorial rule became common throughout Latin America, Asia, and especially postcolonial Africa (particularly since the 1960s). Such dictatorships, often located in the hands of individual military strongmen, rendered whole regions unstable, and allowed for the violent expression of radical ideologies based on ethnic, religious, and even tribal differences, with huge losses of life. The most notorious examples of such dictators have been: Milton Obote (1924–2005) of Uganda, Idi Amin (c. 1925–2003) of Uganda, Jean-Bedel Bokassa (1921–1996) of Central African Republic, Muammar al-Gaddafi (b. 1942) of Libya, Haile Mariam Mengistu (b. 1937) of Ethiopia, Robert Mugabe (b. 1924) of Zimbabwe, Charles Taylor (b. 1948) of Liberia, and the previously mentioned Omar Hasan Ahmad al-Bashir (b, 1944) of Sudan.

Dili Massacre. On November 12, 1991, a massacre took place at the Santa Cruz cemetery in Dili, East Timor. The perpetrators of the massacre were members of the much feared KOPASSUS, the Special Forces of the Indonesian military (the *Tentara Nasional Indonesia*, or TNI). The catalyst for the massacre was a funeral procession for an East Timorese student, Sebastião Gomes (1969–1991), who had been shot dead by Indonesian troops a few days earlier. Tensions were already at a flashpoint by the time of the funeral. A parliamentary delegation from Portugal had been due to arrive in East Timor to investigate allegations of human rights abuses, but when student groups supporting the resistance movement FRETILIN (*Frente Revolucionária do Timor-Leste Independente*, or "Revolutionary Front for an Independent East Timor") threatened to turn the group's arrival into a protest demonstration against Indonesian rule, the authorities grew wary and stepped up the military presence in the capital. As the funeral procession approached the Santa Cruz cemetery, some of the students took the opportunity to unfurl banners calling for independence, showing images of FRETILIN leader Jose Alexandre "Xanana" Gusmao (b. 1946). In the incendiary environment, this was the final justification the KOPASSUS forces needed to clamp down on the procession as an unauthorized political demonstration. As the procession entered the cemetery truckloads of troops appeared and shortly thereafter opened fire on the unarmed crowd. Although figures regarding the numbers killed and wounded in the ensuing violence vary depending on the source, the most commonly accepted numbers are 271 killed, 382 wounded, and a further 250 missing (those who ran away when the shooting began, or were taken into custody and never seen again). The massacre was witnessed and filmed by Western journalists, and, after being smuggled out of East Timor, broadcast around the world to the universal condemnation of Indonesia. The fact that KOPASSUS forces were at the cemetery on the day of the funeral, were heavily armed, and did not hesitate to open fire at an opportune moment, indicated the possibility that the action had been prepared in advance in order to squelch even the slightest expressions of antiintegrationist agitation. The massacre at the Santa Cruz cemetery was a clear statement of the Indonesian government's determination to continue its repression of East Timor, and to maintain its ruthless control over the territory.

Dimensions: A Journal of Holocaust Studies. Established in 1984 by the Anti-Defamation League of B'nai B'rith, *Dimensions* was the successor to *Shoah*, founded by Rabbi Isaac ("Yitz") Greenberg of the National Jewish Resource, New York. The very title of *Dimensions* indicates its focus: exploring the subject of the Holocaust from as broad and varied a perspective as possible. *Dimensions* is now published online.

Dirección de Inteligencia Nacional (DINA). Following the 1973 right-wing military coup in Chile by General Augusto Pinochet (1915–2006), DINA (Chile's National Intelligence Directorate) coordinated the "disappearances" and killings which took place in Chile between 1973 and 1979. In the months immediately following the coup, thousands of individuals were murdered, and between 1973 and 1979, hundreds—primarily political activists, trade unionists, and peasants—"disappeared" following their arrest by the security forces of the army, air force, navy, and *carabineros* (uniformed police). All of the victims were considered to be "enemies" of the regime. In August 1977 the dictatorship closed DINA and replaced it with the *Central Nacional de Informaciones* (CNI), the euphemistic name of the Chilean secret police.

Direct Responsibility. A person may be held individually and directly responsible for graves breaches of the Geneva Conventions, violations of the laws or customs of war, crimes against humanity, and genocide, if he or she plans, instigates, orders, carries out, or otherwise aids and abets in the commission of any of the aforementioned acts.

Dirty War. In certain cases where authorities carry out arbitrary arrests, torture, executions, "disappearances," and/or sporadic massacres against particular groups of people, the actions are referred to as "dirty wars." The murderers can be, and often are, a mix of regular military forces, police personnel, paramilitary/militia units, death squads and/or vigilantes. Among some of the more infamous "dirty wars" in the latter half of the twentieth century were the extrajudicial killings of suspected supporters of guerrillas in Guatemala between 1960 and the mid-1990s, the murder of dissidents in Argentina from the late 1970s through the early 1980s, and the Russian effort to put down rebellion in Chechnya from the mid-1990s to the late 1990s.

Dirty War, Argentina. Known in Spanish by its direct translation (*La Guerra Sucia*), or more colloquially *El Proceso* (the process), the "Dirty War" took place between 1976 and 1983 when Argentina experienced a period of harsh military rule. It has been estimated that between eleven thousand and fifteen thousand people were killed during this time as a result of extrajudicial killings perpetrated by the military regime. One of the most notorious of the killers was naval captain Alfredo Astiz (b. 1951), who commanded a detention center in Buenos Aires—the *Escuela Mecánica de la Armada* (Navy Mechanics' School)—from which operated a murder squad known as Task Force 3.3.2. This squad was one of several operating from the Mechanics' School; overall, the college may have been responsible for half of all those killed during the Dirty War. The murders took place because the victims were known (or suspected) to be opponents of the regime. In most instances they were arrested, tortured, and then "disappeared"—the practice of detention without trial and murder without due process giving the victims their nickname of *Los Desaparecidos* ("the disappeared ones"). Often, as documented cases show, military helicopters would take the victims far out to sea where they would simply be dropped out, never to be seen again. In response, the mothers of those who were missing formed an association called *Las Madres de Plaza de Mayo* (The Mothers of the Plaza de Mayo). Their brave action in standing up to the junta by marching in protest each week, for a period of years, drew world attention to the disappearances. The Dirty War ended in 1983 with the downfall of the junta and Argentina's return to civilian rule. Since then, Argentina has established a Truth and Reconciliation process, and brought to trial some of those responsible for human rights violations during the Dirty War.

During the trial of one Miguel Etchecolatz, a former police officer of the Bonaerense provincial police who was ultimately found guilty of crimes against humanity, the Dirty War was deemed "genocide" by the Argentine court that was trying him.

Disappearances. The concept of "disappearances" refers to the fact that arrests of victims of political repression are often concealed by government officials in order to hide their treatment of the victims. The victims are said to "disappear" because their relatives and friends are unable to ascertain where they are being held and/or what has happened to them. In certain cases, the "disappeared" have been discovered rotting in a prison, while others have been found dead. Political killings and "disappearances" are frequently related. That is, many victims of extrajudicial murder are secretly kidnapped prior to being murdered, and thus the so-called act of "disappearance" attempts to hide or conceal the murder of the victim.

Los Desaparecidos (the disappeared) became a term frequently assigned to the events in Argentina between 1976 and 1983, when between eleven thousand and fifteen thousand people were killed in what has become known as the "Dirty War" (*La Guerra Sucia*), or more colloquially, *El Proceso* (The Process). The victims were referred to as *Los Desaparecidos*, because once arrested, they usually vanished without a trace, murdered by officers of the ruling military.

Discrimination. The act of making a distinction between individuals and/or groups based on criteria other than qualifications or achievements (that is, based on ethnic identity, gender, age, race, religion, nationality, disability, intelligence, political, or sexual orientation versus educational degrees or positions held), and, in turn, using such distinctions to prohibit such persons or indi viduals from realizing their maximum potential physically, intellectually, educationally, socially, or economically. Racism and anti-semitism are, perhaps, the two most well-known forms of discrimination, each with a long history of practice. Education at a very young age is considered to be a primary tool to successfully combat discrimination. Ultimately, however, countering discrimination in all arenas is most successful when it is backed up by the force of legislation and law which prohibit such practices, and, where appropriate, punishments include economic or other sanctions.

Discrimination, Protection from Under International Law. In addition to the "Universal Declaration of Human Rights" (1948), the United Nations has adopted two conventions and one additional declaration designed to reverse centuries of international discrimination against peoples. In 1960 the UN adopted the Convention against Discrimination in Education, entered into force in 1962, affirming that every person has the right to an education, and strongly urging its member states to correct whatever educational deficiencies exist in their educational systems at all levels. In 1979 it also adopted the Convention on the Elimination of All Forms of Discrimination against

Women, which targeted political, economic, social, cultural, and civil discrimination, while also recognizing the unique status of women as child bearers and their consequent health-care needs, as well as their vulnerability to the crime of rape. In 1981 the United Nations proclaimed the Declaration on the Elimination of All Forms of Intolerance and of Discrimination Based on Religion or Belief. Declarations, of course, do not have the force of law with the consequence of punishment. Such conventions, no matter how noble, do not contain within themselves the means of redressing violations, thus leaving all four statements appropriate to a world-deliberative body without the teeth necessary for their implementation.

Disease and Genocide. When scholars speak of disease relative to genocide, they most commonly are referring to lethal diseases that have wrought significant harm to the population size or future size of a group. The great epidemics of history, such as smallpox, cholera, tuberculosis, influenza, leprosy, measles, and bubonic plague were frequently visited upon whole societies as highly infectious viral outbreaks for which there was no immediate cure, and in which hundreds of thousands, and even millions, died. Where the study of genocide is concerned, the most important issue relative to disease is how and to what degree these diseases are, or were, introduced into a population by a perpetrator with the intention of destroying that population. No global conclusions can be drawn regarding this issue, as circumstances have varied greatly throughout the world over the last six or seven centuries. In some situations there is no doubt that viral bacteria were released deliberately into a group with the intention of wiping them out. The vast majority of those who have died over the period in question, however, succumbed due to their vulnerability to the microbes that accompanied encroaching groups, especially immigrants from distant lands involved in imperialist or colonialist ventures. In North America (what is now Mexico and the United States), Australasia, and the Pacific, for instance, local populations from the sixteenth century onward had never before experienced European and Asian diseases, which were brought on ships arriving from Spain, France, Britain, Portugal, and elsewhere. Often, these diseases had wiped out large sections of local populations well before any of those from the encroaching nations had even begun their engagement with the native inhabitants. It is incumbent on all those who comment on this issue to be extremely careful in their use of language when considering it. There is certainly a relationship between disease and genocide, but how far that extends is a matter that can never be taken for granted, and must always be dealt with cautiously.

"Dispersion." A euphemism employed in Queensland (Australia) during the mid- to late nineteenth century, covering a policy of shooting at Aborigines in the rural regions during the colonial settlement of the land with the intention of killing them. The euphemism allowed for the prospect of shooting in the direction of Aborigines so that they might take fright and run away; but, in reality, large numbers of Aborigines were killed deliberately. For the most part, "dispersals" were undertaken by troopers of the Queensland Native Mounted Police, a force comprised of Aborigines recruited from various parts of the colony and commanded by white officers. The policy of "dispersal" came under the spotlight in 1861, when a government Select Committee looked into the matter. It was openly acknowledged that "dispersing" equated with shooting at the Aborigines, and that deaths were frequently caused through indiscriminate hunting down of whole groups of Aborigines without any recognition of individual difference between groups—or even within groups. In testimony offered at the Select Committee, Lieutenant Frederick

Wheeler (d. 1886) stated that "I gave strict orders not to shoot any gins [i.e., Aboriginal women]. It is only sometimes, when it is dark, that a gin is mistaken for a black fellow." Further, Wheeler testified that it was a general order that "wherever there are large assemblages of blacks, it is the duty of an officer to disperse them." It was held that there was "no other way" to remove Aborigines from the path of European settlement than by shooting at them. As with many officers, Wheeler at all times acted "on my own discretion, and on my own responsibility," though this had its negative side—in 1876 he was finally charged with the murder of a ten-year-old Aboriginal boy, was granted bail, and fled the country. Wheeler's case is a good example of how the policy of "dispersal" worked in Queensland, and it is a testament to the "efficiency" of the policy that it was still employed as a strategy carried out by the Native Police as late as 1897. By the end of the process thousands had been gunned down and Queensland had been opened up for white pastoral settlement.

Displaced Persons. *See* Internally Displaced Persons; *also see* Refugees.

Distributive Justice. The concept of distributive justice is based around essential principles that call upon the state to ensure that material goods are allocated fairly across society, relative to demand. Such principles vary, dependent upon indices such as: the type of goods subject to distribution, the socioeconomic nature of those who are receiving the distribution, and the basis upon which the distribution takes place. Insofar as such distribution specifies how the economic productivity of a society is spread, a statement is being made about the values that underpin that society. It is also a means whereby dissatisfaction from deprived sectors can be alleviated, if not deflected altogether. Distributive justice is based upon notions of fairness. Executed effectively, it can make for a harmonious society. Among those who have addressed issues pertaining to distributive justice, the most prominent authors—coming from different perspectives on the issue—are John Rawls (b. 1921), who considers that by "goods" we can include a wide variety of both material and nonmaterial components, and Robert Nozick (1938–2002), who argued that through mixing one's labors with those of others, one can help to create a world of shared outcomes. In this, he was building on the earlier theory of the seventeenth century English philosopher John Locke (1632–1704). In short, distributive justice is a philosophical theory focused on the easing of poverty—and thus on one of the factors, if not ameliorated, that can lead to the emergence of communal tension, violence, and social sectionalism.

Djemal, Ahmed (Pasha) (1872–1922). Military officer in the late Ottoman Empire, and one of the instigators of the Armenian genocide of 1915. A member of the Committee of Union and Progress (*Ittihad ve Terakki Jemiyeti*), Djemal took a major part in the Young Turk revolt of 1908, played a leading hand in the Adana massacres of Armenians in 1909, and was appointed to the important post of Minister of the Navy in February 1914. With this he became a member of the Young Turk triumvirate consisting of himself, Mehemet Talaat (Pasha) (1874–1921), and Ismail Enver (Bey) (1881–1922). These three, in fact, ruled Ottoman Turkey as a dictatorship, in which the role of the Sultan was reduced to one of helpless impotence. Djemal was employed by the regime as a "fixer," who sorted out difficult problems of administration or security, which he was able to do with great success in Adana, Constantinople, and Syria (after the outbreak of World War I). In this latter role he organized the hanging of Arab dissenters, the persecution of Zionist settlers in Palestine, and the general terrorization of the population. As the Syrian Desert was the ultimate destination of Armenian deportees from all over the empire, it was to Djemal that their final dispatch was entrusted, which he undertook with characteristic efficiency. The major killing sites of the Armenian genocide were all within his area of administration, thus installing him as one of its most important murderers. Like Enver and Talaat, Djemal was wanted for war crimes by the Allies at the time of the Turkish capitulation in 1918, and for his own safety he fled to a number of different havens, ending up in Afghanistan via Russia. In absentia, a tribunal sitting at Constantinople sentenced him to death. Ultimately, Djemal was assassinated in 1922 in Tbilisi, Georgia, by two Armenians who had been hunting him down.

Doctors' Trial. A group trial of twenty-three former Nazi SS physicians, medical scientists, and other Nazi functionaries was held in Nuremberg between December 1946 and August 1947. The defendants were accused of conspiring to commit war crimes and crimes against humanity, and of carrying them out through a range of lethal medical experiments and coldblooded murder during the period of the Third Reich. The experiments involved a wide range of tests gauging the effects of high altitude, freezing, mustard gas, sulfur gas, seawater, malaria, typhus, and incendiary bombs on human life. They also involved bone-muscle-nerve regeneration and bone transplantation, skeleton collection, as well as the "T-4," or euthanasia program. All defendants pleaded not guilty to the charges, with the defense arguing that medical experimentation was not a criminal act, owing to the fact that it was being carried out to save the lives of German soldiers. It was also argued, in defense of the euthanasia program, that those being killed—the chronically ill, the old, the disabled, and the weak—were euthanized out of pity and under a piece of legislation that legitimated the process under German law. In the sentences passed down, seven doctors were marked for execution, five received life imprisonment, and the others received sentences ranging from ten to twenty years. From this trial evolved the Nuremberg Code: a set of ten principles outlining the categories of medical experimentation that would henceforth be accepted as permissible. Part and parcel of the new code included the mandatory consent of the participants, a commitment to ensuring that the experimenters would do their utmost to avoid the possibility of harm or injury to the participants, an ability to interrupt or stop the experiments, and that there would be no lasting effects of the experiment upon the participants.

The Doctors' Trial is not to be confused with the International Military Tribunal that also sat at Nuremberg between 1945 and 1946.

Doctors without Borders. *See Médecins sans Frontières.*

Documenting Atrocities in Darfur. Published by the U.S. Department of State's Bureau of Democracy, Human Rights and Labor and Bureau of Intelligence and Research in September 2004, this document delineates and discusses the findings of the U.S. Government's Atrocities Documentation Project (ADP) in Chad, whose express purpose was to ascertain whether genocide had been perpetrated in Darfur against the black Africans by either government of Sudan troops and/or the *Janjaweed* (Arab militia). The report notes that the interviews revealed a consistent and widespread pattern of atrocities committed against non-Arab villagers in the Darfur region of western Sudan. The assessment was based on semistructured interviews with 1,136 randomly selected refugees in nineteen locations in eastern Chad. Most respondents said government forces, the *Janjaweed*, or a combination of the two had completely destroyed their villages. Sixty-one percent of the respondents witnessed the killing of a family member, while 16 percent said they had been raped or heard about a rape from a victim. About one-third of the refugees heard racial epithets while under attack.

Based on these findings, U.S. secretary of state Colin Powell (b. 1937) declared the situation in Darfur to be a case of genocide. Both the ADP and the finding of genocide constituted major precedents: first, the interview project constituted the first time a sovereign state (the United States) conducted a genocide investigation into the actions of another sovereign state (Sudan), and the declaration of genocide constituted the first time a sovereign state accused another sovereign nation of having perpetrated genocide while the atrocities were being committed.

Domestic Genocides. Domestic genocide, a category of genocide distinguished by genocide scholar Leo Kuper (1908–1994), results from major cleavages within a society between class, ethnic, political, racial, or religious groups as a result of situations such as: overt racism, antisemitism, the desire to exterminate perceived or actual enemies, economic expansion, struggles for power, and/or a combination of the latter.

Donor Fatigue. *See* Compassion Fatigue.

Doubling. According to psychologist Robert Jay Lifton in his 1986 study *The Nazi Doctors: Medical Killing and the Psychology of Genocide* (chapter 19, "Doubling: The Faustian Bargain"), "The key to understanding how the Nazi doctors came to do the work of Auschwitz is the psychological principle I call 'doubling': the division of the self into two functioning wholes, so that a part-self acts as an entire self" (p. 418). Accordingly, doubling involves five (5) characteristics: (1) a dialectical relationship between the two part-selves over the issues of autonomy and connection; (2) an inclusive, coherent holistic base in Auschwitz itself; (3) a life and death nexus by which the part-self engaged in the killing-related acts understands itself to do so for survivalist and/or healing of the total self in such a place; (4) an avoidance of guilt; and (5) an unconscious or morally unaware dimension by which such acts could continually be perpetrated. Thus, for the doctors themselves, their rationalizations, seemingly, enabled them to realize such acts as consistent with their medical oaths and commitments, as well as to see them working for the greater and, therefore, common good, in ethically positive and scientifically justifiable ways. Additionally, the general and all-pervasive antisemitism of those who affirmed Nazism, including the doctors at Auschwitz, was also, part of this same elimination of a social, unclean disease (the Jews), which needed to be exterminated. By extension, Lifton's insight into the psychology of those medical healers who participated in these acts of genocide has far broader and less confining implications, in that those outside the medical professions who participate in genocide may also experience these five characteristics and may understand their behavior as ethically sound, if not truly moral.

Draft Code of Offenses against the Peace and Security of Mankind. In the aftermath of the proceedings of the International Military Tribunal (IMT) at Nuremberg in 1945–1946, the International Law Commission (ILC) of the United Nations was charged (1947) with the responsibility of drafting a code dealing with offenses against the peace and security of humanity. The task of the ILC was not only to define aggression, but also to address the issue of criminal jurisdiction. A First Draft was distributed in 1950. The last draft, the Third Draft, was distributed in 1954. A further drafting of this code does not appear imminent, and little further action stemming from the earlier drafts is currently on the horizon. That said, some argue that the International Criminal Tribunal for the former Yugoslavia (ICTY) and the International Criminal Tribunal for Rwanda

(ICTR), as well as the International Criminal Court (ICC), are the concretization of such a code.

Drina Corps. During the Bosnian War (1992–1995) the armed forces of Republika Srpska comprised two distinct segments: the Army of the Republika Srpska (VRS) and paramilitary units of the republic's Ministry of the Interior. The commander in chief was the president of Republika Srpska, Radovan Karadzic (b. 1945); the commanding officer of the VRS was General Ratko Mladic (b. 1942). The VRS was in turn divided into six geographically based Corps, all of which were subordinate to General Mladic. These were the Drina Corps, the First Krajina Corps, the Second Krajina Corps, the Sarajevo-Romanija Corps, the Herzegovina Corps, and the East Bosnia Corps. The Drina Corps was formed on November 1, 1992. Its first commander was General Milenko Zivanovic (b. 1946), who was replaced on or about July 11, 1995 by General Radislav Krstic (b. 1948) though there is some dispute surrounding the date of the handover of command. The Drina Corps consisted of about fifteen thousand troops. Two of the thirteen brigades into which it was divided—the Bratunac Brigade and the Zvornik Brigade—featured significantly in the action for which the Drina Corps will principally be remembered: the Srebrenica massacre of July 1995. The Drina Corps was assisted in its murderous work by an irregular militia unit calling itself the Drina Wolves. The Drina Wolves, though, should not be confused with the Drina Crops itself, as they were distinct entities.

The massacre, and the Drina Corps's role in it, was directly ordered by Mladic, who considered this appropriate in view of the fact that the entire Srebrenica region fell within the Drina Corps's area of operations. Because of the indictment made against Krstic by the prosecutor of the International Criminal Tribunal for the Former Yugoslavia (ICTY), together with his subsequent trial, the Drina Corps itself came under a great deal of scrutiny from the United Nations and the ICTY. Although charges for the Srebrenica massacre have been leveled against specific individuals, no charges have thus far been made against General Zivanovic, under whose command the city of Srebrenica was occupied. Command of the Drina Corps had passed from him prior to the commencement of the genocidal massacre that took place in Srebrenica from July 11 onward. Krstic initially was found guilty of genocide, but on appeal, was found guilty of being an accomplice to genocide. His initial sentence of forty-six years' imprisonment was reduced to thirty-five years. On December 20, 2004, he was transferred to a maximum-security prison in Britain to serve his sentence.

Drogheda, Siege of. *See* Cromwell, Oliver.

Drost, Pieter N. (n.d.). Drost, a Dutch law professor, wrote an early and important work, *The Crime of State* (Leyden: A W. Sythoff, 1959), in which he assessed the strengths and weaknesses of the United Nations Convention on the Prevention and Punishment of the Crime of Genocide. He was particularly scathing in regard to the fact that political and social groups were omitted from the UN's definition of genocide.

Duch (Khang Khek Iev) (b. 1942). Duch is the name of the former interrogator of the Khmer Rouge's Tuol Sleng prison, where innocent people were tortured to death or murdered outright. Along with Ta Mok (1926–2006), who was a senior Khmer Rouge official during the genocide, he is one of only two individuals ever arrested for the crimes of the Khmer Rouge. As of August 2007, Duch was incarcerated in a military prison in Phnom Penh.

Dunant, Henri (1828–1910). A Swiss banker, businessman, and humanitarian, founder of the International Committee of the Red Cross (ICRC), inspiration behind the

Geneva Convention (1864), and inaugural Nobel Peace Prize laureate (1901). A Calvinist Christian by upbringing, Dunant's humanitarian sensitivities were aroused at an early age over the issue of slavery, and he attempted to raise the consciousness of concerned Europeans through a wide-ranging series of lectures during the 1850s. Then, in 1859, he witnessed the Battle of Solferino (June 24) between the army of Austria and that of a combined Franco-Italian force. Shocked by the carnage—at least forty thousand casualties—Dunant was determined to do something to at least help the wounded, even if he could not stop the armies from fighting. The more he reflected on the matter, the more his thoughts became confirmed as to what needed to be done, and these were set down in a book he published in 1862, *Un Souvenir de Solferino* (*A Memoir of Solferino*). Therein he set forth the idea that ultimately would see the birth of the ICRC and the first Geneva Convention of 1864, which produced an international treaty "for the amelioration of the condition of the wounded in armies in the field." From that point onward Dunant's life was on a new course, and he began writing and lecturing on issues as diverse as disarmament, care of innocents in wartime, and the establishment of some sort of international arbitration mechanism to rule on disputes between states. Despite this energetic activity—or more likely, because of it—he lost control of his personal affairs, and he led a life of poverty until his death in 1910. When the first Nobel Prize for Peace was awarded, however, Dunant was not entirely forgotten. For his efforts, he was recognized through the Nobel Committee's sharing of the award between him, and the French economist and pacifist Frederic Passy (1822–1912). Not withstanding his extreme personal financial situation, Dunant donated his prize money to charity.

Dunera Boys. The Hired Military Transport (HMT) *Dunera* was a ship sent from Britain to Australia in 1940 for the purpose of removing enemy alien internees (Germans and Italians) from British areas vulnerable to Nazi attack, thereby helping to secure Britain from possible fifth columnist penetration. A ship displacing 12,615 tons, the *Dunera* carried a total of 2,732 internees, together with 141 guards and crew. The majority of those on board, though technically enemy aliens by virtue of their nationality as Germans, Austrians or Czechs, were, in actuality, Jewish refugees who had found sanctuary in Britain prior to the outbreak of war on September 3, 1939. The Australian government had agreed to house them and guard them in internment camps (at British expense), but not to permit them to be released in Australia. When the British government realized its mistake, it dispatched an officer, Major Julian David Layton (1904–1989) to Australia to arrange their compensation and repatriation to Britain. Those who did not wish to brave the perils of possible Nazi attack on the high seas could remain in Australia, but had to stay interned. All the internees were male, many were in their twenties, and some were as young as sixteen—hence the reference to them as "boys," which continued for the next six decades, even as they aged.

The *Dunera* Boys were joined in internment by a second, smaller contingent of internees: German and Austrian Jewish refugee families evacuated from Singapore on the *Queen Mary* in September 1940, to escape the Japanese threat. Their Australian experience was, in many respects, identical to that of the *Dunera* Boys, except that they included women and small children. Ultimately, all those opting to stay in Australia were released.

Most of the "Boys" joined the Australian Army in a specially raised unit called the Eighth Employment Company. It was this military service that qualified them for permanent residency, then citizenship, at the war's end. Although the journey of the *Dunera* was itself quite shocking—the guards, who had seen some of the hardest fighting around Dunkirk, believed the internees to be Nazi saboteurs and spies, and treated them with such brutality that the *Dunera* became known as a "floating concentration camp"—once the *Dunera* Boys arrived in Australia they were able to make new lives for themselves in the new country. Saved from the Nazis twice (first by leaving Germany, then by leaving blitz-ravaged Britain), the *Dunera* Boys of 1940 became the harbingers of the multicultural Australia that was to receive its kick start after the war. Many went on to become professors, company founders and directors, judges, senior public servants, and leading members of their professions.

Duranty, Walter (1884–1957). A U.S. journalist reporting from the Soviet Union before World War II. English by birth (born in Liverpool), he was controversially awarded the Pulitzer Prize in 1932 for a collection of accounts of life in the Soviet Union that he had written the previous year when he was the Moscow correspondent for *The New York Times*. Altogether, Duranty lived in Moscow for twelve years. In the early 1930s he was sending dispatches back to the United States on events in the Soviet Union. At the time it was the high point of Josef Stalin's (1879–1953) epic reforms, involving extensive industrial expansion and the agricultural collectivization. Because the USSR was not recognized by the government of President Franklin Delano Roosevelt (1884–1945) until 1933, news from the Soviet Union was received with considerable curiosity by the public, who knew next to nothing about the country as a whole, or the Five year Plans (the centralization of all economic, agricultural, and industrial activity according to state-determined targets) in particular, let alone the lethal state violence which accompanied these programs. Ensconced in Moscow, Duranty had a sanitized view of what was taking place outside the capital. Most of his reports were enthusiastic in their praise of the Soviet goals to modernize Russia. His liberal optimism fired his admiration for which he was later honored with the Pulitzer Prize. Crucial to an assessment of Duranty's reportage is what he omitted. It appeared as though he viewed the USSR through rose-tinted glasses: there is, for instance, no hint of the 1932–1933 Soviet man-made terror-famine that raged from the Ukraine to Kazakhstan in Soviet Central Asia. The death of millions caused as a result of this state-induced mass starvation is thus a shocking gap in Duranty's portrait of the USSR. This omission helped cover up a major state crime that was genocidal in scope, and warped the true image of the USSR for many years after the death of Soviet dictator Josef Stalin (1879–1953).

Duranty, who returned to the United States during World War II, died in 1957. Several decades later, on account of his biased reporting, some critics sought the withdrawal of his Pulitzer Prize, owing to what they understood to have been his sycophancy and compliance with Soviet propaganda in the 1930s. The Pulitzer Prize committee did review the award, but in 2003 decided not to overturn the original decision—even though it recognized that Duranty's journalism was of a lower standard.

Dutchbat. The unit name given to a 1,170-strong Dutch paratroop battalion that was deployed to Bosnia to help guard the "safe areas" declared by the United Nations on April 16, 1993. In reality, there were three Dutchbat units; the first and second (Dutchbat I and II) completed their six-month tours in Bosnia unremarkably—guarding UN convoys, negotiating between the warring parties, and so on. Dutchbat III, deployed in 1995, had an altogether different fate. Earlier Dutchbat units had been detailed to safeguard the city of Srebrenica, where the first troops—570 in number—had arrived on March 3, 1994. By

July 1995, Dutchbat III had a complement in Srebrenica of only about two hundred soldiers, nowhere near enough to hold off the advancing Bosnian Serb forces of General Ratko Mladic (b. 1942). As Mladic's troops closed in on Srebrenica, Dutchbat found itself cut off and confined to the vicinity of its compound at Potocari, about five kilometers from Srebrenica itself. In the ensuing Serb advance on the town, Dutchbat did not stop the evacuation of women and children, which was part and parcel of Mladic's "ethnic cleansing" process; did not stop the men of Srebrenica from breaking out of the enclave in the hope of reaching Muslim-controlled territory; did not meet the Serbs head-on to demand that they back away from the UN-protected "safe area"; did nothing to avoid the massacre of some seven thousand to eight thousand Bosnian Muslim men and boys at the hands of the Bosnian Serbs; and stood aside even as the Serbs overran their own (the Dutch) base at Potocari. During this time, the United Nations never provided the air support promised to protect the safe area, even when it was well-known that the safe area was under attack.

Dutchbat's failure at Srebrenica caused a national scandal in the Netherlands, later resulting in the resignation of the entire government in April 2002. Dutchbat, for its part, was withdrawn to Zagreb, Croatia, soon after the fall of Srebrenica, and was thereafter transferred back to Holland. The Dutchbat fiasco will henceforth always be associated with the greatest massacre on European soil since the end of World War II.

E

Early Warning System. Originally a term used by the armed services, it is now broadly used to refer to any type of process or program that monitors pertinent situations in order to collect, analyze, predict, and disseminate information for the express purpose of alerting governmental and intergovernmental organizations and officials, as well as the general public, about potential dangers ranging from natural disasters (e.g., extreme climate conditions such as hurricanes and droughts), to man-made disasters (e.g., ethnic conflict, major human rights violations, and genocide). Among some of the many early warning systems that have been developed over the years are: Global Environment Monitoring System (GEMS), UNESCO's International Tsunami Warning System (ITWS), the PIOOM Program (the Dutch acronym for Interdisciplinary Program of Research on Root Causes of Human Rights Violations), and the former United Nations' Office for Research and Collection of Information (ORCI), which collected and disseminated data on potential massive refugee movements and comparable emergencies. (*See* Genocide Early Warning System.)

East Timor, Genocide in. East Timor is an island nation situated in the Indonesian archipelago between Indonesia and Australia. For three centuries it was part of the Portuguese overseas empire, but in 1975, with Portugal's imperial retreat, one of the East Timorese national movements, FRETILIN, declared the territory independent. Within weeks, Indonesian military forces invaded, declared East Timor to be that country's twenty-seventh state, and began a systematic campaign of human rights abuses which resulted in the mass murder, starvation, and death by torture of up to two hundred thousand people, representing one-third of the preinvasion East Timorese population. For the next two decades the international response to this ongoing human rights disaster was one of indifference. Indonesia's neighbor Australia was especially keen not to antagonize the populous nation to its north, and was the first (and, for a long time, the only) country to recognize the de jure incorporation of East Timor into the body of Indonesia. United Nations resolutions calling on Indonesia to withdraw were ignored, and the United States, anxious lest a hard-line approach toward the annexation be seen by the Indonesians as a reason to look elsewhere for friends with which to side—such as the nonaligned nations—trod very softly on the issue. Only in 1999, after a long period of Indonesian oppression under the rule of President Mohamed Suharto (b. 1921), and an outbreak of genocidal violence after his downfall in 1998 (this time committed by Indonesian-backed militias and units of the Indonesian army), was East Timor freed as a result of Australian and UN military intervention. In 2002 the first parliament, elected by universal suffrage and guaranteed by the United Nations, met in the capital of Dili. Under the name Timor Leste, the country was admitted to membership of the United Nations on September 27, 2002.

Eastern Zone (Kampuchea). An area in Kampuchea (Cambodia) where communist dictator Pol Pot (1925–1998) looked askance at the relative autonomy of the people residing there, and sent in Khmer Rouge troops in May 1978 to "purify" the zone. The "purification" resulted in massacres of the Khmer Rouge's own cadre members, a much more brutal work schedule for those who were allowed to live and remain in the area, and the deportation of tens of thousands to provinces in the northwest.

Economic and Social Council, United Nations. Under Article 64 of the United Nations Charter, the Economic and Social Council has the mandate to "make recommendations for the purpose of promoting respect for, and observance of, human rights and fundamental freedoms for all." It also has the power to develop draft conventions for submission to the General Assembly and to convene international conferences on matters related to human rights. Under Article 68 the Council "shall set up commissions in economic and social fields and for the protection of human rights." The Council has the power to establish ad hoc committees to examine various human rights issues, and also has the mandate to appoint special rapporteurs to analyze and develop reports on matters related to human rights, including genocide. In order to facilitate and expedite work on matters related to human rights, the Council established the Commission on Human Rights and the Commission on the Status of Women. The Commission on Human Rights, in turn, established the Sub-commission on Prevention of Discrimination and Protection of Minorities.

Economic Sanctions. Economic sanctions are imposed against a state by an international organization, regional organization or individual state in order to create hardship (and in some cases, to bring the "targeted" nation's economy to a standstill) in order to induce capitulation to certain demands (e.g., to cease and desist from some aberrant behavior against its own people or others). Among the various types of economic sanctions that are available are: broad trade sanctions (e.g., preventing the targeted nation from selling or trading its main source of revenue such as oil), establishing a moratorium on exports, suspending trade agreements, preventing the transshipment of designated strategic goods to the targeted state, the imposition of fuel embargoes, and banning the import of equipment essential to operating industry and businesses key to running the targeted state's economy.

Economically Motivated Genocide. A close examination of genocide reveals what might be called an economic factor, suggesting that the elimination of a group can, amongst other things, be linked to economic motives. In fact, systematic expropriation and looting is always a part of genocide.

Furthermore, in the ideology of genocide, a major component is the stereotype of the despised group—the "other." Often, the targeted group is associated to some degree as the possessor of excess wealth, of ill-gained property, or of acquisition by stealth at the expense of the innocent poor. Time and again the "other" is demonized as the one who sucks out the economic life-blood of the dominant group. Given this, it is little wonder that acts of genocide are also often accompanied by extortion. The relationship between economic greed, theft, and genocide is a close one, and, although it is too much to say that economics alone causes genocide, it is nonetheless frequently one of a number of motives behind it.

Examples of economically motivated genocide abound. For example, the lethal assault on Armenians by Ottoman Turks between 1915 and 1923 freed large tracts of land once occupied by the indigenous Armenians. Throughout the nineteenth century in eastern Anatolia, the population of Kurds and Armenians outstripped the farming capacity of the land. The elimination of the Armenians was a way of easing this chronic land shortage and offers one reason why Kurds so eagerly participated in the ethnic cleansing of the territory inhabited by Armenians. The success of Armenian businesses in the Ottoman Empire, owing to their industriousness and initiative, also contributed to economically inspired jealousy. The Nazi regime of Germany, between 1933 and 1945, posited numerous reasons for the need to eliminate Jews from the life of the country. Obtaining the Jews' wealth (and their presumed wealth, which far outstripped reality) was a major (though usually unspoken) factor in the Nazis' brutal and, ultimately, genocidal actions. Jews were deprived of their factories, shops and employment, not only to impoverish them, but to enrich Germany. "Aryanization" was thus designed, on the one hand to reduce German Jews to penury, and, on the other to provide Germany with Jewish assets—capital, employment, property, and the like. Innumerable works of art were stolen from Jewish homes and subsequently acquired by German museums and prominent individuals. The Nazi trade in gold confiscated from Jews constitutes a classic case of widespread stealing in the context of the Holocaust.

Another common example of economic factors within the context of genocide is forced labor. For example, between 1939 and 1945 the Nazi state and its component parts used forced Jewish labor to enhance the war effort: Jews built roads, worked in ghetto factories, dug antitank ditches, and engaged in other forms of slave labor. They were hired out to private enterprise by the SS in their hundreds of thousands. Indeed, their forced contribution to the German war economy was significant. At the same time, the conditions of work were so stringent that labor frequently led to their death.

For all the reasons that can be given for the government of Sudan's suppression of its Christian population in the southern part of the country between the mid-1980s and the early 2000s, a major goal was control of the oil deposits located there. Without it the Muslim Arab northern region of Sudan would have remained an economic backwater. In Iraq the murderous assaults of Saddam Hussein's (1937–2006) regime on Kurds in the north and Shiites in the south were driven by a similar concern: access to and control of oil fields. In Rwanda the push against the Tutsi in the early 1990s (which culminated in the 1994 genocide) came partially from the claim that they owned too much land at the expense of the Hutu majority.

Eichmann, Adolf (1906–1962). Born in Solingen, in the Rhineland, Eichmann played a central role in the Holocaust. In the very early 1930s, he joined the Austrian Nazi Party, moved to Germany in 1934, and, in 1935, went to work for the Reich Security Main Office (RHSA) in Berlin. He initially worked on the problem of forced Jewish emigration and mass expulsion, but by 1939, with the start of World War II, he was appointed Head of the Jewish Section for the Gestapo. Having participated in the initial discussions of the "Final Solution to the Jewish Question," he was asked by Reinhard Heydrich (Head of the RHSA) to prepare for the Wannsee Conference of January 1941, where plans for the mass extermination of Jews throughout Nazi-occupied Europe were delineated. The focus of the Wannsee Conference, then, was not, as it is commonly misunderstood, held to plan or debate the merits of the idea of the extermination of the Jews and others, but, since it was a *fait accompli*, to delineate the plan of action.

Eichmann was then tasked with coordinating responsibilities regarding the round-up of Jews and their transportation to the various *Vernichtungslagers* (death camps). He personally took charge of the Hungarian deportations in 1944. After the war he, like many others, went into hiding and was able to make his way to Buenos Aires, Argentina, where he lived with his family and worked as a factory worker under the name Ricardo Klement. In 1960 he was captured by Israeli Security Service agents and taken to Israel for trial for "crimes against the Jewish people" (the only crime for which the punishment is death in Israeli law). Found guilty in 1961, he was hanged, his body cremated, and his ashes scattered at sea.

Eichmann in Jerusalem: A Report on the Banality of Evil. The title of a book published in 1963 by the German-Jewish political scientist philosopher Hannah Arendt. Prior to being published as a book, the report was published as a series of magazine articles in the *New Yorker*, the latter of which had sent Arendt to Jerusalem in 1961 to cover the trial. Argumentative and controversial, Arendt contended, as indicated by the subtitle, that Eichmann himself was merely a banal (read "normal") cog in the bureaucratic machinery of National Socialism, whose own careerist orientation, coupled with his strict sense of following the orders of his superiors, led him to continually refine and perfect the "machinery of death"—and thus, was not necessarily one who was truly antisemitic. Her more negative assessments, however, were reserved for the various leadership groups in the Jewish communities under Nazi domination which attempted to help their people survive, but ultimately failed to do so. These leadership groups, she argued, placed self-serving, competing interests above the actual saving of Jewish lives. Had the opposite been more characteristic, she maintained, the actual number of deaths would have been less. Her book generated intense debate in Israel, among survivors worldwide, and helped generate a serious, scholarly reevaluation of the Nazi period of rule and those most involved, including Jews.

Eichmann Trial. Spirited out of Argentina in 1960, Adolf Eichmann was brought to Israel by Security Service agents to stand trial for "crimes against the Jewish people," which carried with it the possibility of the death penalty. The trial began in April 1961 in the District Court in Jerusalem, under the jurisdiction of a three-judge panel headed by Israeli Supreme Court justice Moshe Landau (b. 1912). The chief prosecutor was Israel's attorney general Gideon Hausner. Eichmann's defense attorney was the German lawyer Dr. Robert Servatius (n.d.), who had previously defended a number of the Nazi elites at the International Military Tribunal, Nuremberg, Germany, 1945–1946.

The Eichmann trial lasted four months. More than one hundred witnesses were called to testify, and more than fifteen hundred documents became part of the court record. While not directly addressing the evidence presented, the defense argued that the trial itself was illegal because the State of Israel itself did not exist during the period of World War II, that the judges themselves as Jews and Israelis were prejudiced, that Eichmann himself was illegally kidnapped out of Argentina, that he was merely "following orders" (a plea rejected at Nuremberg), and the Israeli law charging him with his crimes was itself ex post facto. All these criticisms were rejected by the judges. Found guilty in December, both his appeal of the judges' decision and his plea for clemency were turned down. He was executed by hanging in June 1961, his body cremated, and his ashes scattered at sea.

Eicke, Theodor (1892–1943). Nazi police leader, commander of the Death's Head (*Totenkopf*) Division of the SS, and the prime mover behind the development of the Nazi concentration camp system in Germany from 1933 onward. Eicke joined the National Socialist party in 1928, and in June 1933 was appointed the second Kommandant of the Dachau concentration camp. While there, he systematized the treatment, supervision, and punishment of the prisoners, and instilled a new esprit de corps into the SS guard organization. As Kommandant, he made Dachau a model for the other camps, instituting policies regarding discipline, camp organization and hierarchy, rituals concerning reception and orientation, and regulations concerning capital offenses. In mid-1934 an official body, the Inspectorate of Concentration Camps, was created to coordinate the diverse camps throughout the Third Reich and Eicke was selected by SS chief Heinrich Himmler (1900–1945) to serve as the inspector of concentration camps. Eicke's mandate was to oversee the entire concentration camp system and bring Dachau-style order to the varied systems of hit-or-miss administration, which until then had characterized the camp network. Immediately, he set about transforming the whole concentration camp edifice in accordance with the Dachau model. The treatment of prisoners became standardized, and clear delineations were made within the authority structure concerning the camps' direction and administration. Ultimately, Eicke's routine for Dachau became the archetype for camps all over Germany. Henceforth, for example, Kommandants could instruct their guards to be as imaginative as they liked in matters of prisoner discipline, provided it was imposed within a set of very stringent guidelines. The offenses capable of attracting severe punishment were many, with detailed rules set in place.

In 1939, with the outbreak of war, Eicke took a more active command of the SS *Totenkopf* Division and moved away from the Inspectorate of Concentration Camps. He was succeeded as Inspector by his second-in-command, Richard Glücks (1889–1945). Eicke's command of the *Totenkopf* saw the perpetration of numerous war crimes, particularly against a group of British soldiers in 1940, and later on the Russian front. Eicke died of injuries on February 26, 1943, shortly after being promoted to SS *Obergruppenführer*, or general, as the result of a plane crash during Operation Barbarossa.

Eight Stages of Genocide. While employed at the United States Department of State, Dr. Gregory Stanton (b. 1946), a cultural anthropologist, international lawyer, and genocide scholar, outlined in 1996 what he perceives as the eight stages of genocide: classification, symbolization, dehumanization, organization, polarization, preparation, extermination, and genocide. In an introductory comment to his outline of the stages, he writes: "Genocide is a process that develops in eight stages that are unpredictable but not inexorable. At each stage, preventive measures can stop it. The later stages must be preceded by the earlier stages, though earlier stages continue to operate throughout the process" in a nonlinear way. For an explanation of each stage, see http://www.genocidewatch.org/8stages.htm

***Einsatzgruppen* (German, "Special Action Groups," More Commonly Referred to as "Mobile Death Squads").** During World War II, the *Einsatzgruppen* accompanied the *Wehrmacht* (the German army) into Poland and others parts of eastern Europe, primarily the Soviet Union with "Operation Barbarossa." Their "special function" was to round up any Jews they encountered and exterminate them, murdering men, women, and children, usually after first having them dig large pits in forested ravine areas away from towns and villages, and removing their garments and other possible valuables (e.g., jewelry) so as not to damage such during the course of their murders. The hapless victims were then shot by machine guns and tumbled into the pits that were to serve as mass graves. After the first group had been murdered, each succeeding group was ordered to lie down on top of the previous victims and then they were subsequently sprayed also with machine gun bullets. This murderous procedure was repeated until all Jews in their catchment area were dead. Given that the task of shooting women and children in cold blood was frequently psychologically troublesome to the SS (German, *Schutzstaffel*, "special forces") who carried out these murders, mobile killing vans using carbon monoxide poisoning were eventually introduced, having been tested in a number of locations previously. They were used both to remove the intimacy of contact, and to sanitize the process. Although at times quite inefficient, in view of technical malfunctions and mechanical breakdowns, from an economic perspective such vans were cost-effective regarding the use of both men and matériel.

Divided into four groups, the *Einsatzgruppen's* geographic areas of responsibilities were as follows: Group A, the largest, operated in the Baltic states of Lithuania, Latvia, and Estonia with a force of 1,000 men; Group B operated in Belorussia, and outside of Moscow with a force of 650 men; Group C operated in the Ukraine with a force of 700 men; and Group D operated in southern Ukraine, the Crimea, and Caucasia, with a force of 600 men. It is estimated that between 1941 and 1943 more than 1 million Jews and hundreds of thousands of non-Jewish Russians were murdered by the combined efforts of the *Einsatzgruppen*. Meticulous record keeping of the four groups themselves (three of the four group leaders had earned doctorates) provided a graphic record of their crimes.

After the war, only four of the original twenty-four leaders and subleaders brought to trial were actually executed for their crimes; the majority of those who participated as members of the four *Einsatzgruppen* were never brought to trial. Later, after the International Military Tribunal (IMT) at Nuremberg, Germany completed its work in 1945–1946, West Germany handed down an additional one hundred guilty verdicts, though no death sentences were carried out since West Germany had abolished capital punishment.

Electronic Jamming. In the case of genocide, "electronic jamming" refers to the ability and/or effort of an outside force (e.g., the international community) to prevent perpetrators from broadcasting (over television, radio or other electronic means) messages of hate and lies about its perceived enemies and/or orders and instructions to its group members to take part—in one way or another—in the genocidal process. The international community (both the United Nations and the United States) was roundly criticized for not "neutralizing" (i.e., preventing via "jamming") the hate messages broadcast by *Radio-Télévision Libre des Mille Collines* (RTLM) in Rwanda in 1994 in its (RTLM's) effort to mobilize Hutu to ostracize, hunt down and kill Tutsi and moderate Hutu. Both the United Nations and the United States were well equipped to carry out such an operation, which could have been accomplished from an airborne platform such as the U.S. Air National Guard's Commando Solo airplane.

Eliticide. *Eliticide* refers to the killing of the leadership, the educated, and the clergy of a group. Eliticide often is committed at the outset of a genocide, and is perpetrated in order to deny a group those individuals who may be most capable of leading a resistance effort against the perpetrators. Concomitantly, it is used to instill fear in the citizenry of the targeted group and to engender an immense sense of loss. Over the course of the past century, for example, eliticide was carried out during the Armenian genocide perpetrated by the Ottoman Turks between 1915 and 1923, the Khmer Rouge genocide of their fellow Cambodians between 1975 and 1979, and in various towns across the former Yugoslavia in the 1990s. As for the latter, during the ethnic cleansing of a town or village, a Serb who resided in the town would point out all the Muslims of stature (including lawyers, physicians, business leaders, the police chief, the mayor, among others). Upon being pointed out, such individuals were usually killed immediately by Serb soldiers.

Emergency Rescue Committee (ERC). A refugee-rescue organization formed in New York in 1940 to assist refugees displaced by World War II. The ERC was comprised of activists drawn largely from New York's literati of writers, intellectuals and artists, and received support from influential figures such as Eleanor Roosevelt (1884–1962), wife of Franklin Delano Roosevelt (1882–1945), the president of the United States. The Committee was particularly concerned with the fate of refugees in Vichy France, as they were in the precarious position of living under the threat of deportation to Nazi Germany at a moment's notice. As the U.S. government's policy toward refugees, and particularly Jewish refugees, was at that time restrictive, the ERC saw its role as one of assisting them to find safe havens—places which might include the United States, though not exclusively. The ERC's representative in Marseille, Varian Fry (1917–1976), was charged by the ERC to compile lists of those in greatest need and to attempt to procure visas for their departure through the Vichy French government. Fry's work took on a frenzied air as he attempted to save as many people as possible. He visited the offices of the Vichy authorities daily, purchased visas from the allocations of foreign consuls in Marseille, and, when all options seemed exhausted, smuggled refugees across the border into neutral Spain. For this latter activity, and for not carrying a valid passport himself, Fry was arrested by the Vichy police and deported to the United States in 1941. With this, the ERC's operations in France ceased. During the thirteen months of his ERC tour in Marseille, Fry's efforts saw the salvation of four thousand refugees, including many intellectuals and artists such as: Marc Chagall (1887–1985), Hannah Arendt (1906–1975), Pablo Casals (1876–1973), and Max Ernst (1891–1976). In 1942, the ERC joined with another American body, the International Relief Association, to form the International Rescue Committee, which is still active in refugee relief activities to this day.

Enabling Act. Passed by the German *Reichstag* (Parliament) on March 23, 1933, immediately after Hitler came to power, and based on a provision of the Weimar Constitution, this act "enabled" the Reich chancellor to operate under autocratic decree where the security of the state was at stake. Using the pretext of a fire of highly suspicious origin at the Reichstag on February 27, 1933, Hitler used the Enabling Act to squelch opposition, consolidate power, and reject any legislation not proposed by the Nazis themselves. This Act virtually opened the way to future legislation directed against all future or perceived "enemies" of the Nazi state.

Enclosures. The Tudor period in England (1485–1603) was a time of great religious, social, and political ferment, but few changes had such a profound and lasting impact on the fabric of society than the enclosing of public common land behind fences, with a concomitant amalgamation of small farms into larger estates. The processes begun at this time saw tenants not only thrown off land that had been farmed for generations, but these same tenants deprived of employment and sustenance. The enclosure acts that were passed in the sixteenth century were to increase in number over the next two centuries. Seventy were passed for the benefit of landed aristocrats between 1700 and 1760; in the first thirty years of the reign of King George III (1738–1820), whose reign began in 1760, an astonishing 1,355 more enclosure acts were passed. It has been estimated that the number of acres transferred in the eighteenth century from poor farmers and tenants to prosperous and influential landlords was at least 3 million. The extent and nature of the enclosures brought untold hardships to the dispossessed tenant farmers, converting thousands of independent smallholders into dependent agricultural laborers, and thousands more into slum-dwellers and factory-fodder in the burgeoning industrial centers that were then in the process of revolutionizing English society forever. Although the enclosure movement remodeled the English agricultural population into a landless agricultural and industrial proletariat, its main effect with regard to genocide was, as identified by Holocaust scholar Richard L. Rubenstein (b. 1924), the creation of a "surplus" population that had been rendered vulnerable by legal means. The precedent the enclosure acts created is thus vitally important in the overall history of genocide, even though the acts were not themselves genocidal in nature.

Encyclopedia of Genocide. The brainchild of Israel W. Charny (b. 1931), psychologist and genocide scholar, this encyclopedia was published in 1999 by ABC Clio Publishers. Coedited by Rouben Adalian (b. 1951), Steven L. Jacobs (b. 1947), Eric Markusen (1947–2007), and Samuel Totten (b. 1949), this two-volume work includes entries on a wide range of issues critical to understanding the issue of genocide.

Encyclopedia of Genocide and Crimes Against Humanity. Published in 2004 by Macmillan Reference USA and edited by Dianah L. Shelton, Howard Adelman, Frank Chalk, Alexandre Kiss, and William A. Schabas, this three-volume reference work provides a comprehensive and detailed examination of a wide array of issues germane to genocide and crimes against humanity. In doing so, it highlights and examines the myriad of issues behind the crimes.

Encyclopedia of the Holocaust. Published in 1990, this massive work (1,905 pages) remains the standard comprehensive encyclopedia on the Holocaust. It "seeks to provide, insofar as its format allows, the widest possible scope of information" on the Holocaust. With nearly one thousand entries, its editors (which includes, as its chief editor, the noted Holocaust scholar and survivor of the Warsaw Ghetto revolt Israel Gutman) aim "to make knowledge that was previously available mainly to scholars accessible to the educated public at large" (xvii). For specialist and nonspecialist alike, at all educational levels, from high school through college and university on to graduate school, there remains to this point in time (2007) no comparable set of volumes that address this human tragedy.

Ennals, Martin (1927–1991). Ennals, a passionate defender of international human rights, was the first secretary-general of Amnesty International (AI), and the prime mover and shaker in the establishment of numerous other human rights-based organizations. Included among the latter are International Alert, HURIDOCS, SOS Torture (which became the World Organization Against Torture), and Defence for Children International. Ennals was instrumental in moving AI from an organization that focused on documenting human rights to one that campaigned for the protection of each individual's human rights across the globe. During the course of his leadership with AI, AI's first campaign against torture was undertaken (1973). It was also during Ennals' tenure as secretary-general that AI was awarded the Nobel Peace Prize (1977). Along with Leo Kuper (1908–1994), Luis Kutner (1908–1993), and others, Ennals was instrumental in establishing International Alert (IA), whose express purpose was to focus on the intervention of conflict that had the potential of exploding into genocide.

Enver, Ismail (Bey) (1881–1922). Military officer in the late Ottoman Empire, leader of the Young Turk (CUP) coup d'état of January 13, 1914, and one of the chief instigators of the Armenian genocide of 1915. A man of obscure background (it is believed that he was the son of a railway porter), he was able to rise in the revolutionary ferment of Young Turk politics to become minister of finance and eventually minister of war, to marry into the royal family, and, ultimately, to become one of the three most powerful men in the Ottoman Empire. As minister of war Enver began the process of transforming the Armenians into a vulnerable population by drafting all Armenian men into the army and then ordering them to be disarmed and transformed into labor units. This served to render them defenseless when the army turned on and massacred them in large numbers. Deprived of their men, the Armenian women, children, and elderly became much easier targets in the unfolding genocide. Enver also helped to organize mobile killing units called the Special Organization (in Turkish, *Teskilati Mahsusa*), whose squads were tasked with the singular function of killing Armenians in large numbers. (In this, they prefigured the *Einsatzgruppen* of the Nazis during World War II.) Enver formed one part of a political triumvirate ruling the Ottoman Empire, alongside of Mehemet Talaat (Pasha; 1874–1921) and Ahmed Djemal (Pasha; 1874–1922). At the end of World War I, as a man much sought-after by the Allies for trial, he fled to Germany to escape prosecution for war crimes. In absentia, a tribunal sitting at Constantinople sentenced him to death. Enver moved from Germany to Russia in 1920 to assist the Bolsheviks in achieving their revolution, changed sides, and was killed commanding Muslim troops rebelling against Soviet rule in central Asia in 1922.

Epithets. Perpetrators of genocide often refer to the victim group(s) by derogatory terms that suggest that the members of the target group are less than human and/or traitors. For example, during the 1904 German-perpetrated genocide of the Hereros, the Germans, both the colonial settlers and the perpetrators of the genocide, regularly referred to the Hereros as "baboons." Not only was the average German said to have looked down upon the Hereros as being on the same level as primates, but that the Germans treated the Hereros as inferior. In fact, the Germans espoused and believed that the Hereros only had a right to exist as long as they were useful to the whites. The Kaiser shared such negative attitudes of the Hereros and went so far as to declare that "Christian precepts were not applicable to heathens and savages" (quoted in Bridgman and Worley, 2004, p. 30). During the Armenian genocide (1915–1923), the Ottoman Turks repeatedly referred to the Armenians as *gâvurs* or infidels. It was simply another way of indicating that they were considered worthless by the Turks. During the Holocaust the Nazis referred to Jews, in part, as vermin, lice, parasites, and infections. The use of such terms was used to reinforce and inculcate the perverted notion that Jews were inferior, less than human (*Untermenschen*), and "life unworthy of life." Inferring that the Jews were less than human lent "credence" to the Nazis' exterminatory plans and actions against the Jews. Between 1975 and 1979, during the Khmer Rouge–perpetrated Cambodian genocide, the Khmer Rouge, atheists who detested all religions, denounced Buddhist monks in the country as "leeches" and "bloodsuckers." Prior to and during the 1994 Rwandan genocide, extremist Hutu who attacked and killed an estimated five hundred thousand to 1 million Tutsi and moderate Hutu over a hundred-day period, referred to the Tutsi as *Inyenzi* (or cockroaches"), inciting the Hutu to kill such "vermin." *Inyenzi* was a common term used by Radio Television Milles Collines, the Hutu extremist radio station. For example, during one broadcast, the following transmission/warning/threat was made: "You cockroaches must know you are made of flesh! We won't let you kill! We will kill you!" During the first genocide of the twenty-first century, government of Sudan troops and their *Janjaweed* (Arab militia) allies, regularly referred to their victims, the black Africans of Darfur, as "slaves," "slave dogs," and "Nuba," all of which are considered nasty slurs in the region.

Erdemovic, Drazen (b. 1971). Drazen Erdemovic, a Croat born in Tuzla, had a mixed record of military service prior to becoming the first convicted war criminal in an international tribunal since the end of World War II. When the Bosnian War broke out in April 1992, he joined the Bosnian Army and then deserted because of a dispute over a food ration. He moved to the HVO, the Croatian Army, but was arrested for illegal activities, escaped, and made his way to Bosnian Serb lines where he enlisted in the VRS, the Army of Republika Srpska. Erdemovic's unit, the Tenth Sabotage Detachment, saw close-quarter action in the Serb assault on the eastern Bosnian city of Srebrenica in July 1995. On July 16, where his unit was located on a farm in Pilica, north of the city, he and his fellow soldiers met a convoy of buses arriving from Srebrenica filled with Bosnian Muslim men and boys—civilians all—who had surrendered earlier to the Serb occupiers. Erdemovic's unit led them away in groups of ten, and executed them in a controlled orgy of mass killing. By the end of the process, some 1,200 Bosnian Muslims had been murdered.

On March 30, 1996, Serbian president Slobodan Milosevic (1941–2006) surrendered Erdemovic to the International Criminal Tribunal for the Former Yugoslavia (ICTY), ostensibly to provide evidence against other top-ranking Bosnian Serb leaders. Erdemovic was indicted on May 29, 1996, and appeared in court two days later. He pleaded guilty to the two counts for which he had been indicted, war crimes and crimes against humanity, and, on November 29, 1996, he was sentenced to ten years' imprisonment. More specifically, during the course of the trial, he confessed to having murdered more than seventy civilian men himself near Srebrenica in July 1995. Ultimately, he pleaded guilty to crimes against humanity for his part in the massacre of some seven thousand Muslim boys and men after the safe area of Srebrenica was captured by the Serbs. During the course of his plea, Erdemovic asserted that "I had to do this. If I had refused, I would have been killed together with the victims. When I refused, they told me, 'If you are sorry for them, line up with them and we will kill you too.'"

On appeal—based on the assertion that his original guilty plea was not properly informed—his original ten-year sentence was reduced to five years' imprisonment, and the prosecutor withdrew the count of crimes against humanity. During his appeal he claimed mitigating circumstances, namely his young age when the crimes took place, his remorse, his subordinate status as a private soldier, and the fact that, as a Bosnian Croat, he had been told by his Serb officers that if he did not kill Muslims he would himself be killed. He was transferred to Norway in March 1998 to serve out his sentence. Erdemovic was the first of the accused appearing before the ICTY to plead guilty to the crimes alleged against him, and the first against whom the ICTY handed down a sentence.

Escape from Sobibor. A 1987 made-for-television movie directed by Jack Gold (b. 1930), and starring Alan Arkin (b. 1934), Joanna Pakula (b. 1957), and Rutger Hauer (b. 1944). *Escape from Sobibor* tells the story of the uprising at the Sobibor death camp on October 14, 1943, when over six hundred Jewish inmates, led by Leon Feldhandler (1910–1945) and Alexander Pechersky (1909–1996), broke out of the camp. The escape threatened to ruin the Nazi modus operandi and thereby forced the permanent closure of the gassing facilities that had claimed the lives of at least 250,000 Jews since May 1942. More specifically, the Nazis feared the escapees would make their annihilatory plans public knowledge, thus undermining the subterfuge surrounding the killing at Sobibor. That is, they feared that people might henceforth know what was happening there, and thus resist when the trains arrived at the ramp.

The screenplay of *Escape from Sobibor* was adapted from a closely researched study of the same name written by a non-Jewish author from the United States, Richard Rashke (b. 1934), in 1982. Much of Rashke's work, in turn, was assisted by survivors of the camp and the uprising. Three of them—Thomas "Toivi" Blatt (b. 1927), Stanislaw "Shlomo" Szmajzner (1927–1989) and Ester Terner Raab (b. 1922)—worked as technical consultants on the film. *Escape from Sobibor*, which was filmed on the outskirts of Belgrade, Yugoslavia, garnered two Golden Globe Awards in the United States for Best Made-for-Television Motion Picture and Best Supporting Actor (Rutger Hauer, in the role of Alexander Pechersky). Alan Arkin received a Golden Globe nomination for Best Actor for his portrayal of Leon Feldhandler.

Ethiopia, Genocide in. On September 12, 1974, a military coup took place in Ethiopia, bringing to power a group of military officers calling themselves the Provisional Military Administrative Council, or PMAC. The constitution was suspended, parliament was dissolved, and a socialist course for Ethiopia's future was declared. In 1977, Lieutenant-Colonel Mengistu Haile Mariam (b. 1937) became head of the PMAC, and began to divert the socialist objective into one of stronger military rule. Thousands of political opponents were murdered in a countrywide purge, while private property was confiscated by the state, and military spending was greatly increased at the expense of social programs of all kinds. From 1984 onward, the Mengistu regime conducted a policy of forced relocation of hundreds of thousands of Ethiopian peasant families from barren or near-barren areas to parts of the country with greater fertility. By the end of 1984, about seven hundred thousand people had been forcibly relocated. Although the idea might have been a worthy one (particularly in a country prone to periodic famines), the means employed to effect the population transfers were brutal. At least one hundred thousand people, according to most estimates, perished. Ironically, starvation was a major cause of the deaths; little in the way of resettlement assistance was provided, and those moved were often simply dumped down in regions where no preparatory work had been undertaken. For those "resettled" in temporary camps, conditions were possibly even worse. These camps were run like prisons, and when camp populations complained, they were often attacked by government troops. Underlying the period of the political "red terror" of the late 1970s, and then of the resettlement campaigns of the mid-1980s, was also an ethnic struggle between the ruling regime and separatists in the provinces of Tigray and Eritrea. Movements in these provinces engaged in bitter fighting with the government, resulting in many more deaths caused on grounds of ethnic identity. In 1991, Mengistu was overthrown by a group called the Ethiopian People's Revolutionary Democratic Front, a coalition of rebel organizations led by Tigrayans. Since 1994, a series of trials involving Mengistu-era military and political leaders have taken place, some of the latter of whom have faced charges of genocide under Article 281 (Genocide) of the Ethiopian Penal Code of 1957. Mengistu himself, in exile in Zimbabwe, has escaped justice, though he has been tried in absentia and sentenced to death.

New allegations of genocide against a minority people in Ethiopia, the Anuak, surfaced in late 2003, indicating that ethnic strife is far from over despite the change in government in the 1990s and its avowed commitment to a democratic future for all Ethiopians.

Ethnic Cleansing. In a January 1993 report, a UN Commission of Experts, which was established by the UN Security Council, defined "ethnic cleansing" as "rendering an area ethnically homogenous by using force or intimidation to remove persons of given groups from the area." *Ethnic cleansing*, in fact, is a term that reaches back to at least World War II. During the latter period of World War II, the Nazi-backed Croats used the term to refer to their brutal actions against the Serbs. The Nazis, themselves, also used the term *Säuberung* to denote the "cleansing" of the Jews from countries, towns, and territories. The term *ethnic cleansing* gained wide use during the 1990s to explain actions carried out in the former Yugoslavia, during which various sides in the four wars purposely and systematically forced entire groups of people from their homes, village, towns, and land in an effort to "cleanse" the area of rival ethnic and/or religious groups. Ethnic cleansing in the former Yugoslavia was undertaken via various means, including but not limited to: arbitrary arrest and detention, vile mistreatment of both civilian prisoners and prisoners of war, attacks on hospitals, extrajudicial executions, military attacks or the threat of attacks against civilians and civilian centers, murder, mass murder, rape and others types of sexual assault, torture, the ransacking of homes, and the utter destruction of property, including religious and cultural edifices (e.g., mosques, libraries, and monuments). Article 49 of the Fourth Geneva Convention of 1949 expressly forbids "individual or mass forcible transfers, as well as deportation of protected persons from occupied territory to the territory of the Occupying Power or to that of any other country." It also stipulates that only the security of the civil population or "imperative military reasons" may serve as justification for the evacuation of civilians in occupied territory.

Ethnic Cleansing, Undertaken in the Former Yugoslavia. Like *genocide*, the term *ethnic cleansing* is relatively new, but what it describes is centuries old. The phrase in relation to the former Yugoslavia was originally introduced by reporters covering the Yugoslav wars of disintegration between 1991 and 1995. At first, the term was employed to describe the violence aimed at uprooting Serbian minorities from Croatia, in particular from territories inside historic Croatia such as Krajina and Slavonia. It quickly was expanded to denote any attempt throughout Yugoslavia to force minorities off their lands. Strangely, and euphemistically, ethnic cleansing then became a substitute for genocide in popular discourse, as mass killings proliferated throughout the former Yugoslavia. The many offensives to drive out minority populations intensified with the formation of paramilitary units. Although the end goal was the "liberation" of land from its "alien" inhabitants, greater and greater emphasis was placed on killing as a means of ensuring that those displaced would never return. In other words, mass killings and, in certain cases, genocide, presented themselves as the most efficient way of ridding an area of an unwanted minority. Typically, the policy of ethnic cleansing would begin with the harassment of local citizens of an unwanted group, who would be terrorized and intimidated, often in fear for their lives, to leave their homes. Such terror often included a combination of torture, rape, beatings, mutilation, and extended to the murder of others as an example to the wider population. Sometimes, wholesale murder of much larger numbers was undertaken. Lethal violence as terror, for example, typified the Croatian tactic to expel Serbs from Krajina in August 1995, as it did the Serbs' efforts to evict Kosovars during 1998 and 1999. Once an area had been "cleansed" of its unwanted population, the perpetrators moved in their own people, which altered the character of the region as though the original owners had never existed; in this way, the perpetrators laid claim to the region as of right, with no one able to claim preexisting title through prior occupation. Genocidal violence characterized the Bosnian Serb tactics to destroy the entire Muslim population in Srebrenica and other UN-designated "safe areas." The act of ethnic cleansing in this case is reminiscent of the Nazi-backed Croats' use of the term to describe their brutal treatment of the Serbs during World War II, as well as Nazi declarations during World War II that a city or a region had been made "free" of Jews (*Judenfrei*). The term also echoes the Soviet destruction of a segment of the political strata, the so-called *Chistka* (cleaning, or purge). The psychological implications are the same: ridding society of what is proclaimed to be an "unhygienic" element that must be removed, by mass killings if necessary. In the case of the various parts of Yugoslavia, all of them contained minorities that were unwanted by one group or another. In the desire by zealous nationalists to achieve ethnically homogenous states, ethnic cleansing became a "logical" solution.

Ethnic Conflict. Ethnic conflict can develop in two ways. One is horizontal, as a dispute between two minorities in the same state, for example, Jews and Ukrainians in Imperial Russia in the nineteenth century, or Roma and Hungarians in twentieth century Romania. The second dynamic is vertical, between a minority and a dominant majority, for example, the various Native American peoples and the United States government and its policies favoring the majority of settlers wishing to obtain Indian land during the nineteenth century. Either or both of these categories are present today in a majority of the world's nations, though in most cases such conflict does not spill over into lethal violence. More prevalent are conflicts in many postcolonial states, whose populations are composed of dozens of ethnic groups, for example, Nigeria, Indonesia, India, Papua New Guinea, and Sri Lanka. In all such situations, small and large ethnic populations live precariously side by side. For historical, religious, economic, social, or other reasons, they can be distinctly hostile to each other. Coexistence is a fragile commodity depending on the policies and strengths of the central authorities. Where it is strong, peace prevails; where it is weak, conflict erupts into violence which can easily assume genocidal proportions. In question is the viability of multiethnic or multireligious countries emerging from what are often artificial states created through colonial pasts that did not take into account preexisting differences. The future of such countries depends, at least to a large extent, on the global economy. Poverty intensifies interethnic conflict as food and jobs become scarce, while the competition for dwindling resources is a sure guarantee that differences are amplified where civic culture has not been firmly established. In an environment where regions have become destabilized, economic development has been repressed, and communities have been dispersed in conditions of unmitigated misery, the seeds are sown for future outbreaks of ethnic conflict, even as the current one is being played out. Ultimately, this can lead to genocidal conflict between ethnic groups.

Ethnicity. a group that defines itself and/or is defined by others as being of a common descent and sharing a common culture.

Ethnocentrism. Sociological term describing a range of theories in which one's own race or ethnic group is regarded as more important than (according to a variety of indices) and/or superior to all others. It also involves the propensity to judge other cultures against one's own.

Derived from the Greek *ethnos* (nation), the term finds expression particularly in ideologies that have at base a racial conception of the world (e.g., German Nazism) or a focus on the nation (e.g., local fascisms, especially in Europe, the Americas, and parts of Asia).

Ethnocentric thinking of necessity strives to be inclusive, embracing all members of a specific ethnic group, wherever they may be, to the exclusion of all others; it is highly selective as to what alien influences are permitted entry into the private universe of the in-group; and it is quick to reject those who stand out from perceived group norms. The potential for genocidal outbreaks is thus to be found within ethnocentric ideologies; in situations where those advocating such ideologies attain political office, people finding themselves outside of a specific group are at danger of being marginalized and transformed into a highly vulnerable population

Ethnocide. *Ethnocide* refers to the destruction of a culture without the killing of its population. The term was first introduced by Raphael Lemkin (1900–1959) in a footnote to chapter 9 of his book *Axis Rule in Occupied Europe* (1944). The destruction to which the term refers can involve, for example, such matters as the overt destruction, inadvertent loss, or disintegration of a group's way of life, political and social institutions of culture, language, religion and other customs and traditions, and/or economic existence. Lemkin, himself, understood ethnocide to include both physical and cultural destruction.

Ethnopolitical Conflict. Conflicts that result from grievances held between ethnic groups, usually at an intrastate level. Such conflicts typically involve an ethnic or national minority making demands against a state government, or a government imposing its will on, or purposely neglecting, a minority. Ethnopolitical conflicts have proliferated over the past century and a half, and civilian populations have invariably been the primary targets of groups on both sides of the ethnopolitical divide. This has resulted in widespread violence, intense psychological and physical damage to communities, displacement of populations, and, all too frequently, full-scale civil war resulting in large numbers of deliberately inflicted deaths, massacres, and, in some cases the introduction of genocidal policies by government forces and/or militias operating as government proxies (e.g., Burundi, Rwanda, former Yugoslavia, northern Iraq, Darfur).

Eugenics, Nazi Belief in (German, *Rassenhygiene*). The term *eugenics* was first used at the end of the nineteenth century, and understood to mean the improvement of the human species through selective breeding and the "weeding out" or elimination of those hereditary factors which "diminished" the species. Embraced enthusiastically at the time by biologists, anthropologists, social scientists, and others, nowhere was this more apparent than in Germany. Although the term and concept were originally applied to such issues as paternity, inbreeding, criminal behavior, and the birth of mental and physical defectives, when the Nazis assumed power in 1933 they applied them to so-called racial categories of distinction, specifically aimed at Jews and Roma. Using a variety of techniques, such as visual identification and anatomical measurements, Nazi scientists were able to "prove" the "inferiority" of so-called non-Aryan peoples to their satisfaction, and thus lay the groundwork for the latter's ultimate extermination.

Euphemisms. Used by perpetrators of genocide to mask their murderous activities. During the Armenian genocide (1915–1923), for example, the word *deportations* was used by Ottoman Turk authorities as a "password" indicating their secret intent to "destroy" the Armenian population by force marching them into vast deserts until they died from starvation, dehydration, or attacks by Turk and Kurd brigands. During the Soviet man-made famine in the Ukraine (1933), Soviet officials purposely did not report the huge numbers of deaths, which are now estimated to have been between 3 million and 8 million, that resulted from the famine, as it would have been considered "anti-Soviet." Thus, physicians and others used such euphemisms such as "vitamin or protein deficiency," "heart failure," or "exhaustion of the organism" to describe deaths resulting from what were genocidal actions. During the Holocaust (1933–1945), the Nazis used a host of euphemisms to cover the true intent of their plans and actions. Among some of the many were: "protective custody" (used during the early period of the Nazi regime in place of arbitrary arrest and incarceration in concentration camps); "euthanasia" (to refer to the systematic murder of Germans deemed insane or suffering from mental or physical handicaps); "refractory therapy cases" (to refer to disabled people targeted for killing); "showers" (instead of gas chambers); and "negative population policies," "actions" (or *aktions* in the German), "cleansing," "executive measures," "liquidation," "resettlements," "special treatment," among others (all in place of murder and killing). During the Cambodian genocide (1975–1979), the Khmer Rouge used the term *khchatkhchay os roling*, a term for sociological dissolution which translates to "scatter them out of sight" or "scatter them to the last one," to refer to those groups of people it considered anathema to its "new" society. Essentially, the term referred to the physical destruction of their enemies. During the 1988 Iraqi genocide of the Kurds in northern Iraq (also known as the Anfal), the Iraqi government used the following euphemisms in internal documents to describe what was taking place: "special attacks" and "special ammunition" when referring to chemical warfare. In Rwanda, among the euphemisms used in place of "killing" during the 1994 genocide were: *umuganda*, or "collective work"; "bush clearing" (the order to "chop up men"); and "pulling out the roots of the bad weeds" which referred to the slaughter of children and women.

European Network of Genocide Scholars (ENOGS). Established in January 2005 at a foundational meeting in Berlin, Germany, ENOGS' express purpose is to foster scholarly exchange between individuals and institutions worldwide. Membership is open to researchers from all academic disciplines working on genocide and mass violence from within and outside Europe. Its focus is historical and comparative. At its inaugural meeting, ENOGS' became the official sponsor of the *Journal of Genocide Research*, and a new editorial team was established to reflect such.

European Platform for Conflict Prevention and Transformation. The European Platform for Conflict Prevention and Transformation is a network of approximately 150 key European organizations working in the field of the prevention and/or resolution of violent conflicts in the international arena. Its mission is to facilitate the exchange of information and strategies among participating organizations, as well as "to stimulate co-operation and synergy."

Euthanasia Program of Nazis. Although *euthanasia* literally means "mercy killing," a more accurate term reflecting the intent of the Nazis is *lebensunwertest Leben* or "life unworthy of life." The euthanasia program of the Nazis, initially involved the elimination of German mental and physical "defectives" in the period prior to the start of World War II, and was understood by many to be a "pilot project" for the ultimate goal of the elimination of the Jews. The handicapped were seen as detrimental to both the physical and spiritual well-being of the new Nazi state—not to mention the depletion of economic resources—and the concept of *Volksgemeinschaft* ("folk community"). Estimates of those Germans in mental facilities and hospitals who were murdered by doctors and nurses via lethal injections and gassings exceeded 350,000. Upon their deaths their bodies were immediately cremated and letters were sent to their families indicating a heart attack as the cause of death and need for cremation (the latter ostensibly due to the threat of disease). The program was commonly referred to as "T4" which was the abbreviated version of its address at the Reich Chancellery offices, situated at Tiergartenstrasse 4.

As families of those institutionalized began to protest to their religious leaders, both Catholic bishops and Protestant clergy expressed such concern to the Nazi leadership. In response, the Nazi leadership brought the initial phase to a reported end, but—in reality—never completely ceased its murders of these victims. Indeed, the murder of the physically and mentally handicapped continued apace right through 1944.

Evian Conference. In March of 1938 President Franklin Delano Roosevelt of the United States invited thirty European and Latin American nations, as well as Australia, New Zealand, and South Africa, to meet and consider the resettlement of Jewish refugees from Germany and Austria. Some nations refused to attend such a meeting, while others sent low-level bureaucrats with little or no authority to act. Ultimately, in July of 1938, approximately two hundred persons, including newspaper reporters, met at Evian, France, to discuss the issue. At the end of the nine-day meeting, no resolution had been reached. Great Britain refused to even allow the entrance of Jewish refugees into Palestine to become part of the discussion. With the exception of the Dominican Republic, no other nation agreed to accept refugees into its country. Thus, the conference itself has been viewed, with hindsight, as little more than a public relations ploy for the United States in its own relationship with a concerned Jewish constituency with a modicum of non-Jewish support. More perversely, it affirmed for Hitler and the Nazis the unwillingness of Western democracies to extend themselves on behalf of the Jews.

Excremental Assault. Phrase and concept developed by Colgate University professor of English, Terrence Des Pres (1939–1987) in 1975 in order to help explain the debasements to which prisoners in the Nazi concentration camps and Soviet gulags (widespread network of forced labor and prison camps in the Soviet Union) were subjected as a means of reducing their sense of self-worth. In supporting his use of this concept, Des Pres argued that prisoners were systematically denied the use of toilets, except at certain times of the day; denied facilities to keep clean; fed a diet in which diarrhea was commonplace; and surrounded by diseases also resulting in diarrhea. The prisoners were, under such circumstances, literally assaulted by their own excrement, in what were very often rituals of degradation that had been carefully thought-out by the guards in advance. A deliberate policy which aimed at the complete humiliation and debasement of the prisoners often led them to so revile themselves that they gave up wanting to live. This spiritual and physical destruction, especially in the Nazi camps during World War II, became an end in itself—particularly as the SS guards were able to compare their superior status and clean clothes with the ragged, starving, and filthy prisoners under their unchallengeable rule. It also served the purpose of dehumanizing the prisoners in the eyes of the SS, making the task of extermination easier and less unpalatable. The phrase and concept of "excremental assault," therefore, serves a twofold purpose: to destroy the inner souls and self-esteem of those forced to endure it, and to elevate the status of the guards in their own eyes, while reducing any misgivings they may have had regarding their treatment and the destruction of those whom they saw living in their own filth. For Des Pres, the calculated nature of this strategy only served to make the horrendous situation even more morally appalling and cruel.

Expulsion. "Expulsion" refers to the removal of a lawful resident from the territory of a State by government authorities. Under Article 32 of the 1951 Convention Relating to the Status of Refugees, national security and public order are the only grounds permitted for the expulsion of a refugee. The Convention states that the decision to expel an individual must be fair and just, and the individual must be allowed a "reasonable amount of time" to seek entrance to another State. The act of "ethnic cleansing" (which was carried out throughout the former Yugoslavia in the 1990s and in Darfur, Sudan between 2003 and today, August 2007) was, and is, in clear violation of Article 32 of the 1951 Convention.

Expulsions and Genocide. Expulsion of a population from a specified country or region can serve both as a genocide avoidance device and, depending on the circumstances, an opportunity to engage in genocide. A vast number of examples abound for each. For example, in the United States in the 1830s, the so-called Five Civilized Tribes were expelled by the the U.S. government from their homelands in the southeastern United States and relocated to "homes" in the Indian Territory that was to become known as Oklahoma. An argument can be made that if the Indians were not expelled from their own territory, they would have been annihilated by white encroachment; hence, the argument runs, they were expelled for their own good. Along the way, though, in what has become known as the Trail of Tears, the Indian nations lost large numbers (through disease, cold, and hunger) that numbered close to one-quarter of their total population.

Other expulsions were motivated by less "altruistic" ambitions, and were simply land grabs in which the existing population was considered superfluous and thus "had to be" removed. The best known and most recent examples of this occurred in the former Yugoslavia between 1992 and 1995 (against Bosnian Muslims) and in 1999 (against Kosovar Albanians). It was this form of expulsion—forcing whole populations, in the hundreds of thousands, out of the areas in question—that, when accompanied by killing, became known as ethnic cleansing. Although a relatively new term (it was used during World War II), the practice is an old one.

Yet another form of expulsion, religious removal, has its most famous examples occurring in the Middle Ages. Jews were expelled in toto from England (1290), France (1306), Hungary (1349), France again (1394), Spain (1492) and Portugal (1497). The avowed reason for these expulsions was invariably that the Jews, viewed as guilty of deicide, were incompatible with life in a Christian Europe. More accurately, however, underlying this was a desire to confiscate Jewish wealth or deflect antigovernment criticism (often for quite unrelated reasons such as domestic or court politics, or to redirect public attention away from unpalatable internal policies) by finding a vulnerable scapegoat. Expulsion, in short, can be based on a number of different premises, and, while it need not in all cases seek the destruction of the group as such, as a practice it nonetheless seeks to achieve the group's disappearance from a specific location, through their forced removal to another location.

Extrajudicial Killings. This term, used by Amnesty International (AI), among certain other human rights organizations, refers to those political killings perpetrated by a government's army personnel, police officers, other regular security forces, and/or government-sanctioned assassins and "death squads." The term *extrajudicial* refers to the fact that the killings are carried out outside any legal or judicial process. It is not uncommon for such murders to be carried out on orders from the highest level of government. In many cases, government authorities purposely neglect to conduct investigations into the murders and/or they "condone" the murders by failing to take actions that would prevent further killings. It is not unusual for governments to attempt to hide the fact that they have ordered, committed or condoned such murders. Government officials also frequently deny that such murders have taken place, assert that opposition forces are responsible for such casualties, or argue that they resulted from battles with government forces. AI defines extrajudicial killings (also frequently referred to as "political killings") as: "unlawful and deliberate killings of persons by reason of their real or imputed political beliefs or activities, religion, other conscientiously held beliefs, ethnic origin, sex, colour or language, and carried out by order of a government or with its complicity" (Amnesty International, 1983, p. 5).

Ezhov, Nikolai (1895–1940). Nikolai Ezhov was the head of the main Soviet state security agency, the NKVD (*Narodnyi Komissariat Vnutrennikh Del*, or People's Commissariat for Internal Affairs), between September 1936 and November 1938, and thus the chief of Josef Stalin's (1879–1953) system of repression throughout the most intensive years of the period known as the "Great Terror." Ezhov became a member of the Bolshevik Party in April 1917, and, during the Russian Civil War of 1919–1921 was a political commissar in the Red Army. Elevated to the position of People's Commissar of Internal Affairs (and hence, commander of the NKVD) by Stalin, Ezhov was seen by Stalin every day in a constant briefing about the state of the purges then taking place under Ezhov's direction. During the period of what became known as the *Ezhovshchina* (colloquially, the "Ezhov era"), perhaps up to seven hundred thousand extrajudicial state murders took place, the result of 1.5 million arrests on NKVD orders. For some time afterward, discussion ranged over the extent to which Ezhov operated independently or as Stalin's puppet, but an issue such as this was as much a victim of Cold War considerations as of any serious quest for the truth. The fact is that in the summer of 1938, Ezhov fell from Stalin's favor, and a new favorite, Lavrenti Beria (1899–1953), was appointed by Stalin as Ezhov's assistant. By November 1938 Ezhov had been dismissed as head of the NKVD, and Beria had taken over as People's Commissar of Internal Affairs. On Beria's order, Ezhov was arrested on April 10, 1939, tortured, tried secretly, and executed on February 4, 1940. At the Twentieth Congress of the Communist Party of the Soviet Union in October 1956, in which the crimes of the Stalin period were condemned, Party Chairman Nikita Khrushchev (1894–1971) denounced Ezhov as a criminal and drug addict who deserved his fate. It was only after 1987 that a full state investigation of the Ezhovshchina was made, and several more years before scholars began working on Soviet files sufficiently to bring to public attention the record of Ezhov's crimes.

F

Facing History and Ourselves. Founded in 1976 by William S. Parsons (b. 1945) and Margot Stern Strom (b. 1948), Facing and History and Ourselves is an acclaimed educational program, offering an interdisciplinary approach to citizenship education that connects the history of the Holocaust and other cases of genocide to the moral questions young people face. Its mission is to engage students in civic education—an education that encourages the skills, promotes the values, and fosters the ideals—needed to sustain a democratic society. Facing History "provides middle and high school educators with tools for teaching history and ethics, and for helping their students learn to combat prejudice with compassion, indifference with participation, and myth and misinformation with knowledge."

Failed State. A nation in which its various bodies (e.g., legislative, judicial, and/or military) are either in disarray or have crumbled, and chaos has ensued to such a point that there is no clear sign as to whether or not there is even a governing body. The cause of such failure can result from a wide array of factors, including (but not limited to): violent conflict between the government and one or more actors, an attempt at secession by an actor, economic chaos, civil war, and genocide.

FALANTIL. An irregular military organization that for twenty-five years waged a guerrilla war in East Timor against the occupying Indonesians. The name is an acronym of the force's formal Portuguese title, *Forças Armadas de Libertação Nacional de Timor-Leste*, or National Liberation Forces of an Independent East Timor. FALANTIL was formed in 1975 as an armed wing of the leftist East Timorese political movement known as FRETILIN (*Frente Revolucionária do Timor-Leste Independente*). Its leader, until his capture by the Indonesians in 1992, was Jose Alexandre "Xanana" Gusmao (b. 1946), who was later (in May 2002) to become the first president of an independent Timor-Leste. FALANTIL's struggle to free East Timor from Indonesian rule began on the day of the Indonesian invasion, December 7, 1975. In the first few days following the invasion, two thousand citizens in the capital of Dili were killed and, by the end of 1975, twenty thousand Indonesian troops had occupied the small country. This number rose to thirty-five thousand by April 1976. Confronting the Indonesian army were up to twenty thousand well-armed FALANTIL fighters, who put up a solid guerrilla defense for the next three years, until the last formal outpost of resistance, at Mount Matebian, fell in November 1978. After this, FALANTIL numbers declined, and only the most ardent and seasoned members fled into the mountain regions of East Timor to continue the resistance. FALANTIL reemerged into the open on August 20, 1999, a day designated as FALANTIL Day, when Indonesia was relaxing its hold on East Timor prior to the referendum on independence that took place ten days later. Eighteen thousand people turned out to honor the fighters who had kept the dream of freedom alive. After full independence, on May 19, 2002, the FALANTIL organization formed the backbone of the new Timor-Leste army, though the nascent state faced numerous problems in transforming what had been a rebel guerrilla force into a national military establishment.

Famine. A period of extreme scarcity resulting in widespread starvation and, frequently, accompanying death. When famines occur owing to natural disaster, societies, since ancient times, have responded in one of two ways: either they foresaw scarcity and planned for it (stockpiling reserves and riding out the worst of the famine until circumstances improved), or, more typically, they experienced devastating periods of mass starvation and death, sometimes accompanied by pestilence and disease that often resulted in population collapses. Just as in nature, famine can also occur with catastrophic results when deliberately planned and executed by a government over part of its own population, or the population of a country with which it is at war. Examples abound of such government-induced starvation, from the long-term besieging of walled cities in ancient and premodern times (wherein starvation would set in as food would be prevented from entering cities), to the killing of buffalo herds in the Great Plains of the United States in the nineteenth century, to the killing off of crops through the use of defoliants in Biafra in the 1960s, to the salting of arable land by the Romans at Carthage after 146 BCE. In other instances, perpetrators have destroyed populations more deliberately through the withholding of food, or changing the means of its distribution such that a victim population is deprived of food it normally would have counted on for survival. The key issue to be decided in such cases such is how far the perpetrator's intention is to use famine for the purpose of destroying the victim population as such, or how far its intention is to destroy the victim population's will to resist, or to force resettlement, or otherwise bring about an alteration in the behavior of the victim group. Some instances are clear cut. In Ukraine in the early 1930s, the twin Soviet aims of destroying Ukrainian national identity and redistributing Ukrainian food from the country to the cities had a devastating effect, resulting in the deliberate deaths of millions. Another is that of the Nazis who purposely reduced the daily rations of Jews in the ghettos during the Holocaust, knowing full well that the victims would die of starvation. Intent is thus the most vital determinant of whether a famine situation is genocidal, the more so as regimes throughout history have taken advantage of food shortages in order to "solve" domestic problems involving unwanted populations. Thus, while famine can be an unfortunate result of an act of nature, it can also be deliberately conceived and executed, either to destroy a population, or (more commonly) to address a "problem." Then again, it can be a halfway measure between the two. In assessing famine and genocide, every instance must be measured on a case-by-case basis.

Farben, I. G. German petrochemical conglomerate which, during the Second World War, beginning in 1941, attempted to operate the *Bunawerke* (rubber plant) at Auschwitz-Monowitz concentration camp in Poland with slave labor in the manufacture of synthetic rubber and fuels needed to further the Nazi war effort. Ironically, the production efforts came to practically naught due to the continuous Allied bombing raids and the physical deterioration of the workers themselves. Brought to trial at the end of World War II, most of I. G. Farben's leadership escaped punishment; those who went to prison were all released by 1951. Compensation was paid to Jewish prisoners, whereas none was made to non-Jewish prisoners.

Fascism. A political movement born out of the intellectual ferment following World War I, which was strongest in Europe, but had numerous variants in other parts of the world. Fascism reached its peak in the two decades prior to 1945, though it has prevailed as an important force in many countries since then. Fascism can be characterized as a movement that defines itself more by what it stands against rather than what it stands for; hence, during the period between the 1920s and 1940s, it was anticommunist, antiliberal, anti-Marxist and antiindividualist. Fascism's only goal was the strengthening of the state over the liberalizing forces that could weaken it, and as a result fascists advocated a strong central government (depending on local variants, even a one-party state or a dictatorship), mass obedience, a party army, suppression of trade unions and civil liberties groups, a culture of youth glorification, and a rigorous repression of dissent. Groups adhering to fascism attained political office in a number of European countries before 1945, notably Italy, Portugal, and Spain. It had an impact (sometimes powerfully) on local politics in France, Austria, Britain, Hungary, Romania, and elsewhere; and fascist movements or parties also appeared in most other Western democratic countries. Fascism is a right-wing ideology, but it is not conservative; in its purest form, it can be socially and economically radical, even revolutionary, while always invoking the ideals of a lost "golden age" as something to which the modern nation should seek to return. By manipulating the organs of the mass media, education, and popular culture to the greater glory of the state, fascism offers many people an emotional anchor at a time of increasing social alienation and fragmentation. Its potential as a genocidal force, however, lay in its tendency toward dictatorship, its inclusivity of all members of the nation, its utter rejection of those perceived not to fit into it, its glorification of the military, and its rejection of individualism and humanitarian values in favor of the sanctification and elevation of the state.

Faurisson, Robert (b. 1929). According to numerous Holocaust denialist publications and web sites, Robert Faurisson is presently Europe's leading "scholar" of the Holocaust denial movement. From 1974 to 1990 he was a professor of literature at the University of Lyon, France, but was dismissed because of his denial of the Holocaust. He has extensive publications that both question and deny the historical veracity of much of the Holocaust, including the gas chambers at Auschwitz. He has been subject to physical attack for his views which, he claims, are the result of those who disagree with him. He continues to write and lecture in English; much of his work has been published in the pseudo-scholarly *Journal of Historical Review*, published by the Institute of Historical Review, Newport Beach, California.

Federal Republic of Yugoslavia (FRY). The Federal Republic of Yugoslavia (FRY) was the name taken in 1992 by Serbia and Montenegro, two of the six former Yugoslavian republics, following the dissolution of Yugoslavia. The FRY was known by that name between 1992 and 2003, at which point the country changed its name to the Republic of Serbia and Montenegro.

Financial Sanctions. Financial sanctions are applied against countries by either the international community (e.g., the United Nations), regional organizations (e.g., the European Union), or individual states for what is perceived as egregious behavior by an individual state. The most common types of financial sanctions are those that freeze government funds held in financial institutions outside the targeted nation's direct control. The UN system does not have the legal authority to target individual leaders and their personal assets, but regional organizations (the European Union) and individual nations can and have done such. Some scholars have noted the UN system is weakened by its lack of capacity to freeze the assets of individuals and that the impact of UN financial sanctions will be limited until it is allowed to do so.

In 1999, the Second Interlaken Seminar on Targeting United Nations Financial Sanctions was hosted by the Swiss Federal Office for Foreign Economic Affairs, in cooperation with the United Nations Secretariat. This seminar resulted in the 2001 text "Targeted Financial Sanctions: A Manual for Design and Implementation," which addressed both designing United Nations Security Council resolutions on targeted financial sanctions, and implementing targeted financial sanctions at the national level. Such continuing uses of financial sanctions require the resolve of the international community for their implementation. As is the case with arms sales and the worldwide demand for oil products, individual reluctance on the part of one or more nation-states lessens the effectiveness of such a tool.

Sanctions of all types have been controversial. Some of the many criticisms are that the sanctions have had too many loopholes, various nations ostensibly supporting sanctions have—for whatever reasons—secretly undermined the sanctions effort, and in many cases the sanctions have ended up hurting innocent citizens within the targeted nation, while having little or no impact on the regime itself.

Most scholars studying the use of sanctions have called for the development and implementation of more sophisticated measures. They have also insisted that sanctions must be constantly monitored and adjusted as situations change. Finally, they have noted that a "carrot and stick" approach is generally more effective than a "stick approach."

First Nations. A term describing indigenous populations in many of the lands of recent (1500–1900) European settlement, particularly Canada, the United States, Australia, New Zealand, Argentina, Brazil, and Chile (to name but a few). The term originated in Canada in the 1980s, and, despite the absence of a formal definition, has quasi-legal status in that country. It is most frequently employed in Canada (though the term is growing in popularity in the United States, where the term *Native American* has for many years been the more accepted appellation). The term First Nations is also used by international nongovernmental organizations (INGOs) and by some intergovernmental organizations (IGOs). Because indigenous peoples often refer to themselves according to their own nomenclature, *First Nations* is often used as a blanket term of convenience in some jurisdictions, by both indigenous organizations and government agencies.

First-Person Accounts of Genocide. First-person accounts of genocide in one form or another (e.g., individual written transcripts, books, sound recordings, videotapes) document the thoughts, words, and stories of those individuals (e.g., victims, survivors, journalists, nongovernmental personnel, military personnel) who have witnessed some aspect of a genocide. Among the most valuable documents are contemporaneous documents (e.g., diaries and letters) and the transcripts of the trials of perpetrators (where lawyers have been able to cross-examine witnesses in an attempt to get at the truth). The largest collection of first-person accounts that exist documents the period of the Holocaust (1933–1945). A vast majority of the latter are housed in the archives at Yad Vashem, the Holocaust Martyrs' and Heroes' Remembrance Authority (Jerusalem, Israel) and the United States Holocaust Memorial Museum (Washington, D.C.). Relatively large collections of first-person accounts also exist that document the Ottoman Turk-perpetrated Armenian genocide (1915–1923), the Soviet man-made famine in Ukraine (1933), and the Khmer Rouge-perpetrated genocide (1975–1979). Many fewer first-person accounts exist that document the 1971 Bangladesh genocide, the 1994 Rwandan genocide, and the genocide perpetrated in the former Yugoslavia in the 1990s. Due to the trials being conducted by the International Tribunal for the Former Yugoslavia (ICTY) and the International Tribunal for Rwanda (ICTR), it is safe to assume that over time many more first-person accounts shall be available regarding the 1994 Rwandan genocide and the genocide(s) perpetrated in the former Yugoslavia. Investigators, nongovernmental human rights organizations, and scholars are currently in the process of conducting interviews and oral histories with the black Africans of Darfur who have been under a genocidal attack since 2003 at the hands of government of Sudan troops and the *Janjaweed* (Arab milita).

Foca, Rape Camp. The city of Foca, located on the Drina River east of the city of Visegrad, in far eastern Bosnia, was a major trading center during medieval times on the overland route between Dubrovnik and Constantinople. In 1992, Serbian and Montenegrin militants, in an attempt to "ethnically cleanse" Foca of its Muslim inhabitants, established both rape camps and killing centers there while, at the same time, systematically setting out to destroy any and all evidence of Bosnian Muslim culture (e.g., libraries containing ancient manuscripts, sixteenth- and seventeenth-century mosques, and changing the names of streets with historic Muslim connections) and renaming the city "Srbinje."

Following revelations of the rape camps' existence by U.S. journalist Roy Gutman and British journalist Ed Vulliamy in the summer of 1992, world opinion was alerted to the abhorrent actions of the Serbs. Mass sexual violence henceforth became firmly placed on the human rights agenda of international nongovernmental organizations such as Human Rights Watch, after which advocacy of prosecutions against the perpetrators of such acts was increasingly called for.

Among those brought to trial for war crimes related to the destruction of the city, the killings, and the mass rapes were Dragan Gagovic, Gojko Jankovic, Janko Janjic, Radomir Kovac, Zoran Vukovic, Dragan Zelenovic, Dragoljub Kunarac, and Radovan Stankovic. Others yet to face trial include Savo Todovic, Milorad Krnojelac, and Mitar Rasevic, all of them Serbian leaders in Foca.

A mass grave was also found in Foca close to the destroyed Aladza Mosque (built in 1551), containing the bodies of hundreds of victims of Bosnian Serb militias. In October 2004 an attempt to erect a memorial plaque commemorating the rape of the Muslim women of Foca by representatives of the Association of Women-Victims of War from Sarajevo was stopped by the town's inhabitants.

The year 2003 saw the beginning of the process of returning property (e.g., homes and land) to the victims.

Food Insecurity. The term *food insecurity* refers to those situations where people living in certain regions of the world or states are not sure if there will be enough food to provide life-sustaining sustenance for them and their fellow citizens. Food insecurity is frequently found in nations and regions of the world where the economy depends on agriculture, but the means to make the farmland productive is absent. Increasingly, drought and/or desertification is exacerbating this problem, which many directly relate to global warming. Food insecurity frequently results in instability and is a major root of conflict.

Forces Armées Rwandaises **(FAR).** The national army of Rwanda up to July 1994. The FAR was a composite army, comprised of two forces: the *Armee Rwandaise* (AR), whose responsibility was national security, and the *Gendarmerie Nationale* (GN), which was responsible for maintaining public order throughout the country. Although a composite army, the FAR did not have a unified command structure; its authority derived directly from the minister of defense, and the commander of the FAR was the president of Rwanda (until April 6, 1994, this was President Juvenal Habyarimana, 1937–1994). The FAR included a number of different units, including the Presidential guard, Habyarimana's personal bodyguard. Officers and troops of the FAR were integrally involved in the genocide of Rwanda's Tutsi population (and moderate Hutu who objected to the killing and/or attempted to protect Tutsis), and many of its members were held as alleged génocidaires by the Tutsi-led Rwandan Patriotic Front (RPF) government that came into power after the end of the genocide in July 1994, or were indicted by the International Criminal Tribunal for Rwanda (ICTR) based in Arusha, Tanzania. Of those who were not arrested and/or imprisoned after the genocide, many fled to the Democratic Republic of Congo (formerly Zaire) in order to escape prosecution or (as they feared) revenge from the RPF. The FAR is not to be confused with the current army of Rwanda, which is the reconstituted RPF, which is now known as the Rwandan Defense Forces (RDF).

Forensic Inquiry and Genocide. According to the American Board of Forensic Anthropology, forensic anthropology is the application of the science of physical anthropology to both the legal process and humanitarian agendas primarily involving the identification of skeletal and other human remains, to determine such characteristics as age, gender, identity, evidence of crimes committed, and other traumas. The genocides and genocidal massacres of the 1990s saw attempts after the fact to assess the scale of the killing, plot the distribution of killing sites, and evaluate the means whereby the victims lost their lives. Indeed, in places such as Cambodia, Guatemala, Rwanda, Bosnia, and Kosovo (to name but a few of many), teams of forensic scientists, lawyers, historians, anthropologists, and archaeologists have pooled their skills in order to locate, investigate and chronicle scenes of genocidal crime. Their findings have provided evidence so that legal proceedings can be brought against those indicted for war crimes, crimes against humanity, and genocide. It also provides surviving family members with the remains of their missing loved ones for whom they can perform a proper burial. As a result, forensic inquiry has taken center stage in the investigation of genocidal activity. The work itself involves the study of osteology (or bones) to make both observations and determinations. For example, the Guatemalan Forensic Anthropology Team (GFAT), founded in 1991, investigated the massacres in Tunaja and Río Negro, and estimated the genocidal loses at more than one hundred thousand persons.

Forensic inquiry at genocide sites is an expensive undertaking, and, when not underwritten by international agencies, research teams often rely on charity in order to do this important work. Activities in forensic inquiry range widely. These include, but are not limited to, the following: locating crime scenes; managing crime scenes and laboratory apparatus; excavating crime scenes; analyzing remains, both human and artifact; soil analysis; gathering of witness statements; and recreating crime scene circumstances. Although police forensics is now highly developed in civilian environments in advanced societies, genocide forensics is still developing and requires immense international effort and support in order to achieve the kind of results necessary to be recognized as part of the ongoing campaign to prevent and punish the crime of genocide. Bodies such as the International Forensic Centre of Excellence for the Investigation of Genocide, based at the University of Bournemouth in the United Kingdom, are vitally important organizations in this area of genocide studies, and engage in hands-on endeavors to supplement the ad hoc work of governments and international agencies.

As previously mentioned, the efforts along these lines also serve an important humanitarian purpose in locating the remains of victims whom surviving family members can then bid farewell in an appropriate manner. In this way, an attempt to aid in the psychological healing and closure among both victim families and nation-states, thereby aiding in the necessary acts of reconciliation and rebuilding, can be made.

"Forgotten Genocide." A term often previously applied to the genocide of the Armenian population at the hands of the Young Turk regime between 1915 and 1923. Its "forgotten" appellation was due largely to two factors: first, the ongoing denial by successive Turkish governments, continuing to the present day, that a genocide ever took place; and second, because the Armenian genocide, although claiming up to 1.5 million lives, was eclipsed in both numbers killed and general awareness by the Holocaust of the European Jews between 1933 and 1945. Serious scholarship undertaken on the Armenian genocide since the mid-1980s has seen to it that the term *forgotten* has fallen into disuse.

Forty Days of Musa Dagh, The. The title of a novel published in 1933 by Czech-born Jewish writer Franz Werfel (1890–1945), celebrating the stand made by six Armenian villages at the foot of Musa Dagh (Turkish, Mount Moses; in Armenian, Musa Ler) between July and September 1915. The book is a fictionalized account of a true story, in which the villagers banded together to defend themselves from the Turkish army, which had besieged their mountain retreat. With their backs to the sea, and no possibility of reinforcement or the siege being lifted, the defenders of Musa Dagh had but one hope—rescue. This could only come from the sea, and only in the form of Allied warships. When contact was made with a passing ship from the French navy, deputized Armenian youth leaders swam out to explain the desperate plight of the people on the mountain. Summoning naval assistance, five warships eventually arrived on the scene to rescue the Armenians. Under Turkish fire, more than four thousand men, women, and children were rescued and disembarked at the nearest Allied landing point, Port Said (Egypt). They remained in refugee camps there until the Turkish defeat in World War I in 1918, and then returned home. This inspirational story inspired Franz Werfel to write his novel, which became a best seller. Translated into eighteen languages, it was slated to be produced as a movie by Metro Golden Mayer (MGM) Studios in the United States. However, as part of the ongoing campaign of post–Ottoman Turkish governments to deny the Armenian genocide, pressure was brought to bear on MGM Studios via an intervention by the Turkish embassy in the United States through the U.S. State Department, and the movie project was dropped indefinitely. Despite this turn of events, copies of the book continued to be published and circulated widely, often as a source of encouragement to those suffering persecution. For example, the book was read by many Jews suffering under the Nazis during World War II and was viewed as an allegory of their own situation in the Nazi-established ghettos, and what they might do about it. It was also an inspiration for Jews in Palestine—in particular the followers of Zionist leader Ze'ev Jabotinsky (1880–1940)—while fighting for a state of their own prior to the establishment of Israel in 1948.

Forum on Early Warning and Early Response (FEWER). Following a 1996 international study of the events that led up to and culminated in the 1994 genocide in Rwanda (in which it was revealed that the United Nations and many governments had received ample warning of the impending violence), a group of twenty-six international nongovernmental organizations, academics, UN agencies, and governments involved in conflict research, policy development, and activism joined together to form the Forum on Early Warning and Early Response (FEWER). FEWER is a multisectoral and multidisciplinary network, spanning Asia, Africa, North and South America, and Eurasia.

Frank, Anne. See *Diary of Anne Frank.*

FRETILIN. An East Timorese resistance movement founded in September 1974 for the purpose of securing independence from Portuguese colonial rule. It grew out of an earlier body, a political party named the *Associação Social Democratica Timorense* (ASDT), which was a broad-based, anticolonial association with nationalist leanings. FRETILIN, the *Frente Revolucionária do Timor-Leste Independente* (Revolutionary Front for an Independent East Timor), had a strong radical socialist foundation, and differed from the ASDT in that it sought immediate independence and claimed to speak on behalf of all East Timorese people. By December 1974 it had developed nationwide programs in education, social welfare, health, agriculture, literacy, and the like. FRETILIN ran into opposition from a rival party, the UDT (*União Democratica Timorense*, the Timorese Democratic Union), which was less radical and called for a more progressive and multistage timeline for independence that would be slanted toward a federation model with Portugal. On August 11, 1975, the UDT staged a coup; for three weeks civil war raged throughout East Timor, as forces of the UDT battled with a hastily formed armed wing of FRETILIN, called FALANTIL (*Forças Armadas de Libertação Nacional de Timor-Leste*, National Liberation Forces of an Independent East Timor). Between fifteen hundred and three thousand people were killed at this time. On November 28, 1975, FRETILIN declared East Timor independent, naming it the Democratic Republic of East Timor. Nine days later the country was invaded by Indonesia. In the first few days of the invasion, two thousand citizens of the capital of Dili were killed. Subsequently, Indonesia began a systematic campaign of human rights abuses which resulted in the mass murder, starvation, and death by torture of up to two hundred thousand people—one-third of the preinvasion East Timorese population. In 1996, largely as a result of his efforts to free East Timor from Indonesian rule, FRETILIN leader Jose Ramos Horta (b. 1949) shared the Nobel Peace Prize with East Timorese religious leader Bishop Carlos Felipe Ximenes Belo (b. 1948). Since the departure of the Indonesians and the independence of East Timor, FRETILIN's contributions to the country have been mixed. In elections in 2001—East Timor's first—FRETILIN won only 57 percent of the popular vote, but obtained fifty-five out of eighty-eight seats in the new legislature. Independence showed that, in its transition from being a liberation movement to a political party, the public expected more than FRETILIN could offer, particularly as peacetime issues of poverty and unemployment proved difficult for the party to alleviate.

Frontline: Ghosts of Rwanda. *Frontline*, the highly respected U.S.-based television news show, produced this two-hour documentary on the tenth anniversary of the 1994 Rwandan genocide. It includes interviews with key government officials and diplomats, and eyewitness accounts of the genocide from those who experienced it firsthand. It also shows then U.S. president Bill Clinton's (b. 1946) brief visit to the Kigali airport, which he never leaves, where he apologizes for not responding to the genocide, without ever using the words "I'm sorry." Furthermore, it includes a U.S. State Department official who talked—during the actual course of the genocide—in terms of "genocide-like acts," but refused to call the situation in Rwanda a genocide, announcing, instead, that the State Department was reviewing the appropriateness of using the term in relation to the situation unfolding there. Significantly, *Frontline* examines and discusses various failures by the international community (including the United Nations) to prevent and halt the genocide before extremist Hutu murdered between five hundred thousand and 1 million Tutsi and moderate Hutu in one hundred days.

Fry, Varian Mackey (1917–1976). U.S. citizen who rescued Jews during the Holocaust. Born in New York City, Fry attended Harvard University, where he studied classics. He began his working life as a photographer, but, in 1940, went to Marseille, France, as a representative of an American refugee-rescue organization called the Emergency Rescue Committee. While there, he worked hard to secure passports and visas that would enable refugees to emigrate from Vichy France and reach safety. Fry had no previous experience with the kind of underground activities that would be required to obtain the necessary papers—often forgeries had to be made—but, by the end of his mission, he had saved approximately four thousand people from the hands of the Nazis. Many of these were prominent intellectuals, artists, and musicians, including Marc Chagall (1887–1985), Hannah Arendt (1906–1975), Pablo Casals (1876–1973), Heinrich Mann (1871–1950), and Max Ernst (1891–1976). When his resources for procuring visas dried up, he smuggled refugees from Marseille to nearby Spain, across the Pyrenees. For this, and because he himself did not have a valid passport, Fry was arrested by the Vichy police and deported back to the United States, via Spain, in September 1941. Upon his return to the United States he was reprimanded by the U.S. State Department for his illegal activities, and was given no recognition for his outstanding humanitarian rescue activities. He lived out the next thirty-five years of his life in obscurity, and without appreciation. In 1991—nearly a quarter of a century after his death—Fry received his first official recognition within the United States, from the United States Holocaust Memorial Council. Then, in 1996, he was named by Yad Vashem in Israel as one of the "Righteous Among the Nations" (*Chasidei Ummot Ha-Olam*). To date, he is the only U.S. citizen to be named a Righteous Gentile. For his work in saving thousands, Fry's name is frequently mentioned alongside other major rescuers during the Holocaust, such as Oskar Schindler (1908–1974) and Raoul Wallenberg (1912–1947?).

FRY. *See* Federal Republic of Yugoslavia.

Functionalism. The argument of some scholars—for example, German historians Hans Mommsen (b. 1930) and Martin Broszat (1926–1989), and U.S.-based historian Christopher Browning (b. 1944)—that the Holocaust was not the result of a planned, carefully organized, and orchestrated agenda of Adolf Hitler (1889–1945) because of his overwhelming antisemitism, but, rather, an evolving and sometimes chaotic program of death and destruction, which only began to assert itself after the invasion of Soviet Russia in June 1941 ("Operation Barbarosa"); prior to this, antisemitic activities were undertaken by low-level bureaucrats in a somewhat haphazard and inefficient manner. Thus, functionalists view the Nazi hierarchy as one of competing vested interests and power centers with Hitler not in control. Functionalists also argue that the initial goal of ridding Germany of its Jews, that of compulsory Jewish emigration, had proven unsuccessful, and that, as a consequence, a new and more radical (and more permanent) "solution" to the problem had to be found.

Funktionshäftlinge (German, Prisoner-Functionaries). Concentration camp prisoners incarcerated within the German National Socialist (Nazi) state between 1933 and 1945, who were elevated to positions of authority by the Inspectorate of Concentration Camps to counter the lack of personnel available for administrative purposes. This system was devised in the prewar period. In return for serving as administrative agents for the Nazi police authorities in the camps, the "prisoner-functionaries" (*Funktionshäftlinge*) received more food, had better living conditions, and performed less work than other prisoners, this being mainly restricted to a supervisory role. These "administrative prisoners" were called *Ältester* (elders, or seniors), of which the main figure was the *Lagerältester*— the most senior prisoner in the camp. In each barrack there was a *Blockältester*; in each room, a *Stubenältester*. These latter were, in turn, assisted by a number of *Stubendienst* workers, who acted as room orderlies. In each block was a *Blockschreiber*, a prisoner who acted as a kind of registrar for the barracks and reported to an SS officer in the SS Administrative Department. There were, in addition, other administrative positions, such as the prisoner-doctors (*Haftlingärzt*), camp barbers (*Lagerfriseur*), gatekeepers who operated the gates between compounds (*Torwächter*), and interpreters (*Dolmetscher*). Prisoner-functionaries were utterly dependent on the SS for everything. They, like any other prisoner, could be punished for the slightest infraction of the rules. They had to do exactly as they were told, nothing more and nothing less. They were sandwiched in the middle of camp society; while enforcing SS structures and discipline on those below them, they were never to forget that they were still prisoners of the SS. They could be (and often were) killed by common prisoners as traitors; they could also be killed by the SS on a whim. By creating a prisoner elite, the SS established a system that divided the prisoners in order to rule them. In doing so, they reaped enormous benefits, as they were able to control the inmates with the minimum number of guards required by the Nazi authorities.

G

Gacaca. An indigenous form of local justice in Rwanda that was adapted in the late 1990s and implemented in the early 2000s to try alleged perpetrators of the 1994 Rwandan genocide. The term *gacaca* (pronounced *ga-cha-cha*) is derived from the Kinyarwarda word guacaca, meaning "grass"; hence, *gacaca* literally means "justice on the grass." This is explained through the practice of the session taking place, during the precolonial period, out in the open, frequently on the grass, in the literal sense.

In the aftermath of the 1994 Rwandan genocide, approximately 130,000 alleged génocidaires (French, those who commit genocide) were incarcerated in Rwandan prisons across the country. Various parties estimated that if regular courts tried the cases it would take between sixty and two hundred years to try all the defendants. That was true not only due to the large number of defendants incarcerated in the horrifically overcrowded, filthy and disease-ridden prisons, but to the fact that during the course of the genocide the judicial system of Rwanda had been decimated as most of the prosecutors, defense attorneys, and judges had been killed. Of equal concern was the fact that many of those imprisoned were likely to be innocent. There was also the enormous cost of feeding, clothing, and guarding such an overwhelming number of prisoners, and the fact that such a cost would tax Rwanda's already overwhelmed social system. Ultimately, Rwandan authorities decided to adapt and implement a traditional precolonial system of conflict resolution called *gacaca*. Traditionally, the *gacaca* system was used in villages all across Rwanda to settle family disputes, disputes among neighbors, and conflicts over land, trade, and so forth. The local *gacaca* would meet in the village and a group of elders would make a decision based on the merits of each person's argument.

Significantly, the goals of the new *gacaca* system are many; indeed, *gacaca* has not been put in place solely for the purpose of punishing the guilty, but as a way for the victims to tell their stories, to allow the victims to discover how and where their family members and friends had been killed and/or were buried, to allow perpetrators to confess and ask for forgiveness; and to help bring about reconciliation of the nation's peoples (perpetrators and victims/survivors alike). Initially, attendance at the *gacacas* was voluntary, but when many people failed to attend them, the government made it mandatory for all individuals eighteen years of age and older to attend. The rationale was that *gacacas* are to constitute a participatory type of justice in which the hearings are conducted by, in front of, and for the local people in the very area where the crimes were alleged to have taken place. In each city, town, and village, *gacacas* are held on a special day of the week during which all government offices (with the exception of the police), businesses, and schools close down from 8 a.m. to 1 p.m., so that all individuals can attend and have no excuse to avoid doing so. *Gacacas* are led by "persons of integrity," or those individuals who have been selected by the local people based on their (the person of integrity's) honesty. He or she, of course, cannot have taken part in the genocide in any way whatsoever. The persons of integrity were provided with the rudiments of state law through a number of government-run workshops, though in most areas these have been short in duration, and restricted to a single session.

Neither the perpetrators nor the victims are represented by lawyers, but each is allowed to speak. The persons of integrity are allowed to ask questions of each participant and, if need be, to adjourn a hearing in order to obtain additional information or to call in additional witnesses. All alleged perpetrators—except for those who planned the genocide and/or were major actors in carrying out of the genocide (Category One Prisoners)—are allowed to be tried by *gacacas*. (Category One prisoners are tried in the national courts in Rwanda and the International Criminal Tribunal for Rwanda (ICTR) in Arusha, Tanzania.) Those perpetrators who confess their crimes in public at *gacaca* hearings and ask for forgiveness in a genuine way can have their sentences cut in half. Those who do not confess or are not genuine in asking forgiveness are sent back to prison to complete their full sentence. If it is discovered that an individual has failed to provide a full confession, he or she can, and usually is, given a lengthier sentence than was originally imposed. Significantly, where charges directly relating to the genocide are concerned, *gacaca* courts may only impose custodial sentences, not capital punishment, which is a sentence that can only be reached and enforced by the government within its "classical" or regular court system.

Ultimately, then, the main purposes of the *gacaca* courts are: (1) the reconstruction and recounting of what actually took place during the genocide (who, what, where and how); (2) providing victims with the opportunity to see the perpetrators who harmed and killed their love ones be held accountable for their crimes, thus ending a culture of impunity; (3) speeding up the process of hearing the cases of the alleged perpetrators; (4) freeing the innocent from prison; (5) removing the burden on the national system of courts and thus allowing them to concentrate on trying the planners and leaders of the genocide; and (6) working toward the reconciliation of all Rwandans.

Gacaca is not without its flaws and critics. Some believe that allowing perpetrators to have their sentences cut in half for confessing and asking for forgiveness is unconscionable in light of their crimes. Some believe that the perpetrators will ask for forgiveness whether they are contrite or not. Some have commented that even those who are not guilty of taking part in the genocide, but have been accused of doing so, will falsely admit guilt in order to get out of prison faster than they would have normally. Still others are concerned by the lack of education of the "persons of integrity," as well as a their lack of adequate training for the job they have to perform. And the list goes on. Still, *gacaca* is an innovation implemented by the Rwandan government in an ostensible attempt to be as fair as possible, to as many people as possible, within Rwandan society and to bring about reconciliation in the still fractured land where some five hundred thousand to 1 million Tutsi and moderate Hutu were killed in a hundred-day period.

Gacaca Law. In March 2001, the Rwandan government adopted the *Gacaca* Law, which provided the Rwandan people with the opportunity to take part in and to use a system of participatory justice—a revised form of a precolonial traditional community conflict resolution system—in which alleged suspects of genocide would be tried. Under the *Gacaca* Law, the locally run *gacacas* can try all alleged perpetrators of genocide, except for those who are suspected of having planned and directed the genocide (i.e., Category One prisoners). These were to be tried in national, or traditional, courts within Rwanda, or at the International Criminal Tribunal for Rwanda (ICTR) in Arusha, Tanzania. The *Gacaca* Law includes a provision that those suspects who confess (with the exception of Category One prisoners who are subject to the death penalty) and ask for forgiveness (in a genuine versus an insincere manner) can have his or her sentence reduced by half.

Gacaca: Living Together Again in Rwanda? This film (which was supported by a grant from the Soros Documentary Fund of the Open Society Institute and produced with the assistance of the Sundance Documentary Fund) provides an overview of the *gacaca* process (local tribunals led by "persons of integrity") in which alleged genocide suspects of the 1994 Rwandan genocide are tried in the villages where the alleged crimes took place. The film includes "the intertwining stories of survivors and prisoners, and their visions of the future."

Galbraith, Peter (b. 1950). A senior U.S. diplomat who has held eminent positions in the United States government and the United Nations. The son of noted economist John Kenneth Galbraith (1908–2006), in the 1980s Peter Galbraith was a senior adviser to the U.S. Senate Foreign Relations Committee, and, from an early date, his attention was directed toward the Near East (in particular, Turkey and Iraq). In September 1988 he traveled, with another colleague on the Senate Foreign Relations Committee, to the Turkey/Iraq border, where thousands of Iraqi Kurds had fled from mustard, cyanide, and nerve gas attacks (most commonly referred to as the al-Anfal Campaign) launched against them by the government of Iraqi dictator Saddam Hussein (1937–2006). Interviewing a large number of survivors of these assaults, Galbraith drew the conclusion that the Iraqi campaign was systematic, state-driven, and genocidal in nature. Documentation was collected on forty-nine chemical weapons attacks on Kurdish villagers. Upon his return to Washington, D.C., Galbraith unsuccessfully urged the U.S. government to place sanctions on Iraq. Still, he and others (including journalists with the *Washington Post* and the *New York Times*) had alerted the powers that be in Washington of the Iraqi/Kurdish situation, thus priming the U.S. government to listen more acutely and respond more proactively when the Iraqis carried out further attacks against the Kurds in 1991.

Galbraith's initial report was circulated through the halls of the U.S. Congress and the White House, while he sought every opportunity to keep U.S. attention focused on the murderous policies of the Iraqi government. His work seemed to have yielded results when the U.S. Senate passed a resolution imposing comprehensive sanctions against Iraq later in 1988, though sustained opposition to the proposal from the U.S. House of Representatives and the State Department saw the proposition collapse before the year was out.

Later, in the aftermath of the Iraqi invasion of Kuwait in 1990 and the defeat of Saddam Hussein's forces by U.S.-led United Nations forces in 1991, the Kurds of northern Iraq (along with the Shiites in the south) rose up against the regime. In response, the Iraqi military machine—crushed by the allied forces, but still sufficiently intact to be able to destroy insurgents and civilians—turned against the Kurds. The ensuing carnage—which included aerial bombing and chemical attacks—saw thousands killed, in a deadly revisitation of the al-Anfal campaign of just a few years earlier. The attacks resulted in an estimated fifty thousand to one hundred thousand deaths. The Kurds, themselves, claim that about one hundred eighty-two thousand people were killed. To a large degree the international community, already war-weary after the short war that led to the liberation of Kuwait, appeared to turn its back on the Kurds. More specifically, while the United States had encouraged the Kurds to rise up against Iraq, the United States failed to support the Kurds when the Iraqi government began to carry out a scorched earth policy against the rebels. Fearing that the uprisings would destabilize the area, the United States even refused to provide the rebels with the Iraqi weapons captured during the Gulf War. Only after the Kurds had suffered devastating losses did the U.S. deign it reasonable to establish safe areas and no-fly zones over those areas where the Kurds were huddled.

In May 1992 Galbraith was instrumental in the transfer of some fourteen tons of documents to the United States regarding the Iraqi repression of the Kurds, including the gassing of the Kurds in northern Iraq in the late 1980s. Ultimately, the documents were housed in the U.S. National Archives in Washington, D.C.

Later still, now as U.S. ambassador to Croatia (1993–1998) during the Clinton administration (1993–2002), Galbraith was actively involved in helping to negotiate the peace settlements involving Croatia and Bosnia-Herzegovina. He made a point of being outspoken over a host of issues relating to the violent conflict in the former Yugoslavia, refusing to let them fall by the wayside. More specifically, in a meeting with Mate Boban (1940–1997), a Bosnian Croat leader, Galbraith broached the issue of war crimes being perpetrated in a Croat prison camp, as well as the shelling of civilian targets in Mostar. Though Boban initially denied both charges, the very next day he immediately released some seven hundred prisoners. Galbraith then went on the BBC and claimed that Boban was possibly responsible for war crimes. The interview with Galbraith was rebroadcast in Croatia, and shortly thereafter conditions in various prison camps suddenly improved in significant ways—including a change in the leadership of some camps and the release of some of the innocent people from the camps.

Between January 2000 and August 2001, Galbraith served as a senior official in the United Nations Transitional Administration in East Timor (UNTAET), and later as a Cabinet Minister in the first transitional government in that country. Since leaving the diplomatic service, he has been a professor at Harvard University and the National War College in Washington, D.C. He is generally credited with being the diplomat who kept the U.S. Government's attention focused on the plight of the Kurds, at a time when other concerns—notably, the end of the Cold War—were distracting U.S. policy from humanitarian issues.

Galen, Bishop Clemens August Graf von (1878–1946). Cardinal-archbishop of Muenster, Germany during the period of the Third Reich. He began his career in the Catholic Church in 1904 as bishop's chaplain in Muenster, was ordained as a priest in 1919, and became archbishop of Muenster in 1933. He was an outspoken opponent of Nazi racial doctrine, and set himself up as a key opponent of Nazi ideologue Alfred Rosenberg (1893–1946). As a Catholic religious leader, his creed prevented him from condoning the Nazi euthanasia program, in which people with incurable diseases, mental illness, or disabilities were killed in accordance with state policy. In a public denunciation of the program in 1941, he ran afoul of the Nazi authorities and was subject to virtual house arrest until the end of the war in 1945. In 1944 after the attempted assassination of Adolf Hitler (1889–1945) in the so-called July Plot, von Galen was arrested by the Gestapo and incarcerated in the Sachsenhausen concentration camp. Although von Galen was not part of the plot, the Gestapo used the opportunity presented in the aftermath of the coup attempt to clean up its area of administration by striking at those considered to be dissenters. It was thus claimed that Von Galen had associated with those who were behind the plot. Ultimately, he was released by the Allies in April 1945. In February 1946 he was consecrated a cardinal by Pope Pius XII (1876–1958), and celebrated mass in both Westphalia and Muenster to enthusiastic crowds. A year later he died.

Gas Chambers. The use of the gas chambers was the preferred Nazi method of large scale extermination and annihilation of concentration and death camp prisoners, primarily Jews—but also, to a great extent, Roma and Sinti—in fixed building installations, usually disguised as "showers" (German, *Brausebad*), for the supposed purpose of "delousing" the inmates. Although some of the death camps (e.g., Belzec, Sobibor, Treblinka) continued to use carbon monoxide, the term *gas chamber* is usually associated with camps such as Auschwitz and Stutthof that used the insecticide Zyklon B (hydrogen cyanide, *giftgas*), which was more efficient and more economical, psychologically less stressful for the perpetrators, required fewer personnel, and allowed for more physical distancing from the victim, thus "protecting" the perpetrators from viewing the horrific sight of people scratching and clawing for air as their bodies contorted into frightening shapes and their bodies excreted fluids. A crystalline substance, Zyklon B rapidly became a noxious gas upon contact with oxygen, filling the lungs of those confined. Death for all took place within forty-five minutes. By 1941, gas chamber installations were in use in various concentration and death camps throughout occupied Poland. The Erfurt, Germany, engineering firm of J. A. Topf & Sons won the competition for the construction of the gas chambers at Auschwitz, which would become the primary center for the murders of Jews and others by this method. No final count of those who died in this manner has ever been agreed upon, but is believed to be upwards of 1 million persons.

Gas Vans. Mobile killing units, usually large trucks equipped with sealed chambers into which the victims were forced and then asphyxiated by carbon monoxide poisoning. This method of mass death used by the Nazis ultimately proved unreliable due to frequent equipment breakdowns, the relatively few numbers of victims who could be murdered, and the psychologically negative effect upon the killers upon opening the doors, due to the stench of the victims and the physical disfigurement of the corpses. It was also seen as a waste of gasoline, a precious resource in Nazi Germany. The first gas vans were used in occupied Poland in 1940; the victims were Poles with severe mental retardation and other psychological afflictions.

It is believed that approximately seven hundred thousand victims met their end in such gas vans, half in the area of the Soviet Union by the *Einsatzgrüppen* during "Operation Barbarosa," and half in the area surrounding Chelmno extermination camp, the majority of whom, in both cases, were Jews.

Gendercide. The systematic killing of persons solely because of their gender, either male or female, though gendercide is more often applied to the fate of females than males, as it often refers to the rape and other types of sexual assault and brutalization against targeted female populations.

The term was first used by Mary Ann Warren in her 1985 book *Gendercide: The Implications of Sex Selection*, and was later used by genocide scholar Adam Jones in his research, made even better known through his Web site www.gendercidewatch.com

Gendercide Watch. An international organization based in Canada, Gendercide is a project of the Gender Issues Education Foundation (GIEF), a registered charitable foundation based in Edmonton, Alberta. Gendercide Watch reports that it "seeks to confront acts of gender-selective mass killing (of ordinary men and women) around the world. It also works to raise awareness, conduct research, and produce educational resources on gendercide." It maintains a Web site (http://www.gendercide.org), which constitutes its major means of outreach and public education.

Gender-Related Persecution. Any unjust act or practice that targets or impacts a particular gender.

General Assembly. *See* United Nations General Assembly.

Generalgouvernement (French, absorbed into; German, General Government). When the Germans invaded Poland in September 1939, they divided the country into three parts: the western third was annexed to the Third Reich; the eastern third was controlled by the Soviet Union; and the central third became known as the *Generalgouvernement*. The *Generalgouvernement* was a semi-independent unit ,which the Nazis used as the location for holding, working to death, and exterminating those they considered "unworthy of living." The *Generalgouvernement* comprised five districts: Krakow, Lublin, Radom, Galicia, and Warsaw. In these districts were to be found most of Poland's Jews, and in time the *Generalgouvernement* was utilized as a collection point for Jews deported from all over Europe, often prior to transshipment to the death camps in Poland. It was comprised of approximately 12 million people, 1.5 million of whom were Jews.

Given its location and function, the *Generalgouvernement* was an integral part of the Nazis' "Final Solution of the Jewish Question"; it not only allowed for the concentration of Jews in a specific locale, it was also geographically close to the extermination apparatus— the death camps—set up by the Nazis. Several of the larger and more important ghettos were situated in the *Generalgouvernement*, notably Warsaw, Krakow, and Lublin; Lodz, Lwow, and Bialystok were outside its borders, but nearby. It was anticipated that the *Generalgouvernement* would serve as a reservoir of Jews for forced labor and extermination, but that over time it (along with the rest of Europe) would be emptied of Jews in the final realization of the Nazis' genocidal ambitions.

Following the German attack on the Soviet Union during the summer of 1941, the Nazis added Eastern Galicia to the *Generalgouvernement*, which increased the population by some 3 to 4 million people.

Geneva Conventions. A series of four international treaties, signed in Geneva, Switzerland, in 1864, 1906, 1929 and 1949. Three additional protocols to the 1949 treaty were signed in 1949, 1977, and 2005. Collectively, these conventions establish the humanitarian standards by which nations engaged in war should behave toward the individuals caught up in it, whether as combatants or as civilians. The first of these conventions was the brainchild of Swiss banker Henri Dunant (1828–1910), who witnessed the Battle of Solferino between the army of Austria and a combined Franco-Italian force on June 24, 1859. Shocked by the carnage—at least forty thousand casualties—he was determined to do something to at least help the wounded, even if he could not stop the armies from fighting. His efforts ultimately led to the establishment of the International Committee of the Red Cross, which has since been closely aligned with the conventions that followed. In Geneva, Switzerland, in August 1864, the representatives of sixteen countries met and drew up a treaty (or convention) "for the amelioration of the condition of the wounded in armies in the field." It was the first such treaty of its kind. In the conventions that came after this, the initial principles were broadened, by agreement with the signatory nations and those who had acceded since 1864: the convention of 1906 extended the principles to war at sea, the convention of 1929 concerned the ethical treatment of prisoners of war (who would be granted certain rights with regard to basic care), and involved set rules applicable to all signatory states; in the aftermath of the horrors of World War II, the 1949 convention addressed issues related to the treatment of civilians, both in enemy hands and under enemy control (the difference was an important one to those framing the treaty). The two protocols of 1977 clarified certain issues stemming from the 1949 convention, and considered differences between victims of international armed conflicts and those of non-international armed conflicts. All the conventions of the twentieth century served to build an infrastructure for the new discipline of international humanitarian law, including the Hague conventions (1899 and 1907), together with a slew of such treaties initiated through the United Nations from 1948 onward (one of which was the United Nations Convention on the Prevention and Punishment of the Crime of Genocide 1948).

Geneva Treaty. *See* Geneva Conventions.

Genghis Khan (c. 1167–1227). Mongol chief (approximating both king and emperor) of the twelfth century, whose conquered domains spread from China, through central and western Asia, and into Russia and eastern Europe. His first considerable extension of power from his base in Mongolia was westward; certain larger groups of people (e.g., the Kirghiris and Uighurs) were not so much conquered, as induced to join with him. He then moved into China and, by 1214, had taken Yanjing (later known as Beijing). In 1218 his huge (and ever-expanding) army crossed the Pamir Mountains and swept into Turkestan. The army was well armed and probably included guns and gunpowder for siege work. Famous cities such as Kashgar, Bokhara, and Samarkand all fell in a short period of time. Thereafter, little held him back; the Mongols swept westward to the Caspian Sea and southward as far as Lahore in modern-day Pakistan. By the time his empire appeared on the shores of the Black Sea, a panic set in at Constantinople, at that time still embroiled in the turmoil of the Crusades. Ultimately, the city held out against him and his hordes. In 1227, in the midst of a triumphant career, Genghis Khan died. His empire reached from the Pacific almost to the borders of Poland, and was still expanding. The major characteristic of the empire, in fact, was constant expansion. Like all nomad-founded empires, that of Genghis Khan was founded purely as a military and administrative structure, providing a framework for daily exchange and law—rather than being established on state or government lines. Given this, Genghis Khan's approach to conquest was frequently brutal and extremely bloody. In reducing a besieged city, for example, he would first offer it the chance to surrender; if refusal followed, he would bide his time, attack at an opportune moment, and, upon gaining control of the city, slaughter all its inhabitants (sometimes numbering in the tens of thousands) as a warning to the next city along the road. The empire was of massive physical size, but built on an unmitigated brutality that cost the lives of many hundreds of thousands over the twenty-some years of his rule.

Génocidaire. French term for an individual who takes part in perpetrating genocide.

Genocidal Massacre. A term introduced by noted political scientist and genocide scholar Leo Kuper (1908–1994) in his seminal work *Genocide: Its Political Use in the Twentieth Century* (1981). Noting that the annihilation of a section of a group in a localized massacre (e.g., in the wiping out of a whole village of men, women, and children) contains some of the elements of a genocide, Kuper sought to find a way to give such massacres their proper place within a model of genocide, while recognizing that such events did not, by themselves, constitute genocide. Kuper found the notion of genocidal massacre particularly helpful in this respect. He also found the concept and term useful in describing colonial situations, as the large number of massacres accompanying colonial acquisition pointed clearly to an affinity between colonialism and genocide. Although even an aggregation of genocidal massacres did not necessarily connote a policy of genocide, the motives that underlay such massacres were, in their time-and-place, motivated by a genocidal intent. For Kuper, therefore, the genocidal massacre, while not equal to genocide, was a device for explaining the many examples of destruction that took place during territorial acquisition, maintenance, and decolonization.

Genocidal Rape. *Genocidal rape* is a relatively new term that has entered the vocabulary of genocide studies. Generally, the term genocidal rape is used to suggest the use of mass rape by perpetrators as a weapon against the group they perceive as enemies. In that regard, genocidal rape, itself is largely used as a way to degrade, demoralize, and humiliate both the female victims and their families (not to mention fellow community members and members of their ethnic, religious, national group), as well as to cause physical trauma to the female victims. It has also been used as a means of forced impregnation, particularly in societies where the defiling of women often results in their becoming pariahs, not only in the larger society, but also within their immediate families. Furthermore, it has been used as a means to create "bastards," who not only do not know their fathers who brought them into the world by an act of violence, but are often unwanted by their mothers. Such rape is more a crime of violence than sexuality, both culturally and historically, and made all the more complicated in both Judaic and Islamic communities, which tend to regard the women who have been raped not only unfortunate victims, but blemished religiously and shunned communally.

Although rape is not specifically referred to in the United Nations Convention on the Prevention and Punishment of the Crime of Genocide (UNCG), both sections b ("Causing serious bodily or emotional harm to members of the group") and d ("Deliberately inflicting on the group conditions of life calculated to bring about its physical destruction in whole or in part") are germane to the act and violence of rape. The rationales for the latter assertions are obvious in regard to section b, but less so in regard to section d. As for section d, in many situations across the globe women who have been forcibly impregnated by another group—particularly when the perpetrator group is perceived as "outsiders," enemies, or "infidels"—may result in a woman being forsaken by her own community, and thus not able, even if she so desired, to bear children of her own ethnic group in the future.

In many instances in the near past, mass rape has been used as a tool to carry out warfare, "ethnic cleansing," and genocide. Mass rapes, for example, were perpetrated during the 1971 Bangladesh genocide, the 1994 Rwandan genocide, by Serbs in the 1990s in so-called rape camps against Muslim women in the former Yugoslavia, and by government of Sudan troops and the *Janjaweed* (Arab militia) throughout the course of the genocide in Darfur, Sudan (2003 through today, late 2007).

There is evidence that one of the key purposes of at least some of the abuse in the Serbian "rape camps" in the former Yugoslavia was impregnation. In fact, in certain cases women were detained until their fetus was so far along that abortion was not an option. Among the epithets screamed at the woman by their attackers were "Death to all Turkish sperm" and "You are going to bear little Serbs." Some legal scholars have argued that it is forced impregnation, not rape itself, that constitutes genocide. Others argue that the very act of mass rape that results in females becoming pariahs within their communities, and thus, as mentioned above, unable to bear offspring of their own ethnic group, constitutes genocide.

Genocidal Societies. Coined by the noted sociologist Irving Louis Horowitz (b. 1929), genocidal societies are those in which the state takes the lives of groups of people who it perceives as deviant or dissident.

Genocide: A Critical Bibliographical Series. Created by psychologist and genocide scholar Israel W. Charny (b. 1931), the purpose of *Genocide: A Critical Bibliographical Series* was to publish books composed of critical essays on key issues germane to various facets of genocide, and to provide an accompanying annotated bibliography of major works on the topic addressed in each essay. To date (September 2007) seven volumes have been published.

Among the many topics addressed in the first volume (1988) are the history and sociology of genocidal killings, the Armenian genocide, the Holocaust, genocide in the USSR, the Cambodian genocide, other selected cases of genocide and genocidal massacres, the psychology of genocidal destructiveness, and the literature, art and film of genocide. In the second volume (1991), authors addressed the following: denials of the Holocaust and the Armenian genocide, law and genocide, educating about the Holocaust and genocide, genocide and total war, first-person accounts of genocide, and the language of extermination in genocide. Volume three comprised essays on such topics as democracy and the prevention of genocide, religion and genocide, documentation of the Armenian genocide in German and Austrian sources, genocide in Afghanistan, genocide of the Kurds, the East Timor Genocide, the fate of the Gypsies in the Holocaust, and nongovernmental organizations working on the issue of genocide. The focus of the fourth volume (1997), which was coedited by Robert Krell and Marc Sherman, was medical and psychological effects of the concentration camps on Holocaust survivors.

In 2001 Samuel Totten succeeded Israel Charny as managing editor of the series. The first volume Totten edited, volume five, was titled *Genocide at the Millennium* (2004), which included essays and accompanying annotations on: The 1994 Rwandan genocide, genocide in the former Yugoslavia, international law and genocide, the International Criminal Tribunal for the former Yugoslavia (ICTY) and the International Criminal Tribunal for Rwanda (ICTR), the establishment of the International Criminal Court (ICC), nongovernmental organizations and the issue of genocide, and the United Nations and genocide. Volume six, *The Prevention and Intervention of Genocide* (2008) included essays on past and current efforts vis-à-vis the prevention and intervention of genocide in Iraq, Rwanda, the former Yugoslavia, and Darfur, Sudan; the development of genocide early-warning systems; the efficacy of sanctions; the role of the UN in prevention and intervention efforts; and the concept of an antigenocide regime. Volume seven, *Women and Genocide* (2008), focuses on the plight and fate of women during the course of various genocides (e.g., the Armenian genocide, the Holocaust, the Bangladesh genocide, the 1994 Rwandan genocide, genocide in the former Yugoslavia, the Darfur genocide); international laws germane to such issues as "genocidal rape"; and problems and concerns women face during the postgenocidal period.

Among the many genocide scholars who have contributed essays to the series over the years are: Howard Adelman, Alex Alvarez, Paul R. Bartrop, Israel W. Charny, Vahakn Dadrian, James Dunn, Barbara Harff, Herbert Hirsch, Richard Hovannisian, Curt Jonassohn, Leo Kuper, James Mace, Eric Markusen, Martin Mennecke, Rubina Peroomian, Rudolf J. Rummel, William Schabas, Roger Smith, Greg Stanton, and Samuel Totten.

Genocide and Politicide Project. Based at the University of Maryland-College Park, this project is directed by political scientists Barbara Harff (b. 1942), professor emerita at the U.S. Naval Academy, Annapolis. Its foundation is a data base that includes information on a broad range of genocide and politicides perpetrated between 1955 and 2002—some fifty in all, which have engulfed the lives of at least 12 million and as many as 22 million noncombatants, more than all of the victims of internal and international wars since 1945. The Web site of the Genocide and Politicide Project notes that the following questions cum guidelines were used to help distinguish cases of genocide and politicide from other kinds of killings that generally occur during civil conflicts: "(1) Is there complicity by the state (or, in the case of civil war, either of the contending authorities) in actions undertaken that endanger human life?; (2) Is there evidence, even if circumstantial, of intent on the part of authorities to isolate or single out group members for mistreatment?; (3) Are victims members of an identifiable group?; (4) Are there policies and practices that cause prolonged mass suffering; and (5) Do the actions committed pose a threat to the survival of the group?"

Genocide by Attrition. A phrase that refers to the deliberate denial of adequate water, foodstuffs, and medical attention to a specific group of people by a perpetrator for the express purpose of contributing to the targeted group's demise. This phrase/concept was employed by various genocide scholars to explain a large part of the deaths of black Africans in Darfur, Sudan, who have been attacked, raped, killed, and run off their land by Government of Sudan (GOS) troops and the *Janjaweed* (Arab militia) between 2003 and today (late 2007). The deaths attributed to genocide by attrition are those that resulted from starvation, dehydration, lack of medical care, and similar debilitating, and often deadly conditions. In carrying out death and destruction, the GOS and *Janjaweed* stole the foodstuffs of the black Africans, poisoned their wells by tossing dead animal carcasses and dead human bodies into the wells, and chased the survivors into the wilds of the desolate mountains and deserts of Darfur. The GOS and *Janjaweed* have also purposely prevented foodstuffs, medicine and other supplies crucial to survival from entering many internally displaced camps where the black Africans have sought sanctuary, thus increasing the death toll.

Genocide, Causes of. As with all social sciences, establishing causality is not a scientific endeavor. Only with hindsight is some kind of connection visible between an event and what transpired beforehand. The best one can do is to determine antecedents and circumstances that point toward the event under consideration. This is no less true when analyzing the origins of a particular genocide. Whether one can ultimately arrive at a common denominator of causes true for all genocides remains dubious. Most frequently (though not always), genocides take place in times of war. Of course, there has to be a prevailing ideology (or at least a mood or attitude) that demonizes a target group for elimination. Times of extreme economic stress can contribute to the outbreak of mass violence. Genocidal violence is more likely to erupt where there is an absence of democracy at home and international disinterest. Another condition that may encourage genocidal thought and action is a radical imbalance of power between the génocidaires and the victims; in this environment, an unrestrained state can hurl itself against a defenseless citizenry. Clearly, factors such as these do not automatically lead to genocide. Genocide, like all other human events, is not inevitable before the fact. To take but one example, rabid antisemitism or racism, coupled to a severe economic crisis, need not necessarily lead to genocide, even though racial antisemitism did in the specific instance of Germany between 1933 and 1945. There is no sine qua non without which genocide cannot take place. The "trigger" factor will always vary from case to case. Thus, racism against African-Americans in the nineteenth and twentieth centuries in the United States did not lead to genocide; on the contrary, it evolved away from mass violence and led to the civil rights movement in the context of a democratic society. Similarly, incipient antisemitism under Josef Stalin's (1879–1950) totalitarian rule in the Soviet Union was brutal but not genocidal, whereas in Germany, as previously noted, it did assume genocidal proportions between 1933 and 1945 under the Nazi dictatorship of Adolf Hitler (1889–1945).

Nevertheless, for all the uncertainty about what brings about genocide, and the unreliability of projecting present circumstances into the future, those who seek to anticipate and predict genocidal crises will find knowledge of the background of past genocides useful. Causality in the strictest sense may not exist, but that does not mean that awareness of how a crisis evolved cannot serve as an index of dangers lying ahead. Though causality in the mechanical and philosophic senses does not apply in human history, an informal causality does operate in the affairs of humans. There are connections linking one event to another, not deterministically, but operatively. Thus, for example, the missile attack and subsequent crash of the airplane of President Juvenal Habyarimana (1937–1994) of Rwanda on April 6, 1994, served as a trigger for genocide, but it need not have done so. Indeed, something else altogether could have sparked the genocide against the Tutsi. The will to genocide in Rwanda in 1994 was already present. Without that will, no amount of additional stimuli would have set Rwanda aflame. Thus one genocide's cause is not necessarily another's. Each case of genocide is its own discrete example, with its own set of "causes" and "triggers."

Genocide, Classification in Multiple Categories. One of the major problems associated with applying the term *genocide* to an event or cluster of events relates not only to how it may be defined, but also to which groups are to be included within a definition. As a tool for assisting in the analysis of these important conceptual issues, some scholars have developed structures whereby genocides can be classified and categorized. U.S. genocide scholar Helen Fein (b. 1934), for instance, has concluded that four overall categories of genocide can be discerned: developmental genocide (where perpetrators clear an area of its inhabitants prior to colonization); despotic genocide (where destruction happens so as to clear the way for new regimes to come to power); retributive genocide (where peoples are targeted for reasons based around social dominance and struggle); and ideological genocide (where a population is defined doctrinally as undeserving of life). Other scholars have also sought to broaden the range of categories, such as Eric Markusen (1946–2007) and David Kopf, who add war-related deaths to genocide, or, in the case of R. J. Rummel, find ways of gathering together all instances of massacre, area bombing, state-directed killing of large numbers of people, or mass destruction caused by other agencies or individuals. Locating such actions within a taxonomy of genocide can be useful, but only if an acceptable definition has also been agreed to. And herein lies a problem: grouping genocides for the purpose of plotting, predicting, or planning is a worthwhile task only if scholars can first agree on precisely what it is they are studying. And other than the 1948 United Nations Genocide Convention on the Prevention and Punishment of the Crime of Genocide, which many scholars and jurists regard as inadequate owing to its narrowness, there are no other universally accepted definitions of genocide prevailing today. Grouping examples of mass killing and human rights violations together within a matrix of genocide may be a means to break the impasse, but it has only a limited value in law. Even though conceptually it provides assistance to scholars, classification can only be applied narrowly by lawyers and courts.

Genocide Convention Implementation Act of 1988. The Genocide Convention Implementation Act of 1988, which was named the "Proxmire Act" in honor of Senator William Proxmire (1915–2005), who had arduously lobbied for the ratification of the UN Convention on the Prevention and Punishment of the Crime of Genocide (UNCG), was the title of the U.S. law that made genocide a crime that was punishable in the United States by life imprisonment and fines of up to 1 million U.S. dollars. Although passage of the Genocide Convention Implementation Act of 1988 was hailed as a milestone, many saw it as "tainted," for certain senators insisted that a reservation be attached to the ratification. The reservation basically stated that before the United States could be called before the International Court of Justice (ICJ), the president of the United States would have to consent to the court's jurisdiction. That reservation resulted in the United States being the only country in the world that would decide whether or not it would appear before the World Court.

It is also noteworthy that the U.S. Senate did not ratify the "U.S. version of the genocide treaty" until February 11, 1986, some thirty-eight years after the UN General Assembly unanimously voted on passage of the law. Equally noteworthy is the fact that ninety-seven nations had ratified the UNCG ahead of the United States. Ultimately, it took another two years before the United States' ratification became formal law, for incessant wrangling continued over the implementation legislation that became the "Genocide Convention Implementation Act of 1988."

Genocide, Denial of. Denial of a genocide having taken place (even in the far past, such as the Ottoman Turk genocide of the Armenians and the Nazi extermination of the Jews, Roma and Sinti, and physically and mentally handicapped) is a frequent occurrence. Genocide is first and foremost a crime, and those who commit it, or those supporting the perpetrators' actions, are often eager to seek exoneration by denying that charges of genocide have any veracity. Denial activities have often taken place via the printed word, though most recently this has extended to the Internet and lectures and speeches to receptive (or potentially receptive) audiences.

The motives of genocide deniers are not based on serious or objective scholarship, but rather on political, racist, or bigoted foundations. Often deception is employed in order to "convince" those without deep knowledge that the "accepted version" of history is in fact wrong. Genocide denial is thus not a part of the legitimate quest for understanding in which scholars engage, as denialist activities do not rework or revise, based on new evidence, the endeavors of earlier researchers. Their method, instead, is to deny the very reality of the phenomena to which earlier scholars have directed their attention, or to skew the facts. Concomitantly, genocide denial is frequently an attempt—sometimes made quite crudely—to discredit the victims of genocides by saying their experiences did not take place.

Given the latter, deniers frequently proceed from the belief—often held with passionate conviction—that they are struggling against a massive conspiracy being waged by those alleging the existence of a genocide (two such examples are past and present Turkish governments' reaction to the Armenians' effort to focus attention on the Ottoman Turk genocide of their Armenian ancestors [1915–1923], and neo-Nazi and other Holocaust deniers' repeated claim that world Jewry is attempting to manipulate the world by continued reference to the Holocaust, either for economic gain or political and military support of the state of Israel). Deniers frequently maintain their denialism in spite of all evidence the contrary. Further, they promote the very racism or victimization upon which the historical phenomena (which they say never happened) was based, while "denouncing" a massive "conspiracy" that aims to defraud the world.

Genocide, During Early Modern Period. In the era between the Middle Ages and the modern period, a number of genocidal episodes occurred that were a departure from those of the Ancient World and the upheavals of the great migrations during the first millennium of Christianity. Genocides such as that experienced in the early thirteenth century by the Cathars (or Albigensians) of southern France, which were based on a desire by the Church to uproot what it perceived to be heresy, showed that western Europe had moved far down the road toward becoming a persecuting society established on notions of religious intolerance—a frightening portent of things to come in the modern age. The development of such attitudes, exemplified in a European belief in the undesirability of "the Other," ultimately became internalized as part of European society. It was bolstered by a streamlining of administration as systems of bureaucracy advanced, via the centralization of power as expressed through the feudal system, and through the slow but steady growth of capitalism. Another form of genocidal intolerance came in the form of the two centuries-long Witch Craze of the sixteenth and seventeenth centuries, and in the occurrence of widespread religious persecutions, such as that committed against the Huguenots of France in the sixteenth century, and that in Poland and Ukraine committed against the Jews by the forces of Bogdan Chmielnicki (1595–1657) in the middle of the seventeenth century. Religious persecution resulting in mass death was a constant throughout the early modern period, some of the most terrible examples taking place during the Thirty Years' War (1618–1648). Some areas in the lands that were later to comprise Germany were even depopulated at this time by as much as ninety per cent. In short, the early modern period was an important era of transition in the history of genocide, as human destruction became less a matter of ancillary devastation accompanying territorial conquest, and more an issue of targeted killing on the grounds of what both victim and perpetrator peoples thought or believed. After 1789, ideology would serve increasingly as a determinant as to why genocidal violence happens.

Genocide Early Warning System. A generic term that refers to a process or program whose express purpose is to monitor violent conflict in order to collect, analyze, predict, and disseminate information in order to alert key agencies, organizations, and authorities about a potential genocide. Individual scholars (e.g., Israel W. Charny, Barbara Harff, Helen Fein, and Franklin Littell) have developed theoretical and conceptual models and/or components germane to the development of a genocide early warning system, and over the past decade and a half (1993 to 2007) such organizations as the United Nations, the United States, and the Canadian government have been involved, to one extent or another, in the conception of genocide early warning systems. At this point in time (August 2007), a theoretically sound, well-developed, well-funded, and fully operational genocide early warning system is not a reality.

Genocide Education. Genocide education at the secondary, college, and university levels encompasses all aspects of genocide, including, but not limited to: genocide theory (e.g., definitions of genocide, preconditions of genocide, typologies of genocide); a general history of genocide; specific cases of genocide (e.g., the Ottoman Turk-perpetrated genocide of the Armenians; the Soviet man-made famine in Ukraine' the Khmer Rouge–perpetrated Cambodian genocide of 1975–1979; the Iraqi gassing of its Kurd population in the north in 1988; the 1994 Rwandan genocide; the Darfur genocide in the early 2000s of black Sudanese by Sudanese government troops and Arab militia); comparative genocide (e.g., the Armenian genocide and the Holocaust); the prevention and intervention of genocide, et al.

Four notable works have been published on genocide education: *The Sociology of the Holocaust and Genocide: A Teaching and Learning Guide*, edited and compiled by Jack Nusan Porter and Steve Hoffman (Washington, DC: American Sociological Association, 1999); *Teaching about Genocide: A Guidebook for College and University Teachers—Critical Essays, Syllabi and Assignments*, edited by Joyce Freedman-Apsel and Helen Fein (New York: Institute for the Study of Genocide, 1992); *Teaching about Genocide: An Interdisciplinary Guidebook with Syllabi for Colleague and University Teachers* (second edition), edited by Joyce Apsel and Helen Fein (Washington, DC: American Sociological Association, 2002); and *Teaching about Genocide: Issues, Approaches, Resources*, edited by Samuel Totten (Greenwich, CT: Information Age Publishing, 2004).

"Genocide Fax," January 1994. On January 10, 1994, Lieutenant General Romeo Dallaire (b. 1946), the Canadian Force Commander of UNAMIR (the United Nations Assistance Mission for Rwanda), received intelligence that an extremist Hutu codenamed "Jean-Pierre," was prepared to disclose information regarding a planned genocide of Tutsi. "Jean-Pierre" had been an officer in Rwanda's Presidential Guard, but had left in order to become one of the key men in the *Interahamwe* militia. Upon closer inquiries, it transpired that Jean-Pierre had much to say. He described in detail how the *Interahamwe* were trained, by whom, and where; he added that the militia was in a state of permanent readiness sufficient to kill one thousand Tutsi in the capital, Kigali, within twenty minutes of receiving an order to commence the genocide. As a sign of his goodwill and reliability, Jean-Pierre offered to reveal the location of a large stockpile of weapons somewhere in central Kigali. Dallaire, realizing that these arms had to be confiscated, decided to order an arms raid, and faxed the UN Department of Peacekeeping Operations in New York, headed at that time by Kofi Annan (b. 1938), for authorization. The cable outlined in detail the revelations made by Jean-Pierre. It has frequently been put, with some justification, that, if the authorization had been given, Dallaire's efforts certainly could have forestalled—and perhaps even stopped— the possibility of the genocide that was to break out on April 6, 1994. Dallaire's fax was responded to negatively, however, by those at UN headquarters. More specifically, he was informed (cum ordered) that under no circumstances was he authorized to conduct arms raids. In turn, he was taken to task for suggesting that he exceed his Chapter VI peacekeeping mandate and he was ordered to turn over Jean-Pierre's revelations to the president of Rwanda, Juvenal Habyarimana (1937–1994)—the very man whose anti-Tutsi cause the *Interahamwe* was enforcing. The UN's Department of Peacekeeping Operations, together with the office of the then secretary-general Boutros Boutros-Ghali (b. 1922), decided that legality and process were more important, on this occasion, than action; not only this, but they were concerned for the image of the UN in light of an earlier failed arms raid that took place with heavy loss of life in Mogadishu, Somalia in October 1993. Dallaire adamantly protested the decision, but the UN would not budge—with catastrophic consequences. The "genocide fax" of January 10, 1994 represents a missed opportunity on the UN's part to nip the nascent génocidaires actions in the bud; it was a mistake whose price was the Rwanda genocide three months later in which between five hundred thousand and 1 million Tutsi and moderate Hutu were murdered in one hundred days.

Genocide Forum, The. *The Genocide Forum*, a bimonthly newsletter founded in 1993, was a publication of the Center for the Study of Ethnonationalism located on the campus of the City College of New York. *The Genocide Forum* was intended to serve as a convenient vehicle of exchange to discuss critical issues of common interest to students of Holocaust and Genocide Studies. The founder and editor of *The Genocide Forum* was Professor Henry R. Huttenbach (b. 1931).

Genocide, History of. Genocide is a crime that has been committed throughout the ages. Indeed, every century of recorded history has been marred by genocidal acts. It was not until the twentieth century, though, that this particular act was given the name *genocide*. It is thus a relatively new name for a very old practice. The term was originally coined in 1944 by Raphael Lemkin (1900–1959), a Polish-Jewish jurist who lost most members of his family in the Holocaust. His coinage of the term was accepted and absorbed by the United Nations in order to describe the intentional destruction, in whole or in part, of a specific group of people, in its 1948 Convention on the Prevention and Punishment of the Crime of Genocide.

Genocide as a human activity has taken many forms in the past. The Hebrew Bible contains many passages that refer to mass destruction of a kind which would, today, be identified as genocide. Likewise, the annals of other ancient peoples recount genocidal episodes in great detail, the Greeks and the Romans foremost among them. In central Asia, during the Middle Ages, the Mongols and Turks swept through the deserts and steppes, killing hundreds of thousands along the way. In Europe, as theological differences developed within Christianity, those deviating from the Roman Catholic Church were put to the sword, the gallows, the stake, and the block, and, as Europe extended its physical limits to include the Americas during the sixteenth century, entire areas were depopulated in an explosion of violence and pestilence. Colonial expansion in succeeding centuries saw the destruction of millions on all continents. Such destruction, on a genocidal scale, reached its zenith during the twentieth century, which has become known to many as the "Century of Genocide." Murderous acts of the most intense kind were perpetrated in every decade on at least four different continents (Africa, Asia, Europe and South America), and genocide without killing took place on one other (Australia). Among some of the many genocides perpetrated in the twentieth century were: the German-perpetrated genocide of the Herero in South-West Africa in 1904; the Ottoman Turk genocide of the Armenians, Assyrians, and Pontic Greeks between 1915–1923; the Holocaust (1933–1945); the Bangladesh genocide (1971); the Khmer Rouge–perpetrated genocide in Democratic Kampuchea (Cambodia) between 1975 and 1979; the Iraqi genocide of the Kurds of northern Iraq in 1988; the 1994 Rwandan genocide of Tutsi and moderate Hutu at the hands of extremist Hutu; and the Bosnian Muslim genocide at the hands of Bosnian Serb and Federal Republic of Yugoslavia forces between 1992 and 1995. There were also the almost totally unrecognized genocides of many indigenous peoples across the globe.

The history of genocide has shown that outbreaks of massive destruction have been increasing, but concomitant with this development has been an upsurge in international legislation designed to confront such outbreaks. The establishment of the International Criminal Court in 2002 might be viewed as the ultimate expression, thus far, of the nations of the world to do something effective to outlaw genocide in the future.

Genocide, Misuse of the Concept/Term. Ever since the concept/term *genocide* was first coined by Raphael Lemkin (1900–1959) in 1944, there have been constant disputes within academe over how the concept and term should be, once and for all, defined and interpreted. Although these disputes have been vigorous and, at times, even acrimonious, they have still led to substantial and significant misuse of the term at all levels. Without really appreciating its sophistication, both with regard to international law and international scholarship, many (e.g., some scholars, journalists, activists for various causes, repressed peoples) have added meanings to the word genocide that it was never intended to have. For some, genocide equates directly with war, with language extinction, with colonialist occupation, or with population collapse caused through natural famine or disease. Some argue a case for "accidental" genocide, where a population's numbers are reduced despite the best efforts of others to stop such reduction. Elsewhere, genocide has been misapplied when conflated into other examples of inhumanity or gross human rights violation, such as slavery or political incarceration.

The popularization and misuse of the term genocide has extended into the realms of education and journalism, whereby anyone's definition or understanding of the term is seemingly as legitimate as anyone else's. Departing from universally recognized appreciations of genocide, such as that embodied in the 1948 UN Convention on the Prevention and Punishment of the Crime of Genocide (UNCG), leads to conceptual confusion, and muddies the waters in an area requiring clarity and precision. Thus, for example, in international law there is no such thing as "cultural genocide," as the UNCG does not include cultural groups among those considered as targets for genocide. Yet the notion of "cultural genocide" has become one of those ideas which—though not acknowledged within international law—has been interpreted as a legitimate category.

On a different note, the use of the term/concept genocide has been banalized in a variety of ways. More specifically, all of the following issues/concerns have, at one time or another, been referred to as genocide: "race-mixing" (the integration of blacks and non-blacks); the practice of birth control and abortions among third world peoples; sterilizations and so-called Mississippi appendectomies (tubal ligations and hysterectomies); the closing of synagogues in the Soviet Union; a lack of support by U.S. president Reagan for research on AIDS; the adoption of black children by whites; the U.S. government's drug policy (which purportedly allowed the rampant sale of drugs in the inner cities of the United States), and the rate of abortions in the United States. And in one case, sports hunting was deemed "duck genocide."

***Genocide Studies and Prevention: An International Journal* (GSP).** GSP is the official journal of the International Association of Genocide Scholars (IAGS). It publishes scholarly articles and reviews on all aspects of genocide, and welcomes in particular comparative analyses and articles on prevention and intervention of genocide. GSP is an interdisciplinary, peer-reviewed journal that provides a forum for scholarly discourse for researchers, practitioners, governmental policy makers, educators, and students. The brainchild of Israel W. Charny, GSP was cofounded by the IAGS, and the International

Institute for Genocide and Human Rights Studies (a division of the Zoryan Institute). GSP is published by the University of Toronto Press. The inaugural coeditors of GPS were Alex Alvarez, Herbert Hirsch, Eric Markusen, and Samuel Totten.

Genocide, Theories of. The enormous range and variety of outbreaks that have been termed genocide throughout history have led to a multiplicity of theories attempting to explain it as a human phenomenon. From the time the word was first coined in 1944 by Raphael Lemkin (1900–1959), the scholarly study of genocide has emerged. For many, theorizing about the nature of genocide has become a major intellectual activity; for others, doing so is irrelevant other than to acknowledge that genocide is a crime (for some, "the crime of crimes"), and that as such little theorizing is needed beyond the legislation that has established its criminality (i.e., the United Nations Convention on the Prevention and Punishment of the Crime of Genocide 1948). Although the development of different theories about genocide can take place through the employment of a number of approaches—historical, social, political, psychological, economic, environmental, religious, ideological, military, cultural, and so on—invariably a great deal of genocide theory proceeds from (and all too often, gets bogged down by) discussions relating to definitional matters. Where Lemkin's original conception began with the statement that "By 'genocide' we mean the destruction of a nation or ethnic group," many others have built their discussions around definitions that diverge from this. Some, such as Pieter N. Drost (1959), Frank Chalk and Curt Jonassohn (1990), and Israel Charny (1991) focus on genocide as killing, whereas others, such as Helen Fein (1990) and Irving Louis Horowitz (1976) look at structural issues within the perpetrator state that make a destructive project (regardless of type) possible. Henry Huttenbach (1988) considers "any act that puts the very existence of a group in jeopardy" to be (at least potentially) a genocidal act. Other forms of destruction that do not fit comfortably into these broad theories of genocide have generated even newer terms, proceeding from the approach pioneered by Lemkin: hence, in addition to genocide there now exists such terms and concepts as ethnocide, politicide, democide, omnicide, gendercide, libricide, and autogenocide. Although these notions are often useful in creating models to help approach specific issues, it could be argued that a full appreciation of genocide in all its guises has yet to be exhausted. The establishment of workable theoretical models in order to do so, it can be argued, is just as much a legitimate task today as it was when Lemkin himself first reflected upon the phenomenon of mass human destruction.

Genocide Watch. Genocide Watch, which is based in Washington, D.C., was organized in 1998 to coordinate the International Campaign to End Genocide, a coalition of human rights, legal, religious, and civil society organizations. The International Campaign was launched by ten organizations at The Hague Appeal for Peace in 1999. Genocide Watch maintains the campaign's Web site, fund-raising, monthly news digest, and sponsors its own training programs and conferences. It also proposes genocide alerts to the campaign's members and acts on them with other groups who join in Crisis Groups to lobby governments and international organizations to take action to prevent and stop genocide. Genocide Watch is concerned with all forms of mass murder, not only killing that is legally defined as genocide. It also has an education arm, "Prevent Genocide International."

Geno/Politicide. A term/concept, which was coined and developed by Professor Barbara Harff (b. 1942) of the United States Naval Academy, that refers to "the promotion, execution and/or implied consent of sustained policies by governing elites or their agents—or in the case of civil war, either of the contending authorities—that result in the deaths of a substantial portion of a communal and/or politicized communal group" (Harff, 1992, p. 29).

Gerombolan Pengacau Keamanan (GPK). This term literally means "security disrupting gangs," which is the term that the Indonesian military used in the 1990s to refer to any criminal activity involving violence, including FRETILIN (*Frente Revolucionária do Timor-Leste Independente*, or Revolutionary Front for an Independent East Timor), a socialist-based, anticolonial group with nationalist leanings.

Gestapo. The *Geheime Staatspolizei* or "Secret State Police" was established by Hermann Goering (1893–1946) in April 1933 to combat those opposed to Nazism. From 1934 until his death by assassination in 1942, the Gestapo was commanded by Reinhard Heydrich (1904–1942), but was already part of the Reich Security Main Office by 1939. In early 1934 a "Jewish section," led by Adolf Eichmaan (1906–1962), was established as Section IVB.4, for the purpose of coordinating the rounding up and transferring of Jews to both concentration and death camps. Section I was responsible for organizational and financial matters, Section II with a variety of "enemies of the Reich" (e.g., communists, social democrats, trade unionists), and Section III with counterintelligence activities.

Through the use of torture, terror, and intimidation tactics, as well as so-called protective custody (*schutzhaft*, a code word for torture and imprisonment), the Gestapo became the primary instrument of anti-Jewish activity and repression of others throughout Germany. The Gestapo also had the power to send persons to detention and extermination camps. Furthermore, Gestapo units were part of each headquarters detachments in the occupied areas in Poland, eastern Europe, and later, the Soviet Union. At the International Military Tribunal (IMT), held at Nuremberg between 1945 and 1946, the Gestapo was formally declared a criminal organization and disbanded. Most of those responsible for its activities—the actual torturers and death camp guards—were never brought to trial. Göring, himself, committed suicide before his death sentence was carried out.

Glücks, Richard (1889–1945). Nazi police leader. Glücks was second-in-command to Theodor Eicke (1892–1943) as Inspector of Concentration Camps, an office Glücks took up in November 1939 after Eicke's transfer to a combat command. Born in Düsseldorf, Glücks joined the Nazi party after its ascent to office, and rose in a relatively quick period to become Eicke's aide.

Under Glücks, the Nazi concentration camp network expanded considerably, which was necessitated by German conquests during World War II. In February 1940, Glücks reported to the head of the SS, Heinrich Himmler (1900–1945), that a site had been found for a new camp close by the Polish town of Oswiecim, which in German translated to Auschwitz. By May 1940, upon his orders, the first Kommandant of the Auschwitz concentration camp, Rudolf Franz Hoess (1900–1947), commenced building what would become the largest of all the concentration camps, and a byword for the Holocaust. Glücks introduced a number of new measures to the concentration camps under his direction, including the use of forced foreign labor, and facilities for medical experiments on camp inmates. The full details of his ultimate fate are unclear, though it is believed he committed suicide in Italy in May 1945 to avoid trial at the hands of the Allies.

Goals of Anti-Jewish Administrators through the Ages. In his magisterial three-volume work entitled *The Destruction of the Jews*, historian Raul Hilberg (b.1926) observes that

> the Nazi destruction process did not come out of a void; it was the culmination of a cyclical trend. We have observed the trend on the three successive goals of anti-Jewish administrators. The missionaries of Christianity had said in effect: You have no right to live among us as Jews. The secular rulers who followed had proclaimed: You have no right to live among us. The German Nazis at last decreed: You have no right to live. (Hilberg, 1985, p. 9)

Goebbels, (Paul) Joseph (1897–1945). Holder of a doctorate in literature and philosophy with the intention of becoming a writer, Goebbels joined the Nazi Party in 1924, and, by 1933 Hitler appointed him German Minister of Public Enlightenment and Propaganda because of his talents in this area. A virulent antisemite, among Goebbels's goals was the physical removal of all Jews, not only from Berlin, but from all of Germany, and a campaign for German support for the euthanasia campaign. He also hoped to "Nazify" German art and culture by removing so-called foreign elements (read Jewish), and in 1933 orchestrated the now notorious book burning in Berlin. The primary architect of the infamous *Kristallnacht* of November 1938, the initial destruction of Jewish lives and property, he would, by 1944, be placed in charge of the mobilization of the German people's war efforts. Rather than submitting to capture by either the Russians or the Allies, he and his wife Magda committed suicide in the Fuhrer's bunker after first poisoning their six children.

Goldstone, Richard (b. 1938). For many years in the 1990s and early 2000s, Goldstone served as a justice with the Constitutional Court of South Africa. From August 1994 to September 1996, he also served as the chief prosecutor of the UN International Criminal Tribunals for the Former Yugoslavia (ICTY) and Rwanda (ICTR). He was selected, in part, for the latter position on the basis of his global reputation for his sterling work, while directing a South African Commission of Inquiry that disclosed police violence and abuse against black citizens of South Africa during South Africa's apartheid years.

Golkar. An Indonesian political party. Its name is derived from *Sekretariat Bersama Golongan Karya*, or Joint Secretariat of Functional Groups. The party evolved as an army-backed alliance of nearly one hundred anticommunist groups and organizations in the early 1960s, but it was ineffective so long as Indonesia was ruled by its left-leaning first president, Ahmed Sukarno (1901–1970). After a military takeover of power led by Mohamed Suharto (b. 1921) in 1966, Golkar was reorganized by General Ali Murtopo (1923–1984), head of the army's Special Operations Service (OPSUS) and Suharto's political protégé. The party henceforth became the established party of government, and remained so for more than three decades. Electoral successes in 1971, 1977, 1982, and 1987 saw Suharto's rule entrenched. Between 1971 and 1988, Suharto was unopposed in presidential elections, and Golkar came more and more to resemble a personal political front organization designed to enable him to retain office. Evolving into a mass mobilizing party loyal to Suharto, in some senses it moved away from being the political arm of the Indonesian military alone, though Suharto's ongoing support of the military in most areas tended to blur the distinctions. Yet, as the party leadership tried to distance itself from the army, the military chiefs became increasingly wary of the direction the party was heading, and in the final years of Suharto's rule before his departure in 1998, it was unclear whether or not Golkar would develop into a legitimate party independent of the army. With Suharto's exit as president, and a succession of subsequent presidents that followed until a full and free presidential election in 2004, Golkar's power base was first challenged and then toppled. Although still a leading opposition presence, Golkar—the party that retained Suharto in office for more than thirty years, oversaw the invasion of East Timor in 1975, permitted war to be waged internally against the people of Aceh and Papua, and collaborated with the army to hold the population of Indonesia in what was effectively a police state—has now lost much of the influence (and all of the political power) it once possessed.

Gorazde. A city in eastern Bosnia situated on the Drina River, Gorazde was designated a United Nations "safe area" in 1993. During the Bosnian War (1992–1995) the city was besieged by Army of Republika Srpska (VRS) forces, which were aided by paramilitary and militia units. In April 1994 some 150 peacekeepers, part of the United Nations Protection Force (UNPROFOR) troops helping to safeguard the city, were taken hostage by the Serbs in the hope that this would deter NATO air strikes against Serb positions. The previous week Serb gunners had assaulted the city using heavy weapons taken from the Srebrenica front, causing an enormous amount of damage to urban housing and the city center. NATO delivered an ultimatum to the Serbs on April 22, threatening air strikes unless they pulled back by three kilometers, immediately halted their attacks, and opened the city to all UN forces and relief convoys. The Serbs complied, though whether the NATO actions would have actually followed any noncompliance by the Serbs is open to debate. The UNPROFOR commander, Lieutenant General Sir Michael Rose (b. 1940), and the UN special representative of the secretary-general, Yasushi Akashi (b. 1931), neither of whom evinced the same level of concern about Serb actions as did the NATO forces on the ground, worked hard behind the scenes to prevent further NATO air strikes, and put substantial pressure on the UNPROFOR contributing states not to commit their forces to action against the Serbs. In the end, Gorazde held out as a result of NATO threats and an active local Bosnian Muslim defense. Despite extensive destruction by continued shelling and sniping from Serb positions throughout the remainder of the war, during which Gorazde continued to be besieged, the city did not fall. It was to become the only Muslim town in eastern Bosnia not to be "ethnically cleansed" by the Serbs. Gorazde's role in the annals of international peacekeeping will be assured by another observation: it signaled a parting of the ways between a UN approach that was reluctant to intervene and a NATO approach that was prepared to take action in order to stop Serb aggression. The divide would be played out more fully in March 1999, when NATO went to war with Serbia over the prospect of a genocide taking place in Kosovo.

Göring, Hermann (1893–1946). Born in Bavaria to a wealthy family, Göring distinguished himself as an ace fighter pilot during World War I, and joined the Nazi Party in 1922. In 1933 Hitler appointed him Prime Minister of Prussia and Minister for Police (which gave him authority for the establishment of draconian measures against political opponents), and his designated successor at the start of World War II, September 1939. By 1935 he was also in charge of both German economic policy, and, after 1938, focused increasing attention on so-called Jewish problems. With the failure of the German air force (*Luftwaffe*) against Britain in the years 1940–1941, and its inability to stop the bombing of Germany, his relationship with Hitler began to sour; by 1945 he had been stripped of all power and dismissed from the Nazi Party. Sentenced to death by the International Military

Tribunal at Nuremberg, Germany, he cheated the hangman's noose by poisoning himself in his cell on October 15, 1946.

Gosh, Salah Abdallah (n.d.). A major-general in the Sudanese army, Gosh is director of Mukhabarat, Sudan's intelligence agency. He has been accused by various human rights organizations (including Human Rights Watch) of being the mastermind of the scorched-earth attacks on the black Africans of Darfur by Government of Sudan (GOS) troops and the *Janjaweed* (Arab militia). Gosh is suspected of having overseen the recruitment of the *Janjaweed* militia, coordinated the genocidal actions carried out by the GOS and the *Janjaweed*, and condoned interference with humanitarian aid workers in the Darfur region (the latter of which included threats of violence, acts of violence, and the theft of supplies intended for the black Africans who had been forced from their villages into desolate internally displaced camps [2003 through today, September 2007]).

In May 2005, the United States Central Intelligence Agency (CIA) flew Gosh from Sudan to the United States in a private plane in order to meet with top CIA officials. When a journalist with the *Los Angeles Times* found out about the secret meeting and made the news public, the outcry that followed was met with a statement from the U.S. government that Gosh and his Sudanese counterparts were supplying the United States with important and valuable assistance in the "war on terror" (an effort that the Administration of U.S. president George W. Bush (b. 1946) had undertaken in the aftermath of the terrorist attacks on the United States on September 11, 2001). More specifically, it was asserted that Gosh's agency helped the CIA to question al Qaeda suspects residing in Sudan, dismantled terrorist cells within Sudan, and jailed foreign militants traveling through Sudan on their way to fight in the ongoing war in Iraq (the latter of which, instigated by the United States invasion of Iraq, saw the fall of the regime of Saddam Hussein [1937–2006]). One official, U.S. Representative Donald M. Payne (b. 1934) (D-NJ), was so outraged that Gosh had been flown to the United States by the CIA that he asserted that bringing Gosh "to visit Washington at this time [when Sudan was perpetuating genocide] is tantamount to inviting the head of the Nazi SS at the height of the Holocaust." Notably, Gosh was one of seventeen Sudanese individuals that a UN panel of experts cited as being most responsible for inciting the crisis in Darfur (2003 through today, September 2007), impeding the peace process, and perpetrating war crimes. His name, along with the others, has been submitted to the UN Security Council's sanctions committee. It is also reported that the International Criminal Court, which is investigating the atrocities perpetrated in Darfur, has Gosh's name on their list as one whose actions are under scrutiny.

Grave Breaches of the Geneva Conventions and Protocols I and II. "Grave breaches" refer to major violations of international humanitarian law which may be punished by any state on the basis of universal jurisdiction. Under all four Geneva Conventions, grave breaches prohibit, inter alia, willful killing, torture, rape, or inhuman treatment of protected persons, willfully causing great suffering or serious injury to body or health, and extensive destruction and appropriation of property not justified by military necessity, and carried out unlawfully and wantonly.

Great Dictator, The. One of the classics of cinema history, *The Great Dictator* is a 1940 motion picture produced, directed, written by, and starring Charlie (later Sir Charles) Chaplin (1889–1977). A satire on German Nazism and Italian Fascism, the movie was the first comedy to poke fun at Adolf Hitler (1889–1945) and Benito Mussolini (1883–1945), and by so doing to draw attention to the brutal antisemitism being experienced by Germany's Jews under the Third Reich. Told through thinly veiled code language—Adolf Hitler as "Adenoid Hynkel," Benito Mussolini as "Benzino Napaloni," Der Führer as "The Phooey," Hermann Göring as "Marshal Herring," and so forth—the movie was an enormous gamble for Chaplin, who not only bankrolled its production using his own money, but departed from his career-defining silent movie technique in order to make this his first "talkie." Not only that, it was the first time his signature character, the Tramp—in this case known simply as "a Jewish Barber"—spoke dialogue from a prepared script. The film was well received by U.S. audiences, and was undoubtedly Chaplin's most successful film commercially. Critics were more qualified in their acclaim, some pointing out that Hollywood should refrain from foreign political comment at a time of U.S. isolationism. Others saw Chaplin's comedic portrayal of anti-Jewish persecution as unacceptable bad taste; Chaplin himself was later to write that if in 1940 he had known the full extent of Nazi antisemitic measures (something that could not even be guessed at in 1940) he would never have made the film. However, Chaplin, who was not Jewish, was determined to make Hitler an object of ridicule and he did so in the most effective way he could—through his comic art. *The Great Dictator* was nominated for a number of Academy Awards, including Best Picture, Best Actor (Chaplin), and Best Supporting Actor (Jack Oakie, in his role of Benzino Napaloni). The movie has been selected for permanent inclusion in the U.S. National Film Registry.

Great Purges. A succession of major purges of the Communist Party of the Soviet Union took place at the direction of Josef Stalin (1879–1953), principally between 1934 and 1938. During this period, Stalin's secret police, the NKVD, eliminated hundreds of thousands of opponents, or presumed opponents, of Stalin, cloaked in the necessity to rid the party of dissenters, supposed class traitors or revolutionary "backsliders." The pretext for all the killing was the murder in December 1934 of Sergei Kirov (1886–1934), party secretary for Leningrad. Major trials took place in January 1935, August 1936, January 1937, and March 1938, during which Stalin effectively removed the senior echelons of the Communist Party and the armed forces. It is uncertain whether those executed were killed because of their disloyalty, in Stalin's search for a scapegoat, or to appease Stalin's sense of political paranoia. Apart from the public trials, it has been estimated that at least half a million people were killed owing to lesser prosecutions resulting from denunciation and petty or personal reasons. Over 6 million were sent to Soviet concentration camps, where unknown numbers perished.

With regard to genocide, such enormous destruction presents a paradox; when the 1948 United Nations Convention on the Prevention and Punishment of the Crime of Genocide was originally drafted, the Soviet Union argued successfully against including "political groups" as one of the specific groups protected under the UNCG. The reason, though unstated at the time, is that the leaders of the USSR feared they would be held responsible, under the UNCG, for the past and ongoing persecution of such groups.

Be that as it may, the deaths during the period of the Great Purges must be accounted for in some way. At present, they can best be described as crimes against humanity committed by a regime that was brutal, paranoid, and more concerned about power than the people over whom it ruled. This period established the gulag (a widespread network of forced labor and prison camps in the Soviet Union) as a major characteristic of Soviet society throughout a large part of the twentieth century.

Great Terror, The. The name given to a period of massive turmoil and political violence in the USSR between 1934 and 1938, during which the Soviet secret police, the

NKVD, murdered hundreds of thousands of people alleged to be opponents of the Soviet State. These killings, accompanying what became known as the Great Purges, took place on the order of Soviet dictator Josef Stalin (1879–1953). Ostensibly a strategy to "purify" the Communist Party of the Soviet Union, the terror unleashed throughout the Soviet Union was little other than a reinforcement of the communist stranglehold on total power, after which ordinary Soviet citizens did not dare offer dissent for fear of their lives.

The murder in December 1934 of Sergei Kirov (1886–1934), party secretary for Leningrad, was used as a pretext for initiating a campaign of terror throughout the Soviet Union. The first wave of trials took place in January 1935. A number of close allies of Stalin, among them Gregori Zinoviev (1883–1936) and Lev Kamenev (1883–1936), were tried secretly and given long prison sentences. (Both were later executed after a second trial.) The terror continued through 1937; Karl Radek (1885–1939) and Marshal Mikhail Tukhachevsky (1893–1937) were shot on Stalin's orders, along with many others, while in 1938 it became the fate of such party notables as Nikolai Bukharin (1888–1938), Alexei Rykov (1881–1938), and Genrikh Yagoda (1891–1938). The year 1938 was the last year of the Great Terror period, yet those arrested throughout its four-year term and placed in forced labor camps—not unlike the concentration camps of the Nazis—numbered about 6 million by the end of 1937. Many of these would never be released. The period of the Great Terror saw the executions of perhaps half a million Soviet citizens, with millions more arrested, incarcerated, or with lives otherwise ruined by constant ill-treatment. No one could feel safe; many, indeed, lived in constant fear of denunciation. The Soviet police state built an apparatus of public terror to stop any threats to Stalin before they became too powerful, which was implemented throughout the Soviet Union in a series of ongoing raids, denunciations and investigations. The result was a population weakened by fear, an army crippled by the removal of most of its senior leadership, and a Communist party cowed into meek acquiescence of every one of Stalin's whims. Only after Stalin's death in 1953 was there even a modicum of relaxation for a country that had spent the best part of two decades living permanently on edge.

Grotius, Hugo (1583–1645). Huig de Groot, whose name was Latinized as Hugo Grotius, was a Dutch jurist and philosopher, best known for his contributions to the establishment of a codified system of international law. In fact, he has become known as the "Father of International Law."

A child prodigy born in Delft, Holland, he began studying at the University of Leiden at the age of eleven, and had earned a doctorate from the University of Orleans (France) at the age of fifteen. He began practicing law at the age of sixteen.

A firm believer in natural rights (i.e., that which is right is right in and of itself, and not dependent upon any external power or authority), his fame rests upon his 1625 work *On the Law of War and Peace* (a compilation and commentary on such laws, conventions, and injunctions as had by that stage evolved concerning the ways in which warfare was regulated), in which he argues, first, that all law may be divided into divine law and human law. He argued that disputes may be settled by negotiation, compromise, or, as the last resort, combat. The goal, however, is the preservation of rights and peace.

Grotius's ideas were firmly grounded in a strong Christian belief, and, given the time frame within which he worked, predated the establishment of the modern states system which resulted from the Treaty of Westphalia of 1648. Consequently, while Grotius had a conception of statecraft that was, in many respects, different to that which came later in the seventeenth century (and still prevails today), his ideas nonetheless presaged many that were to be embodied in the later document. Grotius identified the existence of an international society in which rulers and states (who may often be one and the same) are part of a broad community, bound together by an understanding that common rules of interstate behavior exist and are applicable to all. Although enforcement mechanisms to ensure that all comply with this understanding had not yet been well formed during Grotius's time—indeed, owing to the Thirty Years' War (1618–1648) and the Eighty Years' War (1566–1648) between Spain and the Netherlands it seemed as though the international system might be in a state of near collapse—there were enough people who agreed with Grotius for his ideas to stand. The broad notion of an international community was even incorporated into the assumptions that underlay the Treaty of Westphalia itself.

Overall, it can be said that Hugo Grotius was a pioneer of international law (and thus, vicariously, of human rights law), from whom much of the political philosophy conditioning the behavior of states in the modern world derives.

Guatemala, Genocide in. Throughout the late 1970s, 1980s, and early 1990s, Guatemalan government death squads and government-supported militias killed an estimated one hundred thousand to one hundred forty thousand people, primarily impoverished Mayans residing in tiny rural villages. The latter were victims of terror, extrajudicial killings, massacres, and, ultimately, genocide.

Fearful of a leftist takeover, as well as the violent actions of leftist guerrillas, the Guatemalan government under the command of Efrain Rios Montt (b. 1926), a former army general who assumed power in a 1982 *coup d'état*, undertook a vicious campaign which ravaged entire villages. While leftist guerrillas fought and carried out an ongoing insurgency against the government, the slaughter by government forces was in one sense indiscriminate in that it attacked civilian villages and the civilians themselves (men, women, children), but in another it was not indiscriminate at all for it was aimed at those of Mayan descent who eked out an impoverished existence in the highlands where the insurgency was being carried out. For many in the government, the slaughter was an ongoing attempt (which was first undertaken in the 1960s) to quell the desire by the *campesinos* (Spanish, poor farmers) to scratch out more than a meager subsistence. That said, governmental violence in Guatemala against the poor had its origins in the 1950s. More specifically, looking askance at the democratically elected government of Jacobo Arbenz Guzman (1913–1971), the U.S. Central Intelligence Agency (CIA) organized a coup that overthrew Arbenz and replaced him with a right-wing government. Since Arbenz favored radical land reform and was viewed with suspicion by U.S.-owned banana companies based in Guatemala, he became *persona non grata* (as far as the U.S. government was concerned).

The height of military counter-insurgency efforts was carried out in the early 1980s by government forces and paramilitary patrols. In one five-year period (1978–1983) it is estimated that almost one-third of Guatemala's eighty-five thousand Ixil Mayan Indians were wiped out.

In March 1994, the Guatemala government and leftists guerrillas signed a human rights accord. In late December 1996 a peace treaty was signed by the leftists and the government. Part and parcel of the peace agreement was to be the implementation of earlier agreements to establish social equality via economic and agrarian reforms, the protection of human rights, and the establishment of a "Truth Commission" to investigate the atrocities that had been perpetrated over the years. It was also supposed to result in the resettlement of refugees, the recognition of Indian rights, reform election laws, the disarmament and demobilization of rebels, and an assessment about the future of the Guatemalan military. A National Reconciliation Law was also ratified and took effect in December 1996 that protected soldiers and guerrillas from arrest. Human rights activists roundly criticized the law, asserting that the vagueness of its language could prevent prosecution of those accused of atrocities. And, in fact, in late 1996 the Guatemalan government issued a blanket amnesty for those involved in many crimes, but it was to exclude those involved in torture, genocide, and forced disappearance. Up through early 2007, prosecutions of the guilty have been rare and prosecutors seem particularly reluctant to challenge the military.

Guiding Principles on Internal Displacement. Presented to the Commission on Human Rights by the representative of the secretary-general for internally displaced persons in April 1998, the Guiding Principles on Internal Displacement spell out basic standards vis-à-vis the protection of internally displaced persons. Concomitantly, these principles, which are based on international humanitarian law and human rights instruments (though they do not constitute a binding agreement or instrument), are to serve as an international standard to assist governments, international humanitarian organizations, and development groups to assist and provide protection for internally displaced persons (IDPs). Basically, the principles identify the rights and guarantees germane to the protection of internally displaced people in regard to all aspects of displacement. More specifically, the Principles provide protection "against arbitrary displacement, offer a basis for protection and assistance during displacement, and set forth guarantees for safe return, resettlement, and reintegration."

Gulag. Acronym for the Russian term *Glavnoe Upravlenie Lagerei*, or "main camp administration" (of corrective labor camps). During the period of the Soviet Union (1917–1991), the gulags, as all individual forced labor and prison camps (as well as complexes of camps) became known, fell directly under the control of the Soviet secret police forces—consecutively, the Cheka (*V'cheka Vserossiiskaia Chrezvychainaia komissiia po borbe s kontrrevoliutsiei i sabotazhem*, or All-Russian Extraordinary Commission for Fighting Counterrevolution and Sabotage), the GPU (*Gosudarstvennoe Politicheskoye Upravlenie*, or State Political Directorate), OGPU (*Ob'edinennoe Gosudarstvennoe Politicheskoye Upravleni*, or All-Union State Political Directorate), NKVD (*Narondyi Komissariat Vnutrennikh Del*, or People's Commissariat for Internal Affairs), MVD (*Ministestko Vnutrennikh Del*, or Ministry of Internal Affairs), and KGB (*Komitet Gosudarstvennoye Bezopasnosti*, or Committee of State Security).

The system of gulags spread the length and breadth of the USSR, and was a deliberately contrived device initiated and promoted for the purpose of terrorizing the Soviet population into political, social, and economic submissiveness. Although forerunners of the gulag system existed in tsarist times, the gulag itself was essentially a Bolshevik creation that emerged soon after the Russian Revolution and communist takeover of October–November 1917. Evidence exists that the first of the gulags was established with the authority (if not at the initiative) of the Bolshevik leader Vladimir Ilyich Lenin (1870–1924). The system reached its zenith, however, under Lenin's successor Josef Stalin (1879–1953). Although perhaps best known as political counterparts to the Nazi concentration camps during the 1930s, the gulag structure continued to grow during the 1940s and early 1950s, coincidental with Stalin's rule of the Soviet Union. It was an immense penal network, and during the period of Soviet rule comprised no fewer than

476 camp complexes. Overall, these complexes comprised thousands of individual camps, encompassing millions of prisoners who had been arrested for a wide variety of reasons—political, social, economic, racial, religious and national, as well as common crimes. It is uncertain how many prisoners lost their lives during their incarceration in the gulag; some as a result of outright murder, others by brutality, starvation, freezing, overwork, debility, and despair. A figure of 2.7 million deaths has been arrived at, but this is an estimate, at best—and this says nothing for the millions more who suffered permanent disability as a result of their years-long ordeal. The gulag, as it had been administered by the KGB, ceased to be with Stalin's death in 1953; but it was only in the late 1980s that the camps themselves, now transformed into labor camps for anti-Soviet prisoners, began to be dismantled altogether.

Gulag Archipelago, The. Title of a trilogy written by Soviet dissident author Aleksandr Solzhenitsyn (b. 1918), published in English between 1973 and 1978. Solzhenitsyn's trilogy took its name from the gulag, a Russian acronym for *Glavnoe Upravlenie Lagerei*, meaning "main camp administration" (of corrective labor camps). The gulag drew together the massive network of labor camps that were scattered thickly throughout the USSR, like islands of terror forming an archipelago in a broader Soviet firmament. Essentially a critique of the communist state and how it worked in the USSR under Josef Stalin (1879–1953) and his successors, *The Gulag Archipelago* is recognized as a masterwork, though it has been criticized by some for its negativism about the achievements of the Soviet social, economic, and political experiment. A counter-argument is that he had much about which to be critical. In the camps themselves, for example, untold millions lost their lives—whether through the brutality of the guards, the extreme harshness of the Russian and Siberian winters, malnutrition, disease, and, often, violence at the hands of other prisoners in a Hobbesian war of all against all. Solzhenitsyn's work, therefore, is a powerful attempt at bringing to a wider reading public a full appreciation of what it was like to live in the Soviet terror state, a state that devoured its own people through the creation of a system that institutionalized violence for the purpose of maintaining and legitimizing the ongoing revolution required by the Stalinist interpretation of communist ideology. For writing *The Gulag Archipelago*, Solzhenitsyn was arrested, charged with treason, stripped of his citizenship, and deported from the Soviet Union. Earlier, in 1970, he had been awarded the Nobel Prize for Literature; in 1994, after Perestroika had liberalized the USSR and communism had collapsed, all charges were dropped. His citizenship was restored, and he returned to Russia.

Gusmao, Xanana (b. 1946). Jose Alexandre "Xanana" Gusmao was born in a small village in the Manaututo region of East Timor, then a Portuguese colony. He was educated in a Catholic high school prior to attending Jesuit seminaries, and after graduation he worked as a member of the colonial civil service in the Department of Forestry and Agriculture. In 1974, when East Timor's continued status as a Portuguese colony seemed to be about to end, he joined the *Associação Social Democratica Timorense* (ASDT), which was a broad-based, anticolonial association with nationalist leanings. In September 1974 the ASDT transformed itself into a more radical (and socialist) movement, the *Frente Revolucionária do Timor-Leste Independente*, or FRETILIN. Gusmao was elevated to the movement's Central Committee. With the invasion of East Timor by Indonesia on December 7, 1975, Gusmao became a member of FRETILIN's armed wing, the *Forças Armadas de Libertação Nacional de Timor-Leste*, or FALANTIL, that was fighting a guerrilla war against the Indonesians. As a high profile leader of the East Timorese resistance movement, the Indonesian military sought Gusmao's capture as a matter of urgency—which it was able to do only in November 1992. In May 1993 Gusmao was tried, convicted and sentenced to life imprisonment in Jakarta. His incarceration attracted worldwide attention, and he was visited in jail by many leading dignitaries from around the world. (One of these, former South African president Nelson Mandela [b. 1918], likened Gusmao's situation with his own when he was a prisoner of the apartheid regime at the Robben Island jail near Cape Town.) In 1999, with the opening up of possibilities for East Timor's independence via a referendum, Gusmao was released. As the de facto leader of the nation, he stood for, and was elected, the first president of the sovereign Republic of Timor-Leste on May 20, 2002.

H

Habyarimana, Juvenal (1937–1994). President of Rwanda from 1973 until his assassination on April 6, 1994. A Hutu, Habyarimana had been an army officer in the Rwandan military forces (*Forces Armées Rwandaises*, or FAR), rising to the rank of major general. In this capacity he also served as defense minister in the government of his cousin, Gregoire Kayibanda (1924–1976), whom he overthrew in a military coup on July 5, 1973. In the years that followed, the quality of life for most Rwandans improved: there was political stability and the economy improved to unprecedented levels. This "golden age" came at a price, however. Every Rwandan citizen, including babies and the elderly, had to be a member of his political party (the only one permitted), the *Mouvement Révolutionnaire National pour le Développement*, or MRND. This was a party of Hutu exclusivism, and, through it, Habyarimana was able to build what was, in essence, an apartheid-like state in which the Tutsi minority was discriminated against at an official level. The late 1980s saw an economic downturn, however, which destabilized Habyarimana's regime. Although army control ensured that he still held the country in an iron grip, forced budget cuts in 1989—accompanied by a drought in 1988–1989 and a plea for financial assistance to the World Bank—saw domestic pressure brought to bear on Habyarimana to start a slow process towards the liberalization of the political system in Rwanda. An invasion of the country from Uganda in 1990–1991 by rebel Tutsi emigrés known as the Rwandan Patriotic Front, who desired to return to Rwanda from forced exile and demanded a voice in the running of the country, forced Habyarimana to open armistice negotiations, which took on a more formal character when located to Arusha, Tanzania, and carried out under international supervision. Some consider that Habyarimana purposely allowed these negotiations to drag on in order to buy time and thereby reinforce his regime's position at home, the more so as Hutu extremist elements were becoming increasingly frustrated at Habyarimana's "capitulation" to the rebel forces by even entering into negotiations with them in the first place. On April 6, 1994, while returning to Kigali from one of the negotiation rounds in Arusha, Habyarimana's plane, carrying Habyarimana as well as the president of Burundi, Cyprien Ntaryamira (1955–1994), was shot down by two missiles fired from just outside the Kigali airport perimeter. All on board the Falcon 50 jet were killed. Within hours, as if the assassination had sounded a tocsin to the Hutu extremists in Rwanda, the killing of all Tutsi began.

Controversy has swirled around the issue as to who was behind the shooting down of Habyarimana's plane. A French investigation team blamed Tutsi Rwandan Patriotic Front leader—and later president of Rwanda—Paul Kagame. Others, including Kagame, however, have argued it was Hutu extremists.

Hademar. The name of a location in Germany where thousands of people with physical or psychological handicaps, or incurable diseases, were murdered in the Nazi "euthanasia program" between 1941 and 1945. It is estimated that approximately eleven thousand victims were killed at Hademar. Part hospital, part sanatorium, the center had originally been established in 1901 and was extended and refurbished in 1933 as the State Psychiatric Center. Hademar can be likened to the Austrian Hartheim Castle, the center of the Nazi euthanasia program, in which thirty thousand people were killed. Hademar was also utilized for the murder of others: between 1944 and 1945 it was used in order to kill slave laborers who were unable to keep working because of illness or debility, and at other times it was used for the purpose of murdering Allied nationals. Hademar has become a byword for bureaucratic murder masked as medical "improvement" in the name of perverted science. Many of the doctors involved in the killing at Hademar were transferred to the Nazi death camps during World War II, the better to practice their lethal skills: these included Drs. Ernst Baumhardt, Guenther Hennecke, Friedrich Berner, and Hans-Bobo Gorgass.

Hague Conventions. Two conferences relating to issues concerning the conduct of nations at war took place at The Hague, Netherlands, in 1899 and 1907. At these conferences, a basic principle was established formally, namely, that individuals had rights that should be respected as members of the international community. It was recognized at the 1899 conference that alternatives to war should be sought prior to conflict taking place, well in advance of antagonism developing into war. These alternatives could include, it was suggested, such devices as disarmament and international arbitration. The 1907 conference addressed issues that dealt with the laws and customs of war on land. Both the 1899 and 1907 conferences had at base a need to try to diminish the evils of war by revising, where possible, its general laws and customs. The 1907 conference established a series of prohibitions over the behavior of nations engaged in war, with the broad intention of making warfare more humane and respecting the rights of individuals. These included, inter alia, prohibitions on attacking undefended towns or villages, using poison or other weapons that cause "superfluous" injuries, willfully destroying religious or cultural institutions, mistreating civilians in occupied territory, using poison gas in warfare, and violating a nation's neutrality. The 1899 and 1907 Hague Conventions were signed by twenty-six countries, each of which effectively agreed to restrain its behavior in wartime by enshrining a set of actions that were henceforth to be classed as war crimes. The signatories refrained from embracing the notion of an international court, however, preferring to retreat behind well-established principles relating to the absolute sovereignty of nations. A criticism of the Hague Conventions is that nothing was established in the way of an enforcement mechanism for states contravening the laws proscribed by the treaties. The Hague Conventions codified the actions that could be considered war crimes, and although they failed to prevent the outbreak of war in 1914, they retained their attraction as an ideal to which states should aspire and were invoked in discussions throughout World War I and its aftermath.

Hama. A city in central Syria, the location of a genocidal massacre in February 1982. Hama, a city entrenched as a bastion of traditional, landed power and Sunni Muslim fundamentalism, was a long-term opponent of Syria's secular Baathist state. At the beginning of 1982, it had an estimated population of about three hundred thousand people. At the time, relations between the city and the government of President Hafiz al-Asad (1930–2000) were poor. The religious opponents of Asad, the Muslim Brotherhood, directed by charismatic leader Abu Bakr, found themselves besieged by government forces in Hama in February 1982. Bakr gave the order for his forces to break out of the city, thus giving way to a general uprising and *jihad* (holy war) against Asad's rule. Muslim Brotherhood forces held the city for about ten days, during which time they killed the governor and several hundred other city officials. Twelve thousand government troops assaulted Brethren strongholds with artillery and tanks; helicopters attacked the city, conducting sweeps and placing soldiers in strategic areas. Hama was shelled for three consecutive weeks, destroying much of the city. Upon their entry into what was left of the city, government troops then engaged in an orgy of pillage. Up to thirty thousand townsfolk, representing one-tenth of the population, were killed in the campaign. The central issues were twofold: first, to strengthen Asad's rule in a region known for its opposition; and second, to remove the Sunni fundamentalist influence over Syrian life. The government saw that Hama would have to be a last-ditch battle for the future of the country, in which only one side could win. Moreover, as the major supporters of the government were from the minority Alawite sect (a breakaway sect from Shiism, known for their own rigidly doctrinaire approach to Islam), the struggle also assumed the form of an internal religious faction fight for dominance. Given this, it could be said that a case of genocide could be made, under the 1948 UN Convention on the Prevention and Punishment of the Crime of Genocide, for what transpired in Hama on the grounds of Asad's determination to destroy Hama's population for religious reasons, though it was as much a political struggle, or even a rivalry between urban and rural lifestyles, that got out of hand. Hama became a symbol throughout the Middle East for brutal repression by the modern state, and, in serving as an object lesson, it coerced the Muslim Brotherhood and gave the secular state a new lease on life in Syria.

Hamidian Massacres. A series of major massacres committed by the Ottoman government under the direction of Sultan Abdul Hamid II (1842–1918; reigned 1876–1909) against the Armenian community of the Ottoman Empire between 1894 and 1896. The massacres were perpetrated in mid-1894 in the region of Sasun, in southern Armenia; they spread throughout 1895 and showed that the Sultan's government had intensified the nature of anti-Armenian persecution in a dramatic way. The main explanation for the massacres lay in the Sultan's desire to staunch the growth of Armenian nationalism and any calls for reform that could give the Armenians a greater say in imperial affairs. The massacres were thus genocidal in effect (particularly in certain regions of Armenia), but were not genocidal in intent—the preference being to intimidate and terrorize the Armenian population rather than destroy it. Estimates of those killed range widely, from anywhere between one hundred thousand and three hundred thousand, with tens of thousands more maimed or homeless. Most of those killed were men; the killings took place in open areas, in full sight of the community. Vast numbers of Armenians fled the country, and thousands of others were forcibly converted to Islam. In view of the ferocity of the massacres, Abdul Hamid II was nicknamed the "Red Sultan," or "Bloody Abdul," and the massacres were named for him as a way of distinguishing these actions from the later (and much more extensive) genocide of 1915–1923.

Hamitic Hypothesis. The "Hamitic Hypothesis" refers to an explicit racial ideology *cum* "scientific" notion that "white Africans" (as Europeans, based on their colonialist perspectives, referred to so-called civilized or enlightened African tribal communities), from the northeast part of the continent, brought civilization to the rest of the "primitive" continent of Africa. The Tutsi of Rwanda were touted as an example of such a superior race. The latter, according to this "scientific" notion, were born to rule, intellectually superior to all others, and graced with high morals. The Hutu of Rwanda, by comparison, were said to be ignorant, of low morals, and better suited to back-breaking work versus serving as leaders in society.

Heart of Darkness. *Heart of Darkness* is the highly acclaimed novella written in 1899 and published in 1902 by Polish-born author Joseph Conrad, born Josef Teodor Konrad Korzeniowski (1857–1924). The story takes the form of a narrative told by a character named Marlow, who travels down the Congo River longing to meet and talk with the central character, a legendary figure (within the narrative) named Kurtz. Conrad uses the story of Kurtz, the wealth he has accumulated through ivory, and the exploitation of Africans among whom he has enormous power, as a metaphor for European colonialism and misuse of "the dark continent."

Heart of Darkness was based on Conrad's command of a Congo River steamboat for four months, during which time he was able to witness at first hand the savagery of Belgian rule over the Congo. During the 1890s, the entire region served as the private possession of Belgian king Leopold II (1835–1909; reigned 1865–1909), who used it for the sole purpose of wealth creation at the expense of the lives of the local people. Millions died—or, at the least, were horribly mutilated—in the quest for sheer profit. Although *Heart of Darkness*, as a novel, is rich in literary devices that may be interpreted on several levels, its major contribution upon its publication lay in the shock value it provided its readers, many of whom became opponents of King Leopold's regime in the Congo as a result of having read the book.

Two lines attributed to Kurtz—"Exterminate all the brutes!", in the conclusion of a report written by Kurtz to the International Society for the Suppression of Savage Customs; and his dying words, "The horror! The horror!"—have provided generations with material to speculate as to how deeply Conrad felt about the brutality he had himself witnessed and what he was attempting to wipe out. The novel was highly successful in influencing opinion, and Conrad became one of the major intellectual forces resulting in the Belgian government assuming direct control of the Congo from King Leopold in 1908. Although such agitation had begun a couple of years before the appearance of *Heart of Darkness* it was Conrad's contribution that brought the issue before readers of fictional literature, to great effect.

Heavy Weapons Exclusion Zones. In wartime, an area where either the United Nations, a regional force such as NATO (North Atlantic Treaty Organization), or a coalition of nations demarcate an area where no heavy weapons are allowed to exist, let alone operate. During the Bosnian War (1992–1995), heavy weapons exclusion zones were declared from time to time as a means of protecting UN-declared safe areas. These varied in size, though on average they operated in a radius of about twenty kilometers from the center of the city being defended. When Bosnian Serb forces attacked the cities in question—for example, at Gorazde in April 1994, or Sarajevo in August 1994, among others—NATO aircraft received authorization to bomb Serb positions with the intention of driving their heavy weapons capacity away from the cities and closing down the Serbs' ability to so aggress. In enforcing the heavy weapons exclusion zones, NATO developed what became known as Operation Deny Flight, a system of providing close air support for UN troops on the ground, and as a mechanism for heavy weapons exclusion. The concept received a major setback in the aftermath of the fall of the UN "safe area" Srebrenica in mid-July 1995, though air strikes against Serb positions continued to take place until the end of the war was in sight, late in October 1995.

Hegemonial Genocide. A classification of genocide identified by U.S. political scientists Barbara Harff and Ted Robert Gurr in 1988. In Harff and Gurr's taxonomy, genocide can be categorized into two types: hegemonial and xenophobic. A hegemonial genocide—Harff and Gurr's elementary type—is one involving mass murders of specific ethnic, religious, or national groups (and presumably racial groups, though this category is not itemized) that have been forced to submit to a central authority. This could be for reasons of state building or during a period of national expansion; implied within this is the notion that government ("a central authority") is the driving force behind genocidal destruction.

In contradistinction, xenophobic genocide bases itself upon the innate differences between human beings and groups, and, by promoting such differences, encourages fear of the other, potentially leading to genocidal acts.

Hegemony. A term that refers to the domination of a region or the world by a single state. It also refers to the overwhelming power of a single state within the international system.

Heidegger, Martin (1889–1976). Pioneering German philosopher in the fields of phenomenology (the study of human experience) and ontology (the study of human existence), Heidegger was born in southwest Germany and originally had intended to join the Jesuit priesthood. For possible health and other reasons, however, he redirected his energies at Freiburg University from theology to philosophy, receiving his doctorate in 1913. His fame as a philosopher rests, primarily, on his masterwork *Sein und Zeit* (*Being and Time*), wherein he attempted to understand the very meaning of human existence both generally and concretely as activity, despite its inherent limitations.

World War I saw him briefly serving in the army twice, but both times he was discharged for health reasons. In 1923 he was able to secure an academic position at Marburg University. He returned to Freiburg as its rector in 1933, the same year he joined the Nazi Party. During that initial period, he seems to have been a supporter of national socialism, and, in pursuit of Nazi aims, dismissed the Jewish faculty at Freiburg. Though he resigned his position one year later and took no further active political role, controversy continues to surround his seemingly pro-Nazi sympathies, based largely upon his inaugural address as rector ("The Self-Affirmation of the German University"), which stressed the involvement and cooperation of higher education in support of Nazi political and military aims. With Germany's defeat in World War II, he was forbidden to teach from 1945 through 1949 because of his initial involvement with and support of national socialism; after 1949, having completed the Allied program of "denazification," he was then cleared to resume his teaching career.

Even after World War II, he never formally renounced national socialism, its genocidal antisemitism, or his own involvement.

Ironically, for one affiliated with the Nazi party, he was, for a brief time, the lover of his Jewish student, Hannah Arendt (1906–1975), whose own philosophical ideas regarding the role of government were similar to his own. Arendt, herself, never condemned him for his involvements during the years of World War II.

Heng Samrin (b. 1934). Cambodian political leader, best known for his postgenocide activities after the downfall of communist dictator Pol Pot (1925–1998) in 1979. Originally a member of Pol Pot's Khmer Rouge, in which he became a political commissar and divisional commander in the Eastern Zone, Heng defected to communist Vietnam in 1978, where he was groomed as an alternative leader to Pol Pot. From there, he led an anti–Khmer Rouge rebellion, supported by the Vietnamese government. When the Pol Pot regime was deposed, owing to the Vietnamese military intervention in January 1979, Heng oversaw the creation of a new puppet government in his role as Chairman of the Council of State. In December 1981 he became general secretary of the Central Committee of the Kampuchean People's Revolutionary Party (KPRP). Effectively, he co-ruled the country alongside of another former Khmer Rouge leader, now moderate communist politician, Hun Sen (b. 1952). From 1985, when Hun Sen became prime minister, Heng Samrin's influence declined, and, in 1991, when the KPRP reorganized itself and changed its name to the Cambodian People's Party (CPP), he was dropped as general secretary. When Cambodian king Norodom Sihanouk (b. 1922) was restored to the throne in 1993, Heng relinquished his position as head of state. The king granted him the honorific title of *Samdech* (His Excellency), and he was appointed as honorary secretary of the CPP.

Herero People, Genocide of. The German invasion of the Herero people in the colonial possession of South-West Africa (now Namibia) can be termed the first true instance of genocide in the twentieth century. In late 1903, Herero leaders learned of a proposal the Germans were considering that would see the construction of a railway line through Herero territory and the consequent concentration of Herero in reservations. In response, in January 1904, the Herero rebelled with the intention of driving the Germans out of Hereroland. At this time, according to the best estimates, the Herero numbered some eighty thousand. After the German counterattack, reinforcement, and a widespread campaign of annihilation and displacement, which forced huge numbers of Herero of both sexes and all ages into the Omaheke Desert, tens of thousands perished. The situation was exacerbated by the policy of German general Lothar von Trotha (1848–1920), who ordered that all waterholes be located and poisoned in advance of the arrival of those Herero who survived the desert. It has been estimated that some 80 percent of the Herero people perished in the genocide, together with 50 percent of the related Nama population. By 1911, when a count was made of the surviving Herero, only about fifteen thousand could be found. The vast majority of the rest had been killed, either directly or indirectly, by German forces over the preceding half-dozen years, though the majority of the killing had taken place between 1904 and 1905.

Heydrich, Reinhard (1904–1942). Reich Protector of Bohemia and Moravia, assassinated by Czech partisans in Prague. Born in Halle, Germany, and an early supporter of the Nazi Party, by 1936, he was the head of both the Secret State Police (*Gestapo*) and the Security Service (SD), which provided him with the power to unleash his antisemitic hatred. With the outbreak of World War II in September 1939, Heydrich was responsible for the ghettoization of the Jews in Poland, their establishment of self-governing councils (*Judenräte*), and, after the invasion of the Soviet Union in June 1941, the work of the *Einsatzgruppen* (Special Action Squads). In January 1942 he convened the Wannsee Conference to address the plans for the "Final Solution to the Jewish Question." In retaliation for his assassination, six months later the German army (*Wehrmacht*) surrounded the Czech village of Lidice, burned it to the ground, and slaughtered all of its male inhabitants.

Highland Clearances. In the long struggle to clarify the relationship between England and Scotland after the Act of Union on May 1, 1707, the Scots found themselves increasingly subjected to English overlordship as if in a quasi-colonial status. Under the rule of the Hanoverian dynasty, a movement grew within Scotland for a return of the Scottish Stuart royal house, and those known as Jacobites (from the Latin Jacobus, for James, the last Stuart king) staged a number of rebellions from 1715 onwards. The most impressive of these took place in 1745–1746 and, after some success, culminated in the Battle of Culloden on April 16, 1746. This battle was the final death-knell of Jacobite hopes for seeing a Stuart take his place on the restored throne of Scotland. The embers of the rising were stamped out with brutal ferocity. King George II's (1683–1760; reigned 1727–1760) son, William, Duke of Cumberland (1721–1765), made Culloden the start of a period of the most intense repression throughout the Highlands. Jacobites who fled the scene were hunted down; scores were hanged, beheaded, or exiled. Harsh measures were taken to prevent further outbreaks and to establish more settled conditions throughout the country. The clan system was destroyed, as clan chiefs became transformed into a more European-style aristocracy. In the century that followed, Scotland's cities were modernized and developed, and began to benefit from (and participate in) Britain's industrial revolution. In the Highlands, however, few benefits accrued. The establishment of industry foundered, let alone prospered, and the soil was too poor to sustain even the existing population. As the population expanded, it placed intolerable pressure on fixed agricultural patterns. The new landlords in the decades after Culloden, many of whom were either English transplants or absentee Lowland Scots, found it more profitable to transform their holdings into large sheep-runs. Tenant farmers, in the process of being remodeled from a peasantry deriving from the Middle Ages, were evicted from their wretched smallholdings. Scores of thousands left the Highlands forever. At least thirty thousand had emigrated to North America prior to the American Revolution, while more relocated to the Lowlands, where many wound up as lowly factory workers. Although it does not fit directly into the category of genocide, the fate of the Highland Scots during these so-called clearances was nonetheless a tragic illustration of the confrontation that can take place between a backward, tribal society and a progressive, industrializing state in which a people is forever transformed—even destroyed—and replaced by a new way of life.

Himmler, Heinrich (1900–1945). Born in Munich and originally destined for the Jesuit priesthood, Himmler studied agriculture and economics and worked as a salesman and chicken farmer, joining the Nazi Party in the early 1920s. In 1939 Hitler appointed him police president of Munich and overall head of the political police in Bavaria, with authority to reorganize both the SS (*Schutzstaffel*, "Protective Squadron" responsible for internal German security) and the SD (*Sicherheitsdienst*, "Security Service," the intelligence arm of the SS). It was Himmler who organized the first concentration camp in Germany at Dachau in 1933 and was the primary architect of *Kristallnacht* (the unprovoked antisemitic attack on Jewish businesses, synagogues, and persons of the Jewish faith) in November 1938. His racist views, his commitment to "racial purity," and his belief in occult forces enabled Himmler to become the principal instigator of the extermination *cum* annihilation of the Jews, with overall responsibility and implementation for the concentration and death camp system and the so-called medical experiments conducted therein. As World War II was drawing to a close, Himmler foresaw Germany's eventual defeat and attempted to negotiate with the Allies. Captured by the Allies, Himmler committed suicide on May 23, 1945, before he could be put on trial at the International Military Tribunal at Nuremberg, Germany.

Historical Revisionism vs. "Historical Revisionism." It is the legitimate work of historical scholars to amass data, examine evidence, and construct theories to explain what they have uncovered. Furthermore, as additional material is uncovered and presented, and as other scholars participate in the conversation, the original theories may, of necessity, be modified or revised. The process is ongoing, and, thus, the term *historical revisionism* may best be used to describe such intellectual work whereby earlier explanations are revised in the light of new evidence or reworked theoretical approaches. This approach/process is to be distinguished, however, from the self-designated and totally inaccurate use of the term (thus the placement of quote marks around it) by those who, in effect, deny the overwhelming evidence of the Holocaust because of their hatred of Jews and/or Judaism, the State of Israel and Zionism, or their need to "rehabilitate" Hitler and national socialism, and even present-day Germany. Instead of "revisionists," the term *Holocaust deniers* may be a more appropriate description for those advocating such an approach. The various "revisionist" claims include the following: the Holocaust, as such, never happened; if the Holocaust did happen, the numbers of Jewish deaths resulting from it are highly exaggerated (not even close to the 5.8 million historians cite as having been murdered) and that most of the deaths were due to the war, not an extermination process; Nazi dictator Adolf Hitler (1889–1945) knew nothing of the fact of the Holocaust; the wartime concentration camps, where disease was, at times, rampant, had been established for the Jews' own protection against the wrath of the German people; the documentation of the Holocaust is both faulty (e.g., memoirs and diaries) and fraudulent or doctored. All of the latter arguments are false, and legitimate historians have accumulated the evidence that proves the falsity of such.

Today, those who choose to ally themselves with this so-called revisionist movement (which is, as noted above, a denialist movement, as its adherents seek to deny the veracity of the Holocaust rather than legitimately examine new findings and evidence) hold their own conferences, present lectures, publish books and articles, establish Web sites, and attempt to legitimize their views on both college campuses (e.g., using newspapers to "call for free and open debates/discussions on the Holocaust") and in the public arena. In 1978, a group calling itself The Institute for Historical Review was established in California; its pseudo-scholarly publication is entitled *The Journal of Historical Review*, following up on the work of Willis Carto (b. 1926) and his Liberty Lobby and its publishing house, The Noontide Press. The so-called father of historical revisionism is the late Frenchman Paul Rassinier (1906–1967), who was himself a prisoner in Buchenwald concentration camp, but who, after the war, argued that the overall number of Jews murdered was far less than the number usually cited. Among the names associated with this movement are Arthur Butz (b. 1933) and Bradley Smith (b. 1930) (United States); Robert Faurisson (b. 1929) (France); David Irving (b. 1938) (Great Britain); and Ernst Zündel (b. 1939) (Canada).

The use of the Internet has greatly exacerbated the problems posed by such fraudulent scholarship—the slick and sophisticated sites themselves as well as their easy accessibility by students and others naïve and unsuspecting of their true nature. The language the deniers use is not, as one might imagine, shrill but quasi-academic in tone. As a result, the tone and tenor of the words used may lead unsuspecting readers to believe that they are reading the words of historians, thus sucking the unsuspecting reader into a web of obfuscations, distortions, and falsifications. Although Jewish and other concerned organizations have attempted to address these Web sites, shutting them down has not appeared to be successful.

Hitler, Adolf (1889–1945). Born in Braunau am Inn, Austria, Hitler was the son of a government customs official and a mother who later died of cancer. Wanting to be an artistic painter, he moved to Vienna in 1907, where he lived in a low-class apartment house, and applied to the Academy of Arts School of Painting, from which he was rejected because of what was adjudged to be the ordinariness of his work. Moving to Munich in 1913, he enlisted in the German Army, saw action in World War I, served in Belgium and France, and was wounded in a mustard gas attack. After his discharge, he returned to Munich and later joined the renamed *Nationalsozialistische Deutsche Arbeiterpartei* (National Socialist German Workers Party; NSDAP; Nazi), where his oratorical and administrative gifts were put to use. In 1923, Hitler and his followers attempted to seize power but were unsuccessful, and he was sentenced to prison in Landsberg for five years, along with his secretary Rudolf Hess (1894–1987). It was here that Hitler would write his autobiography and political manifesto *Mein Kampf* (*My Struggle*, or *My Fight*). The first volume was published in 1925 and the second volume in 1926. (A third book, published posthumously in 1961, and given the title *Hitler's Second Book*, seemingly spells out Hitler's antisemitism in the context of his racial views, particularly as it applies to his perspective of the conflict of world civilization.)

Released from prison in 1924, Hitler reorganized the Nazi Party, drew about him men such as Joseph Goebbels (1897–1945) and Heinrich Himmler (1900–1945), and began the development and implementation of a serious political agenda. By 1927 the Nazi Party had become the largest political party in a fragmented and fractured Weimar Germany. In 1933, Hitler successfully outmaneuvered the aging war hero General Paul von Hindenberg (1847–1934) to become chancellor of Germany, leaving the presidency for von Hindenberg. Upon Hindenburg's death, Hitler became dictator of Germany by pushing through the Enabling Act of March 23, 1933, which enabled Hitler as chancellor and members of his cabinet to enact laws without consulting the Reichstag (German parliament). Continuing to arrogate power to himself, his Nazi Party, and those of the Party who now occupied increasingly governmental positions, part and parcel of that consolidation process was the evolving antisemitism that specifically dislodged Jews from their former positions in government, universities, businesses, and industries. (Jews were never central players in the military though they did participate in fighting on Germany's side during World War I.)

After having already rearmed the German military in direct violation of the Versailles Treaty of World War I, and having annexed Austria and Czechoslovakia as part of the vision of a "Greater Germany," Hitler launched World War II on September 1, 1939. At the outset, his troops were remarkably successful with their *blitzkrieg* (lightning war). But then, during the fateful winter of 1941–1942, "Operation Barbarossa," the Nazi attack against their supposed ally Soviet Russia, stalled after enormous initial success in the warmer months. This failed military campaign, however, did little to lessen Hitler's antisemitic agenda of initial forced immigration and later extermination/annihilation of Europe's Jews or the continued fighting. After he overcame a nearly successful assassination attempt in 1944, it had become increasingly apparent even to Hitler that the war was going badly. On April 30, 1945, as the Russians were advancing on Berlin, Hitler married his mistress Eva Braun (1912–1945), and on May 1 the two of them committed suicide in the Führer's bunker, with explicit instructions for their bodies to be burned. (Enough evidence has now been released by the Russians to conclude that Soviet troops arrived prior to total incineration and the bodies were taken back to the Soviet Union, autopsied, and their bones preserved.)

Hitler Youth (German, *Hitlerjugend*). The male division of the German youth movement during the Nazi regime from 1933 to 1945. Although it complemented the female League of German Girls (*Bund Deutscher Mädel*), it formed a more important element of Nazi society due to the strict military regimentation it demanded and the socialization it fostered for boys into Nazi ways of thinking and behaving. Given that the encouragement of youth was viewed as the way to the future, the Nazis placed a priority on integrating all youth activities into the structure of the new German Order, and, by 1935, the Hitler Youth movement was a huge institution embracing nearly 60 percent of all German male children. From the ages of ten to fourteen, boys belonged to the Hitler Youth's junior organization, the *Jungvolk*, and, at age fourteen, they were compulsorily enrolled in the Hitler Youth, where they remained until age eighteen. The organization indoctrinated its members with the full range of Nazi ideologies and developed a cult of physical fitness, service to the state, and militarism. The leader of the movement from the very start of the Third Reich until 1943 was Baldur von Schirach (1907–1974), who was convicted at Nuremberg for his antisemitic activities and sentenced to twenty years' imprisonment.

Hoess, Rudolf Franz (1900–1947). Commandant of the Nazi concentration camp at Auschwitz, Hoess was born in Baden-Baden to a middle-class Catholic family. In 1922 he joined the German Nazi Party, and, in 1934, he became a member of the SS. Between 1934 and 1938 he worked as a guard at the Dachau concentration camp in Germany, where he learned about camp administration from Theodor Eicke (1892–1943). In 1938 Hoess was promoted to the rank of captain and transferred to the Sachsenhausen concentration camp; and then, in May 1940, he received his first posting as Commandant when ordered to establish a new camp at Auschwitz. His initial order was to build a transit camp capable of accommodating ten thousand prisoners at Auschwitz, using the existing complex of buildings that had originally been a Polish army barracks. After employing prisoners from other camps as slave labor to build the camp, Hoess saw Auschwitz receive its first permanent inmates on July 14, 1940.

Ultimately, at Auschwitz, Hoess was given the responsibility of carrying out the Nazi "Final Solution of the Jewish Question" through the industrial mass murder of Jews sent from across Europe. He oversaw the installation of gas chambers at Auschwitz and the use of the prussic acid gas Zyklon B for the purpose of killing Jews more "efficiently." Highly commended by the senior Nazi hierarchy, in 1945, he was appointed as deputy to Richard Glücks (1889–1945), the inspector of concentration camps for the Third Reich. In 1945, Hoess was arrested by U.S. troops and transferred to Polish jurisdiction. While awaiting trial in 1946, Hoess wrote his autobiography (published in English in 1960 as *Commandant of Auschwitz: The Autobiography of Rudolf Hoess*), in which he showed himself to be a devoted husband and father, dedicated employee, diligent administrator, and sensitive individual—even though his actions showed him to be an efficient mass murderer. The Polish court sentenced him to death on March 29, 1947, and he was hanged on April 16 of the same year.

Holbrooke, Richard (b. 1941). One of the more important U.S. diplomats and negotiators of the late twentieth century, Richard Holbrooke has engaged in a diverse range of activities in a career spanning four decades. After graduating from Brown University in 1962, Holbrooke entered the United States Foreign Service. From 1962 until 1969, he was involved in U.S. diplomatic work in Vietnam and, between 1967 and 1969, was part of the American delegation to the Paris Peace Talks. In 1977 he became assistant secretary of state for East Asian and Pacific Affairs in the government of U.S. president Jimmy Carter (b. 1924), where he remained until 1981. In 1993 he was appointed U.S. ambassador to Germany—a position in which he stayed for only a short time, prior to his further appointment as U.S. assistant secretary of state for European and Canadian affairs in 1994. (In accepting this position, he became the only person up to that point in time to hold the position of assistant director in two regional offices of the State Department.) In 1995, while in this latter role, Holbrooke oversaw the U.S. involvement in bringing about the peace settlement that ended the Bosnian War, resulting in, respectively, the signing of the Dayton Agreement on November 21, 1995, and the Paris Protocol on December 14, 1995. These agreements, though bringing peace, were controversial in that they appeared to reward the Bosnian Serbs territorially for having engaged in ethnic cleansing. Because of this, Holbrooke—seen by many as being the major architect of the settlement—was criticized in some quarters. In 1998 and 1999 he was U.S. president Bill Clinton's (b. 1946) special envoy with responsibility for the direction of U.S. policy toward the Kosovo-Serbia quandary. By March 1999, after numerous visits to Belgrade and one-on-one negotiations with Serbian president Slobodan Milosevic (1941–2006), it was Holbrooke who conveyed the final offer of peace to the recalcitrant Serbian leader. The Kosovo Intervention, between March and June 1999, precipitated the ethnic cleansing of the Kosovar Albanians by Milosevic, but almost certainly stopped a major genocidal outbreak. In the aftermath of the Kosovo Intervention, Holbrooke became the U.S. ambassador to the United Nations (1999–2001), after which he retreated from a life of public service and entered the private sector.

Holiday Inn Sarajevo. The Holiday Inn Sarajevo, a hotel belonging to the Intercontinental Hotels group, was built for the 1984 XIV Winter Olympic games held in that city, which was then part of Yugoslavia. It is a modern ten-story structure, incorporating conference rooms, shops, restaurants, and bars, while also housing corporate offices of other firms. During the siege of Sarajevo between 1992 and 1995, the Holiday Inn acted as a central location for journalists from the international news agencies covering the siege and the Bosnian War generally. Numerous international aid organizations and elements of the United Nations were also based there. The Holiday Inn stands on Zmaja od Bosne Street, right across from the former Bosnian parliament building—an edifice that was bombed mercilessly during the siege and remains a blackened shell. The Holiday Inn itself frequently came under sniper fire during the siege, as Bosnian Serb forces targeted the hotel as part of the broader campaign to reduce the city to ruins. It was from the Holiday Inn that the first shots of the war were fired in the spring of 1992, when Serb paramilitaries shot into a mass demonstration of Bosnians rallying prior to democratic elections. The first casualty of the war, and the siege, was a young nurse named Suada Dilberovic (1968–1992). The role of the Holiday Inn Sarajevo during the war was celebrated in the 1997 motion picture *Welcome to Sarajevo* (directed by Michael Winterbottom and produced by Graham Broadbent and Damian Jones), providing a representative snapshot of what life was like for the journalists who based themselves there throughout the siege. The hotel has now been fully restored and again forms an important part of the Sarajevo landscape.

Hollerith Machine. Purportedly, this was the first punch-card counting mechanism. It was developed by Herman Hollerith (1860–1929), a German-American who worked for the U.S. Census Office in the late nineteenth century. The Hollerith machine was first used to conduct the U.S. census in 1890. Later, Hollerith started his own company, which was bought out by a company that eventually became known as International Business Machines (IBM). A German company, Deutsche Hollerith Maschinen Gesellschaft, of which IBM controlled 90 percent, developed a more sophisticated and faster Hollerith machine, one that was able to process huge quantities of data in a very short span of time. Historians are not sure whether the Hollerith was used to develop deportation lists of Jews in Germany, but it is known that in many concentration camps the Gestapo's political arm used the machine to process the records of those incarcerated therein.

Holocaust. The English-language term that has been most closely identified with the nearly successful attempt by the Nazis of Germany under Adolf Hitler (1889–1945) and their allied minions during the period of World War II (1939–1945) to exterminate the Jews of Europe. Final estimates of their destructive methods center on the figure of 5.8 million Jews, with 1 million of those being children under the age of twelve and an additional one-half million between the ages of twelve and eighteen. As a word, it is derived from the Greek *holokauston* and understood to be a Hebrew biblical reference to any sacrifice totally consumed by fire; for example, I Samuel 7:9 references "a burnt offering to God," the Hebrew term for which is *olah*. Said to be first used by Nobel Laureate and author Elie Wiesel (b. 1928) as a solo word reference to the Jewish tragedy, the term continues to be problematic because of its religious and theological associations (the vast majority of Jews and Christians do not affirm that the deaths of so many were intended as offerings to God).

Equally problematic in English is the linking of the word with both Jews and Nazis to describe the event—one continues to find writers using the expression *Jewish Holocaust* as well as those who use the term *Nazi Holocaust*.

Historically, Jews themselves have identified their various tragic historical experiences by the use of the Hebrew word *churban* or "catastrophe," Hebrew as a language having no capital letters as such. Though first used already in 1940 to describe the horrendous situation of Jews in Europe, the increasingly preferred term is *sho'ah* in Hebrew, also meaning "catastrophe" and rendered as *Shoah* (with or without an apostrophe) in English as "catastrophe." Regardless of which term is used, however, it must also be noted that such an attempt at a descriptive and meaningful term does not address the tragedy of the Roma peoples, who have their own term *Porrajmos* or "devouring," as well as others who suffered under the Nazis (male homosexuals, Jehovah's Witnesses, so-called asocials, Christian dissidents, political opponents, and others).

In the 1980s and 1990s the term *Holocaust* also began to be used by various scholars (e.g., historian Sybil Milton) and organizations (e.g., the United States Holocaust Memorial Museum) to describe the Nazis' attempt to exterminate other groups, specifically, the Roma and Sinti and the mentally and physically handicapped.

Holocaust Analogy. As the former Yugoslavia began to splinter in the early 1990s and degenerate into war, ethnic cleansing, and genocide, various individuals began to use the destruction and horror of the Holocaust as a "tape measure" of sorts in order to support their positions for or against outside intervention. Thus, for example, a producer with the British Independent Television News (ITN) asserted the following about photographs of prisoners at a camp named Trnopolje: "After viewing their [the camera-men's] ten tapes, I advised that the image that would wake the world was of skeletal men behind barbed wire. . . . They sparked thought of Auschwitz and Belsen" (cited in Power, 2002, p. 276). An editorial in the *New York Times* editorial asserted, "The chilling reports from Bosnia evokes this century's greatest nightmare, Hitler's genocide against Jews, Gypsies and Slavs" (*New York Times*, 1992, p. A18). An editorial in the *Chicago Tribune* posed the following question: "Are Nazi-era death camps being reprised in the Balkans? Unthinkable, you say? Think again . . . The ghost of World War II genocide is abroad in Bosnia" (*Chicago Tribune*, 1992, p. 24). On the other hand, U.S. secretary of state Warren Christopher (b. 1925), a member of the Clinton administration (1994–2000), made the following comment on May 19, 1993, to the U.S. House Foreign Affairs Committee: "There are atrocities on all sides. As I said in my statement, the most—perhaps the most serious recent fighting has been between the Croats and the Muslims. . . . You'll find indications of atrocities by all three of the major parties against each other. The level of hatred is just incredible. So you know, it's somewhat different than the Holocaust. It's been easy to analogize this to the Holocaust, but I never heard of any genocide by the Jews against the German people" (quoted in Power, 2001, p. 308).

The Holocaust analogy was also used to compare and contrast nations' reactions to the deportations and killing by Nazi Germany and the ethnic cleansing and killings taking place in Bosnia. For example, berating the leaders of those nations that capitulated to the perpetrators' demands, *Time* magazine scorchingly said, "The ghastly images in newspapers and on television screens conjured up another discomfiting memory, the world sitting by, eager for peace at any price, as Adolf Hitler marched into Austria, [and] carved up Czechoslovakia" (quoted in Power, 2002, p. 278). The *New York Times* columnist Anthony Lewis (1992) went so far as calling President George H.W. Bush (b. 1924) (1988–1992) a "veritable Neville Chamberlain" (p. A19).

Holocaust and Genocide Studies: An International Journal. Launched in 1986 and originally published by Pergamon Press of Oxford and New York, in association with both the United States Holocaust Memorial Museum, Washington, D.C., and Yad Vashem, the Holocaust Martyrs' and Heroes' Remembrance Authority, Jerusalem, Israel, it remains the primary journal for those at work in Holocaust studies. Although initially almost totally focused upon the Holocaust itself, it has seen its work broadening somewhat to include work on genocide, in both articles and reviews. According to its first editor, Yehuda Bauer, *Holocaust and Genocide Studies* was to "be interdisciplinary and addressed to a variety of constituencies—students, survivors, teachers, academics, and those seriously interested in the subject itself." Currently, *Holocaust and Genocide Studies* is published by Oxford University Press and is associated solely with the United States Holocaust Memorial Museum. Its current editor is historian Richard Breitman of American University, Washington, D.C.

Holocaust Denial. *See* Historical Revisionism vs. "Historical Revisionism."

Holocaust, United States' Response to. The response of the United States to the devastating brutalization and annihilation of almost 6 million Jews and more than 5 million others during World War II under the hegemonic leadership of Adolf Hitler and the Nazis of Germany and their allied minions may best be characterized as one of ambivalence and too little, too late. Prior to World War II, as the United States was still recovering from its own economic Great Depression (1929–1933) and there was a strong sense of isolationism on the part of both governmental leadership and populace, antisemitism was a fact of life in the United States, though far from a dominating one. A generalized reluctance to admit foreigners, and resistance and inhospitality to the world's immigrants, ironically in a country originally founded as a so-called safe haven from oppression, became the foundation upon which the U.S. State Department and others were able to thwart refugees seeking asylum on these shores.

Prior to the United States' entry into World War II, its involvement in such conferences as that held at Evian, France, addressing the refugee question, resulted in little or no practical benefit for the Jewish refugees of Germany and Austria trying to extricate themselves from the Nazis' grasp. (Even the Bermuda Conference of 1943 did not appreciatively change America's refugee policies.)

With the United States' commitment to defeating the Nazis and Japan, the latter following the Japanese attack on Pearl Harbor, Hawaii, priority was given to a speedy end to the conflict rather than to addressing the plight of the victims directly. For example, the request to bomb the rail lines leading to the Auschwitz death camp in southeastern Poland remains, even today, a controversial question, as does the refusal of the United States to enter into negotiations with Adolf Eichmann (1906–1962), who was willing to sell the Jews of Hungary late in the war, with funds to be raised by American Jews.

Only in 1944, under pressure both inside and outside his government, did then U.S. President Franklin Delano Roosevelt (1882–1945) call into being the War Refugee Board, which ultimately was responsible for the saving of two hundred thousand victims.

Horizontal Inequality. Horizontal inequality, a major underlying cause of conflict, refers to the inequality that exists amongst groups. There are three major types of horizontal inequality: economic, political, and social. Although each can result in jealousy and conflict, the three are often interwoven and have a tendency to either induce and/or reinforce the others in areas hard-hit by a lack of jobs, food, political input, and/or opportunities to better oneself as a result of being a member of a specific group. The most explosive situations involving horizontal inequality are states verging on collapse and/or those that have collapsed.

***Hostis Humani Generis* (Latin, "an offense against all mankind").** This term is often used to provide an explanation of the rationale for universal jurisdiction, the latter of which indicates that a state is willing to have any defendant, including its own citizens, tried under foreign trial procedures due to the fact that the nature of the crime is so serious as to constitute a crime *hostis humani generis*. Genocide is one crime to which the concept of *hostis humani generis* is applicable.

Hotel des Mille Collines. The Hotel des Mille Collines is located in Kigali, Rwanda. It was established by, and for many years belonged to, the SABENA group (controlled by SABENA Airlines, the Belgian national carrier), until SABENA was bought by Swissair. The Mille Collines is a modern and elegant five-story structure, incorporating conference rooms, restaurants, bars, an elegant pool area, and 112 guest rooms. During the Rwandan Genocide in 1994, the Hotel des Mille Collines stood as an island of refuge for many "internationals" (individuals from countries outside of Africa) and a select few Tutsi, the latter of whom were threatened with extermination. This resulted largely on the initiative of the hotel manager, a Hutu named Paul Rusesabagina (b. 1954). For eleven weeks, the hotel was a place of refuge for no fewer than 1,268 people from Hutu militias bent on their destruction. Throughout the genocide, the hotel, in a garden setting at the intersection of the Avenue de la République and the Avenue de l'Armée, in central Kigali, was protected by UNAMIR (the United Nations Assistance Mission for Rwanda) under the command of General Romeo Dallaire (b. 1946), though the force was at all times inadequate and far too small to have defended the hotel should the besiegers have pressed home their attack. The hotel's story became the subject of an award-winning Hollywood motion picture on the genocide, *Hotel Rwanda* (director/writer/producer, Terry George, United Artists, 2004). The Mille Collines has now been fully restored and continues to take guests, its place as one of the premier hotels in Rwanda reinstated.

Hotel Rwanda. *Hotel Rwanda* is a harrowing feature film about the 1994 Rwandan genocide. While relating the story of the genocide, it focuses on the true story of hotel manager Paul Rusesabagina (b. 1954) (played by actor Don Cheadle [b. 1964]), who managed to save 1,268 lives while all around him tens of thousands of Tutsi were being brutally murdered by Hutu. The film focuses on both the horrific specifics of the "machete genocide" as well as the passivity of the international community as the genocide unfolded before its very eyes. Remarkably, some of the very victims of the genocide—including Tutsi women who had been raped—play themselves, where they are crowded into a holding pen like animals, just as they were in real life. However, like most feature films based on a true person/story, this one takes certain liberty with the truth and thus fictionalizes aspects in order to "fill out the story." Initially, Rusesabagina is depicted as a wily businessman as he ardently works to maintain the sense that his hotel in central Kigali (the capital of Rwanda), Hotel des Mille Collines, is a lap of luxury untainted by surrounding events. Continuing on in this way as long as possible, he simply focuses on the needs and desires of his wealthy clientele, while keeping a blind eye to the reality of the killing just outside the doors of the hotel. Despite the fact that his friends and neighbors are facing slaughter, Rusesabagina (a Hutu) is out to save only his wife (a Tutsi) and their children. Ultimately, however, as his home becomes surrounded by violence, he chooses to move his family and friends into the hotel. As he gets increasingly desperate, he begins making urgent pleas over the phone for help from foreign governments but all fail to intervene. As the killing increases in intensity and the Europeans flee Rwanda, Rusesabagina begins purchasing the safety of his Tutsi neighbors and obtains a modicum of protection from the raging mobs by bribing military officers with the hotel's cash, liquor, and other goods.

Although the movie was touted by viewers as captivating and thought-provoking, it was also criticized by scholars and others for not providing contextual details: Why do the

Hutu hate the Tutsi to the extent that they do? What are the roots of the conflict? What are the politics behind the conflict and killing?

Lieutenant Colonel Romeo Dallaire (b. 1946), the UN commander of the peacekeeping force with the limited and inadequate mandate in Rwanda during the 1994 genocide, also complained that the writers portray his decisions and actions—shown through the character played by Nick Nolte (b. 1941)—inaccurately. Finally, many in postgenocide Rwanda have complained that Rusesabagina was not as altruistic as Hollywood has portrayed him. Indeed, they say that it provides a romanticized and inaccurate picture of Rusesabagina's actions. More specifically, it has been said, for example, that he actually charged Tutsi to remove water from the swimming pool to drink, cook their food, and wash themselves and their clothes.

Huguenots. A Protestant sect in France, whose Christian practices were based on the teachings of the French exile John Calvin (1509–1564). Basing himself in Switzerland for most of his career after breaking with the Church of Rome (also known as the Roman Catholic Church), Calvin believed in the doctrine of predestination, according to which every individual's salvation or damnation was predestined by God—but also according to which, in spite of this, it was humanity's duty to practice virtue and goodness for its own sake. Calvin's teachings appealed to a small but influential number of the French population; the lower nobility, some merchants and businessmen, and other members of the middle stratum of the French elites conformed to his approach openly, and, at its peak, perhaps from 20 to 30 percent of the total French population embraced Calvinism. The Huguenots, as the French Calvinists were called, also carried political weight in French society, as it was the moneyed and those with financial interests who were on the whole attracted to this new sect. The wider their appeal spread, the greater was the extent of Catholic alarm at this movement, which effectively broke with the Catholic Church on matters of ritual, dogma, and theology. Anti-Huguenot feelings spilled over into massive violence on the night of St. Bartholomew's Eve, August 24, 1572, when a massacre of Huguenots took place in Paris at the instigation of Queen Catherine de Medici (1519–1589), the mother of King Charles IX (reigned 1560–1574). Over the next few weeks, the massacres spread to the provinces, and it is estimated that anywhere between a low of three thousand and a high of ten thousand people lost their lives as a result. The St. Bartholomew's Day Massacres and the great emigration that followed did not destroy Protestantism in France, but it dealt it such a blow that by 1598 the Church felt confident enough to grant a guarantee of religious toleration, the Edict of Nantes. The liberal measures thereby conceded were not to last, however; in 1685 King Louis XIV (reigned 1643–1715), a fervent supporter of traditional Catholicism, revoked the Edict, reversing a policy that for nearly a century had made France a leading country in the practice of religious toleration. Henceforth, the Catholic Church would rule in all matters spiritual, and Protestantism would remain a minority (and barely condoned) religion in France. The tolerant and free-thinking Huguenot approach to social interaction played a role during the Nazi Holocaust in the 1940s, when villagers in the small Huguenot community of Le Chambon-sur-Lignon shielded up to five thousand Jewish children, saving them from certain death.

Human Destructiveness. The 1948 United Nations Convention on the Prevention and Punishment of the Crime of Genocide embodies the notion of destructiveness in its very definition ("with intent to destroy . . ."). Such destructiveness is a psychological process in which human cruelty and physical devastation are important characteristics. There is a variation of opinion regarding the reasons behind human destructiveness, ranging from those who consider it to be the result of social or psychological frustrations—that is, a learned behavior in response to an external stimulus—to those who hold that violence and destructiveness is innate in all humans and that there are few predictable reasons to explain when or why it emerges. Moreover, the fact as to why aggressive behaviors have so often resulted in ferocious brutality is itself a subject of debate, particularly among psychologists who study abnormal behavior. What is clear is that in situations of civil disturbance, war, and genocide, the historical record has shown that the restraining influences of societal morality or religious values take second place to the more powerful (and more deeply located) forms of brutality, violence, and irrationality. There is no definitive position regarding the essential foundations of human destructiveness, but there is no doubt that the ongoing study of human behavior by behavioral scientists, psychologists, psychiatrists, and sociologists is necessary if modern society is to work towards developing an appropriate set of strategies for arresting the violence that has had such a devastating effect on humanity.

Human Rights. Human rights, which are set out in the Universal Declaration of Human Rights (UDHR) (1948), are those inalienable rights to which all individuals and groups of people, everywhere and without distinction, are entitled. Such rights include the following: the right to life, liberty, and security; the right to be recognized as a person before the law; the right to equality before the law; the right to freedom of movement and residence within the borders of each state; the right to leave any country, including [one's] own, and to return to [one's] country; the right to seek and to enjoy in other countries asylum from persecution; the right to freedom of thought, conscience, and religion; the right to freedom of opinion and expression; the right not to be held in slavery; the right not to be tortured; and the right not to be subjected to arbitrary arrest, detention, or exile.

Human Rights Internet (HRI). Founded in 1976 by Laurie Wiesberg and Harry Scobie, Human Rights Internet (HRI) specializes in the exchange of information within the worldwide human rights community. HRI is dedicated to the empowerment of human rights activists and organizations, and to the education of governmental and intergovernmental agencies and officials and other actors in the public and private sphere, on human rights issues and the role of civil society. Based in Ottawa, Canada, HRI communicates by phone, fax, mail, and the Internet with more than five thousand organizations and individuals around the world working for the advancement of human rights. HRI's objectives are as follows: facilitating the application of new technology toward the furtherance of human rights through transferring knowledge and expertise, particularly to nongovernmental organizations (NGOs) and other civil society organizations; producing and providing access to human rights databases and a comprehensive documentation center; carrying out human rights research and disseminating the results to concerned institutions and activities; producing human rights resources, including the *Human Rights Tribune*, annual publications, and directories in digital, hard copy, and microfiche formatting and making them available to NGOs and international institutions; fostering networking and cooperation among NGOs, as well as other civil society organizations, to integrate human rights with social and sustainable development issues; and supporting the roles of NGOs in the promotion of civil society and assisting governmental and intergovernmental organizations in the application of good governance practices and the projection of human rights through technical assistance.

Human Rights Law. Human Rights Law constitutes the following: (1) the collective body of customary international laws; (2) human rights conventions, treaties, and other instruments; and (3) national law that recognizes, honors, and protects human rights. More specifically, it refers to those laws that consider and deem all individuals of the human family, *Homo sapiens*, as having basic cultural, social, civil, political, and economic rights. They are rights each and every individual is entitled to due to the simple but profound fact that they are human. Human rights law, which some have referred to as "the conscience of mankind" [*sic*], is a direct result of the UN Declaration of Human Rights, which was ratified on December 10, 1948.

Human Rights Watch (HRW). Human Rights Watch, the largest human rights organization based in the United States, is dedicated to protecting the human rights of people across the globe. HRW is based in New York but has offices in various overseas locations. HRW was founded in 1978 as Helsinki Watch, with the express purpose to monitor compliance of Soviet bloc countries with the human rights provisions of the Helsinki Accords. In the 1980s, Americas Watch was established for the purpose of focusing on human rights abuses in Latin America. Eventually the organization expanded to other regions of the globe, and ultimately, in 1988, all the "Watch" committees were collectively placed under the umbrella of "Human Rights Watch."

Human Rights Watch promotes itself as one that "stands with victims and activists to prevent discrimination, to uphold political freedom, to protect people from inhumane conduct in wartime, and to bring offenders to justice." Its main activity is the investigation of human rights violations throughout the world.

Researchers with HRW conduct fact-finding investigations into human rights abuses in all parts of the world. The organization exposes such violations in published reports and in meetings with officials at the United Nations, the European Union, and various capitals across the globe. It publishes an annual state-of-the-world report, naming states that abuse human rights and holding them accountable before the bar of world opinion.

In crisis situations in which egregious violations of human rights are being committed, Human Rights Watch may call for the withdrawal of military and economic support from governments.

HRW reports that it was among the first to call for an international war crimes tribunal for the former Yugoslavia (the International Criminal Tribunal for the Former Yugoslavia, ICTY). Once the ICTY was established, HRW worked extensively with the ITCY's investigators and prosecutors, and six of the seven counts on which the tribunal finally indicted Yugoslav president Slobodan Milosevic (1941–2006) in 1999 were cases that HRW had documented in Kosovo. HRW also provided extensive evidence to the International Criminal Tribunal for Rwanda (ICTR) of human rights abuses during the 1994 genocide in Rwanda. HRW also was involved in the legal action against former Chilean dictator Augusto Pinochet (1915–2006) in London and helped to support the principle that former heads of state can be held accountable for heinous human rights crimes. Finally, HRW led a global campaign to push for the ratification of the treaty of a permanent International Criminal Court (ICC) to prosecute those accused of war crimes, crimes against humanity, and genocide.

Humanitarian Action. A concept that refers to a wide array of activities to assist nations and groups that are embroiled in a humanitarian crisis of some sort. Among such activities are development projects; diplomatic efforts; the establishment of safe areas, safe havens, and no fly zones; provision of emergency relief supplies and other types of assistance; and/or implementation of peace enforcement, peacekeeping, peace-building efforts, and other such actions.

Humanitarian Assistance. Nonmilitary assistance in times of genocidal and other conflicts may include food, water, clothing, shelter, medicines, fuel, hospital equipment, and so on, and the appropriate personnel to deliver much-needed supplies and to maintain and support such delivery systems. Among the difficulties of rendering humanitarian assistance are working with corrupt governments and/or opposition forces in delivering such material; gauging the efficiency and/or effectiveness of such work in terms of those receiving such aid; political bickering and infighting among those various groups involved in the delivery of such aid; questions of accountability; the always-present and larger question of neutrality on the part of humanitarian organizations (e.g., UN, ICRC); economic chaos in areas where the vast influx of aid workers changes the face of the political landscape; religious, political, and other agendas on the part of both combatants and aid workers; the vast sums of monies required to purchase such aid and transport it where necessary; the misuse of such aid for political agendas on the part of both combatants and countries involved in delivering the aid; postconflict continuation of humanitarian assistance; and the like. In regard to the issue of genocide, there is the larger question of whether or not military intervention itself is ultimately a form of humanitarian assistance—that is, does bringing such atrocities to a speedy conclusion constitute the first step in supplying aid to the victims?

Humanitarian Intervention. As with many terms used by social scientists, the term *humanitarian intervention* is often defined in different ways by different scholars and policy officials, depending on their world outlook and respective positions/offices. Some define humanitarian intervention as the use of outside military force within the borders of another sovereign nation against the latter's will in order to protect a portion of the state's population from inhumane treatment. Others define humanitarian intervention as an action by an outside agency in the "internal" political affairs of a state with military force against the will of the government of the state for the express purpose of halting gross human rights infractions by the said state. Still others have defined humanitarian intervention as a way of raising the cost of a government's committing gross human rights violations/atrocities and as a means to halt such from being perpetrated.

Discussions and decisions surrounding such intervention, especially in regard to gross violations of human rights, have, of late (the mid-1990s to 2007), largely focused on the conditions that need to be evident in order to override the sovereignty of the state where the violations are being committed. More specifically, the concept of "the responsibility to protect" has become popular in some circles (but, as might be surmised, disparaged in others). Basically, "the responsibility to protect" is the concept that sovereign states have a distinct responsibility to protect their own citizens from conflicts and violent actions carried out by groups and/or governmental entities, and if and when sovereign states are either unwilling or unable to do so, that responsibility must be held up by the international community or constituent parts of it.

Hussein, Saddam (1937–2006). Saddam Hussein was dictator of Iraq from 1979 until 2003. He was born near Tikrit and received his law degree from the University of Baghdad in 1971. While still a university student, Hussein joined the revolutionary Baath party and gained a name for himself in the aftermath of the overthrow of the Iraqi monarchy in 1958, when he took part in a plot to assassinate a top Iraqi official. Upon discovery of the conspiracy, Hussein fled Iraq. Following a Baath coup d'état in 1963, Hussein returned to Iraq and again became involved in Baath party politics. However, with a few short months, the Baath party was overthrown and Hussein was subsequently imprisoned. He remained in prison until the Baath party carried out another coup in July 1968 and regained power. Within five years, in 1976, he rose to the rank of general in the Iraqi Armed Forces. Through great cunning, Hussein managed to gain a spot on the ruling Revolutionary Command Council. Ultimately, he became Iraq's president in 1979 (and as soon as he gained power, he had his opponents put to death), adding the title of prime minister in 1994.

Always bellicose, he embroiled Iraq in a war in 1980 with Iran that lasted for close to ten years and that resulted in a bloodbath for both states. Hussein precipitated the war by having his troops carry out a surprise attack on Iran in an effort to capture the Shatt al-Arab waterway leading to the Gulf. He believed a victory would make him a superpower within the region. During this protracted war (1980–1988), in which millions were killed, he is said to have authorized the use of poison gas against the Kurds, both those who allied themselves with Iran and those who did not, brutally repressing the latter, a now-recognized genocide and one of the strongest charges against him during his trial, conviction, death sentence, and execution. The genocide of the Kurds resulted in the deaths of between fifty thousand and one hundred eighty thousand men, women, and children. Over one thousand Kurdish villages were also totally destroyed.

Also, in response to a rebellion in the south, he had entire towns burned to the ground and drained a huge area of precious swampland that was inhabited by the Ma'dan people, known also as the Marsh Arabs, virtually wiping out their habitat and way of life. The latter, too, constituted genocide.

Throughout his dictatorship, Hussein was ruthless in his treatment of those he suspected of a lack of loyalty and/or those who constituted a threat to his rule. He and his two sons (Uday Saddam Hussein al-Tikriti [1964–2003] and Qusay Saddam Hussein al-Tikriti [1966–2003]), who were equally ruthless and brutal, controlled every aspect of Iraqi life through the constant threat of torture and death. Hussein was so feared by his own people that no one dared mention his name in public unless they were praising him. He, on the other hand, was so paranoid about being assassinated that he reportedly had numerous look-alikes dress up as him and make appearances in his stead. Always suspicious of anyone but his closest advisors, he brooked no opposition and dealt with any and all factions with swift and brutal retribution.

Constantly suspected of harboring a desire as well as the means to develop weapons of mass destruction (nuclear, biological, chemical), Hussein came under intense pressure in 2002 by U.S. president George W. Bush (b. 1946) to allow international weapons inspectors to search Iraq for the materials to develop such weapons. Though no weapons of mass destruction were ever found, Hussein played enough of a cat-and-mouse game with the international community to make the latter even more suspicious of his intent and actions. Following the terrorist attack on the United States by Al Qaeda on September 11, 2001, the Bush Administration began a campaign to convince the world that Hussein was not only hiding weapons of mass destruction but also harboring members of Al Qaeda on Iraqi soil. Utterly convinced of the danger posed by Hussein and his regime, Bush, in March 2003, led the United States, Great Britain, Australia, and several other states in the invasion of Iraq to overthrow Saddam.

Shortly after the invasion Hussein's two sons were killed, but he disappeared. Months later, on December 13, 2003, U.S. forces discovered and captured Hussein hiding in a small underground bunker on a farm north of Baghdad, near the town of his birthplace, Tikrit.

In late 2005, Hussein, along with his stepbrother Sabawi Ibrahim al-Hassan (n.d.) and other members of his regime, was put on trial by an Iraqi special tribunal for the alleged murder of 148 Shiite Muslim boys and men in the town of Dujail in 1982 following an alleged assassination attempt on Hussein. On November 5, 2006, Hussein was convicted and sentenced to death by hanging for crimes against humanity. Hussein appealed the conviction and sentence, but on December 26, 2006, Iraq's highest court rejected his appeal and stated that the former dictator was to hang within thirty days. Saddam Hussein was duly executed on December 30, 2006. Hussein was scheduled for a second trial charging him with genocide and other crimes for his gassing of Iraqi Kurds in northern Iraq, but since that trial was adjourned until January 8, 2007, only his codefendants shall be tried for those crimes.

Hutu. An ethnic group inhabiting the Great Lakes region of central Africa, particularly in Burundi and Rwanda. The Hutu form a numerical majority in the region, significantly larger than their neighbors, the Tutsi. Hutu number between 12 and 13 million, composing about 90 percent of the population of Rwanda (the percentage was less than this prior to the 1994 Rwandan genocide perpetrated by extremist Hutu against the Tutsi and moderate Hutu) and 85 percent of the population of Burundi.

It has been estimated that a Hutu presence first appeared in the region around the first century CE. Traditionally, Hutu life was founded on a clan basis in which small kingdoms prevailed, but, after the arrival of the Tutsi sometime in the fifteenth century, a feudal system was established in which the Hutu were reduced to vassal status and were ruled over by a Tutsi aristocracy headed by a *mwaami* (king). The fundamental division between Hutu and Tutsi was, therefore, based more on a form of class difference than on ethnicity, particularly as a great deal of intermarriage took place; despite this, Hutu are generally of a smaller stature than Tutsi. The language spoken by both peoples is Kinyarwarda. Although the relationship between the Hutu and their neighbors prior to the 1950s had been essentially one based on hierarchy and dominance—the Hutu, a farming people, were exploited by a tithe system as well as other feudal disadvantages imposed by the Tutsi, a wealthier, cattle-raising community—Hutu-Tutsi relationships were, for the most part, peaceful. The divisions between Hutu and Tutsi were reinforced under the colonial rule of Belgium after 1919. The Belgians actually added to the privileged position of the Tutsi by granting them the right to run the country as proxies for the colonial administration. Moreover, as hereditary cattle owners (and thus the main possessors of wealth in Rwandan society), the Tutsi saw themselves as socially elevated compared to the Hutu. This only served to exacerbate the divisions and animosity prevailing in the country. This notwithstanding, Hutu dissatisfaction, where it existed, was expressed nonviolently. After Rwanda's and Burundi's independence from Belgium in the early 1960s, however, frequent Hutu persecutions of Tutsi took place in Rwanda, while the Tutsi elite committed large-scale massacres of Hutu in Burundi. The relationship between the Hutu and Tutsi is inextricably intertwined within the Great Lakes region: since 1994 there have been renewed efforts at reconciliation and the establishment of a harmonious future. Owing to the existence of radical elements among certain sectors of the Hutu population in both countries, however, such efforts have been slow in making lasting progress.

Hutu Power. A virulent Hutu-supremacist philosophy. In 1957 Hutu leaders in Rwanda published a Hutu manifesto espousing the virtues of the Hutu and denigrating the Tutsi. In the 1990s, *Kangura*, Rwanda's "hate-newspaper," which maligned the Tutsi in every way possible, published the "Hutu Ten Commandments." The "commandants" were nothing more than yet another way to malign the Tutsi and warn Hutu that any friendliness or kindness shown Tutsi was frowned upon and would be considered traitorous.

In 1991, the term *Hutu Power*, which conveyed the absolute supremacy of the Hutu over the Tutsi in all matters of life (political, social, economic, and religious), was coined. Not content with words, extremist Hutu formed groups such as the *Interahamwe* (Hutu youth militias), which translates to "those who stand together" and/or "those who attack together." These groups were indoctrinated with Hutu power beliefs and in the process were filled with the poison of hatred for all Tutsi and moderate Hutu. Ultimately, those espousing Hutu power were behind the planning and execution of the 1994 Rwandan genocide that resulted in the mass murder of between five hundred thousand and 1 million people in one hundred days (April–July).

Hutu Ten Commandments. A catalog of ten admonitory instructions that were to be followed by Hutu in order to destroy Tutsi influence over Rwandan society and guarantee Hutu hegemony. Published by Hassan Ngeze (b. 1961) in issue number 6 of the extremist Hutu screed *Kangura*, in December 1990, the "Ten Commandments of the Hutu" were written by Hutu extremists. The "Ten Commandments" could, in many respects, have been adapted directly out of the Nazi Nuremberg Laws. The Hutu Ten Commandants were as follows:

1. Every Hutu male should know that Tutsi women, wherever they may be, work for the interest of their Tutsi ethnic group. As a result, a Hutu who marries a Tutsi woman, befriends a Tutsi woman, or employs a Tutsi woman as a secretary or concubine shall be considered a traitor.

2. Every Hutu should know that our daughters are more suitable and conscientious in their role as woman, wife, and mother. Are they not beautiful, good secretaries, and more honest?

3. Hutu women, be vigilant, and try to bring your husbands, brothers, and sons back to reason.

4. Every Hutu should know that all Tutsi are dishonest in their business dealings. They are only seeking the supremacy of their own ethnic group. Any Hutu who engages in business dealings or partnerships with the Tutsi is a traitor.

5. All strategic positions—political, administrative, economic, military, and security—should be entrusted to the Hutu.

6. The education sector should be majority Hutu.

7. The Rwandan armed forces must be exclusively Hutu.

8. The Hutu should stop having mercy on the Tutsi.

9. Hutu, wherever they may be, must have unity and solidarity and be concerned about the fate of their Hutu brothers.
10. The 1959 revolution, the 1961 revolution, and the Hutu ideology must be taught to Hutu at all levels. Every Hutu must spread this ideology widely. Any Hutu who persecutes his brother Hutu for having read, spread, and taught this ideology is a traitor.

I

I Will Bear Witness: A Diary of the Nazi Years—1933–1941 and *I Will Bear Witness: A Diary of the Nazi Years—1942–1945* by Victor Klemperer. *I Will Bear Witness* (two volumes) (New York: Random House, 1998 and 1999, respectively) by Victor Klemperer (1881–1960), a German Jewish classics professor married to an "Aryan" woman, is one of the most detailed diaries produced during the course of the Nazi reign of terror. It includes with one revelatory observation/fact after another in regard to the Nazis' declarations and actions, both in Germany and in the "East"; the ever-increasing suffocation he experienced as a Jew in Germany; and the reactions of family members, friends, neighbors, and a whole host of bystanders to the events of the day in Germany and beyond.

IAGS. *See* International Association of Genocide Scholars.

ICMP. *See* International Commission on Missing Persons.

ICRC. *See* International Committee of the Red Cross.

Identity Cards, Rwanda. Under Belgian colonial rule in Rwanda, identity cards bearing an individual's ethnic group—Hutu, Tutsi, or Twa—were introduced in 1933. Not only the ethnic background, but also the bearer's place of residence was recorded on these cards—and, over and above that, the name of the person on the card could not relocate to another address without approval from the colonial authorities. After Rwanda's independence in 1961, the identity cards were retained as a means of "positive discrimination" in favor of the Hutu majority. This was a complete turnaround from the previous Belgian policy, which had been to elevate the Tutsi minority to positions of social, political, and economic hegemony.

During the 1994 genocide in Rwanda, the identity cards became literally a death warrant for their Tutsi bearers, though this was not new; for the previous three decades (ever since 1959), but especially since the ascent to power of the regime of Juvenal Habyarimana (1937–1994) in 1973, Tutsi had been continually segregated, persecuted and, on occasion, massacred on account of their group identity, which was clearly delineated on their identity cards. It can be argued that the existence of the cards was an important factor hastening the speed and spread of the genocide, as the entire population had been conditioned for generations to carry them and produce them when required to do so. Thus, when the extremist Hutu demanded to see an individual's identity card and the latter was identified as a Tutsi on the card, he/she was almost automatically killed—sometimes after the females were raped and brutalized and the men beaten. The soldiers generally shot and killed those Tutsi they caught, whereas the *Interahamwe* killed their victims with machetes.

By singling out the victims as different from the killers on the basis of an official ethnic designation, the cards also enabled the Hutu to distance themselves psychologically from the Tutsi, further facilitating the murder process.

Ideological Genocide. Helen Fein (b. 1934), a sociologist and genocide scholar, coined the term *ideological genocide* and defines it as "a particular ideology, myth, or an articulated social goal which enjoins or justifies the destruction of the victims" (Fein, 1990, p. 27). Continuing, Fein (1990) states, "Besides the above, religious traditions of contempt and collective defamation, stereotypes, and derogatory metaphor [all suggest] the victim is inferior, sub-human (animals, insects, germs, viruses) or super human (Satanic, omnipotent), and outside the universe of obligation of the perpetrators" (p. 27). According to Fein, three "classic" cases of "ideological genocide" were the Ottoman Turk genocide of the Armenians (1915–1923), the Nazi-perpetrated Holocaust against the Jews, Gypsies, and mentally and physically handicapped (1933–1945), and the Khmer Rouge–perpetrated genocide against the Cambodian people (1975–1979).

Mass killings along the lines of genocide are often motivated doctrinally. Extermination is justified by absolutist ideas. The most convenient way of creating an out-group is to establish hard and fast categories setting off completely one group from another as implacable foes. The most common ways of constructing such polarized relationships are through the invocation of nation, race, clan, ethnicity, and religion. Religion is one of the oldest devices with which to establish an unbridgeable gulf within and between populations. The medieval crusading centuries unleashed unremitting violence, with Catholics against Orthodox, and Christians against Jews and Muslims; in turn, the Protestant Reformation brought on near-genocidal wars between Catholics and Protestants. In the name of faith, merciless wars of extermination were fought. Nationalism introduced a new collectivity, the nation. Across the nineteenth century, earlier forms of identity hardened into modern nationalism, which established specific criteria that excluded those lacking the prerequisites for inclusion within the group. Over the decades, such nationalism became increasingly intolerant, forcibly rejecting national minorities. By the time of World War I (1914–1918), states waged wars against their minorities who were considered inassimilable. Class lay at the heart of Marxism; indeed, class struggle was the central dynamic in the Marxist dialectical understanding of social progress. With the rise of the Soviet Union, its leaders—most notably, Josef Stalin (1879–1953)—used class definitions as a guideline for aggressive domestic policies. Thus, for instance, in the Ukraine, when it came to uprooting the peasantry from their ancestral lands, unprecedented state violence was applied, especially as the peasants forcefully resisted the government. After four or five years of confrontation, millions had lost their lives. Peasants who refused to comply were labeled as "kulaks," promoters of private ownership, bearers of "bourgeois" values, and, thus, as enemies of the working class. In order to defeat the peasants, the Soviet state employed genocidal means, including the man-made terror-famine of 1932–1933 in Ukraine, which claimed, at a minimum, over four and a half million lives. Race has proven to be another ideological tool with which to classify populations, as was the case in Germany's Third Reich between 1933 and 1945. Nazism set up a vertical hierarchy of "races." At the top were the Aryans, the most pure of the races; on the lowest rung of the ladder were the Jews, who were dubbed nonhuman, the antirace. As the so-called master race, it was the Aryans' duty to extirpate Jews from the population, resulting in the "Final Solution of the Jewish Problem" (*Die Endlösung des Judenfrage*). Jewish identity was determined biologically, with a hierarchy ranking Jews from full Jews in the first generation to quarter-Jews if they possessed a single Jewish grandparent. According to the Nazi scheme, eventually all categories of Jews had to be eliminated in order to safeguard the Aryan race. In this case, racial ideology was used as a device with which to eventually justify genocidal behavior.

Ieng Sary (b. c.1924). Ieng Sary (real name Kim Trang) was born in Tra Vinh province, in southwestern Vietnam. His friendship with Saloth Sar (1922–1998)—who changed his name to Pol Pot as a revolutionary *nom de guerre*—had deep roots. They first met when they were school students at the Lycée Sisowath in Phnom Penh, and they both later received a government scholarship to study in France. It was in France that they first encountered the ideology of communism, which they were to import to their native Cambodia upon their return. Ieng Sary's wife, Ieng Thirith (b. c.1922), was the sister of Pol Pot's wife, Khieu Ponnary (1920–2003).

Upon his return to Indo-China, Ieng Sary, like Pol Pot, became a schoolmaster, teaching history and geography. Instrumental in the opening phases of the struggle of the Khmer Rouge, he transferred himself to Kompong Cham, in northeastern Cambodia, and took up a revolutionary life in the jungle. Ieng Sary became a leading figure in the Communist Party of Kampuchea (CPK) in 1971, when he represented the Khmer Rouge in China. In 1972 he became the commander in chief of Khmer Rouge forces in the northeast. As the exiled monarch of Cambodia, Prince Norodom Sihanouk (b. 1922), traveled the world seeking support against the military dictatorship of U.S.-backed strongman Lon Nol (1913–1985), Ieng Sary would often accompany him. The experience he gained on these trips enabled him to claim the position of foreign minister after the Khmer Rouge took power in April 1975; in this capacity, he also served as deputy prime minister under Pol Pot.

When Phnom Penh fell to invading Vietnamese forces in January 1979, Ieng Sary fled to Thailand. From there, he became recognized by the United Nations as the accredited representative of the Democratic Republic of Kampuchea in exile. After 1982, he lost political influence within the Khmer Rouge, and, in 1996, he left the party altogether. An aging ex-revolutionary in declining health, he emerged from exile and returned to a life of affluence in Phnom Penh, to live out his days surrounded by barbed wire and security guards.

IFOR. A multinational military force sanctioned and established in Bosnia by the United Nations for the purpose of overseeing implementation of the military aspects of the Dayton Peace Accords of December 1995. IFOR took its name from the simplest of premises: it was, quite literally, an implementation force. Its tasks were fourfold: to bring about an end to hostilities between all warring parties in Bosnia-Herzegovina, and to oversee the maintenance of the peace; to separate the armed forces of Bosnia-Herzegovina and Republika Srpska, the two entities of the new Bosnia; to supervise and facilitate the transfer of territories awarded to the two entities under the Dayton agreement; and physically to remove the military hardware of the warring parties' armed forces into approved storage arsenals. Advance units of IFOR were deployed as early as six days after the signing of the Dayton agreement on December 14, 1995, and at its height it grew to a maximum complement of sixty thousand personnel. All its objectives were achieved by June 1996. As an implementation force, IFOR's intended duration was always viewed as temporary, and the success of its mission proved this to be the case. By the end of 1996, IFOR was replaced by a new UN-approved mandate, SFOR (Stabilization Force), which was to continue IFOR's work and extend its scope to incorporate the next stage of the peace-building process—most importantly, preserving the security environment that had been created by IFOR. Such was IFOR's success that SFOR's complement could be reduced by stages; by 2001 it was down to twenty thousand, only a third of what it had been five years earlier.

Igbo People, Genocide of. The Igbo people, formerly known as the Ibo, are a large ethnic group concentrated in southeast Nigeria. The Igbo can trace their presence in the region back to the ninth century CE. After Nigeria's independence from British colonial rule in 1960, thousands of Igbo migrated to the Muslim-dominated north of the country in search of work, where they lived in communities that were strictly segregated from the Muslim majority. In early 1966, the Igbo were held responsible—falsely—by the federal government of Nigeria, led by military dictator General Yakubu Gowon (b. 1934), for the murder of several military officials. The false accusations resulted in murderous riots aimed directly at the Igbo. Violence escalated throughout the year and the deaths rose from hundreds to thousands, provoking a wholesale flight of Igbo from the north back to their traditional home in the southeast. This, in turn, led to calls for an Igbo secession movement, in large measure because the central government seemed unable to curb anti-Igbo violence. Encouraging the Igbo in their belief that a viable breakaway state could be established in Nigeria's Eastern State was the knowledge that large reserves of high-grade oil lay beneath it. In May 1967, the Eastern State finally seceded and, under the leadership of Lieutenant Colonel Chukwuemeka Odumegwu Ojukwu (b. 1933), created an Igbo majority state called Biafra. Immediately, the Nigerian Federal Army invaded the breakaway state, with the intention of dragging it back into the Federation. The civil war that ensued, from the summer of 1967 onward, escalated rapidly. One of the weapons employed by the government of Nigeria—and acknowledged openly by ministers and military figures alike—was to cut off food supplies to the civilian population of Biafra. Igbo leaders, both in Biafra and abroad, labeled the killings as genocide, and appeals were made to the UN to recognize Biafra and to intervene so as to save the population. It was the first time the charge of genocide was made in the international environment since the term was codified into international law in 1948. The UN turned down the Igbo request to be heard on the ground that UN membership was limited to recognized states and that Biafra had not yet achieved such recognition. The Nigerian civil war was dubbed a domestic matter and, therefore, outside the scope of the UN. The war lasted from June 1967 until the sudden collapse of Biafran resistance in January 1970 and took a terrible toll on the Igbo people. The fate of Biafra saw the death of up to a million people, mostly Igbo (including vast numbers of children), and the effects did not end with the military collapse. Civilian infrastructure—roads, bridges, schools, hospitals, towns, homes—had been utterly destroyed throughout Nigeria's southeast. The Eastern State was split into a number of smaller administrative districts, and control was placed in the hands of non-Igbo. Large numbers of the Igbo intellectual and economic elite, who should otherwise have been looked on as a natural leadership for a country under stress, left in fear of their lives, forming an émigré diaspora in Europe, North America, and various African countries.

In large measure, the Biafran genocide and the Nigerian Civil War have effectively been written out of history, overshadowed by events such as the Vietnam War, the various Middle East conflicts, the end of the Cold War, and the genocidal outbreaks of the last two decades in Iraq, Rwanda, Bosnia-Herzegovina, East Timor, and Darfur.

Imperialism. A political and economic philosophy whereby a powerful state extends its control, directly or indirectly, over another (quantifiably weaker) state or territory. Such extension of control can take place in many different ways—through physical conquest, through market penetration and economic domination, through colonial invasion and settlement, and through an offer of "protection" from other imperialist powers—in return for which the weaker state will grant certain specified "concessions" that will incrementally strip it of its autonomy. The term gained popular currency after the middle of the nineteenth century, when the so-called Age of Imperialism saw the extension of European (which later included U.S. and Japanese) rule over most of Asia, almost all of Africa and the Pacific, and other parts of the world (with the exception of Latin America, which was nonetheless largely controlled by the imperialist states economically). Although the Age of Imperialism saw huge colonial population movements from Europe to many lands of recent European settlement such as the United States, Canada, Australia, South Africa, New Zealand, Argentina, and Chile, often this colonialism was accompanied by significant violations of human rights against the indigenous populations that had already been living in the conquered territories. Often, this led to massive population collapse—sometimes through the introduction (deliberate or not) of diseases for which the indigenous populations had no immunity; sometimes through premeditated policies of genocidal killing; and sometimes, in spite of the colonial government's preferences, through settler depredations (e.g., raping the women, pillaging, destroying abodes). In the quest to maximize exploitative economic profits, imperialist governments on occasion brutalized colonial populations (through forced starvation and/or by subjugating them to a slave-like existence) in order to induce them to work harder and give up more and more land. Again, these violations of human rights led to population loss that their descendants and some scholars today refer to as being genocidal in character. Ultimately, imperialism's expansion of European political, cultural, economic, and military hegemony throughout the world was bought at an enormous human cost whose effects are still being felt today.

Implementation Force (IFOR). The NATO-led multinational force that was mandated by the UN to uphold and enforce the Dayton Peace Accords of November 1995, the purpose of which was to bring peace to Bosnia and Herzegovina owing to the intentional and civil wars that raged between 1992 and 1995 as a result of the dissolution of the former Yugoslavia. IFOR, an undertaking codenamed Operation Joint Endeavor, existed under a one-year mandate operational between December 20, 1995, and December 20, 1996.

Implementation Force for Bosnia-Herzegovina. *See* Implementation Force (IFOR).

Impuzamugambi (Kinyarwarda, "those with a single purpose"). A Hutu militia movement comprising youth and run by the political party *Coalition pour la défense de la république* (CDR). The youth were recruited, trained, armed, and led by Rwandese Governmental Forces. Formed in 1992, it was most active during the Rwandan genocide between April and July 1994.

Essentially, the *Impuzamugambi* constituted an armed wing of CDR, the latter of which was a Hutu extremist party dominated by a fanatically anti-Tutsi agenda. One of the CDR's leaders, Hassan Ngeze (b. 1961), was also the publisher of the anti-Tutsi newspaper *Kangura*. Jean-Bosco Barayagwiza (b. 1950), another CDR leader, was also closely involved in running the *Impuzamugambi*. Both were later tried and found guilty of genocide and crimes against humanity by the International Criminal Tribunal for Rwanda (ICTR).

The *Impuzamugambi* is often overlooked by commentators of the Rwandan genocide, primarily because its smaller numerical size saw its actions engulfed by the larger and more visible *Interahamwe*, the militia wing of the *Mouvement Révolutionnaire Nationale pour la Developpement* (MRND), led by Jerry Robert Kajuga (b. 1960). The two militia groups worked closely with each other throughout the genocide, though the members of each remained conscious of their separate political identities. Responsible for uncounted scores of thousands of deaths, members of the *Impuzamugambi* fled before the advance of the Rwandan Patriotic Front (RPF) forces in May and June 1994, with most seeking refuge across the border in the Democratic Republic of Congo. Individual *Impuzamugambi* members have been apprehended and tried in *gacaca* courts, although, like many *Interahamwe* killers, most have managed to reconstruct their postgenocide lives with impunity.

In Rwanda We Say: The Family That Does Not Speak Dies. A fifty-four-minute documentary produced in 2004 in Rwanda, *In Rwanda We Say* focuses on the release of a genocide suspect following a *gacaca* hearing (the adaptation of a traditional, village-based mediation process to try alleged suspects of the 1994 Rwandan genocide), "tracking the effect of his return on a tiny hillside hamlet (where he had formerly lived and where the atrocities had been committed). While the government's message of a 'united Rwandan family' permeates the language of the community, the imposed coexistence brings forth varying emotions, from numb acceptance to repressed rage." When the film was produced, already close to sixteen thousand genocide suspects had been released across the country due to having confessed to their crimes and having served the maximum sentence the *gacaca* tribunals would eventually impose.

In the Beginning Was the Ghetto: Notebooks from Lódz. A highly acclaimed diary about life in the Lódz Ghetto by Oskar Rosenfeld (1884–1944). A Prague intellectual, Rosenfeld provides a detailed view of the harrowing misery experienced by those imprisoned in the Lódz Ghetto from February 1942 to July 1944. In doing so, he speaks of the gnawing hunger, the diseases that swept through the ghetto, the debilitating forced labor imposed on the weak and infirm, the degrading circumstances of life and death, and the ever-present threat of deportation. But he goes beyond that and also speaks about the Herculean efforts by the Jews to retain their sense of self and dignity by carrying on, as best they could, with their cultural, religious, and social lives. Upon liquidation of the Lódz Ghetto, Rosenfeld and over seventy thousand remaining Jews were deported to Auschwitz, where he was murdered.

Incentives, and Diplomatic Practice. Incentives, often referred to as "carrots" (as in "carrots and sticks"), are positive economic and/or political inducements to bring about cooperation from a state that is perceived to be belligerent and/or in contravention of international law or mores. Incentives are offered to an actor in the hope that the latter will be more cooperative and open to changing its behavior, or they (incentives) may be offered on the condition that the recipient responds or acts in a manner specified by the party offering the carrot. Among some of the many positive inducements are the promise or actual granting of debt relief, foreign aid, subsidies vis-à-vis exports or imports, tariff reductions, most-favored-nation status, and/or the lifting of sanctions.

Indian Removal Act, 1830. In 1830 U.S. president Andrew Jackson (1767–1845) signed the Indian Removal Act, a law ordering the compulsory relocation of Native American peoples living east of the Mississippi River to a designated territory to the west. These peoples were known as the "Five Civilized Tribes," comprising the Cherokee, Choctaw, Creek, Chickasaw, and Seminole nations. These nations had adapted to certain European ways by taking that which most suited their quality of life while at the same time retaining their sovereign integrity and folkways. After the passage of the Indian Removal Act, however, these nations were forced to cede their lands to the United States and move to other territories many hundreds of miles away. Of the individual treaties signed following the Indian Removal Act, the first was between the United States and the Choctaw nation at Dancing Rabbit Creek, in 1830. Between 1831 and 1834, most members of the Choctaw nation were forced westward at the point of federal bayonets and in appalling conditions; because federal expenses for removal were inadequate, there were shortages of food, unsatisfactory means of transportation, and little in the way of warm clothing or blankets. At least a quarter of the Choctaw nation died before they reached the new Indian Territory in modern-day Oklahoma. A similar fate befell the other nations. In the case of the Creeks, an experience resembling civil war broke out between supporters and opponents of removal. The Chickasaw people were also removed, but, unlike the Creeks, their experience before and during the journey was less traumatic—owing to their closer proximity to the new Indian Territory, just under a quarter of the population died of exposure and disease as the trek proceeded—but they perished in large numbers after their arrival owing to disease.

For as long as they were able, the Seminoles managed to resist removal and during the Seminole Wars (1835–1842) made U.S. troops pay a heavy price for their invasion of the Seminole nation. Nonetheless, several thousand were eventually transferred to Indian Territory. The Cherokees, the most numerous of the Five Civilized Tribes, did all they could to avoid deportation, arguing their case in the highest U.S. tribunals, including the U.S. Senate and the Supreme Court. Still, as a result of the Treaty of New Echota (December 29, 1835), which ceded all Cherokee territory to the United States and prepared the grounds for removal, they too were forced to leave by 1839. Approximately one-quarter of the Cherokees perished between 1838 and 1839, in what became known as the "Trail of Tears." The term now stands for the forced removal and suffering of the Five Civilized Tribes, generally—during which time tens of thousands of people died as a direct result of U.S. government actions and failures to act.

INDICT Campaign. A British campaign established in late 1996, seeking, as its major aim, the creation of an ad hoc international criminal tribunal for Iraq similar to those established by the UN in the aftermath of the Yugoslav wars of secession (1991–1995) and the 1994 Rwandan genocide. INDICT was set in motion by the House of Commons (it was joined later by the U.S. Senate) in order to bring Iraqi officials to trial following the first Gulf War of 1991. It remained dependent upon voluntary donations until it received financial backing from the U.S. Congress in December 1998, through passage of the Iraq Liberation Act. Saddam Hussein's (1937–2006) dictatorial regime in Iraq had used poison gas against the Kurds in the north and had brutally killed thousands of Shiite Arabs (the Ma'dan people) in the south for having rebelled against him. In the intervening years, no attempts had been attempted to render him accountable, except for a long succession of failed efforts made by the nongovernmental humanitarian organization Human

Rights Watch. Meanwhile, UN tribunals were being established for Bosnia and Rwanda (the International Criminal Tribunal for the Former Yugoslavia and the International Criminal Tribunal for Rwanda, respectively). In both these instances, new successor regimes had begun turning some of the indicted criminals over to these tribunals. Until he was deposed in 2003 as a result of the U.S.-led invasion, Saddam Hussein lay beyond the reach of international law, though INDICT explored a number of legal avenues designed to impede the functioning of his government. The INDICT campaign was backed by U.S. president Bill Clinton (b. 1946). Three former British prime ministers, Baroness Margaret Thatcher (b. 1925), Sir John Major (b. 1943), and Tony Blair (b. 1953), also lent support to the campaign. With the capture of Saddam Hussein on December 13, 2003, and the ongoing trial of him and several members of his former Baath Party, many of the objectives of the INDICT campaign could be said to have been met, though its ambitions for a truly international court were stymied owing to the decision to make the trial a wholly Iraqi affair (though under international supervision). Ultimately, in late 2006, Saddam Hussein was found guilty of crimes against humanity for ordering the 1982 murder of 148 Shiite men and boys as a reprisal for an assassination attempt against him. He was hanged on December 30, 2006.

Indigenous Groups and Genocide. Owing to European colonization of the Americas, Africa, Asia, and the Pacific, many situations arose in which local peoples found themselves vulnerable to exploitation and genocide. Colonization itself was often deliberately genocidal, with untold millions of people across half a millennium losing their lives through outright murder or the imposition of conditions calculated to destroy their capacity to continue functioning as members of identifiable groups. Colonization by itself, though, was not the only force affecting indigenous peoples in a genocidal manner: decolonization no less than colonization has been responsible for massive destruction. Furthermore, not all indigenous peoples in postcolonial societies have experienced genocidal forms of destruction, though many have. Still others have found themselves at risk of destruction through a creeping violation of their human rights. Often, especially in the aftermath of colonial control and the postcolonial succession period, indigenous peoples have suffered not only genocidal forms of physical destruction, but existential threats to their culture, belief systems, habitation, languages, and identity.

The scope and extent of indigenous groups facing genocide is broad and ranges from non-Western tribal peoples in central and South America, West Papua, India, Burma, and many parts of Africa, to more settled peoples such as the Kurds, the Maya, and the Acehnese. To a certain extent, the experiences of indigenous peoples in the past have sensitized many in the First World to the need to take especial care to see that genocidal forms of destruction are not visited upon those in a colonized environment again. As a result, a push for human rights recognition has developed in many places, deliberately drawing attention to the plight of indigenous people so as to safeguard their position in the face of the expansionist tendencies of modern society that could otherwise see a reduction in the status of indigenous lives. For many, the fate of indigenous populations is a "front-line" issue in the struggle to create a genocide-free world.

Indigenous Peoples. Indigenous peoples, who are sometimes referred to as "First Nations" or "Fourth World" peoples, are those who are aboriginal or native to the countries in which they live. Although there is no single definition acceptable universally, it could be said that indigenous peoples are those who have a historical connection with a given region or territory and who inhabit (or have inhabited) that region or territory and have retained, at least in part, a cultural, linguistic, or social association with it. Additionally, indigenous peoples are those who identify themselves as such and are recognized by others as indigenous. The term *indigenous* is controversial, as an argument can be put that everyone is indigenous to somewhere; with this in mind, some argue that it is thus inappropriate to single out as indigenous only those aboriginal peoples who have been subjected to colonialism.

Precise estimates for the total population of indigenous peoples composing the "Fourth World" are difficult to determine, though at the beginning of the twenty-first century, it has been estimated that they make up approximately six percent of the world's population, a figure of about 300 to 350 million people. They are located all across the globe. Many indigenous peoples, whose lands are considered to be traditional lands of indigenous occupation, have suffered greatly at the hands of foreign colonizers or their successors. Often their land has been stolen from them; their culture has been wiped out (or nearly wiped out); and they have been forced to lead an impoverished life that has led to early death. Issues of concern to indigenous peoples around the world today include land rights, linguistic and cultural preservation, autonomy, environmental degradation, poverty, incarceration rates, health, exploitation of natural resources in traditional lands, and racial, ethnic, or cultural discrimination in all fields.

Individual Responsibility, Concept of. The concept of "individual responsibility" was one of the most significant aspects of the post–World War II trials (e.g., Nuremberg and others conducted to try the perpetrators of crimes committed during World War II). In other words, defendants such as those who planned, oversaw, and/or carried out crimes against humanity, crimes against peace, and/or war crimes (at the time, genocide was not included as a crime under international law) were not allowed to claim—as part of their defense—that they were simply following "superior orders." Furthermore, no longer were alleged perpetrators allowed to assert that their actions had constituted "acts of state" and have it accepted as a statement of defense. Also, no longer were alleged perpetrators, including national leaders, allowed to claim "sovereign immunity" as a defense. The rejection of this so-called Nuremberg defense (as it came to be known) has become enshrined in judicial practice ever since and is now a given in war crimes, crimes against humanity, and genocide prosecutions.

Indonesia and Genocide. In the last third of the twentieth century, Indonesia perpetrated genocide both inside and outside its own country under its first two presidents. The Indonesian government was never universally condemned by world public opinion, nor have its leaders and perpetrators been brought to justice for their crimes.

Between late October 1965 and March 1966, approximately half a million members of the PKI (*Partai Komunis Indonesia*, Indonesian Communist Party) were murdered by the Indonesian military, and perhaps an equal number supportive of the aims of the party were also killed in a direct confrontation between the United States–backed Indonesian military and Indonesia's first president, left-leaning Ahmed Sukarno (1901–1970). There is ample evidence that the United States may have supplied the Indonesian military forces with actual names of both communist party members and supporters. (Though political parties were specifically excluded from the 1948 United Nations Convention on the Prevention and Punishment of the Crime of Genocide, there is no doubt whatsoever that Indonesia's intent to destroy all members and supporters of this one group constitutes genocide in the broader understanding of the term.)

In December 1975, under President Mohamed Suharto (b. 1921), Indonesia's military forces invaded the former Portuguese colony of East Timor and annexed it in a brutal show of force. Between 1975 and 1999, when East Timor finally gained its independence, the Indonesian military murdered approximately one-third of the tiny territory's population.

In 2006, citizens of the Indonesian province of West Papua (formerly known as Irian Jaya), which has been under Indonesian control since 1969, began fleeing to Australia, claiming massive human rights abuses (including politically inspired deaths) by the Indonesian military. However, as of this writing (mid-2007), it is too early to assess whether this is a genocidal campaign against the native Papuans and thus a return to Indonesia's earlier genocidal practices.

There are numerous and complex reasons why Indonesia has not yet been condemned, including but not limited to the following: its friendship with the West within the earlier Cold War environment; its population as the largest non-Arab Muslim constituency in the world (and thus a supposed bulwark in the new, as of 2001, so-called war on terror); more recently, its perception within the global environment as a bastion of democracy in Asia; and its continuing denial of genocide.

Indonesia, Mass Killing of Suspected Communists. On October 1, 1965, six senior Indonesian generals were kidnapped and murdered by junior officers. The Indonesian Communist Party (PKI) was blamed for this act, which was portrayed by the military and its leading spokesman, Major General Mohamed Suharto (b. 1921), as an attempted coup d'état designed to entrench the power of left-leaning President Ahmed Sukarno (1901–1970). Suharto led a successful countercoup, resulting in widespread reprisals against the communists—even though the role of the PKI in the coup attempt, at the time and since, was unclear. On October 16, 1965, Sukarno appointed Suharto as minister for the army and army commander in chief, after which General Suharto ordered his forces to destroy the PKI and the threat it allegedly represented. In the months that followed, an unprecedented explosion of violence swept the country as PKI members (many of whom were, coincidentally, ethnically Chinese) were rounded up, tortured, and executed. Families of suspected communists were also targeted by the military, military-endorsed militias, and even civilian mobs. Estimates of the number killed varies widely; most accounts put the number at about half a million, though some have speculated that it was as high as 2 million. Hundreds of thousands more were imprisoned without trial, often for periods of twenty years or longer.

Under Suharto the military forces were purged of what were viewed as pro-Sukarno elements, and Sukarno's power base effectively collapsed. On March 11, 1966, Suharto assumed supreme authority throughout the country, displacing Sukarno, and introduced what became known soon afterward as the New Order (*Orde Baru*). The next day, the PKI was officially banned, PKI members of parliament were purged, the press was gagged, and trade unions were forbidden. The upshot of what became known as "The Year of Living Dangerously" was that, between 1966 and 1998, Indonesia was basically ruled as an authoritarian quasi-democracy, with one president, one ruling party, and few elections. The country became increasingly militarized, and the military forces received a permanent place in the running of the country. Suharto's rule possibly saved Indonesia from going communist (the certainty of this will never be truly known); but, by doing so, the Indonesian people suffered over thirty years of repression, censorship, and state-sanctioned violence.

Inducements, as Part of a Sanctions Policy. In regard to the implementation of sanctions, inducements (or inducement sanctions) refer to the introduction or use of positive incentives for the express purpose of enhancing the likelihood of compliance by the party being sanctioned. The use of inducements are also based on the notion that a sanctions policy solely composed of a series of extremely heavy and punitive pressures can become counterproductive in that the sanctioned state may end up perceiving the sanctions as unfair and dismiss them out of hand; on the other hand, if incentives are added to the approach, it may increase the likelihood of compliance. Put another way, the stick-and-carrot approach is predicated on the notion that what the "stick" is unable to achieve alone, the addition of the "carrots" will (i.e., tempt the targeted nation to capitulate).

Part and parcel of inducements can, and often does, involve the following: (1) the suspension of sanctions for renewable periods (e.g., every ninety-day period an assessment is made to ascertain if the targeted state is in compliance; and, if it is, the suspension of certain sanctions are renewed, but if it is not then the sanction(s) that have been suspended are reinstated); (2) the easing of certain sanctions (e.g., allowing the targeted state to either export or import a higher volume of goods than previously allowed); and (3) receiving financial benefits for compliance.

Some scholars and policymakers look askance at inducements, asserting that they provide a poor and potentially dangerous example to other states in that inducements may come to be perceived by some as a way of obtaining favors for not engaging in unlawful actions.

***Inkotanyi* (Kinyarwarda, "warrior," or colloquially, "fierce fighter").** A self-descriptive name used by soldiers of the Rwandan Patriotic Front (RPF) beginning with its formation in 1990. During the Rwandan genocide of 1994, it came to be applied to the RPF by the Hutu Power regime, always employed in a derogatory fashion. Its use by the Hutu was such as to describe the RPF as a bunch of rebellious traitors. The name originally was derived from that given to warriors serving in the army of nineteenth-century Rwandan Mwaami (King) Kigeri IV Rwabugeri (who reigned from 1853 to 1895).

Inquisition. A term traditionally associated with the Roman Catholic Church to describe a specially convened ecclesiastical institution for the purpose of rooting out, suppressing, and combating heresy (i.e., falsity in belief, doctrine, and/or practice). The term is usually associated with the Middle Ages. Although inquisitions took place throughout Christian Europe during this period, especially Italy and France, Spain is the country that has been most closely identified with "The Inquisition," particularly as regards the case of those called the *marranos* (pigs), Jewish converts to Catholicism who were perceived as insincere. Begun during the royal reign of King Ferdinand (1452–1516) and Queen Isabella (1451–1504), Pope Sixtus IV (1414–1484) granted them permission to establish such an inquisition; its judges were appointed by them in 1480. Father Tomás Torquemada (1420–1498) was the true organizer and, thus, named the Grand Inquisitor of Spain. Under his authority, both "false" Jewish and Muslim converts were rooted out, sentenced, and put to death. The actual number of such victims cannot be fully established.

Institute for the Study of Genocide (ISG). Founded in 1988 by Dr. Helen Fein (b. 1934), a sociologist and genocide scholar, the Institute for the Study of Genocide is an independent nonprofit education corporation founded to promote and disseminate scholarship and policy analyses on the causes, consequences, and prevention of genocide. As part of its effort, the institute hosts conferences on various aspects of genocide, issues working papers, and publishes (semiannually) *The ISG Newsletter*.

Institute of Turkish Studies (ITS). An institute founded in Washington, D.C., in 1982, established by a grant from the government of the Republic of Turkey. It advertises itself as a nonprofit educational foundation devoted solely to supporting and encouraging the development of Turkish Studies in American higher education. It is based at Georgetown University, Washington. Its founding director, Heath Lowry (b. 1942), established the Institute in Washington, D.C. so as to provide researchers with the opportunity to avail themselves of research and travel monies provided by the Turkish government. In attempting to promote Turkish Studies, the ITS has lobbied U.S. government officials and submitted articles to newspapers and journals with the intention of painting Turkey in the best possible light, along the way utilizing its position, as a respectable-sounding research institute in the national capital, to deny the excesses of the Armenian Genocide.

Institute on the Holocaust and Genocide (Jerusalem). The Institute on the Holocaust and Genocide was founded in 1979 by Israel W. Charny (b. 1931), Shamai Davidson (1926–1986), and Elie Wiesel (b. 1928). The Institute was one of the first to link the two concepts of Holocaust and genocide, and one of *the*, if not the, first devoted to genocide scholarship. Among some of the many projects undertaken by the Institute are the convening of the International Conference on the Holocaust and Genocide in Tel Aviv (1982); the development and publication of the series titled *Genocide: A Critical Bibliographic Review* (1988–); the development and publication of *The Encyclopedia of Genocide* (1999); and the cofounding of *Genocide Studies and Prevention: An International Journal* (2006), the latter of which is published by the University of Toronto Press.

Integrated Network for Societal Conflict Research (INSCR) Program. Based at the Center for International Development and Conflict Management (CIDCM), University of Maryland, College Park, INSCR was founded in 1998 as an organizational framework to better integrate and coordinate quantitative research initiatives investigating various aspects of complex societal conflicts and as a network platform for establishing closer contact and collaboration with similar research enterprises in other locations around the world. The INSCR program builds upon the research foundations developed by Ted Robert Gurr including the Polity, Minorities at Risk, and State Failure research projects.

Intentionalists. Those scholars who argue that the Holocaust, the genocide of the Jews, was primarily centered in the person of Adolf Hitler, his antisemitism, and his commitment to bringing to realization a world free of Jews (German, *Judenrein*) are commonly referred to as "intentionalists" (i.e., those who adhere to the intentionalist theory). Critical to their understanding are Hitler's many public speeches vilifying the Jews and promising them harm, as well as his own "masterwork" *Mein Kampf*. (It must be noted, however, that no actual document signed directly by Hitler ordering the physical destruction of the Jews has ever been discovered, and such a document, most probably, was never written.) Most famous of these was his speech of January 30, 1939, to the German Reichstag, where he publicly affirmed that if "international Jewry" (a fallacious notion to which Hitler and many other Nazi antisemites referred to throughout the period of the Third Reich) would be the cause of yet another world war—the inference that "Jewry" had caused World War I was a fraudulent claim that Hitler and the

Nazis used as propaganda to instill hate and dissension—"then the result would not be the Bolshevization of the earth and with it the victory of Jewry, it will be the annihilation of the Jewish race in Europe." The intentionalists also argue that with the invasion of the Soviet Union in June 1941 (Operation Barbarossa) and the Wannsee Conference of January 1942, Hitler was able to mobilize the Nazi effort to carry out his long-sought agenda.

Intentionalists'/Functionalists' Debate. Primarily a debate among historians, which has now subsided somewhat, based on two schools of thought in regard to whether the Nazi annihilation of the Jews was an early and overt plan of the Nazis based on the thinking and aim of Hitler himself or whether the "Final Solution" was a policy that evolved slowly over time. The so-called intentionalists (a term first coined by historian Christopher Browning [b. 1944]) have argued that Hitler's own vision, consistent with his ongoing antisemitism, was part of a strategic plan from the very beginning of his drive for political power and dominance. The intentionalists rely on Hitler's writings (including *Mein Kampf*) and numerous public statements and speeches in which his hatred and contempt for Jews is abundantly clear. One of the clearest and most well-known examples of the latter is found in a speech Hitler made on January 20, 1939, during which he asserted the following: "If the international Jewish financiers outside Europe should succeed in plunging the nations once more into a world war, then the result will not be the bolshevization of the earth, and thus the victory of Jewry, but the annihilation of the Jewish race in Europe." The so-called functionalists, on the other hand, see the Nazi leadership and administrative apparatus as one of competing vested interests, at times chaotic and self-serving, and often working at cross purposes, with Hitler standing "above the fray" and entering into it only when necessary, more as an arbiter than a leader. Although the functionalists, too, agree upon the importance of Hitler's public antisemitism and his desire to "do away with the Jews," they argue that his own lack of specific and concrete ideas left such work to his underlings, and thus the annihilation of European Jewry was more the result of historical circumstance than directives from the top. The lack of actual documentation from the Führer himself only adds to the difficulty of assigning one approach primacy over the other.

Intentionality. Ever since the genesis of the development of the UN Convention on the Prevention and Punishment of the Crime of Genocide (UNCG), there has been heated and constant argument as to how investigative bodies and courts should assess the intent of alleged perpetrators of genocide, especially when there is no record (paper, audio, video, etc.) indicating such and/or no witnesses who can or will attest to hearing of plans to carry out such a crime. Over the years, international law specialists, genocide scholars, and others have argued that, in reality, "intent" can be inferred from the various criminal acts themselves. In other words, if a perpetrator singles out a specific group of people and undertakes actions seemingly to destroy them, in whole or in part, then intent can and should be inferred from the act itself. (For a more in-depth discussion of this issue, see William A. Schabas's *Genocide in International Law*, Cambridge University Press, 2000.)

Interahamwe (Kinyarwarda, variously, "those who stick together," "those who work together," and "those who attack together"). The *Interahamwe* was an extremist Hutu paramilitary unit that was fundamental to the Rwandan genocide of 1994 and was the most important of the anti-Tutsi militias prevailing throughout the country. The movement's genesis could be found in a number of junior soccer clubs, one of which, the *Loisirs* (Leisure) club, was coached by one Robert "Jerry" Kajuga (b. 1960). Under his direction, the *Interahamwe* was transformed from a youth organization when it was founded in 1990, to a radical Hutu killing machine. Originally trained by the French at the request of the government of Rwandan president Juvenal Habyarimana (1937–1994), the *Interahamwe* formed the shock troops of the Hutu war of extermination against the Tutsi. The *Interahamwe* was the most radical of the many factions opposed to the Arusha peace process of 1992, in which Habyarimana found himself negotiating with the émigré Tutsi organization known as the Rwandan Patriotic Front (RPF). In the pregenocide years of 1992–1994, the *Interahamwe* engaged in lethal street fights hoping to upset the social order. Their source of weapons was funneled to them through the army, allowing them to engage in daily murder sprees employing machetes and other implements. To keep the *Interahamwe* in check, there were periodic purges of the most extreme members, who wished to proceed at a pace faster than that preferred by their political leaders. When the call for action finally came after Habyarimana's assassination on April 6, 1994, none were more bloodthirsty than the *Interahamwe*. From April 6 forward, *Interahamwe* killing units were left to their own devices; they knew their instructions and required no further prompting. Only one word describes them: merciless. The other killing factions such as the *Impuzamugambi*, another anti-Tutsi extremist militia that worked closely with the *Interahamwe*, were also brutal. Right up to the end of the genocide, all members and cells of the *Interahamwe* were carefully monitored by Joseph Nzirorera (b. 1950), the secretary-general of the *Mouvement Révolutionnaire National pour le Développement* (MRND, the National Revolutionary Movement for Development), even though the day-to-day affairs of the *Interahamwe* were coordinated by its vice president, Georges Rutaganda (b. 1958). The *Interahamwe* forcefully recruited peasants in order to encompass as much of the population as possible within the genocidal project; in this way, genocide became civic virtue, of sorts, to be practiced by all. When the killing ceased, many of the *Interahamwe* members managed to escape to eastern Congo. What is most significant about the existence of the *Interahamwe* is that it demonstrated that the genocide was far from spontaneous; indeed, it was a carefully planned campaign of extermination that had its executioners prepared and waiting to go into action long before the trigger on the night of April 6, 1994.

INTERFET. An initiative by the Australian government of prime minister John Howard (b. 1939) to reestablish a peaceful regime in East Timor after the failure of the United Nations Security Council's own mandated peacekeeping operation, UNAMET (United Nations Mission in East Timor), to curb militia and other violence prior to and during the territory's referendum on independence from Indonesia in September 1999. INTERFET (International Force in East Timor), the largest single deployment without reinforcement of Australian combat troops since the Second World War, was commanded by Lieutenant General Peter Cosgrove (b. 1947), subsequently the head of the Australian Defence Force. It was a multilateral force involving twenty-two countries in all. The deployment was successful in establishing peace and security through a credible and deterrent presence in all parts of East Timor, including the West Timor enclave of Oecussi. INTERFET's tasks included reconstruction activities following the widespread militia-generated destruction accompanying the referendum, assistance with administration, policing and law and order functions, and detection and investigation into allegations of human rights violations. As a UN Security Council–backed mission, INTERFET was equipped with a Chapter VII mandate (a peace enforcement mandate versus a softer peacekeeping mandate), signaling the determination of the UN on this occasion to prevent the large-scale abuses that had characterized other situations requiring UN intervention in the 1990s (e.g., in Rwanda in 1994 and Srebrenica in 1995, to mention but two). INTERFET remained active in East Timor until February 2000, when its operations gave way to the United Nations Transitional Administration in East Timor, or UNTAET. The purpose of this latter body was to administer the territory and exercise legislative and executive authority during the transition period leading up to East Timor's independence on May 20, 2002.

Intergovernmental Organizations (IGOs). Intergovernmental organizations are multistate institutions formed by treaties or other formal agreements. Such organizations share perceived and actual interests (be they political, economic, social, or otherwise). IGOs serve as a conduit for dialogue between states, a source of information gathering and dissemination for its membership, and a means for establishing guidelines to which the states are expected to adhere. IGOs serve a wide variety of other functions as well, including but not limited to those that are economic, humanitarian, social, and security in nature. The most notable IGO is the United Nations. Other examples of IGOs are the African Union (AU), the Association of South East Asian States (ASEAN), the European Union (EU), the North Atlantic Treaty Organization (NATO), the Organization of American States (OAS), and the Organization for Security and Cooperation in Europe (OSCE).

Internal Displacement. The involuntary movement of individuals and groups of people inside their own country. Such displacement is the result of various situations, including but not limited to threats of mass violence, outbreaks of mass violence, systematic massacres, and/or the threat and/or reality of genocide.

Internal Refugees (also referred to as internally displaced persons [IDPs] or displaced persons). This term, like its counterpart, internally displaced persons (IDPs), refers to those who are fleeing armed conflict or internal strife and/or persecution (or the fear of persecution) but have not crossed an internationally recognized state border and are thus still residing within the territory of their own country.

Internally Displaced Persons (IDPs) (also referred to as internal refugees or displaced persons). *See* Internal Refugees.

International Alert (IA). In 1985, International Alert—a standing International Forum on Ethnic Conflict, Genocide and Human Rights (IA)—was established by a group of experts concerned with the need to anticipate, predict, and prevent genocide and other mass killings. IA basically has two main aims: First, the organization is concerned with conflict resolution and conflict avoidance (conflicts of interest between ethnic or other groups within recognized states that have already resulted in violence or are likely to do so unless solutions or accommodations are found) in accordance with international standards. In that regard IA aims at promoting internal peace and conciliation through dialogue. Second, as its name implies, it works to "alert" international opinion to situations of ethnic violence which are assuming genocidal proportions.

International Association of Genocide Scholars (IAGS). A global, interdisciplinary, nonpartisan organization that seeks to further research and teaching about the nature, causes, and consequences of genocide and to advance policy studies on genocide prevention. Founded in 1994, IAGS meets biennially in a conference format to consider comparative research, new directions in scholarship, case studies, the links between genocide and massive human rights violations, and prevention and punishment of genocide. Since being established, conferences have taken place at (or under the auspices of) the College of William and Mary (Williamsburg, Virginia), Concordia University (Montreal, Canada), the University of Wisconsin-Madison, the University of Minnesota (Minneapolis), the National University of Ireland (Galway), Florida Atlantic University (Boca Raton, Florida), and the University of Sarajevo (Bosnia-Herzegovina). The aim of IAGS conferences is to focus more intensively on questions of genocide than is possible in the existing two-hour format of most conferences and to draw colleagues from different disciplines into an interdisciplinary conversation. In addition to the biennial IAGS conferences, the association has also published scholarly works under its own imprint. *Genocide Studies and Prevention: An International Journal* is the official organ of the IAGS. The association has affiliate relationships with other like-minded organizations such as the Institute for the Study of Genocide (New York) and the Institute on the Holocaust and Genocide (Jerusalem, Israel). Membership in the IAGS is open to scholars, graduate students, and other interested persons worldwide.

International Bill of Rights. The International Bill of Rights, developed and established under the auspices of the United Nations, is composed of three seminal parts: The Universal Declaration of Human Rights of 1948, and two international covenants adopted by the General Assembly in 1966—one on economic, social, and cultural rights and the other on civil and political rights (and the means of implementation that are part and parcel of the "Optional Protocol" to the Covenant on Civil and Political Rights).

International Commission on Intervention and State Sovereignty (ICISS). In response to a challenge from UN secretary-general Kofi Annan (b. 1938), Canada's prime minister Jean Chrétien (b. 1934) announced the establishment of the International Commission on Intervention and State Sovereignty during the United Nations Millennium Summit in September 2000. The mandate of the commission was to encourage and undertake a comprehensive global debate on the relationship between intervention and state sovereignty, with an attempt at "reconciling the international community's responsibility to act in the face of massive violations of humanitarian norms while respecting the sovereign rights of states."

The ICISS was given the mandate to examine, analyze, and debate a wide array of questions related to a host of legal, moral, political, and operational issues vis-à-vis the question as to when, if ever, states can legitimately, collectively or individually, carry out coercive—and, in particular, military—action against another state for the express purpose of protecting people at risk in that state. The latter, then, constitutes the so-called right of humanitarian intervention. An international research team conducted extensive research in order to collect, examine, and present the latest and best thinking on the issues of intervention and sovereignty and the relationship between the two. Ultimately, the report's primary theme became "The Responsibility to Protect," the concept that sovereign states have a distinct responsibility to protect their own citizens from conflicts and violent actions carried out by groups and/or governmental entities, and if and when sovereign states are either unwilling or unable to do so, that responsibility must be upheld by the international community or constituent parts of it.

The ICISS issued a final report entitled *The Responsibility to Protect*, which was a result of the aforementioned research, consultations with various bodies from around the world, and deliberations by the commission's members. On December 18, 2001, the report was formally presented to Secretary-General Kofi Annan and the member states of the United Nations.

International Commission on Missing Persons (ICMP). ICMP is an intergovernmental organization (IGO) established in France in 1996. Its fundamental purpose has been to locate the whereabouts or the fate of those missing as a result of the wars accompanying the disintegration of the former Yugoslavia, namely, Slovenia and Croatia, in 1991, Bosnia-Herzegovina between 1992 and 1995, Kosovo in 1998–1999, and the crisis in the Former Yugoslav Republic of Macedonia (FYROM) in 2001. A good deal of ICMP's work is in the area of forensic identification of bodies located at mass gravesites where massacres have taken place, particularly in Bosnia-Herzegovina. Its Exhumations and Examination (E & E) program undertakes the tasks of detecting these sites, recovery and anthropological examination of human remains, and the use of scientific methods in order to compile a snapshot of how the victims were killed. The Identification Coordination Division takes responsibility for the collection of DNA samples from the relatives of those who are missing and passes these on to the ICMP's laboratories for cross-matching with data collected by the E & E researchers. The ICMP is also heavily involved in tracing those who are missing on account of war and genocide in the region but whose fate is unknown; it thus acts as an investigative unit tracking down the missing, and reuniting families. ICMP's activities, beyond those for which it is mandated, are many and include consciousness-raising about missing persons, empowerment of those searching for their relatives, establishment of missing persons search networks, and representation of the interests of families to governments, other IGOs, and nongovernmental organizations (NGOs). The head office of the ICMP is located in Sarajevo, with other offices situated throughout several of the other countries of former Yugoslavia.

International Committee of the Red Cross (ICRC). An international humanitarian organization established in Geneva, Switzerland, in 1863, by Henri Dunant (1828–1910), a Swiss businessman who had witnessed at first hand the terrible carnage caused to soldiers of both sides in the Franco-Austrian Battle of Solferino (1859). In 1864, at Dunant's urging, the Swiss government convened a sixteen-nation international committee for the purpose of establishing a set of universal norms that would allow for humane treatment of both the wounded in battle and prisoners of war. This was the first of several Geneva conventions. The ICRC works alongside of the Red Cross and Red Crescent societies that exist in individual countries. ICRC delegates are usually permitted access to all sides of a dispute because of the respect most nation-states have for the ICRC's fidelity to a key principle that has guided all ICRC operations since its establishment—the principle of absolute neutrality and confidentiality. Throughout its history, the ICRC has acted as a silent witness to some of the worst excesses of state and nonstate behavior, never deviating from the aforementioned core principles. The position it advocates by way of justification for its silence is a straightforward one: if the ICRC were to speak out publicly about what it has witnessed after having been allowed access to prisons, detention centers, concentration camps and the like, violators of human rights norms could simply refuse ICRC delegates continued access—in which case, prisoners and other populations at risk would be denied the succor that the ICRC can bring to such situations. Where it is given access, the ICRC's neutrality enables it to do much good for those unable (for various reasons) to provide for their own basic needs, and, with this in mind, ICRC delegates are often extremely reluctant to leave a dangerous area, even after their continued presence has become a liability. Sometimes delegates are killed, either in crossfire or deliberately. But to bear arms, even for self-defense, is anathema to the ICRC, as it sees this as compromising its neutrality. The ICRC's ability to see to its core tasks—monitoring of prisoner conditions, carrying messages between prisoners and their families, advocating more humane conditions, providing food and other "comforts" for prisoners, delivering emergency aid to victims of armed conflicts, among others—has enabled it to achieve admiration unsurpassed among humanitarian aid agencies. Yet its policy of confidentiality has come under increasing criticism in the face of genocide, and many around the world are of the opinion that perpetrators of genocide must not be greeted with silence.

International Court of Justice (ICJ). Based at The Hague in the Netherlands, the ICJ is the principal judicial organ of the United Nations. It began its work in 1946 and replaced the Permanent Court of International Justice, which had operated since 1922. Its primary responsibilities are twofold: (1) to decide legal disputes according to the principles of international law of those nation-states that both submit their requests and agree to abide by the decisions rendered, and (2) to give advisory opinions to duly recognized international agencies and organs when invited to do so. It is composed of fifteen justices, each of whom is elected by the UN General Assembly and the UN Security Council for nine-year terms. No more than one judge can be elected from any one nation-state.

The court's services are available to all states that are parties to its statute, which include all members of the United Nations and Switzerland. The only parties allowed to have cases heard at the ICJ are states; in other words, it does not hear cases involving private individuals, other bodies/entities, or international organizations. The court's jurisdiction applies to all disputes, issues, and questions that member states refer to it, as well as any and all matters provided for in the United Nations Charter, international conventions, and international treaties. Thus, for example, it can, and has, heard cases on all of the following: territorial sovereignty, noninterference in the internal affairs of nation-states, diplomatic relations, hostage-taking, asylum, nationality issues, land frontiers and maritime boundaries, and rights of passage. It has also offered advisory opinions on such questions as judgments rendered by international administrative tribunals, status of human rights rapporteurs, and the legality of the threat of nuclear weapons. Based on its statute, the ICJ decides disputes by adhering to and applying the following: international conventions establishing rules expressly recognized by the contesting states, international custom based on general practice accepted as law, the general principals of law recognized by nations, and judicial decisions.

International Covenant on Civil and Political Rights (ICCPR). Adopted by the United Nations in 1966, the ICCPR entered into force as international law ten years later (1976). The ICCPR recognizes "the inherent dignity and the inalienable rights of all members of the human family" as "the foundation of freedom, justice, and peace in the world" and the obligation of the member states of the United Nations to promote such. Its mandate allows it to address a host of concerns, including: the right of self-determination; discrimination based upon "race, color, sex, language, religion, political or other opinion, national or social origin, property, birth or other status"; the inherent right to life; torture, cruel, inhuman, or degrading treatment or punishment; slavery; access to the legal system;

freedom of movement and residence; freedom of expression and opinion; peaceful assembly and association; and the centrality of family and marriage.

Unfortunately, the reality of the contemporary political world, including both the United Nations itself and the signatory nations to the ICCPR, is that, despite the force of international law, the ICCPR has little, if any, impact on the general international improvement of human rights, most especially in totalitarian nation-states under dictatorial regimes. The latter is true due to the fact that such nation-states more often than not ignore pleas from international human rights organizations and the international community to halt their egregious human rights violations and figure that in the long run they can do as they wish as few will effectively challenge their actions, let alone their rule.

International Covenant on Economic, Social, and Cultural Rights (ICESCR). Similar to the United Nations International Covenant on Civil and Political Rights, the ICESCR was adopted in 1966 and affirmed in international law in 1976. It, too, recognizes "the inherent dignity and inalienable rights of all members of the human family" as "the foundation of freedom, justice, and peace in the world," but directs its focus on the three areas of economics, social, and cultural rights. It affirms the rights of workers to receive a fair wage for their work; the right to establish unions; the right of families, especially mothers and children, to protection; the right of all human beings to an adequate standard of living regarding food, clothing, and shelter; freedom from hunger; the right to both physical and mental health; the importance of access to education; and the rights of persons to access their cultural heritage and derive benefit from scientific achievements. Signatory nations are expected, at the invitation of the secretary-general of the United Nations, to submit reports to the Economic and Social Council of their present achievements and future goals.

International Covenant on the Elimination of All Forms of Racial Discrimination (ICEAFRD). Adopted by the United Nations in 1965, the ICEAFRD entered into the force of international law in 1969. The ICEAFRD resolves "to adopt all necessary measures for speedily eliminating racial discrimination in all its forms and manifestations, and to prevent and combat racist doctrines and practices in order to promote understanding between races and to build an international community free from all forms of racial segregation and racial discrimination." Signatory parties are, therefore, expected to practice no forms of racial discrimination, to encourage other nation-states to eliminate such discrimination, to condemn such where it exists, and to educate their own constituencies about discrimination and ways to eliminate such.

International Criminal Court (ICC). The idea for the establishment of an international criminal court reaches back into the nineteenth century when Gustav Moynier (1826–1910), one of the cofounders of the International Committee of the Red Cross, suggested the need for such a court to uphold the Geneva Convention of 1864. From that point onward, the idea for such a court was raised many times (e.g., during the course of the Versailles Peace Conference of 1919, by the Committee of Jurists in 1920 under the auspices of the League of Nations, several times during World War II, and in the post–World War II years), but to no avail. It was not until the late 1980s and early to mid-1990s that actual headway was made in establishing such a court, "helped" along no doubt by the genocidal atrocities that were being perpetrated, first, in the former Yugoslavia, and then in Rwanda in 1994.

The International Criminal Court (ICC) was established officially on July 17, 1998, by the United Nations after sixty member nations became parties to the Rome Statute of the International Criminal Court.

According to its mandate, the ICC is an independent judiciary charged with responsibility to try persons accused of genocide, crimes against humanity, and war crimes. Although critical concerns have surfaced regarding political biases of Court members, issues regarding legal due process, potential interference with national processes of reconciliation, and jurisdictional questions, they have thus far not prevented its work.

As of mid-2007, 104 nations have become signatories to the document. As for the United States, it wavered back and forth, time and again, in favor of and then against the establishment of the ICC. A major objection voiced by its leaders and military personnel was that the way the ICC was worded would leave U.S. officials and military personnel open to possibly being charged with war crimes and/or crimes against humanity, if not genocide, even though it might be engaged in a humanitarian effort that involved combat. Thus, in 1998 the United States voted against the Rome Statue (the treaty establishing the International Criminal Court). It was only one of seven nations to do so, the other six being China, Israel, Iraq, Libya, Qatar, and Yemen.

Then, on December 31, 2000, U.S. president Bill Clinton signed the treaty, basically agreeing to support the creation of the ICC. But then, on May 6, 2002, U.S. president George W. Bush's administration basically "unsigned" the agreement by withdrawing the United States' signature from the treaty. In November 2002, in an attempt to explain the latter move by the Bush Administration (as well as the administration's continued opposition to signing the treaty), John R. Bolton, undersecretary for arms control and international security, made the following comments:

> The problems inherent in the ICC are more than abstract legal issues—they are matters that touch directly on our national security and our national interests.
>
> For a number of reasons, the United States decided that the ICC had unacceptable consequences for our national sovereignty. Specifically, the ICC is an organization whose precepts go against fundamental American notions of sovereignty, checks and balances, and national independence. It is an agreement that is harmful to the national interests of the United States, and harmful to our presence abroad.
>
> U.S. military forces and civilian personnel and private citizens are currently active in peacekeeping and humanitarian missions in almost one hundred countries at any given time. It is essential that we remain steadfast in preserving the independence and flexibility that America needs to defend our national interests around the world. As President Bush said, "The United States cooperates with many other nations to keep the peace, but we will not submit American troops to prosecutors and judges whose jurisdiction we do not accept. . . . Every person who serves under the American flag will answer to his or her own superiors and to military law, not to the rulings of an unaccountable International Criminal Court."

Numerous human rights activists, international lawyers, and others within and outside of the United States have countered the U.S. government's current position but to no avail.

According to the ICC's Web site (under the heading "The States Parties to the Rome Statute"), as of January 2007, the following nations were some of the many that had not yet become signatories to the ICC: China, Egypt, Guatemala, Iraq, Israel, Libya, North Korea, Russia, Sudan, Syria, the United States, Yemen.

Among some of the key investigations already under way by the ICC are the crisis situations in Uganda, the Congo, and Sudan.

International Criminal Tribunal for Rwanda (ICTR). The ICTR was established by the United Nations Security Council on November 9, 1994, and is located in Arusha, Tanzania. The ICTR's first trial began in January 1997, with the case of former journalist Hassan Ngeze (b. 1962). Generally speaking, progress in securing judicial verdicts has been slow. The tribunal has handed down judgments on less than forty accused since its inception. This is not to say, however, that these have been minor: the first successful prosecution in an international court, specifically for the crime of genocide, came from the ICTR in 1998. This concerned the former mayor of the Rwandan village of Taba, Jean-Paul Akayesu (b. 1953). The judgment on this occasion extended genocide case-law, ruling that rape could henceforth be considered within a general legal framework of crimes against humanity and genocide. Other precedents established by the ICTR emerged in the trial of former Rwandan prime minister Jean Kambanda (b. 1955). Kambanda, who pleaded guilty to the crime of genocide (and was the first accused to do so in any international setting), was the first head of government to be convicted for this crime.

The ICTR comprises a tribunal of eminent judges from a wide range of countries and is truly international in scope. It possesses an open and transparent appeals procedure. By its Security Council mandate, the ICTR is currently scheduled to have completed all of its major investigations by the end of 2008 and will be wound up in toto by the end of 2010.

International Criminal Tribunal for the Former Yugoslavia (ICTY). The ICTY is an international court pertaining to the wars accompanying the dissolution of the former Yugoslavia between 1991 and 1999. In response to the extreme violence inflicted on civilians, the United Nations Security Council resolved to establish a special *ad hoc* court to try those charged with three types of offences, namely, grave breaches of those sections of the 1949 Geneva Conventions relating to war crimes, crimes against humanity, and genocide. The crime of genocide was introduced because of the specific kind of mass killings of ethnic groups that took place during these wars in concentration camps, in rape camps, through the mass murder of civilians, and through the brutal practices associated with forced deportations and "ethnic cleansing." The accused being tried by the ICTY come from all four of the major ethnicities involved in the war: Serbs, Croats, Bosnian Muslims, and Kosovar Albanians. The accused from each ethnic group, it is alleged by court indictments, had engaged in some kind of genocidal violence in their quest for territory and their determination to expel en masse inhabitants of a rival ethnicity—a process that is commonly referred to as ethnic cleansing. By far the majority of those indicted, however, were Serbs, both from Serbia and from the ethnic Serb entity in Bosnia-Herzegovina, Republika Srpska.

The ICTY was established by the United Nations Security Council by UNSC Resolution 827 on May 25, 1993. It is located in The Hague, Netherlands. Its purpose is to render justice to the victims, to deter further crimes, and to contribute to the restoration of peace by holding accountable those found responsible for serious violations of international humanitarian law. The tribunal's judges and officials are drawn from a pool of prominent international jurists.

At the outset, the ICTY suffered setbacks, both budgetary and administrative: costs outpaced the income of the court; reviewing evidence in preparation for each trial proved time-consuming; and each trial got bogged down in repeated postponements or recesses. Most troublesome was the process of locating and detaining the indicted themselves, whose arrests frequently depended on the cooperation of the governments of Bosnia-Herzegovina,

Croatia, and Serbia, the latter of which shielded not only its own nationals but also those from Republika Srpska. The court has no marshals with the power to arrest in these countries, meaning that some indicted are still living in hiding or are living in the open, out of reach of the tribunal.

Despite these obstacles, the court has managed to try suspected criminals from all combatant nationalities and to convict both high- and low-ranking criminals, particularly those associated with the war in Bosnia. Its most notable indictment and trial to date was that of Slobodan Milosevic (1941–2006), the former president of Serbia. He was the first head of state ever accused and tried for genocide, an unprecedented step in judicial history. (The trial did not conclude with a verdict, however, as Milosevic died of a heart attack while in custody during the trial.)

It is anticipated that the ICTY will have completed the trial process of all those indicted by the end of 2008, with all appeals completed by the end of 2010. This might, however, be extended should currently pending warrants be met by the arrest of leading indictees yet to be apprehended, such as Radovan Karadzic (b. 1945) and Ratko Mladic (b. 1942).

International Crisis Group (ICG). The International Crisis Group (or, in colloquial usage, Crisis Group) is an international nongovernmental organization committed to strengthening the capacity of the international community to anticipate, understand, and act to prevent violent conflict. The ICG is, in the first place, an information-gathering body that sends investigators to the world's trouble-spots whenever there appears to be a threat of large-scale violence on a group, communal, or interstate level. The investigators gather information from a wide range of sources and assess local conditions. Based on the data submitted, ICG generates situation reports and analyses that it forwards to political leaders in the affected countries, to other world leaders, and to international organizations deemed to have an interest in the matter at hand. Its reports are also, generally, made available over the organization's Web site (http://www.crisisweb.org).

ICG was founded in 1994 by three men with substantial experience in global affairs: Mark Malloch Brown (b. 1953), Morton Abramowitz (b. 1933), and Fred Cuny (b. 1944), all of whom were major figures in the area of disaster relief and international statecraft. Today, ICG employs nearly 120 staff members on five different continents. Its current chief executive is the former Australian foreign minister, Gareth Evans (b. 1944); its cochairmen are the former European commissioner for external relations, Christopher Patten (b. 1944), and former U.S. ambassador Thomas Pickering (b. 1931).

Besides its headquarters in Brussels, Crisis Group has major offices in Washington, D.C., New York, London, and Moscow, plus fourteen other offices throughout the world.

International Force in East Timor. *See* INTERFET.

International Humanitarian Law (IHL). IHL is the body of law, principles, and regulations that pertains to and governs situations of international or noninternational armed conflict. The heart of international humanitarian law is the four Geneva Conventions (August 12, 1949), and their two Additional Protocols (June 8, 1977). Every single state across the globe is a party to the Geneva Conventions of 1949.

International Intergovernmental Organizations (INGOs). International intergovernmental organizations (INGOs) are composed of members who are either nonstate organizations or individuals. The focus and work of INGOs is eclectic: cultural, economic, political, professional, and religious, among others. Among some of the most noted

INGOs are Amnesty International, Human Rights Watch, and the International Red Cross. Many such organizations have a profound impact on both national and international politics.

International Law. A body of laws, rules, or legal principles generally based on custom, treaties, and conventions, and legislation that pertain to and govern relations among states. Such laws are generally accepted as binding in relations between states and nations.

International Military Tribunal (IMT). Known colloquially as the "Nuremberg Trials," the victorious Allies (France, Great Britain, the Soviet Union, and the United States) in World War II convened this tribunal from October 1945 through October 1946, in Nuremberg, Germany, to try twenty-two leaders of the Nazi hierarchy as well as six Nazi organizations (the Nazi Party, the Gestapo, the SA, SD, the Reich Cabinet, and the Army General Staff). Ultimately, Nuremberg was chosen because of its infamous association with the Nazi racial laws of 1935. Each of the Allies provided two judges for the IMT.

Under Article 6 of its charter, the individual charges included the following: (1) crimes against peace, (2) war crimes, and (3) crimes against humanity. The organizational charges included the following: (1) commitment to wage a war of aggression, (2) violation of commonly accepted rules of warfare, and (3) participation in criminal organizations. Most significantly, the IMT rejected as a defense position that of "following orders" from above, emphasizing, instead, the principle of individual responsibility.

Twelve of the defendants were sentenced to death: Herman Göring (Luftwaffe commander), Joachim von Ribbentrop (foreign minister), Wilhelm Keitel (army chief of staff), Ernst Kaltenbrunner (chief of the security police), Alfred Rosenberg (minister of the Eastern Occupied Territories), Hans Frank (governor-general of Poland), Julius Streicher (editor and publisher of *Der Stürmer*), Fritz Sauckel (plenipotentiary-general for labor mobilization), Alfred Jodl (army chief of operations), Martin Bormann (Hitler's deputy, in absentia), Arthur Seyss-Inquart (governor of the Netherlands), and Wilhelm Frick (minister of the interior). Göring committed suicide before he could be hanged.

Sentenced to life imprisonment were Rudolf Hess (Hitler's deputy; who committed suicide in 1987), Walter Funk (president, Bank of Germany, who was released in 1957), and Erich Raeder (naval commander; who was released in 1955).

Sentenced to various length prison terms were Albert Speer (armaments minister; served twenty years), Konstantin Freiherr von Neurath (governor of Bohemia and Moravia, served eight years and was released in 1954), Karl Döenitz (navy commander, served ten years and was released in 1956), and Baldur von Schirach (leader of the Hitler Youth, served twenty years).

Acquitted were Fritz von Papen (ambassador to Austria and Turkey), Hjalmar Schacht (minister of economics), and Hans Fritzche (head of broadcasting).

Heinrich Himmler (head of the SS) committed suicide in May 1945. Also indicted was Robert Ley (leader of the German Labor Front), but he committed suicide prior to the start of the trials.

The IMT was not without controversy; indeed, some—not only Germans, but some jurists as well—saw it as an example of "victors' justice," according to which the victorious Allies were exacting vengeance on a defeated enemy and masking it as *justice*. With its stress on both individual responsibility in times of war and the legality of war itself (self-defense against aggression), however, the IMT set the stage for not only the United

Nations Convention for the Prevention and Punishment of the Crime of Genocide (1948) but also the later International Criminal Tribunal for the former Yugoslavia (ICTY) and the International Criminal Tribunal for Rwanda (ICTR) in the 1990s.

The IMT's massive record, including both documents and testimonies, remains a fruitful source for much scholarly investigation.

International Network on Holocaust and Genocide. Published under the auspices of the Centre for Comparative Genocide Studies and the leadership of Professor Colin Tatz, Macquarie University, New South Wales, Australia, this newsletter was published eighteen times between the years 1993 and 2001. Over the years it addressed such topics as "Holocaust versus Genocide" (2001); "Genocide in Australia" (2000); "Kosovo" (1999); "Cambodia" (1997); "Denial" (1996); "Memory and Policy: America's Response to the Challenge of the Armenian Genocide" (1996), and other important topics. With the shift of the center from Macquarie University to the Shalom Institute in the year 2000 and the creation of an independent educational entity titled The Australian Institute for Holocaust and Genocide Studies, this newsletter as such ceased publication and was replaced by individual volumes of articles (e.g., *Genocide Perspectives I & II*).

International Panel of Eminent Personalities (IPEP). An independent inquiry established by the Secretary-General of the United Nations, Kofi Annan (b. 1938), with support from the United Nations Security Council, to establish the facts related to the response of the United Nations to the 1994 genocide in Rwanda (April–July) and to make recommendations to the secretary-general on this issue. The inquiry was carried out by Mr. Ingvar Carlsson (b. 1934; former prime minister of Sweden), Professor Han Sung Joo (b. 1940; former foreign minister of the Republic of Korea) and Lieutenant General Rufus Kupolati (ret.; b. ? –died 2005) of Nigeria. The report of the panel was released on December 15, 1999. Basically, the independent inquiry found that the response of the United Nations before and during the course of the 1994 Rwanda genocide failed in numerous and fundamental ways. More specifically, it asserted that the failure of the United Nations to first prevent and then halt the genocide "lies with a number of different actors," in particular the secretary-general, the secretariat, the Secretariat Council, UNAMIR, and the broader members of the United Nations.

International Workgroup for Indigenous Affairs (IWGIA). IWGIA, which was founded in 1968 by human rights activists and anthropologists, is an independent, international organization that supports indigenous peoples in their struggle against oppression. IWGIA publishes the IWGIA Documents Series and the *IWGIA Bulletin* (English) (each of which is published four times annually), and the *IWGIA Yearbook*. IWGIA's main office is in Copenhagen, Denmark. It has additional offices in Göteborg, Sweden; Lund, Sweden; Zurich, Switzerland; and Paris, France.

Internet on the Holocaust and Genocide. The *Internet on the Holocaust and Genocide*, the first international newsletter to join the two subjects of the "Holocaust" and "genocide" and to "serve as a bridge between different peoples and between different professions concerned with genocide," was founded by Israel W. Charny (b. 1931) in 1985. For ten years (1985–1995), it was published under the auspices of the Institute on the Holocaust and Genocide. Its target audience was the then nascent community of scholars, professionals, institutes, nongovernmental, and governmental and international agencies involved in the effort to understand, intervene in, and prevent genocide. Fifty-six issues in toto of the newsletter were published. Among its many special issues were "The United Nations Report on Genocide" by Ben Whitaker; "Genocides and Politicides Since 1945: Evidence and Anticipation" by Barbara Harff and Ted Robert Gurr; "Power Kills, Absolute Power Kills Absolutely" (which compared the history of totalitarian and democratic countries in committing genocide) by R. J. Rummel; "Denial of the Holocaust, Genocide and Contemporary Massacres" edited by Israel W. Charny; and "Educating about Genocide" edited by Samuel Totten.

Inyenzi (Kinyarwanda, "cockroaches"). Monarchist Tutus in exile who periodically carried out guerrilla-like raids into Rwanda in the 1960s referred to themselves as *inyenzi*, or cockroaches, as a way of denoting their furtive movements, toughness, and resilience. Eventually, *inyenzi* became an epithet used by Hutu to denigrate those same Tutsi guerrillas.

In the 1990s the term was reintroduced by Hutu Power ideologues to describe members of the Rwandan Patriotic Front (RPF) fighters (primarily composed of exiled Tutsi). Ultimately, both prior to and during the 1994 genocide, all Tutsi came to be referred to as *inyenzi* as a way to dehumanize them.

Radio Télévision Libre des Mille Collines (RTLM), the government radio station that broadcast extremist Hutu propaganda often sent out the following message: "The *inyenzi* have always been Tutsi. We will exterminate them. One can identify them because they are of one race. You can identify them by their height and their small nose. When you see that small nose, break it."

Iraq Genocide of Kurds in Northern Iraq. *See* Anfal.

Iraq Special Tribunal for Crimes Against Humanity (IST). Also known in some circles as the Supreme Iraqi Criminal Tribunal, or SICT, this is an *ad hoc* court of law established by the Iraqi Governing Council in Iraq in December 2003, for the purpose of bringing to justice Iraqis accused of war crimes, crimes against humanity (including torture, assassination, extra-judicial executions, forcible relocation of residents, and the use of chemical weapons), and genocide under the regime of Iraqi dictator Saddam Hussein (1937–2006). Pursuant to Iraqi Law Number 10 of 2005, the Tribunal has three main purposes: adjudication, investigation, and prosecution. Each of the three functions was undertaken by a separate body of prosecutors or judges. The IST's jurisdiction is framed within the period between July 17, 1968 and May 1, 2003 (the date on which the United States declared the end of its war, "Operation Iraqi Freedom," to overthrow the regime of Saddam Hussein). These dates correspond to the period of rule by the Ba'ath, a secular Arab nationalist political party.

The tribunal's most important cases have been the trials of Saddam Hussein, his cousin Ali Hassan al-Majid (b. 1941, known in the Western world by the nickname "Chemical Ali"), former vice-president in the Hussein regime Taha Yassin Ramadan Al-Jizrawi (1938–2007), former deputy prime minister Tariq Aziz (b. 1936), and eight other leading members of the former dictatorship. The fact that this court is specifically Iraqi, and not an international tribunal, is significant; it provides local ownership over the process of justice and, it is hoped, will be an important institution in the process of rebuilding Iraq after decades of brutal dictatorship, corruption, war, and genocide. This notwithstanding, concern has arisen among international lawyers and human rights activists that the trials have not been as objective as they could and should have been, and thus have resulted in what has been deemed "victor's justice."

On November 5, 2006, the court found Saddam Hussein guilty of crimes against humanity in ordering the deaths of 148 Shi'ite villagers in the town of Dujail in 1982. It sentenced him to death by hanging, and the sentence was carried out on December 30, 2006. Numerous commentators, including genocide scholars, have noted that the quick execution of Saddam extinguished the possibility of trying him on charges of genocide, and thus the international community lost a golden opportunity of furthering international law vis-à-vis the issue of genocide.

Irish Conquest, 1649. *See* Cromwell, Oliver.

Irredentism. A term used in international relations, the word *irredentism* signifies the desire and intent of a nation to annex territory of another nation-state on the grounds that the population resident in the second nation-state is related to the population in the first by nationality, language, ethnicity, race, or shared historical experience. The classic example would be that of Nazi Germany's *anschluss* (German, "union") of Austria in 1938 and its annexation of the Sudetenland of Czechoslovakia that same year. The German term *lebensraum* (German, literally "living room" or "living space") is a reasonably proximate synonym for the Italian *irredenta*. The term itself is believed to have been derived from the Italian *Italia irredenta* (Italian, "unredeemed Italy"), referring to disputed territory between itself and the Austro-Hungarian empire in the late nineteenth and early twentieth centuries.

A popular and politically volatile way to make such claims involves the use of the word *greater* by both governmental and political leaders (e.g., Greater Germany, Greater Italy) A number of nation-states have enshrined such concepts within their constitutional documents—for example, Argentina (Article III, Section 1); People's Republic of China (Preamble & Article 4); Comoros (Article 1); and the Republic of Ireland (Article 2 and Article 3). The recent genocide in Croatia, Bosnia-Herzegovina, and Kosovo all bear witness to the tragic consequences of this idea.

Irving, David (b. 1938). David Irving is perhaps the most well-known denier of the Holocaust, primarily because of his voluminous publications dealing with the Second World War. Having lived and worked in Germany as a steelworker in the Ruhr Valley, and fluent in German, Irving has neither the training nor the credentials to be taken seriously by the scholarly community of historians. His initial academic work on World War II involved a prodigious amount of research and, although criticized for certain inaccuracies, overall was deemed a reasonable attempt at serious scholarship. Later works by Irving on Adolf Hitler (1889–1945) and Hitler's role as the leader of Germany during World War II, although again the products of prodigious research, have been seriously criticized for selectively using partial quotations and drawing highly specious conclusions. By 1988, coincident with the trial of Canadian Holocaust-denier Ernst Zündel (b. 1939) on charges of denying the fact of the Holocaust (a crime in Canada), Irving was fully ensconced within the Holocaust-denial movement, the result of what he maintained was an honest and serious reconsideration of the accepted evidence and the conclusions mainstream historians had drawn from it. However, his reputation as a legitimate historian within the academy was being called into question as a result of mounting and continuing criticisms not only of his work but also of his appearances before Holocaust denial groups (e.g., the Institute for Historical Review in the United States), as well as his contacts with neo-Nazis in Germany.

In 1996 Irving filed a libel suit in Britain against U.S. scholar Deborah Lipstadt (b. 1947) of Emory University, Atlanta, Georgia, for her comments about him in her 1993 book *Denying the Holocaust: The Growing Assault on Truth and Memory*. In the same suit, he sued Lipstadt's British publisher Penguin Books, Ltd. In May 2000, Judge Charles Gray rendered his verdict, dismissing the suit and labeling Irving both an antisemite and a Holocaust-denier. Irving was ordered to pay legal fees in excess of nearly 2 million British pounds (U.S. $3.8 million). In 2001 he was denied a request for a new trial by an appeals court. He continues, however, to write and lecture about World War II and his denialist version of the events associated with the Holocaust, questioning such matters as the numbers of Jewish victims, the usage of the gas chambers at Auschwitz death camp in Poland, and related topics. He also maintains his own Web site to promote both himself and his publications.

In Austria in 2006, Irving was sentenced to three years imprisonment for denying the Holocaust by a Viennese court but was released by the end of year and stated that his position had hardened during this latest incarceration.

"Israel." Compulsory middle name that the Nazis required all male Jews to adopt in Germany. The designation was made law under the "Second Decree Supplementing the Law Regarding the Change of Family Names and First Names," passed on August 17, 1938. The law became operational as from January 1, 1939. Henceforward, all Jewish males were required to add the name into their passports and other official documents, and to all identity cards. In like manner, Jewish females were forced to add the name "Sarah" to their own.

Ittihad ve Terakki Jemeyeti. *See* Committee of Union and Progress.

Izetbegovic, Alija (1925–2003). President of Bosnia-Herzegovina between 1990 and 1996, a period traversing the last days of communist rule in united Yugoslavia and the establishment of the independent Republic of Bosnia-Herzegovina. Izetbegovic was born in Bosanski Samac, a town in northern Bosnia. During World War II he was a member of a Bosnian Islamic organization called *Mladi Muslimani,* or Young Muslims. The latter organization was a party of Islamic renewal, but the aftermath of the war saw the imposition of the communist regime of Josip Broz Tito (1892–1980), which suppressed ethnic and religious distinctiveness. Izetbegovic was arrested in 1946 for political reasons related to his advocacy of Muslim separateness in a state that was at that time being transformed into a communist dictatorship, and jailed for three years. Upon his release, he began to work tirelessly for Muslim rights within the Yugoslav state. In 1970 he published a manifesto titled *The Islamic Declaration,* which again reinforced his Islamic fidelity. His opponents would later look at this work as an affirmation of his fundamentalism—and thus, by extension, of Islamic extremism. Although Tito died in 1980, the repression of religious and ethnic separateness continued, and Izetbegovic, along with others, was again imprisoned, this time sentenced to fourteen years in 1983. He was pardoned, after a drawn-out appeals process, in 1988. By then, Izetbegovic had become the de facto leader of Bosnia's Muslims. In 1989, he was instrumental in establishing the Stranka Demokratske Akcije (SDA), or Party of Democratic Action; while this was not specifically a Muslim party, it was nonetheless a party that attracted the largest following among Muslims.

As Yugoslavia began to unravel through the early 1990s, Izetbegovic looked inwardly to shore up Bosnia's rights against those of Serbia in the rapidly changing environment. In mid-February 1992 he arranged a referendum on Bosnia's independence; on February 29, 1992, he declared Bosnia's independence from Serb-dominated Yugoslavia (in a situation where minority populations might well suffer reprisals as the Serbs resisted the fragmentation of the state), to take effect on April 7. The day before this, however, Bosnian Serb and Yugoslav forces crossed into Bosnia with the intention of bringing the new country back into the federation. For the next three years, Izetbegovic strove hard to retain Bosnia's territorial integrity in the face of invasion, ethnic cleansing, and genocide, fighting three and sometimes four enemies at once. He consistently promoted the idea of a multiethnic Bosnia (an ideal that has become Izetbegovic's major legacy through to today), but waging war to guarantee Bosnia's survival was at no stage something he could achieve without foreign intervention and a negotiated settlement. Peace finally came only at the end of 1995, when Izetbegovic signed the Dayton Peace Agreement (November 21, 1995) and the Paris Protocol (December 14, 1995) alongside other regional and world leaders. Remaining in power until October 2000, Izetbegovic died three years later, recognized as the father of Bosnian independence. He is buried in Sarajevo.

J

"J." Tenth letter of the alphabet; stamped on all German passports and other official documents from October 1938 onward during the period of the Third Reich, whereby the bearer was identified as a Jew according to Nazi legislation. The idea for a *J* stamp came from the Swiss government in negotiations with the Nazis, and the stamping of the letter *J* on the passports of German Jews thus served the purpose of assisting restrictive immigration policies and regulating the entry of Jewish refugees into countries bordering Germany.

Jackson, Robert H. (1892–1954). Born in Pennsylvania, Jackson, after attending classes for only one year at Albany Law School (New York) and apprenticing himself to a lawyer, spent forty-two years in Frewsburg, New York, practicing his chosen profession. In 1934, President Franklin Delano Roosevelt (1882–1945) invited him to become general counsel for the Internal Revenue Service. He went on to become U.S. solicitor general, U.S. attorney general, and a U.S. Supreme Court justice. He was the primary author of the London Charter, which created the legal basis for Nuremberg. In 1945, while serving as a justice at the U.S. Supreme Court, Jackson was asked by U.S. president Harry S. Truman (1884–1972) to serve as the chief U.S. prosecutor at the International Military Tribunal, Nuremberg, Germany, where twenty-four high-ranking Nazis were about to be tried on four counts: (1) conspiracy to wage aggressive war; (2) waging aggressive war, or "crimes against peace"; (3) war crimes; and (4) crimes against humanity.

Jackson's role in the Nuremberg Trials was crucial. He was seen as a tireless and energetic man of conscience, committed to the rule of law and the development of the principles under which the trials were framed, specifically, crimes against humanity and the rejection of orders above morality.

Responding to those critics who opposed the trials, both Allies and Germans, and the accusation of the application of so-called victor's justice (German, *Siegerjustiz*), Jackson responded, "We must make clear to the Germans that the wrong for which their fallen leaders are on trial is not that they lost the war, but that they started it."

Jackson wrote two books about the trials: *The Case Against the Nazi War Criminals* (New York: Alfred A. Knopf, 1946) and *The Nürnberg Case* (New York: Alfred A. Knopf, 1947).

Upon the completion of the tribunal (October 1945–October 1946), Jackson returned to the Supreme Court for eight more years, participating in the now-famous 1954 desegregation decision *Brown v. Board of Education*. Shortly thereafter, in 1954, he suffered a fatal heart attack. His body was interred in the Maple Grove Cemetery in Frewsburg, New York, beneath a simple headstone on which was inscribed, "He kept the ancient landmarks and built the new."

Janjaweed. An Arabic composite of *jinn* (spirit/ghost) and *jawad* (horse) that was traditionally used to describe wild outlaws that run amok. In the early 2000s it was the appellation given to the "Arab" militiamen who carried out genocidal attacks (early 2003 to the present or late 2007), in conjunction with government of Sudan (GOS) troops, against the black African population of Darfur, Sudan. In Darfur, *Janjaweed* colloquially translates to "evil horseman," "horsemen with guns on horseback," and/or "devils on horseback."

The *Janjaweed* generally attack, along with the GOS, the villages of black Sudanese on camel and/or horseback (and, to a lesser extent, as passengers in Sudanese army vehicles). The initial attacks (meaning in 2003) carried out by the GOS troops and the *Janjaweed* were in retaliation for attacks on the government by black Sudanese rebels who were incensed over the poor treatment black Sudanese citizens received at the hands of the Sudanese government. However, instead of solely attacking the rebels' strongholds, the GOS and *Janjaweed* have systematically and ruthlessly attacked village after village of common citizens and noncombatants. In the course of the attacks, tens of thousands of black Africans have been killed, village after village has been burnt to the ground, women and girls have been raped, and over 2 million people are now internal refugees. Several hundred thousand more have sought refuge in refugee camps in Chad.

On September 9, 2004, the U.S. government accused the GOS and *Janjaweed* of having committed genocide against the black Africans (particularly those members of the Massaliet, Fur, and Zaghawa tribes).

Jasenovac. A location in central Croatia and the site of a notorious concentration camp during World War II. It was not a Nazi concentration camp, but was instead established by the *Ustashe*, a radical Croatian right-wing nationalist movement. The *Ustashe* controlled wartime Croatia as a puppet government under the presidency of Ante Pavelic (1889–1959). The Jasenovac concentration camp, which was set up in August 1941, was headed by Miroslav Filipovic (1915–1946), also known as Miroslav Majstorovic. Over time, Jasenovac grew to become a complex of five subcamps and three smaller compounds, including a camp for children at Sisak and a notorious camp for women at Stara Gradiska, east of the main Jasenovac complex. Generally speaking, Jasenovac was a camp in which the *Ustashe* confined scores of thousands of victims, mainly Serbs, Jews, and Roma.

Jewish Question. For Adolf Hitler (1889–1945), other Nazis and their allies, two thousand or more years of hateful rhetoric, texts, and behaviors convinced them that the Jews were, indeed, the enemies of all civilization, responsible at its core for all of its ills, racial parasites, and a cancer on the body politic that must be destroyed. The battles between them were elevated to "cosmic contests", and the annihilation and extermination of the Jews—men, women, and children—as the only possible outcome. Perceiving the issue as a "question" thus necessitated answers and solutions to a solvable problem.

"The Final Solution to the Jewish Question" (German, *Die Endlösung der Judenfrage*) became the Nazi coded expression, or euphemism, for the murderous plan to eliminate the

Jews of Europe. Early on, Hitler's own antisemitic agenda was made fully manifest in his 1925 political autobiography *Mein Kampf*.

Upon assuming the chancellorship of Germany in 1933, beginning with the infamous Nuremberg Racial Laws of 1935, and aided by theories of eugenics (i.e., the improvement of the species), social Darwinism (i.e., survival of the fittest) and post-Enlightenment thinking vis-à-vis the progress and scientific perfectibility of the human person, the Nazis turned to the sciences and their practitioners (legal, medical, biological, physical, chemical) for such answers. From early experiments in the mass killing of his own people (the so-called T-4 or euthanasia program of mental and physical defectives), followed by the now infamous Wannsee Conference of January 1942 (where plans of the annihilation of the Jews were delineated), the program of the extermination/annihilation of the Jews, after unsuccessful attempts as large-scale emigration, evolved through the use of extermination squads (*Einsatzgrüppen*) and mobile gas vans into the ultimate gas chambers and crematoria of the death camps that were located in Poland.

By the end of the war nearly 6 million Jewish women, men, and children (1 million younger than twelve years of age; one-half million between the ages of twelve and eighteen) had been murdered, along with others, including Roma, Poles, political dissidents, Russian prisoners of war. Nation-states had been conquered and subjugated by the Nazis who, in turn, essentially made them *Judenrein* or "Jew free." For the Nazis and their collaborators, the "Jewish Question" had been successfully answered by the murder of the Jews.

Journal of Genocide Research (JGR). JGR (founded in 1999 by Henry Huttenbach [1931], a historian based in the United States) was the first journal to promote an interdisciplinary and comparative approach to the study of genocide. In early 2000 it became the official journal of the European Network (ENOGS) of Genocide Scholars (later renamed the International Network of Genocide Scholars [INOGS]).

Journey to Darfur, A. A documentary that actor George Clooney (b. 1961) and his father, journalist Nick Clooney (b. 1934), filmed during their visit to the Chad-Sudan border in 2006, where hundreds of thousands of refugees had fled from the ongoing genocide in Darfur, Sudan, when government of Sudan troops and *Janjaweed* (Arab militia) carried out a scorched earth policy of burning down villages and raping and killing the black Africans of Darfur. The documentary was initially broadcast on January 15, 2007, on American Life TV Network in the United States.

Jud Süss (German, a colloquial term that, euphemistically, approximates "suspect Jew"). Novel written in Germany by Jewish author Lion Feuchtwanger (1884–1958) in 1925, and translated into English as *Power*. Feuchtwanger, whose writings had been suppressed during World War I because of what was held to be their revolutionary content, became one of the earliest critics of Hitler and the Nazis and was subsequently forced into exile in London by the Nazis in 1934. In *Jud Süss*, he chronicled the story of a powerful ghetto businessman, Oppenheimer, who believes himself to be a Jew. His ruthless business practices result in the betrayal of an innocent girl; for this, he is arrested and sentenced to death, the victim of anti-Jewish laws. Rather than declare his non-Jewish identity, which he discovers through a set of letters given to him by his mother revealing that his father was in fact a Christian nobleman, he dies on the gallows, with dignity and honor, as a "Jew."

Feuchtwanger intended the book to be an attack against antisemitism, an allegory of German society during his own day. It was, however, transformed by the Nazis into a viciously antisemitic movie in 1940. It was directed by Veit Harlan (1899–1964) and starred Werner Krauss (1884–1959) in the title role. The plot was twisted to make Oppenheimer a real Jew portrayed according to Nazi stereotypes: greasy hair, hooked nose, unscrupulous, bearded, cowardly, and a rapist. At his arrest and execution, he is seen as screaming and unmanly; by contrast, his executioners appear to be upright, solid citizens. After Oppenheimer's execution, the rest of the Jews of the city are driven into exile. As a piece of propaganda cinema, the movie had a powerful effect on its audiences, helping to prepare the German public for further atrocities against Jews. Many viewed it as though it were a documentary and were driven to acts of violence against Jews in the street after having seen it.

Tellingly, Heinrich Himmler (1900–1945), the head of the SS, ordered all members of the various official bodies under his command to see the movie; this extended to local police and concentration camp guards. Its effectiveness as a propaganda tool was thus not limited to the general public, as it was used to achieve specific dehumanizing goals regarding the perceived racial enemy and to whip up violence against that enemy.

Veit Harlan was later tried for crimes against humanity by the Allies at Nuremberg, but his case was dismissed due to a lack of direct evidence implicating him in the destruction of the Jews.

Judenfrei **(German, literally, "free of Jews").** A term used by Nazi leaders responsible for Germany's anti-Jewish measures during World War II, employed for the purpose of indicating that a successful liquidation of a Jewish area had taken place. The term was often employed alongside of (or synonymously with) the word *Judenrein* (clean of Jews) by SS (*Schutzstaffel*, or "Security Police") leaders such as Heinrich Himmler (1900–1945), among many others.

Judenrat **(German, "Jewish council").** Among the more controversial issues surrounding the fate of the Jewish victims of the Second World War/Holocaust remains the role of the Judenrat, the "Jewish self-governing councils" that existed in many of the larger and a number of the smaller Jewish ghettos under the Nazis. Though the tradition of Jewish self-governance is historically well-grounded, and many of those who served on the Judenrat found themselves in the horrendously ambivalent position of serving their Nazi masters at the same time as trying to act as a buffer between their overlords and their fellow Jews, doing what little they could to attempt to save a dying people, many have argued strongly that the Judenrat complicitly aided in their own demise. That argument becomes problematic in that their options were limited, their own activities tended to be more cautiously conservative and secretive, and some among their collective leadership were prone to corruption and self-serving ends, all, ultimately, in an effort to prolong life.

The first of these councils was already established in Poland in the fall of 1939, within a few short weeks of the start of World War II (September 1, 1939) under the following mandate: "Jewish population centers 10,000 persons and under led by twelve-person councils; over 10,000 persons twenty-four person councils." While the elections of the twelve-person council were to be an internal matter, the Nazi leadership had to approve such persons. Once established and overseen, their focused activities were directed primarily to organizational-administrative matters (data and census collection), economic and production matters (factory and workshop production and labor quotas), and social service delivery systems (healthcare, welfare agencies, food allocations, residence permits). From their (Jewish) perspective, many of these leaders truly believed that by establishing their economic worth and value to the Nazis, they would be allowed to maintain their communities, even under such severe and repressive conditions. However, with the beginnings of the mass deportations in 1942, the tide began increasingly to turn against the Jews, and questions of refusal or compliance began to surface as the real agenda of death became more and more known. According to the article titled *Judenräte* in the *Encyclopedia of the Holocaust* (Gutman, 1990, p. 766), the patterns of behavior of the various *Judenräte* fell into four categories: refusal, acquiescence, resignation, and compliance. Thus, any truly accurate historical assessment of these councils must take into consideration: the geographical location of the ghetto communities; the actual resources available; the different behavioral patterns of the Judenrat, Jewish populations, and Nazi officials; and the specific years of activity under analyses.

Judenrein (German, literally "Jew free," i.e., free of Jews). German term used to describe a geographic location where Jews had been physically eliminated, through emigration, deportation, or murder. Later understood as the ultimate goal of the entire Nazi program of extermination/annihilation—a Europe free of Jews. (*See also* Jewish Question.)

Jus ad Bellum (Latin, "laws for going to war"). *Jus ad bellum* is the international law dealing with the decision to go to war, in which self-defense is considered the sole legitimate reason for declaring war.

Jus Cogens (Latin, "compelling law"). *Jus cogens* refers to a normative law that may not be violated by any state. *Jus cogens* norms thus refer to those principles of international law that are so fundamental that no state can ignore them or opt out of abiding by them. A classic example of a jus cogens norm is that no nation, legally or morally, can refuse to abide by the principles forbidding such abhorrent crimes as genocide. *Jus cogens*, though, is honored more in theory than in practice; nation-states have, at times, closed a blind eye to acts of genocide practiced by others.

Jus in Bello (Latin, "laws during the waging of war"). *Jus in bello* is the humanitarian law dealing with the conduct of war. It demands that states at war must make a clear distinction between noncombatants and combatants and must take into consideration proportionality in carrying out the war.

Just War Theory. This doctrine, embracing the notion that under some circumstances the waging of war is a just act, can be traced to Biblical times. The ancient Israelites went to war in the name of their god, the Lord of the Universe; early Christians overcame their pacifism by fighting in the name of the crucified Jesus, when, in 313 CE, Emperor Constantine (272–337 CE) thought he saw a cross in the shape of a sword on which was inscribed the words "In this sign thou shallst triumph." Several centuries later, St. Thomas Aquinas (c. 1225–1274) refined the notion of a just war, following the campaigns of the crusaders against the Muslims in the quest to recapture Jerusalem. In turn, Islamic theologians coined their own rationale for a morally condoned war, the *Hegira*, dying in the name of the Prophet Mohammed (c. 570–623 CE). In early modern times, wars pursued by absolute monarchs were automatically justified by the doctrine of the Divine Right of Kings, according to which God's will flows through the sovereign. More recently, nationalism has contributed to the notion of a legitimate war, one that is in the interest of the state; in this, the doctrine of *realpolitik* is invoked to justify military action. By this logic, an aggressive war is *ipso facto* a war in the defense of the nation. The just war idea is thus grounded firmly within considerations of moral philosophy and stands outside that of such normally accepted rationales governing statecraft as would be explained by political realists, who see the world in terms of *realpolitik*.

According to international law, interventionist action to stop genocide is condoned by the UN Convention on the Prevention and Punishment of the Crime of Genocide. All signatories are obliged to act if genocide, once identified officially, is taking place. In such circumstances, military intervention is justified and supersedes the traditional rights of sovereignty accorded by the modern states system established at the Treaty of Westphalia in 1648. The concept of a just war has gradually transformed into a newer category, that of "humanitarian intervention." Just war theory, for the most part, approaches issues of war and intervention from the twin perspectives of *jus ad bellum* (under what circumstances it is right to go to war) and *jus in bello* (what may be done in order to wage war). Again, while the reality of conducting wars for justice seems to be both a contradiction and fairly recent, the roots of discussions regarding it go deep. Noteworthy in this regard was the Dutch philosopher Hugo Grotius (1583–1645), whose 1625 work *De iure belli ac pacis* (*On the laws of war and peace*) codified the rules by which a just war could be fought and outlined the rights of those taking part. His was a very early foundational document in what would emerge in the twentieth century as a burgeoning literature of human rights.

K

Kagame, Paul (b. 1957). Paul Kagame first became president of Rwanda in March 2000 and was elected in a landslide on August 25, 2003. A Tutsi, Kagame was born in Gitarama in 1957 and as a child became a refugee as his family fled to Uganda in the face of Hutu attacks on Tutsi in his home country. In 1985, as a young, English-speaking Tutsi refugee burning to return to Rwanda, he and his friend Fred Rwigyema (1957–1990), established the Rwandan Patriotic Front (RPF), a political organization with an armed wing named the Rwandan Patriotic Army (RPA). The RPA comprised mostly Tutsi who had fought in Uganda with the National Resistance Army (NRA) in the overthrow of President Idi Amin (1928–2003) in 1979. In 1986, Kagame became head of NRA military intelligence, and actively participated in the 1990 invasion of Rwanda. In 1990 it was strong enough to launch an invasion of Rwanda from Uganda, supported by Ugandan president Yoweri Museveni (b. 1944). Rwigyema was killed during the invasion, which failed after a French-led intervention force stopped its advance after an appeal for help from Rwandan president Juvenal Habyarimana (1937–1994). After Rwigyema's death, Kagame became the commander of the RPF, which continued to carry out raids on Rwanda throughout the early 1990s. Kagame's role in negotiations with the Habyarimana regime throughout the 1990s was important, and certainly contributed to the signing of the Arusha Accords, a peace settlement between the RPF and the Rwandan government. He, in fact, took part in the signing of the Arshua Accords as he signed them on the behalf of the RPF on August 4, 1993. Habyarimana's assassination on April 6, 1994, however, destroyed any possibility that these accords would be implemented. (One accusation after another has been made in regard to who ordered the plane shot down, as well as who actually carried out the action. Hutu have accused Tutsi, Tutsi have accused Hutu, and even some Tutsi have accused other Tutsi. To date, evidence has not been located to definitively prove who was behind the downing of the plane.) With the subsequent start of the Rwandan genocide as a result of Habyarimana's death, the RPF again invaded Rwanda and, on this occasion, was successful in beating back the Rwandan National Army (the FAR) and the anti-Tutsi militias such as *Interahamwe* and *Impuzamugambi*. By the end of May 1994, the RPF had taken over much of the country, though UN general Roméo Dallaire (b. 1946) was also critical of Kagame for not increasing his military strikes during the genocide itself.

In July its forces occupied the capital, Kigali. It was a brilliant and timely victory, and resulted in the RPF becoming the government. Kagame became vice president and minister of defense in a new administration led by Pasteur Bizimungu (b. 1950). After a period of political infighting and Bizimungu's resignation and later imprisonment, Kagame became president in March 2000 and was overwhelming reelected in August of 2003.

Especially since his electoral victory in 2003, Kagame's presidency has been devoted to issues of postgenocide justice and reconciliation. He remains a strong critic of the UN and France for their failures during the genocide, and, although a Tutsi himself, prefers to downplay this identity in favor of his Rwandanness.

Kaganovich, Lazar Moiseevich (1893–1991). Kaganovich was an Old Bolshevik from Ukraine and served as Soviet dictator Joseph Stalin's (1879–1953) chief lieutenant. Kaganovich served twice as first secretary of the Communist Party of Ukraine (1925–1927 and 1947). During the period of the Soviet man-made famine in Ukraine (which constituted genocide) in 1933, he served as secretary of the All-Union Central Committee section on agriculture and also headed, in November 1932, a special mission to the North Caucasus. According to Soviet historians who published their works in the 1960s, Kaganovich personally oversaw the deportation of Cossack settlers in the rural areas of the North Caucasus in 1932. Eventually, he was removed from power in 1957 for opposing Soviet dictator Nikita Khrushchev (1894–1971).

Kajuga, (Jerry) Robert (b. 1960). The founder and national president of the Rwandan youth militia known as *Interahamwe* ("those who stick together" and "those who attack together"). The movement's genesis could be found in a number of junior soccer clubs, one of which, the *Loisirs* (leisure) club, Kajuga coached. Kajuga's father was a highly respected Episcopal priest of Hutu background who had married a Tutsi woman. Kajuga was thus the child of a mixed marriage.

Under Kajuga's direction, *Interahamwe* was transformed from a youth organization when it was founded in 1990, into a radical Hutu killing machine as the anti-Tutsi campaign of hatred fostered by Rwandan president Juvenal Habyarimana (1937–1994) intensified throughout 1992 and 1993. After Habyarimana was killed in a plane crash as the result of a missile attack on April 6, 1994, it was *Interahamwe* that took the lead in the massacre of Tutsi throughout the country. Kajuga justified the role of the organization of which he was national president on the grounds that Rwanda's Tutsi were waging a concerted offensive, through the Rwandan Patriotic Front (RPF), to destroy the Hutu. A fanatic of the most extreme caliber, Kajuga was active throughout the genocide not only in running the *Interahamwe* but also in his close personal association with the various Hutu Power cliques directing the genocide and with Rwanda's interim (Hutu) government. As the forces closed in and put the *Interahamwe* to flight, Kajuga fled along with many thousands of his militia members. It is possible that he might have slipped into Zaire, but his true fate remains unknown.

Kambanda, Jean (b. 1955). An extremist Hutu in the *Mouvement démocratique républicain* (Democratic Republican Movement), Jean Kambanda was sworn in on April 9, 1994, as prime minister of the interim Rwandan government that was set in place after President Juvenal Habyarimana (1937–1994) and Prime Minister Agathe Uwilingiyimana (1953–1994) had been assassinated. (Habyarimana's death was the catalyst for the start of the genocide; Uwilingiyimana, a Hutu moderate, was one of its first victims.) Kambanda remained prime minister throughout the period of the genocide until the victory of the Rwandan Patriotic Front (RPF) army defeated the forces of the interim government on July 19, 1994.

Throughout his term as prime minister, he directed government policy with regard to the Hutu genocide of Rwanda's Tutsi population by broadcasting messages of hate on *Radio-Télévision Libre des Mille Collines* (RTLM) and inciting Hutu to kill Tutsi and urging Hutu to construct roadblocks throughout Rwanda in order to prevent Tutsi from fleeing the country. He also provided weapons and ammunition to Hutu militia and others for the express purpose of having the latter murder Tutsi. Furthermore, he reportedly traveled throughout the country for the express purpose of inciting the genocide and directing the killing process. As the head of government, he also contributed indirectly to the killing by failing—or rather, refusing—to condemn militia groups such as the *Interahamwe* (an extremist Hutu youth group that became the lead killers during the 1994 Rwandan genocide) when they broke the law by killing Tutsi and destroying property in vast quantities.

After the RPF victory, Kambanda fled Rwanda. He was arrested in Nairobi, Kenya, on July 18, 1997, and transferred immediately to the jurisdiction of the International Criminal Tribunal for Rwanda (ICTR) in Arusha, Tanzania. He was arraigned on a variety of charges (including inciting massacres, ordering the establishment of roadblocks for the purpose of rounding up Tutsi, and distributing weapons for the express purpose of carrying out the genocide) and pleaded guilty, on May 1, 1998, on all counts (genocide, conspiracy to commit genocide, direct and public incitement to commit genocide, complicity in genocide, and two counts of crimes against humanity) by the International Criminal Tribunal for Rwanda (ICTR).

Ultimately, on September 4, 1998, he was found guilty of genocide and crimes against humanity and was sentenced to life imprisonment (the maximum penalty that can be imposed by the ICTR). He, however, withdrew his confession and appealed his conviction on the ground that his legal counsel had misrepresented him. Controversy surrounded the appointment of Kambanda's counsel, who was chosen by the ICTY Registrar from a limited list which excluded French and Canadian Francophone lawyers, and forced Kambanda to defend himself for four months. This led to allegations that Kambanda was subjected to a "show trial." Kambanda's appeal was dismissed on October 19, 2000, and the original verdict was upheld on all counts. He is currently serving his sentence in the Bamako Central Prison, Bamako, Mali.

The trial of Kambanda was noteworthy on numerous fronts. First, it was the first time a head of state admitted in a court proceeding direct participation in a genocide. It also constituted the first time a head of government pleaded to guilty to genocide. His sentence also constituted only the second time since the adoption of the United Nations Convention on the Prevention and Punishment of the Crime of Genocide that someone was found guilty of genocide. His conviction, though, constituted the first time a head of government was found guilty of genocide.

Kangura. An anti-Tutsi popular newspaper (sometimes also referred to as a magazine) in Rwanda prior to the 1994 genocide. Its first issue appeared in May 1990, and its last in February 1994—two months before the Rwandan genocide began. This periodical became an instrument in the preparation of the Hutu population of Rwanda for the genocide of the Tutsi population that took place during the one hundred days that followed April 6, 1994. *Kangura*, which in Kinyarwarda translates as "Wake them up," was published by Hassan Ngeze (b. 1961), a Muslim of Hutu ethnicity. Ngeze, who was later prosecuted by the International Criminal Tribunal for Rwanda (ICTR) and convicted for facilitating genocide, always asserted that he was a businessman and entrepreneur rather than a Hutu Power ideologue, but the pages of *Kangura* constantly showed him to be much more than what he claimed to be. Perhaps the most infamous piece he published in *Kangura* was a catalog of ten admonitory instructions that were to be followed by every Hutu in order to destroy Tutsi influence in Rwandan society, and guarantee Hutu hegemony. These "Hutu Ten Commandments," as they were called, could in many respects have been adapted directly out of the Nazi Nuremberg Laws, and their repetition through the pages of *Kangura* served as an important means in the ongoing conditioning of the Hutu against the Tutsi of Rwanda. Elsewhere, *Kangura* published material which referred constantly to Tutsi as *Inyenzi* (cockroaches) and drove home the message that these *Inyenzi* (including those from outside, the *Inkotanyi*, or rebels, from the Rwandan Patriotic Front) were about to enslave all the Hutu and/or exterminate them. The required response, it put rhetorically (and frequently), was to preempt the Tutsi, protect themselves, and wipe out the Tutsi attackers. Prior to ceasing publication, *Kangura* also published the names of Hutu deemed to be politically suspect—with the insinuation that they should suffer the same fate as the Tutsi—and exhorted all other Hutu to take all measures to ensure that they would predominate now and into the future. Editorials and articles also attacked the United Nations Assistance Mission in Rwanda (UNAMIR) by making a variety of vicious and defamatory claims.

Employing sensationalism at every turn, and with a readership many times greater than its circulation figures suggested, *Kangura* was an important agent in developing a consciousness for genocide, notwithstanding that it had ceased publication by the time the genocide actually began. By then, *Kangura*—along with the other purveyor of hate messages, the radio station *Radio-Télévision Libre des Mille Collines* (RTLM)—had done its job, and the idea of Tutsi annihilation was firmly implanted on the Hutu worldview.

Kapos (Latin, *capo* for "head of"). Within the Nazi concentration camp system, discipline and punishment over the prisoners could not have operated without the compliance (sometimes willing, sometimes not) of inmates who acted in a correctional role. The individuals who carried out such roles were known as Kapos. The Kapo was an inmate appointed by the SS to serve as the foreman of a labor detachment. Kapos were chosen amongst the prison population, regardless of the type of crime (e.g., murder, assault and battery, robbery) for which they were incarcerated.

The Kapos are mainly remembered as fearsome and harsh, renowned for their brutality and frequent sadism. It is worth noting that Jews served as Kapos over other Jews, and some were vicious in their treatment of their fellow prisoners. No task set by the SS— beating a fellow prisoner mercilessly, selecting prisoners arbitrarily for hazardous work details, distributing food to SS "favorites" (thereby discriminating against others, and in doing so placing their lives in jeopardy)—was worth too much if it meant the continuation of the incumbent's position. Indeed, not only did Kapos wield a brutal form of immediate power over their fellow prisoners, but they also received enormous benefits from their positions. They usually had more to eat than those over whom they had authority, and their food was often of a higher quality. The Kapos supervised the common prisoners at work while doing little work themselves. They had more time to sleep than the others and could requisition any item from the prisoners. In the blocks, which were mostly overcrowded after 1939, the Kapos often had their own rooms, sometimes single beds of their own, and at times even lockers for their personal property. They were allowed facilities to wash regularly, to change their linen, and, in at least one recorded instance, even to change their underwear. Concessions like these were worth too much to lose, and the natural instinct was to try to keep them.

There was the added factor that if an SS order went unheeded, or was not satisfactorily completed, the functionary could lose much more than just his position. This made the Kapos just that more vicious, and thus detested by their fellow prisoners. Kapos could be (and often were) killed by the common prisoners as traitors, and could equally by killed by the SS owing to their status as detested enemies of the Third Reich.

In February 1944, SS head Heinrich Himmler (1900–1945) issued an official order preventing Jews from serving as Kapos. He did so in order to bring Nazi ideology into alignment with acceptable practice; that is, that no Jews should ever be placed in a position of authority over a non-Jew, even someone who was a prisoner of the Nazis and therefore not normally deserving the same treatment as one who was a respected citizen. The Nazi world view could not accept Jews "ruling" over non-Jews, no matter what.

Karadzic, Radovan (b. 1945). Bosnian Serb leader. Born in Montenegro, Karadzic's father had been a Serb patriot and anticommunist who fought against Josip Broz Tito's (1892–1980) partisans during World War II. A psychiatrist by training and a poet by inclination, Radovan Karadzic made himself the leading proponent of Bosnia's Serbs. As a poet he is said to have come under the influence of Dobrica Cosic (b. 1921), a Serb nationalist writer. It was Cosic, in fact, who convinced Karadzic to enter the world of politics.

In 1990, he was a founder of a pro-Serbian nationalist party, the Srpska Demokratska Stranka (SDS), or Serbian Democratic Party. His express goal in founding such was the establishment of a Greater Serbia. In 1991, much like Hitler threatened the Jews in 1939, he warned that Bosnia's Muslim population would "disappear from the face of the Earth" if it chose to "opt for war" by establishing an independent Bosnia-Herzegovina. At a later point in time, he asserted that "Muslims are the most threatened . . . not only in the physical sense . . . rather, this is also the beginning of the end of their existence as a nation."

In the aftermath of the Bosnian declaration of independence from Yugoslavia on April 6, 1992, Karadzic declared the Serbian-peopled sections of the country independent, as Republika Srpska, or the Serbian Republic. Backed by Serbia's Slobodan Milosevic (1941–2006), between 1992 and 1995 Karadzic then waged a murderous war against the Muslims of Bosnia-Herzegovina. It was Karadzic who orchestrated the three-year-long siege of Bosnia's capital city, Sarajevo. Day after day, he ordered a barrage of artillery to rain on the defenseless city. From his headquarters in Pale, in the mountains overlooking Sarajevo, Karadzic ordered the systematic destruction of historic Muslim targets such as the National Library, not to mention the killing of unarmed civilians congregated in open-air markets. His most egregious crime was the offensive he ordered in 1995 against the six so-called safe areas under UN protection (Sarajevo, Tuzla, Gorazde, Srebrenica, Zepa, and Bihac). In the worst of these, and in full view, Karadzic's senior military officer, General Ratko Mladic (b. 1942) fell on the city of Srebrenica. Systematically, militias and troops from the Army of Republika Srpska (the VRS), the Bosnian Serb army, captured as many men and boys between the ages of ten and sixty-five as they could find, led them out of the city, and killed them in the surrounding hills, burying them in mass graves. The women and children of Srebrenica were sent outside the borders of Republika Srpska. This was one of the most blatant acts of genocide, in the context of the Yugoslav wars, for which Milosevic was held accountable indirectly, and in which Karadzic was the primary executor. Karadzic has yet to be tried. The International Criminal Tribunal for the Former Yugoslavia (ICTY) has indicted him as a war criminal, and called for his immediate arrest and trial. So far, he has found safe haven in the Serbian-controlled territories in Bosnia; to many Bosnian Serbs, he remains a hero, and no one has dared apprehend him for fear of retribution. NATO troops supervising the peace settlement in Bosnia, lacking the inclination to go after him, have been totally ineffectual in making an arrest.

Karamira, Froduald (1947–1998). Radical Rwandan politician prior to and during the 1994 Rwandan genocide. Born in Mushubati, central Rwanda, Karamira's mixed ethnic ancestry could have seen him claim either Tutsi or Hutu ethnicity; starting with the former, he switched to the latter as he grew older. Entering Hutu society provided him with opportunities to advance himself politically and economically, and by the late 1980s he was the owner of several properties in downtown Kigali. A highly placed member of the ruling Mouvement Démocratique Républicain (MDR) party, in July 1993 Karamira engineered a split in the party. More specifically, Karamira's perspective was that the MDR was not sufficiently pro-Hutu and that any form of negotiation with the rebel opposition Rwandan Patriotic Front (RPF) was an intolerable ethnic betrayal. The newly formed MDR-Power, with Karamira as vice president, espoused a radical Hutu Power ideology, and, after April 6, 1994, it participated actively in the genocide of Rwanda's Tutsi and moderate Hutu. Prior to this, on October 23, 1993, Karamira made a highly inflammatory speech in which he called on the Hutu to rise up and "take the necessary measures" to target "the enemy amongst us." When the genocide began, Karamira became a member of Rwanda's interim government, and broadcast frequently on *Radio-Télévision Libre des Mille Collines*, the rabidly anti-Tutsi private radio station. His messages were hate-filled incitements to commit mass murder. It has been alleged that he was personally responsible for hundreds of murders, and directly answerable for the deaths of at least thirteen Tutsi members of his own family. As the rebel forces of the RPF closed in on the interim government in June and July 1994, Karamira fled. In June 1996 he was arrested in Mumbai, India, and extradited, via Addis Ababa, to Rwanda. On January 13, 1997, his trial for crimes against humanity, murder, conspiracy, and genocide began in a Special Trial Chamber in Kigali; and on February 14, 1997, he was found guilty and sentenced to death. Appeals were rejected on September 12, 1997, and he was executed by firing squad in a public exhibition at the Nyamirambo Stadium, Kigali, on April 24, 1998, along with a number of other convicted génocidaires.

Karski, Jan (1914–2000). Underground name for the Polish non-Jew, Jan Kozielewski, who smuggled himself into the Warsaw Ghetto and the Belzec death camp to mentally record the details of the plight of the Jews and then smuggled the information out to the West to give firsthand testimonial evidence of their fate. Arriving in London in 1942, he was able to present his information both to the Polish government-in-exile and to British prime minister Winston Churchill, later traveling to the United States to present his findings to then president Franklin D. Roosevelt. His 1944 book *The Story of the Secret State* detailed his own experiences, that of the Polish underground, and the plight of the Jews as then understood. After the war, he remained in the United States, ultimately becoming a professor of diplomacy and political science at Georgetown University in Washington, D.C. In 1982, Yad Vashem, Israel's Holocaust Memorial Authority, named him a "Righteous Gentile" (the latter is the term used to describe non-Jews who risked their own lives trying to save Jews during the Holocaust years).

Ka-Tzetnik 135633. The pseudonym of writer and poet Yehiel Dinur (1917–2001). The pseudonym was derived from the German slang "KZ" (*konzentrationslager*, "concentration camp"); the number was his Auschwitz registration number.

Dinur was born in Poland and active in the Orthodox Jewish community of Sosnowiec. In 1931, he published his first book of poems in Yiddish. After having survived two years in Auschwitz, he emigrated to Palestine in 1945 and settled in Tel Aviv, later testifying at the trial of Adolf Eichmann in 1961, where he dramatically collapsed. A writer of considerable talent, he saw his "mission" as telling the story of what happened in the Holocaust on behalf of those who did not survive. Among his more well known works are *House of Dolls* (1956), *Star of Ashes* (1967), and *Shiviti: A Vision* (1989). His books have been translated into more than twenty languages.

Ke Pauk (1933–2002). Ke Pauk, a longtime warlord in Cambodia, was the military commander and deputy of the Northern Zone under the Khmer Rouge's totalitarian and genocidal rule of Kampuchea (1975–1979). He was considered by many to be one of the most murderous of the Khmer Rouge leaders. He was a member of the Khmer Rouge's standing committee and the military commander who was possibly most responsible for the mass purges carried out by the Khmer Rouge. He died in February 2002 of natural causes, not having spent a single day in prison for his crimes.

Kemal, Ismail (Bey) (1844–1919). An official in the Ottoman Turkish regime during the anti-Armenian persecutions of 1894–1896, and then in the Young Turk regime from 1909 onward. Ismail Kemal had a long career as an anti-Christian administrator, and the main focus of his activities centered on the destruction of Armenian aspirations, and, ultimately, lives. Among his major genocidal acts was organizing and overseeing the massacre of Armenians at Yozgat, in northwestern Turkey, in 1915. On April 12, 1919, after an Allied-convened trial in Constantinople, he was hanged in public. He was the first person in history to be executed for having been found guilty on the charge of "crimes against humanity."

Kenney, George (b. 1958). George Kenney (b. 1958), an acting Yugoslav desk officer within the U.S. State Department, resigned, on August 25, 1992, in protest over what he considered the Bush administration's (1988–1992) totally inadequate response to the crisis in the former Yugoslavia. A front-page article in the *Washington Post* quoted the following from his letter of resignation: "I can no longer in clear conscience support the Administration's ineffective, indeed counterproductive, handling of the Yugoslav crisis. . . . I am therefore resigning in order to help develop a stronger public consensus that the U.S. must act immediately to stop the genocide."

Khang Khek Iev. *See* Comrade Duch.

Khieu Samphan (b. 1931). Born into an elite family in Svay Rieng province, Cambodia, Khieu Samphan was a Khmer Rouge killer possessed of great longevity, and, as such, an important figure in Cambodian political life during the second half of the twentieth century.

Like many other bright young Cambodians during the period of French colonialism, Khieu won a government scholarship to study in France during the 1950s, leading, in his case, to a doctoral degree in political economics. While studying, he was drawn to left-wing student politics, becoming a founder and secretary-general of the Khmer Students' Union. His connections with other Cambodian students Saloth Sar (1925–1998), who later took the name Pol Pot, and Ieng Sary (b. c.1931), helped forge a radical relationship that would come to fruition in the most devastating way in the 1970s. (Through marriage,

Khieu also became the brother-in-law of both Pol Pot and Ieng Sary.) Upon his return from Paris in 1959, Khieu became a professor of economics at the University of Phnom Penh, and founded a left-wing newspaper, *L'Observateur*. In 1962 and 1964 he was elected to the National Assembly and served in the cabinet of Prince Norodom Sihanouk (b. 1922). He achieved an envied reputation for his efficiency and incorruptibility in government. With the overthrow of Sihanouk's government by military strongman Lon Nol (1913–1985) in 1970, Khieu fled to the jungle along with Pol Pot and the other members of the Khmer Rouge. There, in 1973, the Khmer Rouge joined with Sihanouk in order to create a united front against Lon Nol and his American backers. This union, known as the *Gouvernement Royal d'Union Nationale du Kampuchéa* (GRUNK), or Cambodian Royal Government of National Unity, became the alternative government, though it was never recognized formally outside of Cambodia and possessed no authority other than in the areas it controlled by force. Khieu Samphan served in a variety of roles in the GRUNK, including deputy prime minister, minister of defense, and commander in chief of the Khmer People's National Liberation Armed Forces (despite not having any military experience). After the Khmer Rouge victory in the civil war against Lon Nol's government in April 1975, Khieu became president of the State Presidium of Democratic Kampuchea, a position translating to head of state. He remained in that position until December 1978, when Vietnamese forces invaded the country and the Khmer Rouge regime fled in disarray into the jungles of western and northwestern Cambodia. Khieu Samphan was evacuated through Beijing, and played a leading diplomatic role on behalf of the Communist Party of Kampuchea (CPK). He became the public face of the former regime at the United Nations and in world capitals and, in 1985, succeeded Pol Pot as titular head of the CPK. He represented the Khmer Rouge in Paris in October 1991 at the signing of the Peace Agreement relating to the organization and conduct of free and fair elections in the postgenocide, post-Vietnamese occupation of Cambodia and became the senior Khmer Rouge representative on the Supreme National Council established to guide Cambodia to a peaceful future. This was not to last, however, as political differences saw the breakup of the harmony all had looked for in Paris.

Continuing governmental instability, coupled with both internal and external military action between 1980 and 1992, eventually resulted in the imposition of a United Nations elections supervisory authority in 1993. Subsequently, in July 1994, Samphan fled Phnom Penh with several thousand loyal troops. Returning to the Khmer Rouge–controlled regions of Cambodia, he was named prime minister in a Khmer Rouge–proclaimed provisional government. Ultimately, though, in December 1998, Khieu Samphan defected to the Cambodian government of Hun Sen (b. 1952), alongside Pol Pot's deputy, Nuon Chea (b. c.1923). Upon his defection, he apologized for the killings and then abruptly said that the Cambodian people should "let bygones be bygones." Undoubtedly because he chose to defect to the government, unlike some of the other Khmer Rouge leaders, he was not imprisoned or even put under house arrest but was warmly welcomed by the government and allowed to live free in the semiautonomous region run by Ieng Sary, another former Khmer Rouge leader/killer. That said, it is still possible that he could be brought to trial should the current effort to establish a tribunal in Cambodia to try former perpetrators of the genocide comes to fruition. In February 2004 he released a short book in French, Khmer, and English entitled *The Recent History of Cambodia and My Successive Positions*, which many regard as both self-serving and a sanitized version of historical events.

"Khmer Noir." A pejorative term used in 1993 and 1994 by conservative French government and military opponents when referring to the Rwandan Patriotic Front (RFP). Use of the term was intended to project onto the RPF the stigma of Cambodia's murderous Khmer Rouge of the 1970s and 1980s. The RPF was thereby vilified as a terrorist body bent on mass murder, specifically, of Rwanda's Hutu population. Reference to the RPF as a "Khmer Noir" was highly disparaging and was used essentially for propaganda reasons by those in France supporting the Hutu Power regime. It showed little understanding of the fundamental differences between Cambodia's Khmer Rouge and the RPF and at no time could be said to carry any credibility. The irony to be found in the use of this term lay in the fact that the actions of the very Hutu killers the French conservative establishment was supporting most resembled Cambodia's Khmer Rouge's genocidal actions.

Khmer Rouge. Cambodia's extremist communist party army before and during the Cambodian civil war of 1970–1975, and then the primary coercive instrument of the rule of dictator Pol Pot (1925–1998) under the regime of the Communist Party of Democratic Kampuchea between 1975 and 1979. Leaders of the Khmer Rouge, apart from Pol Pot, included Nuon Chea (b. 1923), Ieng Sary (b. c. 1924), Ta Mok (1926–2006), Khieu Samphan (b. 1931), and Son Sen (1930–1997).

The Khmer Rouge (KR), or "Red Khmers" (i.e., Red Cambodians), was originally a term of ridicule coined by Cambodian king Norodom Sihanouk (b. 1922) to describe his left-wing political enemies, and the term stuck. Most commonly recognized as the merciless body responsible for the Cambodian genocide during Pol Pot's rule, KR cadres were the principal bearers of Pol Pot's communist ideology, and were the ones who brutally imposed his rule throughout the country in order to achieve his ambition of returning Cambodia to "Year Zero." It was the Khmer Rouge that carried out the radical policy of clearing the cities and forcibly removing their inhabitants into the countryside; of establishing communal farms and abolishing private property, family structures, and all Western-influenced trappings of Cambodian society; and of imposing a murderous reign of terror throughout the country, in which at least 1.7 million (and possibly up to 2 million) people died through starvation and deliberate murder in what became known as Cambodia's "killing fields."

The entire fabric of communist Kampuchea was dominated by the Khmer Rouge, and the country was characterized by mass murder, intimidation, exploitation, torture, oppression, and a total disregard for human life. In 1997, Cambodia established a Khmer Rouge Trial Task Force that would lay the groundwork for legal procedures to be brought against such Khmer Rouge leaders as were still alive. Progress proved slow, however, and it was only in May 2006 that a judicial bench was established to try Khmer Rouge suspects charged with crimes against humanity and genocide. Trials are expected to begin sometime in 2007 or 2008.

Kielce Pogrom. In the aftermath of the Holocaust and the liberation of the Jews from Nazi captivity, many of those who had survived returned to their home towns searching for loved ones and/or in the quest to reestablish their lives. About two hundred of these returned to the city of Kielce, in southern Poland. They arrived at a time that was not favorable for Jews. Many Poles were opposed to a Jewish return, and a deep-seated antisemitic tradition, dating from well before World War II, did not create welcoming conditions for them. Some, if not many, Poles also feared they would have to surrender their illegal possession of Jewish property and homesites that they had acquired upon the deportation and/or arrest of the Jews. Furthermore, Jews were increasingly seen as agents for the occupying Soviet troops and the Polish communists who had been installed in Warsaw on orders from Moscow. An extremist right-wing group, *Narodowe Siły Zbrojne* (National Defense Force), was even known to have pulled returning Jews off trains and murdered them. Across Poland, it was estimated that up to four hundred Jews were murdered between February and September 1946.

On July 4, 1946, a nine-year-old Polish boy, Henryk Blaszczyk, was reported missing in Kielce. His father accused returning Jews of kidnapping his son, and the townsfolk, emulating anti-Jewish pogroms from earlier times, began to clamor for the destruction of the entire Jewish community. A blood libel was invoked that the Jews had wanted the boy's blood for ritual purposes. Marching into the Jewish quarter—which was already largely depopulated because of the losses of the Holocaust—the mob, which comprised townsfolk of all ages, went on a violent rampage. Synagogues and homes were burned, and the Jewish Community Center was besieged. Police assisted in luring Jews out of their hiding places, only to hand them over to the mob. Ransacking the Jewish district lasted throughout the day and well into the night. At the Jewish Community Center, the panic-stricken pleas of the community leaders over the phone to the local bishop, and other nearby figures of authority, fell on deaf ears. By the time the mob's frenzy had abated, forty-two Jews, most of them survivors of Nazi concentration and death camps, had been murdered. About fifty others were injured, some seriously. As for Henryk Blaszczyk, the boy whose disappearance had initiated the pogrom, it was later discovered that his father had earlier sent the boy away to the next town in order to support the prearranged kidnapping story. The Kielce Pogrom was a tragic addendum to the Nazi Holocaust, and a signal to Jews throughout Europe that Poland was no longer a country in which they could feel safe.

Kigali Memorial Centre. The Kigali Memorial Centre, which was opened on the tenth anniversary (April 2004) of the 1994 Rwandan genocide, is located on a hillside where over two hundred fifty thousand people are buried. The Museum at the Centre, which was created by a joint partnership of the Kigali City Council and the British-based Aegis Trust, contains three permanent exhibitions: one of the Rwandan genocide, one of other genocides perpetrated in the twentieth century, and one that provides unique insights into the mass killing of young, innocent children at the hands of the perpetrators. Included within the Centre's complex are The Education Centre, Memorial Gardens, and National Documentation Centre of the Genocide.

"Kill Them All. God Will Know His Own!" *See* Amaury, Arnold.

Killing Fields, The. A term coined to refer to both the mass killing perpetrated by the Khmer Rouge in Cambodia between 1975 and 1979 and the location of the mass graves of those killed during that genocidal period. The killings and graves were and are, respectively, located in virtually every region of the country, evidence of the genocidal character of the Khmer Rouge's policy of a total eradication of all those (outside of the most senior echelons of the Communist Party of Kampuchea) who had been influenced by foreign ideas, education, and customs. The goal was to reconstruct an authentic Khmer society and culture, literally from the roots up. Aerial photography has helped locate many of the main mass gravesites, the best known of which is to be found at Choeng Ek, about seventeen kilometers south of the capital of Phnom Penh. Most bodies at that location have been disinterred as a way of determining the totality of the victimization that took place during the genocide. Estimates overall consider that up to 2 million people—one-quarter of the population—were killed and buried. Although the term *killing fields* is most commonly applied to the murder sites of Cambodia, it has entered general parlance more widely in recent times. Hence, reference is known to have been made to the killing fields of Ukraine, Bosnia, Iraq, East Timor, Rwanda, and Sudan in contemporary scholarship.

Killing Fields, The. *The Killing Fields* is a major feature film about the story of one man caught up in the genocide perpetrated by the Khmer Rouge in Cambodia (1975–1979). It tells the story of one Dith Pran (b. 1942), who had served as an assistant to noted *New York Times* journalist Sydney H. Schanberg (b. 1934), and who, with Schanberg, chose to remain in the capital city of Phnom Penh as it was being overrun by the Khmer Rouge on April 17, 1975. Ultimately, Schanberg was allowed to leave Democratic Kampuchea (which the Khmer Rouge rebels had renamed Cambodia), but Pran was forced out into the countryside with millions of other Cambodian citizens, where the Khmer Rouge worked and starved them to death and/or murdered them at will. It is estimated that between 1 and 2 million of Cambodia's 6 to 7 million perished during the rule of the Khmer Rouge.

Kim Il-sung (1912–1994). Communist dictator of the Democratic People's Republic of Korea (DPRK) from its establishment in 1948 until his death in 1994. Under his absolute rule, vast numbers of people were killed by deliberate action for purely political reasons. After fighting for the Soviet Union during World War II (rising to the rank of captain), and with long-standing connections in the Chinese Communist Party, Kim was appointed prime minister of the DPRK upon its independence. On June 25, 1950, with the authorization of the Soviets and Chinese, Kim launched an invasion of the Republic of South Korea, whose president at that time was Syngman Rhee (1875–1965). In the resultant Korean War (1950–1953), hundreds of thousands of people on both sides were killed and millions were displaced. It is next to impossible to calculate how many murders were committed in Kim's name or on his orders, but it is known, for example, that prisoners of war were murdered in their tens of thousands. After the war, Kim tightened his control of the country by purging his party and establishing a vast ring of political labor camps—the North Korean gulag—throughout the country. Millions were mobilized into huge economic infrastructure projects (road making, dam construction, bridge building, irrigation drainage, and the like), during which scores of thousands died as a result of exposure, starvation, and overwork. As Kim developed a "personality cult" around himself, more people were murdered by the state as dissenters, more were sent to the gulag, and more died of starvation and overwork as major projects were created in the "Great Leader's" honor. When, in the 1960s, Kim launched the DPRK on a policy of *juche*, or "self-reliance," the country slid further into despair owing to a massive reduction in what few economic relationships remained after two decades of war, centralized economic control, and repression. The future, by 1980, was one of unmitigated gloom. But this would be for Kim's successor—his son, Kim Jong Il (b. 1942)—to have to deal with. On July 8, 1994, Kim Il-sung died of a heart attack. U.S. political scientist R. J. Rummel (b. 1932), attempting to provide some sort of estimate of the number of killed under Kim's rule, has calculated figures of "perhaps from 710,000 to slightly under 3,500,000 . . . with a mid-estimate of almost 1,600,000" (http://www.hawaii.edu/powerkills/SOD.CHAP10.HTM). Per head of population, this places Kim Il-sung in the forefront of mass killers during the twentieth century.

Kishinev Pogrom. In April 1903, the most notorious pogrom in early twentieth century Russia took place in the city of Kishinev, the capital of Bessarabia, in Russia's south. It is estimated that some fifty thousand Jews lived in the city (nearly half of the overall population), and, although they had previously experienced some degree of antisemitism, the pogroms that had beset Russian Jewish communities since 1881 had so far bypassed by Kishinev's Jews. On the night of April 6–7, 1903, however, the situation in Kishinev took a turn for the worse, prompted largely by the antisemitic rabble-rousing of P. A. Krushevan (1860–1909), the editor of the reactionary local newspaper *Bessarabets*. On that night, and in another pogrom on April 19–20, fifty-one Jews were killed on the spot, and eight more died subsequently. Eighty-six were seriously wounded or raped, and another five hundred received lesser injuries. More than fifteen hundred Jewish-owned properties (homes and businesses) were destroyed outright or otherwise damaged. Although there was a measure of Jewish self-defense, it was ultimately ineffectual owing to the intervention of the Russian military on the side of the pogromists.

The horror of the Kishinev pogrom was reported throughout Russia and the rest of the world. The most influential Russian thinker and writer of the age, Leo Tolstoy (1828–1910), saw Kishinev as an issue worthy of tsarist condemnation. The man who would later be dubbed the poet laureate of the Jewish people, Chaim Nachman Bialik (1873–1934), wrote one of his most famous poems on the pogrom ("On the Slaughter") after he had gone to the city to investigate for himself what had happened there. The leader of the Zionist movement, Theodor Herzl (1860–1904), traveled to Russia a few months after the pogrom to try to convince the minister of the interior, Vyacheslav Konstantinovich von Plehve (1846–1904), to relax restrictions against Jews trying to develop the Zionist movement seeking a homeland in Palestine. In western Europe and the United States, the Kishinev pogrom turned the spotlight directly onto the conduct of the tsar's government and held it up as the kind of regime that could not be trusted to look after its own people.

The death of those at Kishinev inaugurated the new twentieth century as one in which Jews throughout Russia (and Europe) would suffer as no other Jewish community had ever before suffered; but the irony is that the outrage expressed by democratic nations in 1903 was not to be carried very far forward when persecution of Jews intensified to proportions hitherto unforeseen during the period of the Holocaust years (1933–1945).

Klemperer, Victor (1881–1960). *See I Will Bear Witness: A Diary of the Nazi Years—1933–1941* and *I Will Bear Witness: A Diary of the Nazi Years—1942–1945* by Victor Klemperer.

KOLAKOPS. KOLAKOPS is an acronym for the Indonesian military unit Komando Pelaksanaan Operasi TNI, or Operations Implementation Command for the TNI (Indonesian armed forces). Essentially responsible for counter-insurgency activities, KOLAKOPS units were established during Indonesia's rule over East Timor (particularly between 1989 and 1993), and continued to be used in Indonesia's long-running war for the control of its breakaway province of Aceh during 2001. In most cases, they are under the command of senior officers of the TNI or KOPASSUS, the much feared Special Forces. The fact that KOLAKOPS commands are specially created and sit outside of regular military command structures gives them wide discretionary powers not normally found in the Indonesian military's rules of engagement; consequently, abuses of civilians, torture of prisoners, and even massacres of local folk can and do take place under KOLAKOPS administrations with impunity. (An example of the latter took place in November 1991, when mourners at the Santa Cruz cemetery in Dili, East Timor, were fired upon by KOPASSUS troops, with substantial loss of life.) KOLAKOPS commands have not been established in all areas where Indonesia has experienced civil or separatist strife (e.g., in Papua), but their presence in specific conflicts has indicated a special determination on the part of the military to deal with such conflicts with a vigor not usual in regular commands of the TNI.

Kosovo Force (KFOR). The international force especially formed and headed up by NATO to enforce a diplomatic settlement/agreement in Kosovo between warring Kosovar Albanians and Serbs in the late 1990s.

Kosovo Intervention, and Allegations of a Serb-perpetrated Genocide. In the aftermath of Serbia's failed wars to retain Slovenia and Croatia, and the drawn-out and bloody conflict in Bosnia-Herzegovina between 1992 and 1995 (resulting in a quarter of a million deaths), it was hoped by many that Serbia's nationalist regime, led by Slobodan Milosevic (1941–2006), would rejoin the world of peaceable nations. In March 1998, however, violence once more erupted, this time in Serbia itself—or, more specifically, in its southern province of Kosovo. The long-term ethnic and religious animosity between minority Serbs and majority Kosovar Albanians in the province led to the establishment of a self-defense organization, the Kosovo Liberation Army (KLA), that engaged in terrorist activities in order to attract international attention to their cause and at the same time intimidate Serbs in the province to leave Kosovo. Serbian responses took a military form, with widespread killings of Kosovar civilians taking place—particularly, though not exclusively, in areas well-known as KLA strongholds such as the Drenica Valley. Increasingly, the United States and its European allies saw a need to intervene before this state-initiated killing got totally out of hand: the result was the decision by NATO, after many serious attempts at negotiation, to commence military action against Serbia in March 1999. The hope was that this would coerce Milosevic into halting the attacks against the Kosovars, but the opposite took place: rather than succumbing, Milosevic took the chance afforded by NATO's intervention to attempt to "ethnically cleanse" Kosovo of Albanians. During Serbia's war with NATO, 1.3 million Kosovars were forcibly driven from their homes, and eight hundred thousand were physically expelled from Kosovo. Thousands were killed, raped, and maimed in the process. It is from these actions that accusations of genocide have their roots.

Kosovo Intervention, Serb Claims of Genocide. Accusations of genocide committed by NATO during its military intervention into Kosovo for the purpose of stopping the ethnic cleansing being perpetrated against the province's Kosovar Albanian population by the Serbian regime of Slobodan Milosevic (1941–2006), during the spring of 1999. Such accusations emerged both during and after the conflict. This was one of a number of tactics employed by the Serbian government of Slobodan Milosevic (1941–2006) to discredit NATO's war effort and turn world opinion against NATO. During the conflict, Serbian authorities in Belgrade and abroad claimed that NATO had carried out war crimes against civilians, in particular through the use of cluster bombs against civilian targets and attacks on facilities with dual civilian and military usages—for instance, the state-run Serb television headquarters in Belgrade. In another example, there was evidence of use being made of depleted uranium weapons by NATO aircraft, though this was not considered to be a war crime under existing international laws of war. The NATO campaign did cause serious damage to the environment, and questions were certainly raised in international arenas regarding NATO's selection of bombing targets, particularly later in the war. More importantly for Serb claims of genocide was the targeting of urban concentrations, with the attendant civilian deaths caused by direct military action. Estimates of the number killed vary; Serb sources calculated anywhere between twelve hundred and five thousand civilian deaths, whereas a Human Rights Watch report from February 2000 concluded that about five hundred civilians died. Although such deaths are of course a tragedy, there is no evidence to show that they were caused by a NATO policy of genocide—though in some instances specific incidents could come very close to a definition of war crimes (and, perhaps, of crimes against humanity). The Serb claim of genocide was for the most part an element of a broader anti-NATO propaganda campaign waged during the conflict.

Kosovo Liberation Army (KLA). The Kosovo Liberation Army (KLA), or, in Albanian, *Ushtria Çlirimtare e Kosovës* (UÇK), was a paramilitary body composed of Kosovar Albanians during the 1990s. Though labeled a terrorist organization by the Serbs, it functioned more as a guerrilla or insurgent army, and, in 1998, was estimated to have a membership of almost twenty thousand troops, including former Yugoslavian military, and mercenaries, from such countries as Albania, Saudi Arabia, Yemen, and Afghanistan. Ideologically committed to a separatist nationalist outlook, the KLA found some of its adherents comfortable in the fascist camp, whereas others favored a more communist line; politically, however, the KLA continued to suffer from a lack of both leadership and unity. Their military modus vivendi, however, was always and increasingly violent. Their announced intention was to unite all Albanians into a greater Albania, including independence for Kosovo itself. Founded in Macedonia in 1992, the KLA was an underground movement organized by Kosovar Albanian militants, which began carrying out armed attacks against Serbian police in 1995. The KLA was, at first, comprised of several hundred radical Kosovar secessionists who opposed the more moderate majority, led by their prime minister-in-waiting, Ibrahim Rugova (1944–2006), whose preference throughout the 1990s was to seek compromise with Serbian president Slobodan Milosevic (1941–2006) in order to avoid violence. Following the bloody events in Bosnia between 1992 and 1995, the KLA rejected this as utopian. Receiving arms smuggled from Albania, the KLA launched its own campaign of reprisals, prompting Milosevic, in March 1999, to set in motion what became known in the West as "Operation Horseshoe," a campaign in which Serbian military and paramilitary forces were sent into Kosovo to initiate another round of ethnic cleansing. Within days, nearly 1 million Kosovars fled their homes, crossing into Macedonia and Albania. The attack was halted by NATO bombings of Serb positions, first in Kosovo and then in Serbia itself, between March and June 1999. The aftermath, in which Milosevic surrendered the province, saw the insertion of UN peacekeeping troops, allowing the refugees to return. In 1999, after the fall of Milosevic, the KLA was supposed to be demilitarized, but this was never fully accomplished. Indeed, under the cover of the UN, the KLA then waged a war of its own, seeking to expel Serbs, Roma, and non-Albanian Muslims from Kosovo. Repeated calls from the UN troops for the KLA to disarm and disband were defiantly ignored. Instead, the KLA continued to "cleanse" Kosovo of its ethnic minorities. To date, few Serbian refugees have managed to return. Many who have stayed live in fear for their lives; ethnic killings by the KLA are frequent and carried out with impunity, as KFOR (Kosovo Force), the NATO led and UN-authorized international peace-enforcement force responsible for establishing and maintaining security in the province, has often shown itself unable to curb the killing.

Since the KLA's formation, the militants have won the support of a clear majority of the Kosovar Albanians. The former moderates seem to have lost popularity. Politically, those sympathetic to the KLA cause have gained commanding social and political posts. The KLA is now the de facto army of Kosovo, poised to make independence a reality before foreign troops leave.

Kristallnacht **(German, "Night of the Broken Glass").** *Kristallnacht* refers to the far from spontaneous Nazi pogrom carried out in Germany and Austria on the night of November 9–10, 1938 (and into the day of November 10), against Jewish stores and synagogues in retaliation for the fatal wounding of the third secretary of the German embassy in Paris, Ernst vom Rath (1909–1938), by sixteen-year-old Hershel Grynszpan (1921–1943?), whose parents and sister, originally from Poland, were relocated across the border where they were forced to live in destitute and squalid conditions. There is ample evidence that proves that the attacks themselves were carefully orchestrated by the Nazis (including Josef Goebbels [1897–1945], minister of propaganda), with the apparent consent of German dictator Adolf Hitler (1889–1945) and with the collusion of the police. The term *Kristallnacht* itself is an invented one, and does not appear anywhere in official Nazi documents.

According to a report by the SS (in German, *Schutztaffeln*, or "protective unit," Hitler's private body guard that was notorious for its vicious treatment of the Nazis' perceived enemies) report, more than thirty thousand Jews were arrested (many of them later released), eight hundred fifteen shops and twenty-nine department stores owned by Jews destroyed, many more than two hundred sixty synagogues and cemeteries vandalized, and ninety-one Jews killed outright (with many others in the concentration camps themselves). It has also been estimated that more than seven thousand five hundred Jewish-owned businesses were vandalized overall. The actual cost of the damages inflicted was more than 25 million Reichmarks, for which the Jews themselves were held liable, as well as a fine of more than 1 billion Reichmarks as "reparations." Western outrage at these events, particularly the United States, did not appear to have any appreciable effect upon the Nazi agenda of forced takeover of Jewish businesses, the speeding up of Jewish emigration, or the increasing violence against, and incarceration of Jews. These events are now understood to have paved the way for the near-successful annihilation of European Jewry in the years that followed.

Kristof, Nicholas D. (b. 1959). A political scientist, author, and a columnist for *The New York Times*. Kristof traveled to Darfur, Sudan, during the period of the genocide there (2003–2007) and wrote one article after another about the genocidal actions of Government of Sudan (GOS) troops and the *Janjaweed* (Arab militia), the plight and fate of the black African victims, and the inaction by the international community to halt the genocide. For the powerful series of articles he wrote on Darfur, Kristof won his second Pulitzer Prize (the first was for his and his wife's coverage of the Tiananmen Square Massacre in China in 1989). In awarding the 2006 Pulitzer to Kristof, the Pulitzer Committee noted that it was "for his graphic, deeply reported columns that, at personal risk, focused attention on genocide in Darfur and that gave voice to the voiceless in other parts of the world."

Krstic, Radislav (b. 1948). Radislav Krstic was born in Vlasenica, Bosnia-Herzegovina, and became a career soldier. After the secession of Bosnia from Yugoslavia on April 6, 1992, he was appointed chief of staff and deputy commander of the Drina Corps, one of six geographically based corps in the Army of Republika Srpska (VRS), under the command of General Milenko Zivanovic (b. 1946). In this role, Krstic was closely involved in the Bosnian Serb attacks on the city of Srebrenica, a United Nations–protected "safe area," in July 1995. Sometime between July 11 and July 13—there is disagreement as to when the transfer of command took place—Krstic was placed in command of the Drina Corps, at the height of the Serb assault. By this stage, Srebrenica was in the process of being "ethnically cleansed" in line with the declared policy of VRS commander general Ratko Mladic (b. 1942). On July 12 and 13, women, children, and the elderly, then sheltering in the UN base at Potocari, about five kilometers from Srebrenica, were put onto buses and deported en masse to Bosnian lines far from Srebrenica; such men as had not yet fled the city were separated from the women, children, and the elderly, loaded on buses and trucks, taken out into the hills surrounding the city, and slaughtered. Ultimately, troops under Krstic's command murdered between seven thousand and eight thousand Muslim men and boys, which is now regarded as Europe's worst atrocity since the Holocaust of World War II. When the Srebrenica operation began, Krstic was in charge of planning and executing the campaign, under Zivanovic and Mladic, and it was for the crimes committed during this campaign that Krstic was indicted by the International Criminal Tribunal for the Former Yugoslavia (ICTY) on October 30, 1998.

Through November 1998, Krstic led an open life in Republika Srpska, being promoted to the rank of general major and placed in command of the Fifth Corps of the VRS in April 1998. On December 2, 1998, however, he was arrested by soldiers of the United Nations Stabilization Force for Bosnia-Herzegovina (SFOR), and was transferred for trial to The Hague the next day, where he was charged with genocide, crimes against humanity, and war crimes. On August 2, 2001, Krstic was found guilty on all counts and sentenced to forty-six years' imprisonment, but, on appeal, his sentence was reduced to thirty-five years as the appeals court found that he was an accomplice to the crimes he had committed and not their instigator. He was transferred to the United Kingdom on December 20, 2004, where he is currently serving his sentence.

Kulak. Traditionally, the use of the word *kulak* in the Soviet Union referred to those peasants who were relatively well off economically. Officially, it was used by Soviet officials to refer to "'a rural capitalist who hired labor,' a 'generic rural class enemy,' or a member of the upper socio-economic stratum of the village" (Commission on the Ukraine Famine, 1988, p. 230). During the 1932–1933 Soviet man-made famine in Ukraine, kulak, however, was used by Soviet officials to refer to anyone, no matter how poor, that they (the officials) wanted to disenfranchise in the Ukraine. In fact, if the "'class enemy' marked for 'liquidation' was too poor for the term kulak to be used, he would be disenfranchised as a subkulak" (Commission on the Ukraine Famine, 1988, p. 230).

The Soviets had multiple goals in carrying out the famine, but three of the major ones were: (1) the forced collectivization of agriculture on the basis of the liquidation of the kulaks as a class; (2) the destruction of the Ukrainian nation as a political factor and social organization; and (3) a move toward rapid industrialization.

Ultimately, those who were starved to death during the man-made famine included anyone residing in the Ukraine (no matter how impoverished they were) who appeared in any way, shape, or form to resist the forced collectivization of agricultural.

Kuper, Leo (1908–1994). Considered one of the doyens of genocide studies, Kuper, a South African sociologist and lawyer who last taught at the University of California at

Los Angeles (UCLA), was the author of two early and influential works on genocide: *Genocide: Its Political Use in the Twentieth Century* (New Haven, CT: Yale University Press, 1981) and *The Prevention of Genocide* (New Haven, CT: Yale University Press, 1985).

Kurdish Genocide in Northern Iraq. The Kurdish population of Iraq in the mid-1980s numbered some 4 million, or about 22 percent of the overall Iraqi people. For much of the rule of Iraqi dictator Saddam Hussein (1937–2006), the Kurds, a non-Arab Muslim people, were discriminated against and, at different times, subjected to policies of ethnic cleansing and genocide. In March 1988, Iraqi aircraft bombed the Kurdish city of Halabja with chemical weapons, the most dramatic (though not the only) instance of many uses of such weapons in the first phase of the Iraqi campaign against the Kurds which had begun the previous year. A series of offensives were launched against Kurdish guerrillas fighting alongside Iranian troops as part of the wider Iran-Iraq conflict (1980–1988), and entire villages were leveled. Men were separated from women and children, with the latter concentrated in internment camps. It was later estimated that some one hundred thousand men had been killed, and buried in mass graves far to the south; at least four thousand Kurdish villages were destroyed, and with them much of the fabric of Kurdish society in the areas targeted by the Iraqi military.

Kurdish Genocide in Northern Iraq, U.S. Response to. Well aware of the genocidal (*Al-Anfal*) campaign (1986–1989) waged against the Kurds in northern Iraq by Iraqi president Saddam Hussein (1937–2006), the U.S. government of President Ronald Reagan (1911–2004) chose not to condemn Hussein's policy for fear of alienating him and placing the continued supply of Middle East oil in jeopardy. Concomitantly, during the Iran-Iraq War between 1980 and 1988, Washington took the position that those fighting the ayatollahs in Iran were to be supported, and this meant Saddam Hussein's Iraq—the same government that was persecuting, gassing, and slaughtering the Kurds living in the north of the country. The Kurds' situation was not helped by the fact that they were themselves siding with Iran in its war with Iraq.

Proposals in the U.S. Congress for the imposition of economic sanctions against the Iraqis were effectively killed off by the White House, supported behind closed doors by influential lobby groups from big business interests. The most common response by the United States to allegations of genocide by Iraq was for the United States to announce that a fact-finding mission or investigative team was being put together to inquire into the allegations. The United States' policies were thus dictated by *realpolitik* concerns, not by humanitarianism in the face of genocide and gross violations of human rights.

Kutner, Luis (1908–1993). A lawyer and author, Kutner was a cofounder of the noted human rights organization Amnesty International (1961), and was a strong advocate of World Habeas Corpus, an international tribunal established to resolve conflict between nations. Among his most noted writings are *World Habeas Corpus: A Proposal for an International Court of Habeas Corpus and the United Nations Writ of Habeas Corpus* (Chicago, IL: World Freedom Press, 1958), and *World Habeas Corpus* (Dobbs Ferry, NY: Oceana Publications, 1962).

L

Land of Wandering Souls. This 1999 film, which was produced by Rithy Panh, who, as a teenager, fled the Khmer Rouge takeover in Cambodia, is about a group of survivors of the Cambodian genocide (1975–1979). It depicts some Cambodian families digging trenches amid "human minefields" (the wasted and the dead) in order to lay a fiber-optic cable network from east to west. In doing so, the group not only travels across the countryside but retraces their history.

Language and Genocide. The language and syntax employed by those engaging in genocide ranges from the use of extremely blunt language to deceptive euphemisms. In some cases, it is the combination of the two. For example, the Nazi phrase "The Final Solution of the Jewish Question" (*Die Endlösung des Judenfrage*) embodies both elements.

The finality of genocide is often expressed in absolutes: *annihilate, eradicate, destroy*. Such words convey the violence of physical destruction associated with genocide. In contrast, *deportations, resettlement, special treatment*, and *shower* have all served as euphemisms for killing.

Most, if not all, genocides use a vocabulary to depict the hated target, the one to be obliterated. For example, *subhuman, cockroach, microbes, dogs, pigs, cancer, virus, life-unworthy-of-life*, and *excrement* were used by various perpetrators of genocide in the twentieth and early twenty-first centuries. Although some of the latter terms depict a target that is less than human, others depict something that is dangerous and harmful to humanity and needs to be removed for the sake of humanity's safety.

The language of genocide is always an egregious exaggeration of reality and fantasy, and the genocidal mind expresses itself in apocalyptic terms and in polarized terms such as "us versus them." Indeed, it sees the world in terms of rival races, nations, religions, and classes. In the language of genocide, there is also often an element of pornography, with references to perversity as a means of further demonizing the stereotyping of the hate-object—the easier to justify carrying out extreme measures.

Ultimately, the language of genocide serves as a prelude to physical violence; it is its precursor, resorting to words that rationalize and exhort a population into accepting that turning to violent means is legitimate. Given its two faces of extremism and euphemism, the language of genocide can and does veer from the brutal to the benign, from the cruel and the threatening to the seemingly condescending. Its practitioners are adept at both, creating an atmosphere of profound uncertainty, insecurity, and isolation in the ranks of the victims.

Last Days of the Jerusalem of Lithuania: Chronicles from the Vilna Ghetto and the Camps, 1929–1944. Written by Herman Kruk (1897–1944), *The Last Days of the*

Jerusalem of Lithuania: Chronicles from the Vilna Ghetto and the Camps, 1929–1944, is an extremely informative and valuable diary that constitutes one of the major sources available on the life and death of the Jews of Vilna during the Holocaust. An acute observer, Kruk writes about the problems and dilemmas faced by the ghetto's leadership, the efforts of the resistance movement, and the Vilna Jews' incredible efforts to maintain a strong cultural, ideological, and social life in the midst of degradation, despair, and death. The journal covers the period of the ghetto from September 7, 1941, through its liquidation in July 14, 1943. It also chronicles the collapse of Poland (September 1939–June 1941), the destruction of Jewish Vilna (June 22, 1941–September 6, 1941), and life in various camps in Estonia (August 1943 and September 1944). Kruk wrote his final diary entry on September 17, 1944, just before he and other inmates were shot to death.

Last Just Man, The. This 2001 documentary focuses on the life and thoughts of Canadian lieutenant general Romeo Dallaire (b. 1946), the man who was in charge of the UN peacekeeping mission in Rwanda prior to, during, and following the 1994 genocide when some five hundred thousand to 1 million Tutsi and moderate Hutu were killed in one hundred days. *The Last Just Man* portrays Dallaire as a haunted man who continues, years after the horrific genocide that he witnessed up close, to question whether he could have done more to attempt to halt the genocide. Making use of interview footage and scenes from Rwanda, the film does a good job of recapturing the turmoil—political, civil, and emotional—of the 1994 Rwandan genocide and the harrowing impact it has had on Dallaire as a man.

Laval, Pierre (1883–1945). Four-time prime minister of France (1931–1932, 1932; 1935–1936, and 1942–1944), Pierre Laval last served under the pro-German, antisemitic, and collaborationist Vichy government of Field Marshal Philippe Pétain (1856–1951), first as vice premier and then as prime minister, for which, after World War II, he would be tried as a traitor to France and executed. During his fourth term in office, he suffered an assassination attempt, having been shot four times while reviewing troops in Paris.

Originally opposed to Nazi Germany during its early years, Laval unsuccessfully attempted to enter into an alliance with the Italy of dictator Benito Mussolini (1883–1945) to strengthen his own political power. With the German occupation of France (1940), however, his allegiance turned, and he wholeheartedly supported Vichy France's pro-Nazi and antisemitic positions. In fact, he is credited with designing and implementing the antisemitic policies of the Vichy government, including the roundup and transport of French Jews to the death camps in Poland. At the end of World War II, he fled to Spain, was extradited to Austria, and was turned over to U.S. troops, who handed him over to the French for trial and execution.

Law for the Protection of German Blood and German Honor (German, *Gesetz zum Schutz des deutschen Blutes und der deutschen Ehre*). Adopted unanimously on September 15, 1935 (out of the Nazis' concern for "safeguarding" the "purity" of "German blood")—the same day the *Reichstag* (German parliament) unanimously adopted the Nuremberg Laws on Citizenship and Race (the so-called *Reichsbürgergesetz*)—the Law for the Protection of German Blood and German Honor consisted of the following seven sections: (1) marriages between Jews and German nationals or those of "kindred blood" were forbidden; (2) relations outside of marriage between Jews and German nationals or those of kindred blood were also forbidden; (3) female German nationals or those of kindred blood under the age of forty-five could no longer be employed in Jewish households; (4) Jews were henceforth forbidden to hoist the German and Reich flags or "present the colors of the Reich," though they could present "the Jewish colors"; (5) punishment for violations of sections [1] and [2] were to be imprisonment with hard labor; violations of sections [3] and [4] were imprisonment of one year and monetary fines; (6) implementation and supplementation of this law was the responsibility of the Reich minister of the interior; and (7) the law was to take effect on September 16, 1935, with the exception of section [3] which was to become effective on January 1, 1936. The law was signed into effect at the Nuremberg Party Rally of Freedom by Führer and Reich Chancellor Adolf Hitler (1889–1945); Reich Minister of the Interior Wilhelm Frick (1877–1946); Reich Minister of Justice Dr. Franz Goertner; and Deputy of the Führer Rudolf Hess (1894–1987). (For the purpose of this and other Nazi legislation and related activities, a "Jew" was defined as someone with least three Jewish grandparents. This was the Nazi definition.)

Law for the Restoration of the Professional Civil Service (German, *Gesetz zur Wiederherstellung des Berufsbeamtenteums*). This was one of the earliest, most significant, and devastating anti-Jewish laws passed by Nazi Germany (April 7, 1933). It mandated that "civil servants of non-Aryan descent must retire." It also meant that Jews could no longer be employed as teachers in schools, professors in universities, or judges in the court system. As a favor to President Paul von Hindenburg (1847–1934), those Jews who had served as frontline soldiers in World War I were exempt from this anti-Jewish law (but this was to be short-lived).

The law was passed by the Nazi-controlled government of Germany, barely two months after Adolf Hitler (1889–1945) took office. The law itself was originally written by Interior Minister Wilhelm Frick (1877–1946), who was later executed for war crimes by the Allies at Nuremberg. Upon von Hindenburg's death in 1934, the law was amended to include all Jews yet remaining in governmental positions.

Relatively brief, consisting of only seven sections, divided into four parts, the antisemitic heart of the legislation was Part 3, Section 1, which stated: "Civil servants who are not of Aryan descent are to be retired; if they are honorary officials, they are to be dismissed from their official office." (As originally written, Section 2 stated the following: "Section 1 does not apply to civil servants in office from August 1, 1914, who fought at the Front for the German Reich or its Allies in the World War, or whose fathers or sons fell in the World War.")

Lawyers Committee for Human Rights. The Lawyers Committee for Human Rights, which has offices in New York City and Washington, D.C., works in the United States and abroad in an effort to create a secure and humane world by advancing justice, human dignity, and respect for the rule of law. It supports human rights activists who fight for basic freedoms and peaceful change at the local level; protects refugees in flight from persecution and repression; and helps to build a strong international system of justice and accountability for the worst human rights crimes.

Le Chambon-sur-Lignon. Le Chambon-sur-Lignon is the Huguenot Protestant village in southern France which sheltered and saved between three thousand and five thousand Jews during the Nazi period, 1941–1944, under the direction of its pastor André Trocmé (1901–1971). The heroism of the villagers and their leader have acquired international fame as a result of Phillip Hallie's (1979) book *Lest Innocent Blood Be Shed: The Story of Le Chambon and How Goodness Happened There*, and Jewish survivor Pierre Sauvage's (who was born in the village) 1989 documentary film *Weapons of the Spirit*. Many of the inhabitants, including the Pastor Trocmé, have been designated "Righteous Gentiles" (i.e., the phrase for non-Jews who risked their lives saving Jews during the Holocaust) by Yad Vashem, Israel's Holocaust Memorial Authority.

League of Nations, and Intervention. The League of Nations was formally established in 1919, a direct consequence of World War I (1914–1918) and the failure of international diplomacy to maintain the peace. In its attempts at creating a new order for the world based on open diplomacy, fairness, and the rule of law, the League adopted a procedure based on dialogue, conferencing, and negotiation rather than multilateral intervention in order to reduce the risk of conflict. The principle of nonintervention was rooted in a preexisting belief in the inviolability of the state, as guaranteed by the Treaty of Westphalia (1648). The League, so closely bound up in the post–World War I peace settlements, found itself a prisoner of the very structures it was attempting to control—*realpolitik*, a states system, secret diplomacy, and the impunity of states acting contrary to the common international good. The League was only ever as powerful as the resolve of its member states, and none were at any stage prepared to surrender any portion of their sovereignty in favor of an international ideal that had never before been tried. The key doctrine determining the League's attitude toward global security was thus an extension of the old idea of collective security, only now it was on a much bigger scale than had ever been the case in the past. In this sense, the League was not as revolutionary as many initially hoped it would be; but its novelty lay in the fact that it was the first attempt of its kind, and, as such, it did not act as much more than an experimental undertaking in an untried area of international cooperation. Given this, such notions as multilateral intervention for the purpose of peace making, peace enforcement, or peacekeeping were neither suggested nor tried under the League of Nations. It took the failure of that body, a second world war, and a new international organization—the United Nations—to realize the necessity of cutting through the structures that had so impeded the League's ability to act.

Lebensborn **(German, "Fountain of Life").** The Nazi program of selective breeding of its population to produce a superior or "master" race. Without benefit of marriage, German women who met stringent physical standards were urged to produce children with SS men who met the same standards of height, weight, blond hair, blue eyes, and athleticism. Upon conception, these women were sent to special maternity homes where they were cared for until the birth of their children. The program, however, did not prove successful, and, in 1942, the term *Lebensborn* became a code term for the kidnapping of Polish and other children who met these idealized characteristics and were placed in German families. After the war, many of the actual records of such births and kidnappings were lost; thus, no actual numbers in either category can be accurately assessed.

Lebensraum **(German, "Living Room," or "Living Space").** A cornerstone of Nazi foreign policy was the belief of the inherent "right" of the so-called master race to appropriate whatever lands needed, primarily to the East, for the settlement, survival, and growth of its population. Not only the lands themselves but their populations were viewed as resources to be exploited. The concept itself preceded the rise of Adolf Hitler (1889–1945) and the Nazis and was already taught in German universities in the early 1920s, one possible adumbration of the political implications of social Darwinism. Hitler himself advocated such in his book *Mein Kampf*, with his argument of Germany's "moral right" to acquire such lands and resources. Thus, the annexation of Austria, the takeover of the Sudetenland in Czechoslovakia, Poland, and parts of the Soviet Union may all be assessed from this understanding.

Lemkin, Raphael (1900–1959). Polish Jewish refugee, lawyer, and legal scholar, Lemkin was born in rural village of Bezwodene and is best remembered as the individual who coined the word *genocide* and who served as the motivating force behind the (1948) United Nations

Convention on the Prevention and Punishment of the Crime of Genocide (UNCG). It was Lemkin's enormous energy and resolve, and his personal commitment, above all else, that ultimately led to the passage of the UNCG. Indefatigable in his efforts, he wrote and rewrote drafts of legislation, cornered ambassadors and officials in the halls of power, and undertook voluminous correspondence encouraging individuals of note (e.g., governmental and religious officials) to support the development and ratification of the UNCG.

Lemkin studied law at the universities of Lvov, Poland, and Heidelberg, Germany, becoming, in 1927, Secretary to the War Court of Appeals. From 1929 to 1935 he served as Secretary of the Committee on the Codification of the Laws of the Polish Republic while maintaining a private legal practice. After the beginning of World War II and the invasion of Poland in 1939, he served briefly in the Polish underground, traveled to the United States in 1941, where he first taught law at Duke University and later at Yale University. Lemkin also served as adviser to the U.S. War Department, U.S. Board of Economic Warfare, and United States Supreme Court Justice Robert H. Jackson (1892–1954) in the latter's capacity as chief U.S. prosecutor at the International Military Tribunal, Nuremberg, Germany, 1945–1946.

Lemkin's (1944) magnum opus, *Axis Rule in Occupied Europe: Laws of Occupation, Analysis of Government, Proposals for Redress*, clearly spelled out his concerns with genocide (Chapter 9), though the origin of his thinking arose in his childhood and was part of his overall orientation already in the 1930s.

He died in 1959, unable to get his adopted country, the United States, to ratify the Genocide Convention.

A lengthy excerpt of Lemkin's unpublished autobiography, *Totally Unofficial Man*, has been published in Samuel Totten and Steven Leonard Jacobs's (Eds.) *Pioneers of Genocide Studies* (New Brunswick, NJ: Transaction Publishers, 2002, pp. 365–399).

Lenin, Vladimir Ilyich Ulyanov (1870–1924). Russian revolutionary, leader of the Bolshevik Party, and first premier of the Soviet Union. The son of a senior school inspector (which qualified him for one of the categories of hereditary nobility based on service), Vladimir Ilyich Ulyanov took the name "Lenin" as a revolutionary *nom de guerre*. In light of the terror he was to unleash in Russia, the name is not a little ironic in that it is based on the Russian root of *Lena*, the name of a peaceful Russian river in Siberia that he discovered while living in exile.

Lenin qualified for a career in law, but, by 1894, had become a full-time revolutionary, inspired by communist ideals. Arrested in late 1895 by the tsarist secret police, he was exiled to Siberia between 1896 and 1899 and then lived in self-imposed overseas exile for two periods, 1899–1905 and 1907–1917. As a revolutionary, Lenin made ends meet by lecturing, through party donations, and as editor of his party's newspaper, *Iskra* (*The Spark*). He returned to Russia for two years owing to the 1905 revolution but left again upon realizing that the *Duma* (parliament) did not fit his model of a true revolutionary body. When Russia collapsed into constitutional democratic revolution in February–March 1917, Lenin returned from exile in Switzerland as a result of a deal struck with the Germans: if he managed to attain power in Russia, he would extract it from the war against Germany. The coup d'état of the Bolshevik Party against the Provisional Government of Russia in October–November 1917 was exclusively Lenin's brainchild and achievement.

As a revolutionary leader Lenin quickly adopted totalitarian methods in order, first, to secure the Bolshevik Party's dominance throughout Russia and, second, to stave off the possibility of counterrevolution. He instituted a police state (and created a new secret police force in order to achieve it, the *Cheka*) and suppressed all dissent ruthlessly. It was under Lenin's rule that the system of political concentration camps known as the gulag was established, and he initiated genocide against a Russian minority population known for their support of the tsar, the Cossacks. Under his reign of terror, millions of Russian and Soviet citizens died in the name of the Bolshevik Revolution. There is evidence that Lenin knew much of the extent of the destruction his party and its ideals had wrought, but this was not something that concerned him; for Lenin, the end—revolutionary success and the maintenance of the Soviet regime—justified whatever means were necessary to achieve it. The events his government set in motion by way of precedent enabled his successor Josef Stalin (1879–1953) to take the revolution to new and horrific levels of destruction.

Leopold II, King of the Belgians (1835–1909). Louis Philippe Marie Victor Saxe-Coburg, king of the Belgians, reigned from 1865 until his death in 1909. In 1876 he engaged an Anglo-American explorer and journalist, Henry Morton Stanley (1841–1904), to penetrate the interior of the Congo basin region of central Africa, having first established an International Association for the Exploration and Civilization of the Congo—a front for what can otherwise be referred to as a land grab. The subsequent creation of the Congo Free State, assented to by the European powers at the Berlin Conference of 1884–1885, enabled Leopold to transform the region into his personal empire. In the drive to exploit the Congo's resources, Leopold authorized all measures to be taken against the population in order to ensure maximum generation of wealth. Slave labor, floggings, mass mutilation for the most trivial of offenses, depopulation of whole districts in favor of land cultivation; anything was permissible. In minerals, in ivory harvesting, but above all in the manufacture of rubber, Leopold's agents spread throughout the country sowing devastation, mayhem, and death on a massive scale. Although all this contributed to Leopold's personal fortune, it also damned him in the view of international opinion once the worst excesses of his regime were exposed by critics from around the world. The first revelations came from an Englishman, Edward Dene Morel (1873–1924), but it was the investigative work of British diplomat Sir Roger Casement (1864–1916)—later to be hanged for his alleged role in Ireland's 1916 uprising—that mobilized world opinion against Leopold. Other critics included Joseph Conrad (1857–1924), Sir Arthur Conan Doyle (1859–1930), Mark Twain (1835–1910), and Booker T. Washington (1856–1915).

The world outcry was sufficient to force the Belgian government to take control of Leopold's Congo Free State in 1908. Under direct Belgian rule the worst excesses of Leopold's rule were slowly reduced, though little was done to develop the country for the Africans themselves. Even at the beginning of the independence movement, in the late 1950s, Leopold II's legacy still haunted the Congo—a legacy of massive death and devastation the country is still yet to surmount.

Lepsius, Johannes (1858–1926). Born in Potsdam, Germany, Lepsius was an evangelical Protestant clergyperson who, in 1895, established the *Deutsche* (German) Orient Mission to run orphanages for Armenian children who had survived the Ottoman Turk–perpetrated massacres of 1894–1896. The following year he published his *Armenians and Europe*, wherein he detailed the atrocities committed under Sultan Abdul Hamid II (1876–1909). With the privately published *The Condition of the Armenian People* in Turkey in 1916, after the Ottoman Turk genocide of the Armenians (1915–1923) had begun, Lepsius fled from Germany to Holland, where he continued his activities. There, he published his *Germany and Armenia 1914–1918*, documenting German complicity in the genocide.

In Berlin, in 1921, he testified at the trial of Soghomon Tehlirian (1897–1960), the acquitted assassin of Talaat Pasha (1879–1921), Turkey's former minister of the interior, and one of the triumvirate responsible for the genocide. He died in Italy in 1926 and is, today, much regarded by the worldwide Armenian community as a true "righteous hero."

Lewis, Bernard (b. 1916). Professor emeritus at Princeton University, in the Department of Near Eastern Studies. Born in Britain, Lewis has had a long-standing reputation throughout the world as a knowledgeable and highly influential scholar of Middle Eastern history. In 1962, in his book *The Emergence of Modern Turkey*, Lewis described the events of the Armenian genocide as "the terrible Holocaust . . . when a million and a half Armenians vanished." Over time, however, his views did an about-face, such that he began downplaying the fact of the genocide of late Ottoman history to the extent of actually denying a genocide took place at all. In June 1995, Lewis was found guilty, in a French court, for statements he made denying the Armenian genocide. In a civil case in which he was charged with causing damage to another party owing to his failure to address his responsibilities as a scholar, the court found him negligent of recognizing the truth of the issues he was discussing regarding the Armenian genocide. He was ordered to pay a fine of 10,000 francs for punitive damages (i.e., damages by way of "punishment" for offensive conduct) and court costs, and one franc to each of the two plaintiff parties to indicate that while the parties presented their cases successfully, they only deserved a symbolic amount of damages. Although the decision provoked a series of mixed reactions in U.S. and French newspapers (where *Le Monde* was forced by the court to report the decision, given that it was that paper that had originally published Lewis's denial statements) regarding academic freedom and historical controversy, the decision was nonetheless an acceptance by a French court that the Armenian genocide was a judicial fact, and that as such it was not to be challenged for political or ideological reasons.

Libya, Genocide in. In January 1929, the Italian North African colonies of Tripolitania and Cyrenaica (now Libya) were united under the control of a fascist governor, General Pietro Badoglio (1871–1956). The imposition of close military rule over the colony by committed fascists, ready to obey the will of Italian dictator Benito Mussolini (1883–1945), met with resistance from Libya's Arab population. Some Arabs had already been resisting Italian rule, based on both religious and nationalistic grounds; now, a wider assault on Italian colonialism developed. In response, between 1929 and 1932, a policy of what some have since described as genocide was inaugurated by Mussolini's regime against the Libyans. The main perpetrators of the brutal suppression of the Libyan uprising were Badoglio, General Rodolfo Graziani (1882–1955), General Luigi Federzoni (1878–1967), and Mussolini himself. The acts undertaken included the gassing of villages, bombing of civilian areas from the air, and the introduction of concentration camps throughout the colony. These latter, at their maximum, incarcerated up to one hundred thousand people (men, women and children), at least half of whom died from violent treatment, neglect, disease and malnutrition. Overall, up to a hundred thousand people may have died throughout the colony during the fascist campaign. Contemporary Italian press reports, approved by the fascist censors, referred to the process as *cleansing*. Behavior such as that exhibited by Mussolini's regime in Libya (and also later, after Italy's 1935 invasion of Ethiopia) affirms the genocidal (and extremely violent) tendencies to be found within the ideology of fascism—tendencies that were to be further realized in the early 1940s through the actions of the German variant of Italian fascism, Nazism, in its campaigns against Jews, Roma and Sinti, Poles, and other peoples.

Lidice. A Czech town located in Bohemia, not far from Prague. The town was selected as the target of a reprisal against the Czech people (and to serve as a warning by example) for the assassination of Germany's Reich Protector of Bohemia and Moravia, Reinhard Heydrich (1904–1942), in early June 1942. On June 10, the Nazis targeted Lidice as the location that would suffer the full wrath of their vengeance for Heydrich's death, basing their decision on the erroneous belief that the inhabitants had helped the assassins. German security police began by surrounding the village and blocking all avenues of escape. The entire population was rounded up, and all males over fifteen years of age were imprisoned in a barn. They were shot the next day. Another nineteen men, who had been outside the village at work in a mine, and seven women previously undetected, were sent by the Nazis to Prague, where they were also shot. The rest of the women of Lidice were transferred to concentration camp at Ravensbrück, where about a quarter of them died before the liberation of the camp in 1945. The village's children were taken to a concentration camp in Lodz; a few, considered to be assimilable into German families as "Aryans" (the ideal German racial model), were sent on to Germany. The fate of the rest of the children is uncertain, though it is possible that they may have been sent to other Nazi extermination camps in Poland. Overall, estimates converge on a figure of some 340 people from Lidice who were murdered by the Nazis in this massacre, with 192 men, 60 women, and possibly up to 88 children slain. After destroying the people, the Nazis then moved in on the village itself, which was systematically destroyed and its name removed from all maps and official documents, as though it had never existed. The martyrdom of Lidice became a byword for Nazi savagery (even during the most savage war in history), its fate known around the world within a relatively short period.

Lieber, Dr. Franz (Francis) (1798–1872). A German American jurist and academic and author of the Lieber Code, a seminal statement regarding the behavior of soldiers in wartime. Migrating from Prussia to Boston (via a stay in Britain) in 1827, Lieber became a professor of history, economics, and political science in South Carolina, before moving to Columbia University, in New York, in 1856. During the American Civil War (1861–1865), Lieber's allegiance was to the Union (his son, however, fought for the Confederacy and was killed at the Battle of Williamsburg in 1862). At the request of U.S. President Abraham Lincoln (1809–1865), Lieber prepared a set of guidelines in 1863 entitled *Instructions for the Government of Armies of the United States in the Field*; it was published as General Order No. 100 and nicknamed the Lieber Code or Lieber Instructions. The document was divided into ten sections: behavior in a time of martial law; protection of civilians, civilian property, and punishment to transgressions; deserters, prisoners of war, hostages, and war booty; partisans; spies and traitors; truces and exchange of prisoners; parole of former rebel troops; the conditions of any armistice, and respect for human life; assassination and murder of soldiers or citizens in hostile territory; and the status of individuals engaged in a state of civil war against the government.

The Lieber Code was the first important foundational document in respect of U.S. military ethics, declaring that people in enemy or occupied territories were entitled to humane treatment. It addressed issues relating to the ethical entitlements of the combatants on both sides of a conflict, and was, therefore, a momentous harbinger of the 1864 Geneva Conventions (which were subsequently amended over the next century-and-a-half), and the Hague Conventions of 1899 and 1907. The Lieber Code, modified to suit local conditions, was later adopted by military establishments in other states. After the

Civil War, Lieber became a principal archivist working on the captured papers of the Confederacy, and ended his career in a diplomatic capacity on behalf of the United States.

Life is Beautiful. An Italian-made movie made about the Holocaust, *Life is Beautiful* (in Italian, *La Vita è Bella*) was the brainchild of actor-director Roberto Benigni (b. 1952). The film was produced in 1997 and focuses on an Italian Jew in the 1930s, Guido Orefice, who falls in love with and marries a non-Jewish woman, Dora (played in the film by Benigni's real-life wife, Nicoletta Braschi (b. 1960), to great effect). After the Nazis have occupied Italy and imposed the full weight of German antisemitic legislation, Guido and his infant son, as "racial" Jews, are sent to a concentration camp. At her request, Dora is permitted to join them. In order to maintain his child's morale—in effect, in order to give him the will to live—Guido convinces his son that everything that is happening to them is actually part of a big game, in which the winner of the first prize wins an army tank. In a tribute to the other great comedy about the Nazi persecution of the Jews from 1940, Charles Chaplin's (1889–1977) *The Great Dictator*, Benigni gave his character Guido the same concentration camp prisoner number as that on the uniform of Chaplin's character, the Jewish Barber. The popular and critical acclaim for *Life is Beautiful* was little short of phenomenal. It won the Grand Jury Prize at Cannes, and Oscars for Best Foreign Film, Best Actor (Benigni), and Best Original Dramatic Score for the music of Nicola Piovani (b. 1946). Although it is not a "Holocaust movie" in the strict sense of historical fiction or documentary, *Life is Beautiful* is nonetheless an important movie that extends the boundaries of cinema about the Holocaust into areas of fantasy and fable.

"Life Unworthy of Life" (German, *Lebensunwertes Leben*). German Nazi term for those afflicted with hereditary illnesses, including the mentally ill, who were perceived as a political and economic burden to German society and worthy of "euthanasia." The July 1933 Law for the Prevention of Offspring with Hereditary Diseases was passed by the Reichstag, establishing euthanasia centers to carry out the deaths—via medical means—of those labeled "unworthy of life." Actual killing centers were established at Brandenburg, Grafenek, Hartheim, and Sonnenstein. Between two hundred thousand and two hundred seventy-five thousand were murdered. Another three hundred thousand to four hundred thousand German nationals were sterilized under this program. The "T-4" program was the code name for the implementation of the "euthanasia" program, its headquarters being located at Tiergartenstrasse 4. *Lebensunwertes Leben*, itself, was first used in a 1920 book by German jurist Karl Binding and German psychiatrist Alfred Hoche, *The Permission to Destroy Life Unworthy of Life*.

Linguicide. Linguicide refers to any act or series of acts committed with the intent to destroy, in any way whatsoever, or to prevent, the natural development of a language or dialect.

Lon Nol (1913–1985). Cambodian military general and politician, who, in March 1970, overthrew the rule of Prince Norodom Sihanouk (b. 1922), in a U.S.-backed coup d'état. This event was to lead directly to the Cambodian civil war of 1970–1975 and to the victory of communist dictator Pol Pot (1925–1998) and his murderous Khmer Rouge movement.

Lon Nol was born in Prey Veng province, and received a standard French colonial education. He became a civil servant, rising to provincial governor, and, under Sihanouk, became, over time, Cambodian chief of police, chief of the general staff of the Cambodian military forces, minister of defense, and prime minister on two occasions (1966–1967 and 1969) prior to his coup. Following the coup, he abolished the monarchy and declared Cambodia a republic, with himself as president. His new regime was closely aligned with the

West, and among his first acts was a demand for the evacuation of all North Vietnamese and Vietcong forces from Cambodian sovereign territory, and the closure of all access points (by land and sea) supplying communist Vietnam. These actions escalated Cold War violence in Cambodia, and drew the United States more deeply into Cambodian events—at a time when the war in Vietnam was raging. If the U.S. intention was to set Lon Nol up as a bulwark against communism, it was a strategy that failed. In 1971 he suffered a debilitating stroke, and, in the aftermath of his slow recovery (during which he retained office), he proved an incompetent and inconclusive leader. Lon Nol's rule saw a massive U.S. bombing campaign against Vietnamese bases in eastern Cambodia, which drove large numbers of Cambodians into the arms of the anti-Western, anti-U.S. Khmer Rouge. As the civil war intensified, Lon Nol's regime showed itself to be riddled with corruption, and he was himself revealed as a poor military leader. By the spring of 1975, Khmer Rouge forces had conquered all of Cambodia save its capital, Phnom Penh. On April 1, 1975, Lon Nol resigned as president (having insisted that an inducement of US$1 million be placed in his name in a secure American bank account), and he was evacuated from the capital by U.S. forces. Just over two weeks later, on April 17, 1975, Khmer Rouge forces entered Phnom Penh, and the nightmare years of the Cambodian genocide (1975–1979) began immediately. Lon Nol settled at first in Hawaii, but, in 1979, moved to California, where he died in 1985.

London Charter (also known as the London Agreement, the London Accord, and London Charter Conference). On August 8, 1945, the Allied signatories (the United States, France, Great Britain, and the Soviet Union) signed the London Agreement that established the Charter of the International Military Tribunal (IMT). The IMT was the tribunal that was established to carry out "the just and prompt trial and punishment of the major war criminals of the European Axis"—that is, those leaders of the Nazis who were alleged to have perpetrated crimes against peace (i.e., the waging of aggressive war), war crimes (i.e., violations of universally accepted standards of military conduct), and crimes against humanity (i.e., violations of standards regarding civilians) during the course of World War II.

The IMT consisted of the following major provisions: (1) the Tribunal was to consist of four members (and four alternates), one from each of the signatories; (2) all members of the Tribunal must be present to constitute a quorum, with one to be elected president; (3) the crimes and punishments were to be crimes against peace, war crimes, and crimes against humanity; (4) neither holding a position as a head of state or government official nor following superior orders was to be considered as alleviating responsibility; (5) procedures shall follow standard legal and courtroom methods as commonly understood; (6) the Tribunal itself as well as both prosecutors and defense counsels were to, also, follow accepted legal and courtroom procedures; and (7) judgment and sentencing were the responsibility of the Tribunal.

The implementation of the IMT (October 1945 to October 1946) constituted a legal breakthrough in international law, though not without its critics (e.g., accusations of "victors' justice"), and later paved the way for the establishment of the International Criminal Tribunal for Rwanda, the International Criminal Tribunal for the former Yugoslavia, and the International Criminal Court.

Lost Boys of Sudan. A feature-length documentary film made in the United States in 2003. The "lost boys" featured herein are two Sudanese refugees, Peter Nyarol Dut and Santino Majok Chuor, members of the Dinka people of southern Sudan. They were both orphaned owing to the Sudanese civil war (1983–2005) during which the Arab Muslim–dominated government in Khartoum waged war against the black African Christian and animist peoples of Southern Sudan. Peter and Santino are but two of some twenty thousand orphans left by the war, and the film traces their experiences as they struggle through desert and savannah, braving militia incursions, to reach a camp for refugee children in Kenya. Some of these orphans, who became known as "lost boys" to a watching world, were chosen for resettlement in the United States, and this film shows how its subjects go about the process of integrating into contemporary North American society—a world away, both literally and psychologically, from what they had left. *Lost Boys of Sudan* is therefore a film that deals with both genocide and the postgenocide legacy and the impact of such on two young men growing to maturity. Produced and directed by Megan Mylan and John Shenk, who also functioned as sound recordist and cinematographer, respectively, *Lost Boys of Sudan* has been critically acclaimed and has won a number of film and human rights awards in the United States.

Lowry, Heath W. (b. 1942). Atatürk professor of Ottoman and Modern Turkish Studies at Princeton University since 1993 and a leading defender of the Turkish position regarding the Armenian genocide of 1915. Lowry's chair at Princeton was originally funded by the Turkish government, following his directorship of the Institute of Turkish Studies (ITS) at Georgetown University, Washington, D.C. Between 1994 and 1997 Lowry was chairman of the Department of Near Eastern Studies at Princeton, where he came under constant criticism for his ongoing denial of the Armenian genocide. Lowry's activities as director of the ITS at Georgetown and as a professor at Princeton placed him at the forefront of Armenian genocide deniers. Among other activities, he vigorously discredited the memoirs of former American ambassador to Constantinople during the genocide, Henry Morgenthau, Sr. (1856–1946), claiming that they are unreliable and nothing more than wartime propaganda. In 1995, Lowry was exposed as one prepared to suppress intellectual inquiry, when he was found to have ghostwritten (in 1990) a memorandum for the Turkish ambassador to the United States in response to a reference to the Armenian genocide by Robert Jay Lifton (b. 1926) in his book *The Nazi Doctors* (1986). The ambassador's letter to Lifton (drafted by Lowry) both denied the Armenian genocide and discredited Lifton's scholarship for having referred to it. When news broke of Lowry's connection with the Turkish ambassador (and through him, with the Turkish government), his credentials as an objective scholar were reduced almost to zero; in fact, he was seen as little more than a propagandist for the government in Ankara. In 1997, after two years of intense criticism over his denial of the Armenian genocide, Lowry stepped down as chairman of Princeton's Department of Ottoman and Near Eastern Studies. Ultimately, the scandal over Lowry's ongoing denial activities and his lobbying on behalf of the Turkish government seemed to have backfired. It called into question the integrity of Turkish-funded academic chairs and programs and provided those seeking to develop a broader public consciousness of the genocide with inspiration.

Lublin-Majdanek. A concentration and death camp in Poland, Lublin-Majdanek was initially constructed primarily by two thousand Soviet prisoners of war (supplemented by approximately one hundred fifty of the three hundred Jews rounded up in the town of Lublin) in October 1941 as a labor facility. One hundred and forty-four barracks for inmates were built, including some especially for children. In 1942, the camp population was increased with the arrival of more than seven thousand Jews from Slovakia, and more than ten thousand Jews from both the Treblinka death camp and the Warsaw Ghetto. That same year, more than twenty-five thousand Jews were transferred from the death camp Belzec. In the spring of 1943, after the unsuccessful revolt by the remaining Jews of the Warsaw

Ghetto, between eighteen thousand and twenty-two thousand survivors were sent to Lublin-Majdanek. Beginning in October 1943, Zyklon B gas (cyanide) as well as carbon monoxide (CO) began to be used on prisoners in the gas chambers. Earlier that year, six sub-camps (Budzyn, Trawniki, Poniatowa, Krasnik, Pulawy, and Lupowa) were subsumed under its administration. During this same period, Lublin-Majdanek was also used as a major clothing storage depot for goods from Belzec, Sobibor, and Treblinka. Beginning on November 3, 1943, the Nazis shot and killed eighteen thousand Jews in the forest surrounding the town after first forcing them to dig the mass graves for their burial. Eight thousand from the camp itself and the remaining ten thousand housed in the town from other camps made up this number. Both its first Kommandant, Karl Otto Koch (1897–1945), and its second Kommandant, Hermann Florstedt (1895–1945), were executed by the Nazis for their corrupt activities while in charge of the camp; the remaining three commanders (Max Kroegel, Martin Wiess, and Arthur Liebenschel) were all tried and executed after World War II—Kroegel by the British, Wiess by the Americans, and Leibenschel by the Poles. It has now been estimated that somewhere between seventy-four thousand and ninety thousand Jews were transported to this camp, close to sixty thousand of whom were Polish Jews. Jews and others died there as a result of the horrid conditions as slave laborers (e.g., beatings and starvation) or being sent to the gas chambers. The camp was liberated by Soviet troops on July 24, 1944. The actual number of camp victims continues to be difficult to determine, ranging from 1.5 million according to Soviet figures, to the more modest seventy-eight thousand according to the current historian in charge of the records, Tomasz Kranz, to Holocaust scholar Raul Hilberg's estimate of fifty thousand.

Lukic, Milan (b. 1967). Milan Lukic was born in the Bosnian town of Foca. A Serb, during the Bosnian War of 1992–1995 he organized a militia group known as the White Eagles, which operated in and around the town of Visegrad, located on the Drina River. As White Eagles commander, Lukic is alleged to have been responsible for overseeing the "ethnic cleansing" of the Muslim population of Visegrad, in which its citizens were imprisoned, tortured, assaulted, raped, mutilated, deported, and murdered. These activities took place throughout the summer of 1992, until such time as the prewar Muslim population of Visegrad—some fourteen thousand in all—had been removed from the town altogether. This became the first instance of what became known as "ethnic cleansing" in Bosnia.

In August 1998, the International Criminal Tribunal for the Former Yugoslavia (ICTY) charged Lukic with eleven counts of crimes against humanity, and, in September 2003, a Serbian court sentenced him in absentia to twenty years' imprisonment on a different set of charges relating to mass murder of Bosnian Muslims during the Bosnian War. Although he seemingly lived quite openly in Republika Srpska from 1998 onward, attempts to arrest him and bring him before a court were continually stymied. Be that as it may, he held a number of informal negotiations with ICTY officers, and on April 9, 2005, he offered to go to The Hague voluntarily once his superiors had also gone. (It is generally assumed that these would include Bosnian Serb military commander Ratko Mladic (b. 1942) and Republika Srpska president Radovan Karadzic (b. 1945), both of whom remain at large through this writing, September 2007.) Then, on August 8, 2005, Lukic was arrested in Buenos Aires, Argentina. He appeared before a judge the following day, as extradition orders were being cut to have him transferred to The Hague for trial. In 2001, the original indictment against Lukic was amended to include war crimes as well as crimes against humanity, as ICTY negotiators uncovered more evidence against him. At the time of writing, Lukic's judicial fate remains pending.